Endorsements for the Book

Praise for *Innovations in Healthcare Management: Cost-Effective and Sustainable Solutions*

This is a timely and well-considered book. The majority of leadership texts have a Western-centric approach, with Western ideologies and approaches dominating the literature. This book explores Western management philosophies, in particular the Lean approach to management, and applies them to developing countries with a significant focus on the Indian subcontinent. The global approach taken by this book to the substantial challenges faced by nations throughout the world identifies the commonalities and differences in the solutions and implementation of global health care and the major role that leadership plays in both the identification and the application of health-care policy, appropriate to the environment in which they are delivered. Leaders predominantly create context and this wide-ranging text contributes significantly to the analysis of the leadership required to provide sustainable and affordable global health care. I would recommend it to all those with an interest in the global health economy.

Richard Hayward
Course Leader
MSc HealthCare Management
Anglia Ruskin University, United Kingdom

I wish to congratulate Dr. V. K. Singh and Paul Lillrank for their insightful book, *Innovations in Healthcare Management: Cost-Effective and Sustainable Solutions*, highlighting the strengths and pitfalls of the health-care system prevailing in India and in many countries the world over. We at Gulf Medical University and its affiliated network of GMC Hospitals, the first private teaching hospitals in the UAE, focus on innovation: innovation in education, health care, and research. With a reach to a wider population and offering affordable services, we have successfully implemented many trendsetting features over the last decade. I feel services offered through e-health and m-health will be the key in the next decade, which can reach and benefit people in remote areas. Overall, I find this book to be a useful read for all and would open up a dialogue, paving the way for new line of thinking in developing technologies for health maintenance, aligning purpose with people and performance, private–public partnerships, innovations in emerging economies, and innovative approaches to build health-care facilities. I once again congratulate the authors for their efforts.

Thumbay Moideen
Founder President—Board of Governors
Gulf Medical University and GMC Hospitals
Ajman, United Arab Emirates

Congratulations on your marvelous initiative in producing this exciting book. This appears to be a very interesting and ambitious book on health-care management, which must surely be welcome in the current challenging environment for health care worldwide. The list of contributors is very impressive, as all of them are involved in different innovative initiatives in health care around the world. Many of the initiatives are exciting and indicate new directions for the future in making health care sustainable. We can certainly learn from experts from the United States, United Kingdom, India, or elsewhere as the problems faced in health care are common and global.

Dr. Abu Bakar Suleiman
President, International Medical University, Kuala Lumpur
Chairman, IHH Healthcare Berhad
Adviser, Malaysian Society for Quality in Health

This book is eminently practical. Readers will find much to imitate in the numerous and varied case studies. I hope that many will also be inspired by the successes of others to create their own innovations.

David Wittenberg
CEO
The Innovation Workgroup, India

This book is a great tool for anyone across the world. Africa inclusive is planning to improve health-care delivery in a cost-effective manner. It gives the reader most of anything one would want on cost-effective and sustainable solutions in the management of a troubled health-care industry. The authors advocate the use of innovations in health maintenance, health-care management, health prevention, as well as in the health supply chain as a means of changing the way we care about patients with limited resources. The authors give very practical examples that can be implemented easily, thus making the book useful in many settings across the world. This is a book worth reading by health-care workers, particularly health managers and hospital CEOs. Wishing you greater success in this endeavor.

Dr. Marina Alois Njelekela
Executive Director
Muhimbili National Hospital
Dar es Salaam, Tanzania

Admiral Singh and Professor Paul Lillrank have done a great service by conceiving and birthing this exciting book, particularly in assembling a diverse "A Team" of Indian and global experts to write the chapters. The book is very timely, for India and the world are at critical inflection points in health. Enormous challenges are intersecting with the opportunities created by new thinking and new technologies. As this exciting book describes, there are huge shifts underway: sick care to wellness, facilities-based to doorstep health, expert and separate to holistic and person-centered, and artisanal to big data-driven science. India faces horrendous levels of malnutrition and stunting in its youth, an explosion of noncommunicable diseases (NCDs) in its adults, and critical shortages in trained personnel. However, it must find ways to provide wellness to hundreds of millions of citizens at the base of the pyramid; the Western model of medicine simply will not work. From theory to specific proposals to on-the-ground examples, this book shows how India could lead the world by reinventing the provision of well-being. Read it.

David K. Aylward
Senior Advisor, Global Health and Technology
Ashoka—Innovators for the Public
Former First Executive Director of the mHealth Alliance
Arlington, Virginia

I am excited to learn more from your book, *Innovations in Healthcare Management*. I am sure, with the topics you have chosen, it would be of immense benefit to the doctors and engineers who want to get into the field of health care. Affordable innovations are something we require, and should be of extreme help for the poor population of the country. The contributors of this book are internationally and nationally renowned experts in their fields. Wishing you all the best.

Professor Yogesh Chawla
Director
Post Graduate Institute of Medial Education & Research
Chandigarh, India

The editors have put together an impressive group of professionals with deep insight to analyze the present situation and provide directions to optimizing the resources to maximize the benefits of intelligent, innovative, and ground-up approach to health-care delivery. The readers will greatly benefit from the authors' hands-on experience. Health care is dynamic and obsolescence of technology and methodology is rapid. India is a unique country with equal preponderance of communicable and non-communicable (lifestyle) diseases. Medical professionals who provide care to captive populations in state and federally funded hospitals have a unique advantage to follow up with patients for outcomes over a certain period of time. When scientifically planned, such exercises can provide important information on treatment protocols that can be applied at a national level. This will be extremely useful in infectious diseases to prevent antibiotic resistance and save precious resources. Similarly, readers of this book may be inspired to chart new courses in the field of clinical epidemiology, pharmacoeconomics, pharmacoepidemiology, and other emerging disciplines.

Dr. Vijai Kumar
President and Chief Medical Officer
Excel Life Sciences, Inc.
Durham, North Carolina

This book, *Innovations in Healthcare Management*, discusses in depth the challenges posed in various domains of health care, and proposes solutions centered over the Lean principles from a global and also

Indian practice setting. Cost-effectiveness and a sustainable model for primary health care in emerging economies, behavioral changes and health literacy, and so on, are very well discussed. Management tools and techniques have their origins in the manufacturing industry. The characteristics of the health-care industry are unique and need to be specifically calibrated to achieve the levels of success other industries have demonstrated.

This book discusses opportunities of learning from industry and tailors those to suit health-care requirements. Examples of frugal innovation in health care and building an innovative culture through Lean are very interesting. Patients' expectations are constantly on the rise, and so are the health-care costs. Efforts need to be made at the stage of hospital planning and designing to facilitate Lean operations. New tools of information and communication technology (ICT) and evidence-based practice of these concepts are discussed. The various chapters in this book offer the reader the key concepts of Lean in health care with a structured approach, ultimately benefitting all the stakeholders, primarily the patients, in availing better quality and service.

Dr. Murali Rao
Head of Dental Department, Panaga Health Centre
Brunei Shell Petroleum, Brunei Darussalam

Innovations in Healthcare Management answers the need for a critical discourse on global questions pertaining to sustainable health care for all. The golden thread that runs through each of the chapters is clear and highlights the need to do more with less, especially in emerging economies. This book is not only authored by experts in their respective fields in health care, but offers an authentic and thought-provoking insight into a wide range of advances in modern health-care management that provides both conceptual depth and extensive practical application. The text is recommended for both inexperienced health-care professionals and policy makers, as it provides unique perspectives on current health-care challenges, especially relating to sustainable health care.

Professor Dalena van Rooyen
Director, School of Clinical Care Sciences
Nelson Mandela Metropolitan University, South Africa

Addressing one of our times' most important challenges—how to provide affordable and sustainable health care to all citizens—the editors of this book have gathered an impressive group of contributors that together provide a wide array of innovative examples in a broad international setting. It is a vital effort that enhances learning and proliferation of new ways to organize and deliver health care under strong constraints. I recommend decision makers as well as health-care professionals to invest their time in sharing the insights provided and get inspired to turn valuable ideas into a better practice.

Dr. Hans Winberg
Secretary General
Leading Health Care Foundation, founded by the Stockholm
School of Economics, Sweden

The delivery of health care has changed greatly both in form and in function over the last century. Although the delivery of health care was formerly the domain of the local general practitioner (GP) and proximate health systems, today there is an increasingly bewildering choice of doctors and access to global health systems. These changes have brought significant advances to health care but have often left its recipients confused and unsure as to the quality of care they can access. This book has brought together leaders in their respective fields, who have addressed the continuum of care right from preventive medicine, hospital design through to the various modes of health-care delivery. They have discussed interesting innovations worldwide that have driven positive process changes in medical systems. I would highly recommend this book to anyone who is passionate about improving access to cost-effective and efficient health care for patients all around the globe irrespective of location or socioeconomic status.

Dr. Chandy Abraham
Facility Director and Head Medical Services
Health City, Cayman Islands

Innovations in Healthcare Management

Innovations in Healthcare Management

Cost Effective and Sustainable Solutions

VK Singh • Paul Lillrank

CRC Press
Taylor & Francis Group
Boca Raton   London   New York

CRC Press is an imprint of the
Taylor & Francis Group, an **informa** business

A PRODUCTIVITY PRESS BOOK

The cover page was conceptualised by a team at MixORG Consulting and developed by the publisher. Each chapter of the book describes different facets of Innovations in Healthcare Management as the name of the book suggests.The green lines of digital information dropping onto the world map represent the coming together of deep knowledge about the healthcare domain and innovation of various global experts. The digital lines touch the countries of chapter contributors on the map and join to form a unity--all knowledge is ONE. New knowledge creation and its adoption of innovations are possible with cross pollination of ideas and the spirit of sharing.

CRC Press
Taylor & Francis Group
6000 Broken Sound Parkway NW, Suite 300
Boca Raton, FL 33487-2742

© 2015 by Taylor & Francis Group, LLC
CRC Press is an imprint of Taylor & Francis Group, an Informa business

No claim to original U.S. Government works

Printed on acid-free paper
Version Date: 20141223

International Standard Book Number-13: 978-1-4822-5209-5 (Hardback)

Visit the Taylor & Francis Web site at
http://www.taylorandfrancis.com

and the CRC Press Web site at
http://www.crcpress.com

Contents

Summary of Book

V. K. Singh and Paul Lillrank

Health care is a troubled industry all over the world. As Sir Nigel Crisp states,

> the challenges for both rich and poor countries are similar: how to shift focus from cure to prevention; how to integrate various technologies and care pathways; how to maximize the gains from science and technology; how to fund health systems that can provide equitable access to healthcare for whole populations?

To address these challenges, global learning and technology circulation are needed. Developing countries lack not only the resources but also the baggage of history and the vested interests of the advanced world. This book looks into the health-care innovation challenge from a global and an Indian perspective.

Mr. Sam Pitroda, Advisor to Prime Minister of India and Chairman of National Innovation Council, believes India has a tremendous opportunity for innovation. It is a country with over 500 million young people, a rich pool of technology and business talent, and a host of public health challenges present right before our eyes. The National Innovation Council, along with state and sectorial councils, has focused on enabling innovation ecosystems at the bottom of the pyramid, because Western models of resource-intensive consumption cannot suit India's needs. As developed economies enter a period of slower growth, emerging economies have the opportunity to develop examples of how more can be achieved with less.

Dr. Thulasiraj Ravilla and Dr. R. D. Ravindran represent Aravind Eye Care System, a prime example of frugal innovation. Its mission is to eliminate needless blindness by providing eye care to all. To this end, Aravind has through years of hard work and experimentation developed a production system that is efficient, customer friendly, and economically self-sustaining. In the field of cardiac surgery, Dr. Devi Shetty and his team have built Narayana Health (NH), a rapidly growing low-cost, high-quality hospital system, which has expanded to the Americas.

Innovation, like evolution, requires a large breeding ground of variety, from which ideas can be selected, nurtured, and developed. With global information flows, ideas and innovations from different contexts can be brought together. India has become a fertile ground for innovations both in technologies and management.

CHAPTER 1: INTRODUCTION

V. K. Singh and Paul Lillrank

Health care needs innovations, not only in clinical methods, diagnostics, and pharmaceuticals but also in how services are organized, financed, produced, delivered, and distributed. Innovation is something novel, it can be replicated and repeated, and it produces value both to the innovator and users. Innovation is like evolution: it requires variety, repetition, and selection. The role of innovation research is to identify, observe, describe, model, explain, and communicate innovations to accelerate learning and adaptation.

CHAPTER 2: GLOBAL TRENDS IN HEALTH-SYSTEM INNOVATION

Anne Snowdon, Karin Schnarr, and Charles Alessi

National health systems face similar challenges all over the world. The proliferation of noncommunicable diseases changes the demand for services. Simultaneously, information and communication technologies empower patients and turn them into consumers asking to be treated not as partners. Advances in pharmaceuticals, devices, analytics, and methods provide the service supply side with increasingly effective tools.

When more can be done, more is asked for. Health-care costs are reaching unsustainable levels. The trend is toward value-based health systems, health and wellness, patient engagement, prioritization, and quality. This has the potential to undermine the hegemony of the medical model of health. Health-care consumerism enables patients to make informed treatment choices and set their own priorities.

CHAPTER 3: LEARNING FROM INDUSTRY: INNOVATING IN HEALTH-CARE OPERATION

Paul Lillrank

Health-care providers apply management methods. Most of them have their origins in manufacturing, where quality, cost efficiency, and flexibility have improved dramatically over the past half-century. Despite several success stories, the overall performance of health service systems in relation to the resources spent has not improved at the same rate. Health service production needs methodologies based on the specific characteristics of health care. Management-based segmentation methods reveal that emergencies, continuous care, prevention, and cure have different logic of production, value creation, waste, demand, and finance. Healthcare Operations Management focuses on how to organize resources and flows, so that given targets, cost and clinical quality, and patient experience can be achieved with the available resources.

CHAPTER 4: LEAN AND INNOVATION: "THE TWO RESPONSIBILITIES"

Marc S. Hafer, John Gallagher, and Adam Ward

Lean is a management philosophy and a set of methods widely used in health care. The basic principles are to define customer value, identify the value chain, organize processes based on flow, eliminate nonvalue-adding activities, and involve all employees in continuous improvement, that is, the conversion of a current state of affairs into a better one by following known principles aiming at industry best practices.

The first responsibility is to improve based on existing views of patient value by eliminating quality errors, unnecessary steps, and waiting. The second responsibility is innovation in how patient value is created. Lean provides a structured approach for the pursuit of innovation.

CHAPTER 5: CULTIVATING AN INNOVATIVE CULTURE THROUGH LEAN

Tan Ghim Meng and Philip Choo

Lean calls for a profound change in organizational culture. At Tan Tock Seng Hospital (TTSH), Singapore, Lean has proven to be applicable in improving efficiency, as well as building an innovative culture. TTSH distilled key Lean principles into a language accepted by health-care workers: *Faster, Better, Cheaper, and Safer* care. An overall framework, My Care, was established to provide training at various management levels, involve staff, install a system for daily improvements, and conduct specific development projects.

CHAPTER 6: INNOVATIVE APPROACHES TO BUILD HEALTH-CARE FACILITIES

Chris Lloyd

The decisions taken in the design of products, processes, services, and buildings have a lifetime impact on the cost of ownership. Lean hospital design provides a methodology that focuses on patient flows; engages the staff, patients, and stakeholders; is fast and effective; and ensures robust, repeatable, and sustainable operational concepts. The model has five steps: capture the needs, rather than wants of the customer; create the operational model; define the main flows; create the services; and produce the design.

CHAPTER 7: HOSPITAL PLANNING AND DESIGN INNOVATION FOR LEAN OPERATION

S.K. Biswas and V.K. Singh

Hospital design has adopted the principle "Design follows first patients, then functions." New tools and technologies, such as ICT, evidence-based planning, Lean, and life-cycle cost analysis are used. Iris Hospital in Kolkata is the first Indian hospital that has been planned using these concepts.

A hospital information system was developed in-house to ensure that processes standardized at the design stage were followed by the staff, using forms, reports, and tools within the software. Five examples are presented. Value outcomes were identified and tracked through a patient feedback system. Waste in the medication management system was cut out. Just in time was applied in the inventory management system. The value stream was improved in the decentralized billing system. A standard methodology was designed for the discharge system.

CHAPTER 8: PUBLIC HEALTH INNOVATIONS

Vandana Kumar

Distributing basic health services to populations with high level of illiteracy and traditional views on human health takes a lot from the frontline health workers. Two innovations aimed at helping their works are presented.

Mobile Kunji seeks to build support for healthy practices within families and communities by means of an audiovisual job aid, which includes both a mobile service and a deck of 40 illustrated cards, with essential information on pregnancy and newborn health. The frontline health workers use it during counseling sessions with rural families.

SughaVazhvu Healthcare provides evidence-based primary health care to rural India. Early risk assessment is implemented through mobile phones to ensure community-based disease mapping.

CHAPTER 9: BEHAVIOR CHANGES, THE LAST MILE IN HEALTH CARE

Shiban Ganju

Health literacy is the least expensive way to reduce the disease burden. Save a Mother (SAM), an NGO, is working on demand generation by spreading health literacy through social behavior change communication. Maintaining health is as much a responsibility as it is a right. SAM simplifies complex knowledge into a few essential messages. Communities convert these messages into songs and slogans. Volunteers are trained as health activists using disease-based modules. SAM has successfully applied its experience in maternal health to tuberculosis control, population stabilization, and water-borne diseases.

CHAPTER 10: COST-EFFECTIVE, SCALABLE, AND SUSTAINABLE MODEL FOR PRIMARY HEALTH CARE

Ankur Pegu and Sundeep Kapila

Health shocks are the single biggest cause of impoverishment in India, pushing millions of Indian households below the poverty line each year. Swasth addresses this through frugal health centers that provide all primary care services and connect to a network of referral secondary and tertiary care providers. Average expenditure per health episode at Swasth Health Centres is less than half of other urban private providers. Costs are contained through a low-cost drug supply chain, pathology laboratory, and an in-house integrated IT platform for Electronic Health Records and Enterprise Resource Planning. Swasth India demonstrates that the primary health-care needs of urban poor can be met through a cost-effective, scalable, and self-sustaining model.

CHAPTER 11: DOING COMMUNITY GOOD IS GOOD FOR BUSINESS

Bahare Forotan

Access to essential and life-saving medicines is a pressing issue, especially in rural areas in developing countries. Novartis created Arogya Parivar (Healthy Family) in 2007 as a for-profit social business to serve those living at the base of the pyramid in rural India. The initiative offers education on basic health issues, treatment options, and prevention through affordable medicines. Arogya Parivar treats people in low-income bands as individuals with some purchasing power. By increasing health awareness through a market-based approach, companies can better meet their needs, prevent harm, increase their productivity and incomes, and empower their entry into the formal economy.

CHAPTER 12: PROCESS EFFICIENCY BY INNOVATION

Anssi Mikola and Paul Lillrank

Aravind Eye Clinic is one of the best-known health-care innovations in terms of procedures, management, and business models. Aravind has developed a frugal high-volume production system for cataract surgery. Aravind manages demand through two types of inbound logistics: the patients who show up at its facilities and those approached by its outreach program. The latter pose a managerial challenge as flow must be efficient to minimize patients' absence from work, resource efficiency must be maximized as most of these patients do not pay for their care, and quality must be assured to prevent complications and delays. Aravind is a textbook case of how the fundamental drivers of productivity, division of labor, specialization, and standardization can be applied in health care.

CHAPTER 13: STANFORD OPERATING SYSTEM: ALIGNING PURPOSE WITH PEOPLE AND PERFORMANCE

Amir Dan Rubin

Stanford Health Care vision is to heal humanity through science and compassion, one patient at a time. The Stanford Operating System aligns purpose, people, and performance. Its components are strategic deployment, value stream improvement, and active daily management. These are applied in the key domains of complex care, network care, virtual care, and population care.

CHAPTER 14: MANAGING STAKEHOLDERS AND PATIENT EXPERIENCES TO ACHIEVE BETTER OUTCOME

Kavita Narayan

The measure of a health system is the health outcomes of its target population. Outcomes are driven by three different activities: diagnosis and care plan, safe and error-free execution, and patient experience.

Patient experiences can be improved in various ways: coordination of the patient journey, throughput time reduction, focus on stakeholders, the Disney management method, and drawing on Eastern traditions, such as Ayurvedic treatment.

CHAPTER 15: LEAPFROG THROUGH mHEALTH

Sachin Gaur

Connected Health is a delivery model that uses technology to provide services remotely, easing the constraints of location and time. There are close to 1 billion mobile phones in India. With cloud computing and powerful sensors mobile devices can have superior capabilities, such as diagnostic kits that allow the test data to be recorded in real time and backed up on cloud-based storage. The National Health Portal (NHP) provides a single point of access for authenticated preventive health information, housing various digital initiatives.

CHAPTER 16: INNOVATION EXCELLENCE: LEARNING FROM EMERGING AND DEVELOPED ECONOMIES

V. K. Singh

Innovations aim at creating new value or finding ways to produce known value with less waste. Innovations typically have a fuzzy front end of new ideas and combinations, which are not easily managed. The innovation process from the idea to fruition is long and complex, but to an extent manageable with systematic methods, such as Lean and Innovation Excellence. Innovations get adapted in ecosystems that may or may not be supportive. The health-care ecosystems in developed and developing countries are different, thereby creating different types of innovations. Collaborative approaches can open to new insights.

CHAPTER 17: INNOVATIVE APPROACHES OF AFFORDABLE HEALTH CARE IN EMERGING ECONOMIES

Venkataramanaiah Saddikuti, Mohan Gopalakrishnan, and Saji Gopinath

Medical technologies have an important role in the delivery of affordable health care. The case of an Indian medical device manufacturing company is used to illustrate the 4A decision framework. Awareness of preventive care was developed in collaboration with different stakeholders. Access has been improved by directly supplying devices and support services to hospitals. Affordability has increased through cost optimization, high volume, and diversification across the value chain. Adoptability has been demonstrated through close work with governmental and private organizations for improving sales on a large scale through partnerships and collaboration.

CHAPTER 18: SUPPLY CHAIN INNOVATIONS IN HEALTH CARE

Atanu Chaudhuri

Supply chain management integrates supply and demand management within and across companies. Pharmaceutical supply chains were structured to avoid stock outs and to meet regulatory requirements through high inventory levels. There is a need to redesign to improve both cost efficiency and responsiveness. By its nature, supply chain innovations can rarely be accomplished by a single organization and require cooperation from the supply chain partners. Organizations must redesign processes while involving people within and across their organizations. Innovative practices can break the trade-offs.

CHAPTER 19: THREE-DIMENSIONAL HEALTH CARE: "THE NEED OF THE HOUR"

Satish Kr. Gupta

The global burden of disease has shifted from communicable to non-communicable diseases and created misalignment between needs and resources. Need has arisen for a comprehensive model of medical practice and education including spirituality. It should be capable of dealing with health problems in their physical, psychological, social, cultural, and existential dimensions and address the root cause of disease.

Spiritual symptoms may interact with other symptoms. Such synergistic effects have not been widely studied as there is a lack of a common language for spirituality, as well as concerns on ethics, and cultural and religious differences. It is imperative that soul, mind, and body, all three, are addressed. The next logical step for medical science is to address all the three aspects of a human being with a three-dimensional health care model.

CHAPTER 20: INNOVATIVE INITIATIVES IN HEALTH CARE BY INDIAN GOVERNMENT

Vishwas Mehta

The Indian government has taken initiatives toward universal health coverage through health insurance, health-care delivery system, human resource management, knowledge networking, drug procurement, and public–private partnerships. The central government operates through the National Health Mission, constituting of a rural and an urban part. The government has concluded that increasing the number of highly trained medical doctors cannot solve the problems of primary and preventive care. A bachelor of science (community health) degree has been established to create a cadre of middle-level public health professionals, community health officers (CHO). They are deployed to strengthen the public health delivery system at the grassroots level.

CHAPTER 21: INDOVATION: FRUGAL INNOVATION IN INDIAN HEALTH CARE

Sandeep Bhalla and Nimisha Singh Verma

Indovation is an Indian way of frugal innovations attempting to make best use of available resources. Health care is a set of networks connecting government actors, businesses, and charities. They can combine in various ways: public–private partnerships, government–charity collaborations, and social enterprises. These are, like charities, founded on a social vision but adapt a business-like organizational architecture, operating on the premise that customers perceive the value of their offerings and are willing to pay. Several examples depicting various combinations are described.

CHAPTER 22: EMERGING HEALTH-CARE INNOVATIONS

Preethi Pradhan and Keerti Pradhan

Several technical and managerial innovations have the potential to change the future of health-care delivery. Four categories are discussed. First, there are technologies, such as Google Glass, that were developed for consumer or industrial use, but are finding useful applications in health care. Second, there are technologies that are specifically developed to solve known problems within health care, such as noninvasive procedures. Third, there are innovations to empower patients by providing better information such as personal health devices. Fourth, advances in financing assist in converting ideas to fruition faster.

Foreword

Innovation is often seen as the modern-day equivalent to the old model of efficiency. It used to be that global competition made efficiency a necessity for the survival of industries and organizations. In today's economy, however, it is innovation that provides an alternative path to replace simple exercises in efficiency—by crafting, modifying, and transforming the old into a highly scalable and utilized new.

Innovation is not just important to industries that face global competition. In the age of the Internet, people all over the world can see what is happening elsewhere, in real time and from multiple points of view. News of what is possible, as well as what is significant and capable of producing lasting change, travels fast. As a result, innovation is a mandate across industries, organizations, individuals, and even governments.

Today more than ever, India has a tremendous opportunity for innovation—it is a country with over 500 million young people, a rich pool of technology and business talent, and a host of challenges present right before our eyes. Although the climate is challenging, it is also full of possibilities. The President of India has declared this as the Decade of Innovation, and the National Innovation Council, along with state and sectorial councils, are focused on developing and cultivating a culture of innovation across many verticals, including health care. The focus is on incubating ideas and enabling innovation ecosystems at the bottom of the pyramid. This is where India has a unique advantage, because Western models of resource-intensive consumption cannot suit India's needs. As developed economies enter a period of slower growth, it is the emerging economies, like India, that have the opportunity to develop examples of how more can be achieved with less. In essence, India can be a model for innovation at the base of the pyramid.

This book takes a deeper look at a specific industry that has often been overlooked when speaking about innovation—both in India and abroad—and one that is in dire need of innovation across its value chain: health care. It is an industry that is facing challenges the world over as it struggles to find ways to reduce costs and increase value, to improve patient experience while providing increased access to all people. Innovation in the health-care context has often been applied only to the development of new drugs or devices; however, for real change to occur in the industry, innovation must be seen as a broader phenomenon—one that looks at areas previously untouched by change. And that is what this book examines.

Bringing together experience and expertise from across the health-care industry, the writers look at innovations that can bring about real advances in the industry. The book explores the importance of Lean health care and innovation, looking at new concepts, methods, and tools to advance processes and operational flow. Also included are case studies of actual results in health-care innovation from three continents, providing concrete examples of five levels of innovation present in health care. The writers also include information on nontraditional ecosystems of innovation, moving outside of expected technological innovations to include innovations in social persuasion, rural health delivery, and planning and design of hospitals. The book focuses on important issues across the industry, including access to care, demand creation, patient experiences, and data—to fuel and implement new ideas and new models of delivery of affordable care in the context of emerging economies.

The writers of this book cover a lot of ground, offering a comprehensive look at best practices and out-of-the-box thinking and doing. This book provides a timely discussion on what can be done in India and beyond to offer the global population better care, reduced costs, and overall higher quality patient experience, no matter where they live or what unique health-care challenges in the value chain they may come across. The time for true innovation in health care has arrived, and thanks to the many writers involved in this book, we have a launching pad for both discussion and immediate action.

Sam Pitroda
Advisor to Prime Minister of India and Minister
Chairman, National Innovation Council

Setting Tone of Innovation in Health Sector

EVERYONE HAS SOMETHING TO TEACH AND EVERYONE HAS SOMETHING TO LEARN

Nigel Crisp

There are striking similarities in the challenges facing health systems around the world, as well as sharp differences.

Our interdependence globally means that we need to work together to confront the threats of pandemics, conflict, climate change, food scarcity, and large-scale population migrations. Health is interwoven with foreign, economic, development, and security policies worldwide.

The similarities do not, however, end there. We are also facing the same sorts of problems in delivering health care and improving the health of our populations. Changing economic fortunes means that the populations of emerging and growing economies are demanding universal health coverage at the same time as the countries of the developed West are struggling to find ways to maintain coverage for their citizens. The challenges for both are similar:

- How to focus on prevention not cure: managing the growth in long-term chronic conditions and working across sectors to improve health
- How to improve the integration and quality of services
- How to maximize the gains from science and technology development
- How to fund health systems that can provide equitable access to health care for whole populations

To address these challenges, we need to *turn the world upside down*—change our mindsets, abandon many of our preconceptions, and learn from people outside the (sometimes) hidebound health establishments of the high-income countries, including from leaders in low and middle countries who, without our resources and the baggage of our history and vested interests, have developed practices and ideas that have wider application.[1]

There is a whole range of learning to be had from people outside health care, from industry, and other sectors, as well as from young people and pioneers within health. I will concentrate here, however, on learning from low- and middle-income countries and on the importance of combining insights from around the world. My observation is that there are six main areas to consider:

1. Finding ways to engage the community, family, and women
2. Using the resources at hand to develop new service models and new technologies
3. Linking the fields of health, education, and work
4. Developing new social and business enterprises to deliver improvements
5. Linking public health and clinical medicine—a concern for the health of a population as well as an individual patient focus
6. Training health workers for the job in hand and not just for the profession

Examples of Practices and Innovation

Some examples of these approaches are now very well known, such as BRAC (formerly Bangladesh Rural Advancement Committee) in Bangladesh, whose work is based very substantially on empowering women as the agents of change, or Aravind in India, which over almost 40 years has delivered high-quality services to some of the poorest people in the country through a systematic approach to innovation and quality. I will draw attention here to other examples of new service design in mental health, the development of technology, and the widespread redesign of staff roles.

I have recently been collecting examples of practices and innovations in mental health in low- and middle-income countries, which might have application in high-income countries.[2] Among many interesting examples, a series from Jamaica stand out in which Professor Frederick W. Hickling has led the integration of mental health into the Jamaican public health system. It has wide ranging and, sometimes, startling lessons for the development of mental health services elsewhere.

Professor Hickling describes how this has been achieved over 50 years by the combination of four innovative strategies: the gradual deinstitutionalization of the mental hospital, the integration of psychiatry with the public health system, a unique use of medical wards in general hospitals for the treatment of acute psychosis, and the pioneering development of mental health officers who have served as the task shifting catalysts to bring all the elements of this psychiatric/medical assimilation together.

He argues further that the process has catalyzed the development of culturally appropriate methods of treating mental illness in Jamaica. Follow-up services for severe enduring mental illness have been integrated into public health clinics, and into home treatment services. General practitioners now treat mild and moderate mental illness almost exclusively. A National Health Fund guarantees an 80% subsidy on all psychotropic medication. Church-based clinics provide integrated religious counseling alongside psychiatric treatment and care. There is an island-wide child and adolescent treatment service, and a total diversion of treatment of the mentally ill offender from the Correctional Services to the Community Mental Health Services. There has also been the establishment of cultural therapy based on a novel analytic technique, psychohistoriography, pioneered in Jamaica.

Listening to Professor Hickling from a British perspective one cannot help wondering why many mental health patients cannot be treated on general wards. As one aide says "If a patient is treated at St Anne's hospital it is just an episode like everywhere else; if it's at Belleville . . . then he's a madman."

There has been widespread innovation in technology too. A simple low-cost device that helps newborn babies to breathe and has the potential to transform the life chances for thousands of African babies has been awarded the highest prize in the first GSK and Save the Children US$1 million Healthcare Innovation Award. It has been developed by Friends of Sick Children in Malawi—a partnership between the pediatric department of Queen Elizabeth Central Hospital in Blantyre, Malawi; Rice 360°: Institute for Global Health Technologies in the United States; and the University of Malawi College of Medicine.

The life-saving kit, called a *bubble* continuous positive airway pressure, or bCPAP, is used to help babies in respiratory distress, which is often caused by acute respiratory infections like pneumonia. Continuous positive airway pressure (CPAP) devices use air pressure to keep patients airways open, and as there are few wall-mounted air supplies in Malawi hospitals, the newly innovated bCPAP air pump works on its own. Moreover, it is made of durable materials that are inexpensive and easy to repair. A similar version is already commonly used in developed countries where they cost at least US$6000 each. This innovative low-cost bCPAP adaptation can be produced for approximately US$400.

This extraordinary example illustrates the power of institutions working in partnership around the world—each bringing their own special skills to the task in hand. These partnerships are a very common theme in the development of new roles for health workers that have developed around the world. Sometimes called *task shifting, task sharing,* or *skill-mix change*, this approach has been used extensively where there are health worker shortages and major health needs that are not being addressed. Many of these approaches could inspire similar changes in high-income countries and, indeed, we are already seeing community health worker models, pioneered in Africa, being transferred to New York and London.

Not all such practices are successful of course, and I have been involved in a recent study by a British All Party Parliamentary Group that identified the success factors.[3] They are very simple, as Figure 1 shows. There needs to be good preparation and leadership, appropriate job design and recruitment, formal training and scope for progression, good supervision and the ability to refer patients on to more expert health workers, and, finally, there needs to be good teamwork and recognition within the system of the achievements of the workers. It is simple to describe but, of course, difficult to do in practice.

These few examples hint at the rich seam of ideas and practices that have developed and are developing around the world. Some, of course, are not innovations at all but traditional or long-term practices and just new to the Western observer.

There is a need to continue to collect such examples, analyze them, and learn the lessons from them. Examples from one context cannot simply been transferred to another—there are many cultural and contextual differences to take into account—but they can suggest new approaches that will work, offer insights, and, above all else, influence and inspire others.

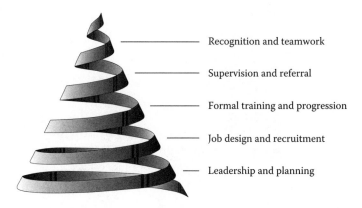

Recognition and teamwork

Supervision and referral

Formal training and progression

Job design and recruitment

Leadership and planning

FIGURE 1
Success factors for skill-mix change. (From All Party Parliamentary Group on Global Health: All the Talents—How New Roles and Better Teamwork Can Release Potential and Improve Health Services, July 2012.)

The Institute for Healthcare Improvement of Cambridge, Massachusetts, has played a major role in importing ideas and practices from industry to health care—some of them innovations and some just new to us. It coined an expression that should guide us all as we explore learning from elsewhere: "Everyone has something to teach and everyone has something to learn."

REFERENCES

1. Crisp N: *Turning the World Upside Down—The Search for Global Health in the 21st Century*. Boca Raton, FL: CRC Press, 2010.
2. Retrieved from www.ttwud.org
3. All Party Parliamentary Group on Global Health: All the Talents—How New Roles and Better Teamwork can Release Potential and Improve Health Services, July 2012. Available at: http://www.who.int/workforcealliance/knowledge/resources/Allthetalents_fullReport.pdf

QUALITY CARE AT AFFORDABLE COST

Devi Shetty

At the advent of the Industrial Revolution some 300 years ago, the main concern was scarcity of everything: food, clothing, and shelter. These daily necessities had all been invented, but the economy did not have the technology and the capacity to produce them in sufficient volumes. The development of industrial management, based on the principles of division of labor, specialization, and standardization, led to a rapid increase in production volume. The engine of growth changed from employing more resources to deploying them more wisely. Productivity-driven growth is to produce more with less. A century or so later the Industrial Revolution started to deliver entirely new products based on scientific discoveries such as the combustion engine and electricity. In advanced economies, the common man now enjoys a standard of living 20–30 times higher than his preindustrial ancestors.

In services in general, and health care in particular, a productivity revolution of the same speed and impact has not yet happened. More is needed to produce more; in advanced countries more resources achieves less health outcomes. There are several reasons, many of them valid. Health care is about patients with varying needs and situations, which require clinical judgment and individual adjustments. Despite advances in therapies and technologies, the core service encounter is still undertaken with a preindustrial craft mode of production: a doctor meets a patient. However, although clinical intuition and individual adjustment is always needed at the core, health care is also a service production system with several support, preparation, and management processes to which Industrial Management methods can be applied.

A large number of people in India are deprived of care that, technically speaking, has been innovated long time ago. The constraints lie in distribution, access, and price. Therefore, the mission of NH is to develop, expand, and continuously improve a service production system that can deliver affordable care to the masses. In fulfilling its mission, NH strives to learn and apply management methods, even those with their origins in other industries.

Management innovations are needed to lower prices, expand access, reduce waste, improve quality, and offer mass customization, that is, standard solutions that can easily be adjusted to individual needs. To do such things successfully, NH needs to be profitable.

The governance model of NH can be described, as Christopher Meyer does in his book *Standing on the Sun*, as the fourth sector.

The first sector is ordinary business that strives to maximize its profits by producing what their chosen customer segment wants to pay for. The second sector is government, with the basic mission to guarantee external security and internal safety, which in modern societies includes safety in cases of diseases, accidents, and misfortunes. The third sector is composed of charities, voluntary associations, and various aspects of the civil society. Charities have a social mission, and fund their activities by soliciting charitable contributions and voluntary labor.

The fourth sector, also called for-benefit producers, combines elements of the first and the third. Like charities, they have a social mission and use revenue models based on progressive pricing. Patients are charged by their ability to pay. Those without means will get services subsidized by those better off. However, the fourth sector players do not want to rely on contributions from donors or governments. Rather they fund their operations through income from paying patients, and raise capital in the ordinary way through retained earnings and capital markets. To do this, they need to expand the market through lower prices while being profitable. In a free market, profit is a reward that satisfied customers grant a producer.

The classical productivity drivers, division of labor, specialization, and standardization can be applied to hospital operations. Best practices can be standardized and disseminated through an organization. Steps in the value chain can be modularized and combined to improve the patient experience. Steps that do not create value can be eliminated to reduce waste.

Surgery is, and for the most part will continue to be a craft, performed by highly skilled specialists. Therefore, economies of scale do not work on the patient process level. However, there are many ways to increase capacity utilization through teamwork. A large hospital has the possibility to share infrastructure and use its volume to create supply chains and business ecosystems to support hospital operations.

Let me give an example. In cardiac surgery, materials are 32% of cost, the rest being labor and facilities. One such material is the gown that surgeons and staff need to wear while in the operating room. For hygienic and handling reasons, disposable gowns made of nonwoven fabric are the best. We used to purchase them from a supplier at INR5000 (US$83) apiece. That is a lot. The alternative is reusable gowns made of linen. They require industrial-strength laundry, and can be washed and reused about 60 times. We calculated the cost per use and arrived at INR1200 (US$20). We contacted the supplier and asked to renegotiate the price, offering INR2000 (US$33) per piece. They refused. So we studied the supply chain of surgical gowns. We found that the fabric was bought in high volumes from Alstom, France, at a fraction of the cost of the final product. The fabric needs to be cut in shape, stitched, and sterilized. NH established a supply company that bought the fabric directly from France and arranged for the processing locally. The cost per gown could be reduced to INR1200 (US$20), and with some process improvements, further down to INR800 (US$13) per piece. A hospital much smaller than NH would not have been in the position to build a supply chain for surgical gowns.

High volume means more patients can be treated with less cost. Therefore, NH intends to keep growing while continuously improving all aspects of hospital services.

PERSPECTIVES AND INSIGHTS FROM ARAVIND EYE CARE SYSTEM

Thulasiraj Ravilla and R. D. Ravindran

Aravind's three and half decade journey in eye care have resulted in a number of innovations. Some of these have been truly innovative technologies, products, or processes, whereas others are a result of continuous enhancements that are perceived as innovations by those seeing them for the first time.

Looking back, innovations have stemmed from two sources:

The first driver of innovations has been *Aravind's purpose* to "eliminate needless blindness by providing eye care to all." As it happens with any organization, there is always a value framework within which the purpose and its fulfillment has to take place. The nonnegotiable values lay down a boundary, which defines what the organization can and cannot do. For Aravind, the nonnegotiable values are "equity, transparency, maintaining human dignity and providing the highest quality of care irrespective of the patient's capacity to pay."

The second source of innovation logically derives from the first. Innovations often appear around the *bottlenecks and challenges* that come up while pursuing the purpose within the value framework. Such bottlenecks often tend to be around resources (human resources, equipment, supplies, or the physical infrastructure), technology, or established external norms.

Although the purpose and bottlenecks are what spur innovations, the innovations come out of the paradigms that we adopt. Broadly, these are about how we look at "customer, cost, quality, and the ecosystem within which we operate."[1]

CUSTOMER VERSUS NONCUSTOMER

In health care, the overarching goal is to provide universal care. We have to be concerned about noncustomers, those who will benefit by a health intervention but are not seeking it. This must become the focus especially when this cohort is significantly larger than those who seek care. Only by providing care to the noncustomer we will achieve the goal. However, most hospitals tend to focus only on those who seek care with them or have systems to woo those who go elsewhere. Very few hospitals do anything to bring into the fold those who are not seeking care but, from a clinical standpoint, need it.

For example, population-based studies have shown that less than 20% of those with significant refractive errors are actually wearing corrective spectacles, whereas 80% who will benefit by it are not. If one seeks to set this right, the real focus has to be on the 80% who today are not seeking any intervention for their compromised near or distant vision. This focus is what gives birth to a number of locally effective innovations.

Aravind, pursuing its purpose to eliminate needless blindness, reached out to people with the help of local communities, education systems, and industries. Outreach screening programs were conducted to reach out to school children, workers in industries, as well as the general community. Such reach out covers over a million people each year, with over a third of them getting some significant intervention such as surgery, laser, glasses, or medications.

Although these activities result in short-term benefits, the longer term impact is positively influencing health seeking behavior, augmenting the customer base for the hospital, and making progress toward universal health care.

COST AND AFFORDABILITY

Cost and affordability are significant obstacles. Here, effective innovations stem from the paradigm of viewing cost from the patients rather than from the provider's perspective. When the cost perspective is limited to that of providers, the interventions are not effective. We see this often. Even when interventions such as immunization are offered for free, we see that the uptake is not universal. In most instances, the patients have to incur significant cost and effort in accessing care or in complying with the prescribed interventions such as medicines, glasses, or surgery.

A recently published article[2] shows that when patients are given a prescription for glasses, less than 25% of them actually end up buying and using them. However, when the system was able to deliver the prescribed glasses immediately, the uptake was over 75%. In both instances the patient paid for the glasses. However, in the later scenario, the innovation was to eliminate the cost of accessing the glasses by providing them on the spot.

Thus, there is a need to systematically get a deeper understanding of the patient's total cost and design systems that will continually reduce it, thus making care more and more affordable.

QUALITY: OUTCOME VERSUS OVERALL EXPERIENCE

In health care, as in most service sectors, the word of mouth propagation about a facility or service based on overall patient experience drives and sustains demand. However, most health-care providers take a myopic view on quality, restricting their purview to just clinical outcomes. What the patients appreciated as good quality is the overall experience in the health system in which the treatment outcomes are a part, granted an important one. The patient experience and the ensuing satisfaction or lack of it comes through many domains—level of patient empowerment, perceptions around value for money, transparency in the care-giving processes, communication, ambience, staff interactions, and so on.

Innovations have to happen in all these domains constantly to strengthen the patient experience.

At Aravind, introducing patient counselors significantly increased compliance to treatment. A total of 95% of those advised in outreach to undergo surgery accept it. Within the hospital, these counselors, who really serve as patient advocates, are able to empower the patients in making the right treatment choices and are with them to address any fear or concerns about surgery or treatment. They were first introduced in 1992 and today there are close to 200 of them working in the hospital. Their introduction to the human resources pool enhanced the compliance to medical advice leading to better clinical outcomes and higher patient satisfaction resulting in continuous increase in the patient volumes.[3]

Maintaining human dignity is also a significant influencer of patient satisfaction. This can be achieved through innovative systems that promote transparency and equity.

The patients are in complete control of where they get care at Aravind. They can choose to go to the free hospital and pay nothing or very little, or go to the paying section by paying the prescribed fee. This has almost eliminated dropouts. Transparency in pricing and knowing exactly how much it will cost and the easily appreciable differences in the facilities explained by the patient counselors have helped the patient to be in control of this decision.

CONSTRAINTS: OBSTACLES VERSUS OPPORTUNITIES

Every organization has to operate within certain constrains that are either unconsciously self-imposed or an external reality. However, innovative organizations are able to recognize such constraints as opportunities rather than as obstacles and overcome them and design the services within the constraints.

To illustrate, in the late 1980s surgery with an intraocular lens (IOL) became the standard of care in the West for those with poor vision due to cataract. This new procedure offered a superior quality of vision and did not require high-powered glasses with thick lenses. However, due to the very-high cost of the IOLs (around US$200 then), the eye care fraternity from the World Health Organization, international funding agencies, and governments were against embracing it on account of the high cost of the IOL; the high investment required for equipment like microscopes, ultrasound equipment, and lasers; and the skills required to perform the surgery with an implant. All these were assumed to be unchangeable parameters. However, the commitment to give the best to the patient led Aravind to explore various options to bring down the cost of IOLs and build the required skills to perform this new technique. This thought process led to the establishment of Aurolab in 1992. It was able to produce world class IOLs then at a price of US$10. Today, the basic IOL is priced at less than US$2, and Aurolab meets over 8% of the global IOL needs, sending its products to over 120 countries.[4]

To address the other constraints, short-term skill development training programs were put in place to help practicing ophthalmologists develop the new surgical technique under close mentorship, thus minimizing the harm to the patients during the learning curve. These training programs were exponentially expanded by training of trainers who then went on to do such training programs in their own places.

Such innovations have helped the global adoption of a radically new technology. In less than a decade, this became the standard of care across all countries.

Adopting the right paradigm or perspective to customer, cost, quality, and constraints drives effective innovation.

ADDRESSING THE BOTTLENECKS

The other drivers of innovation operate at the operational level and these essentially present themselves as bottlenecks in the execution of the purpose. Such bottlenecks are often in the realms of human resources, infrastructure, technology, or established norms.[5]

Human Resources

In most developing countries, there is an acute shortage of skilled human resources, further compounded by concentration in bigger urban centers. In many African countries, it is not unusual to find all the skilled professionals in the country's capital city. In India, it is rare to find a specialist doctor outside the district capital. Although efforts are made to augment the human resources pool and policies are being debated to address the distribution issues, both of these make a difference over a very long time frame. Care to the patients cannot wait till then.

We also need short-term solutions. We have to challenge ourselves to see how we get the most out of the current scarce human resources. We need to ask the following questions:

- Can I make the ophthalmologists perform twice as many surgeries or examine twice as many patients?
- How can I make the ophthalmologists give care to a person in a remote village far away from where the ophthalmologist is located?

Innovations stem out of such self-challenges. When one perseveres to address the challenge and does not give up, innovative solutions emerge.

At Aravind, the entire clinical process was broken down into smaller tasks and it was soon recognized that over 80% of them are routine repetitive tasks involving measurements (intraocular pressure, refractive error) or documentation (imaging). It was then visualized that all such routine repetitive tasks could be offloaded from an ophthalmologist and shifted to another cadre who can be trained to do one or more of these tasks. This led to the development of a new personnel category called mid-level ophthalmic personnel. By deploying them in the right proportion, it was possible to more than quadruple the productivity of an ophthalmologist—the number of surgeries done or patients examined with enhanced quality.[6]

Technology

Technology can play a significant role in addressing some of these bottlenecks. With appropriate technology and work processes, it becomes possible to bridge the geographic gap or the urban-rural divide and provide comprehensive care even at primary levels.

For example, a well-trained ophthalmic technician in a rural village is able to provide comprehensive eye care for over 90% of the patients through a low-cost telemedicine technology. A complete workup is done by the ophthalmic technician and the findings are entered directly into an online electronic medical record. Each of the patients then receives a real-time video consultation with an ophthalmologist sitting in the base hospital in one of the urban centers, who is able to review the medical record and interact directly with the patient and the technician to come up with a definitive diagnosis and treatment advice. The prescription for glasses or medicines is sent by the ophthalmologist to be printed out at the rural Vision Centre.[7]

Through low-cost telemedicine technology, Aravind Eye Hospital today sees over 1,000 patients each day through its network of rural Vision Centres (primary eye care centers) staffed by ophthalmic technicians.

Today, a lot more technological innovations are required as most technology today is designed for use in urban setting with good support infrastructure and for use by skilled doctors. We need technologies that are designed to be used in rural settings by workers with less educational qualifications.

Processes

Challenging existing processes and practices are required to come up with solutions for bottlenecks. Surgical facilities and good surgeons are both at a premium and in acute short supply. Hence, the focus has got to be on getting the maximum out of such scarce resources. The common protocols for surgical facilities are often set by general surgeons and procedures take a long time, involving large incisions with the risk of infections. However, such parameters are not relevant for many other high-volume surgical situations as in ophthalmic surgery.

In ophthalmic surgery, the incisions are very small, measured in millimeters, and the surgery takes a very short time and is almost always performed when the person has no infection. The level of stringency required for avoiding surgical infection is very different in the two settings.

Recognizing this, as well as the need to have a high level of productivity of the operating rooms and surgeons, Aravind Eye Hospital innovated the "two-table surgical system." Each surgeon is allotted two surgical tables within the same operating room and assisted by two scrub nurses, one for each table, and a common circulating nurse. The surgeon is provided six to eight sterile surgical instrument sets. The two tables are placed 5–6 ft apart to allow easy circulation as well as placement of the surgical microscope in the center. Waiting time between surgeries has been completely eliminated by having the next patient prepared on the second table, as the surgeon is operating on the patient in the first table. The surgical outcomes and infection rates are closely monitored. The infection rate is comparable or lower than those reported in the West, where they follow much more stringent protocols that allow only one operating table in an operating room.

The two-table surgical system is a necessity in countries like India with a very high number of patients in need of surgeries. Such innovations came out of the necessity of having to do a lot with fewer resources at no compromise to quality. This results not only in a higher number of patients served but also at much lower cost with no compromised clinical outcomes or infection rates.[8]

Although the above was an example of an innovation that significantly enhanced productivity and thus reduced costs, there are several process innovations that can reduce the overall cost to the patients. One such innovation would be to carry out the complete care cycle for a patient in a single visit. This means that the process design allows for all investigations, cross consultations, diagnosis, and treatment or surgery to happen on the same visit, which could be more than a day.

For example, the management of diabetic retinopathy can be done with a process designed to examine a diabetic patient, do a fundus photo, and perform a laser procedure if indicated, all of it on the same day. Similarly, for a person walking in with a diminished vision diagnosed as requiring cataract surgery, all the investigations can be completed swiftly and the surgery scheduled for the next day. This requires a high level of coordination and scheduling of resources and supplies. In traditional settings, a surgical intervention typically requires four to five visits that cause a significant financial burden to the individuals and the families.

Such process innovations significantly reduce the number of visits a patient has to make for receiving the care, which directly translates to savings in cost and effort for the patient. An added advantage is that it also eliminates a lot of duplicated tasks for the hospital when a patient is made to make multiple visits for the same condition.

SUMMARY

Innovations that are driven by a broader public health purpose and patient-centric perspectives tend to be very effective not just in the hospitals where such innovations are born but well beyond them. Looking at the challenges and the current situation with a patient-centric paradigm results in the right innovation.

REFERENCES

1. Thualsiraj R. D., Sanil J. How can hospital programs be strengthened to enhance achievement to vision 2020 objectives? *Middle East African J Ophthal.* 2011;18(2): 102–108.
2. Ramasamy D., Joseph S., Valaguru V., Mitta V. P., Ravilla T. D., Cotch M. F. Cluster randomized trial to compare spectacle delivery systems at outreach eye camps in South India. *Ophthalmic Epidemiol.* 2013;20(5):308–314.
3. Lindfield R. Improving the quality of cataract surgery. *Community Eye Health J.* 2014;27(85):9–11.
4. Ibrahim M., Bhandari A., Sandhu J. S., Balakrishnan P. Making sight affordable (Part I): Aurolab pioneers production of low-cost technology for cataract surgery. *Innovations.* 2006;1(3):25–41.
5. Govindarajan V, Ramamurti R. Delivering world class health care, affordably. *Harvard Business Review.* 2013;8(11):1–7.
6. Comprehensive planning of human resources for eye care to meet the goals of vision 2020: The right to sight. World Health Organization. *SEA-Ophthal.* 2002;120.
7. Qureshi B. M., Mansur R., Al-Rajhi A., Lansingh V., Eckert K., Hassan K., Thulasiraj R. D., Muhit M., Khanna R. C., Ismat C. Best practice eye care models. *Indian J Ophthalmol.* 2012;60(5):351–357.
8. Venkatesh R., Muralikrishnan R., Balent L. C., Prakash S. K., Prajna N. V. Outcomes of high volume cataract surgeries in a developing country. *Br J Ophthalmol.* 2005;89(9):1079–1083.

Acknowledgments

I always skipped this page while reading a book, but while writing a book I realized how important the acknowledgments page is. We could not have completed this book without the support of the people mentioned here. I was toying with the idea of writing a book but could not take the plunge alone. It seemed like a herculean task to create a literary piece. Then I shared my thoughts with Professor Paul Lillrank, known to me for many years, a great academician and researcher. He kindly concurred immediately, and it would have not been possible to complete this long-cherished dream without his support.

This book is a collection of the ideas and practices of both thinkers and doers at the frontline of health-care innovation. We would like to thank each contributor of the book for sharing their experience and knowledge for the benefit of readers.

We had a team of people assisting us along the way. We would like to acknowledge the contributions of Katy Dowd, director of marketing, Simpler. She helped us to identify a dynamic publisher and created a social media network to popularize our work. She patiently rendered professional advice at each stage. Michael Sinocchi, executive editor of Productivity Press, was very quick to take the responsibility of publishing through CRC Press. Jessica Vakili, senior project coordinator, was dedicated to coordinating our project with the publishing house. She gave us documents to peruse to understand the art and steps of publishing and was always available for quick advice when it was needed most. Cynthia Klivecka, project editor at CRC Press, and her team always make things simple for us in moving forward. I cannot forget to mention Ramya Gangadharan, project manager, and her team at diacriTech, ever willing to walk the extra mile to ensure the quality and timeline of the project; it has been pleasure to work with her. Shikha Bassi, a long-time professional associate, looked at each chapter critically and formatted as per requirements of publishers. Gaurav Verma, an expert in health care IT, helped us put technology writings in the right perspective. Divya Singh, a professional and prolific reader, provided advice on what readers might be expecting from the book.

Neerja Singh, who has a background as a scientist, scanned through literature and advised in appropriate naming of chapters. Vishal Singh, an expert on management turnarounds, provided constructive criticism on both content and style.

We would like to thank Simpler Consulting LLC for providing wholehearted support for publishing and making this project successful.

Authors

Dr. Vijai K. Singh superannuated as Surgeon Rear Admiral after 37 years in national and international assignments. He earned MBBS, Masters in Hospital Administration, Diplomate National Board in Hospital and Health Care Management, and M Phil. He was awarded a Distinguished Services Medal for services in Zambia by the President of India and commendation by Zambia. He had been deputy chief medical officer of the United Nations, adjunct professor of the Massachusetts Institute of Technology (MIT), Zaragoza, Spain, and consultant to the National Disaster Management Authority. He was president of the Academy of Hospital Administration, founder director of the International Institute of Health Management Research, chairman of the Health Care Division of Quality Council of India, and member of the International Group on Biosafety. He developed a European Foundation for Quality Management (EFQM) model for Healthcare in India released by Union Health Minister.

Presently, he is Adjunct Research Professor at the International Health Innovation Center, Ivey School of Business, Canada, and Director of Healthcare Asia for Lean Healthcare Excellence-Simpler. He is a member of the National Public Health Committee of Confederation of Indian Industry (CII) and visiting professor of the Indian Institute of Management, Management Development Institute, and Public Health Foundation of India. e-mail: surgravksingh@gmail.com

Paul Lillrank has been a professor of quality and service management at Aalto University since 1994. He earned his PhD from Helsinki University in 1988 after postgraduate studies in Japan, where he studied quality management in Japanese industry. He has worked at Science University of Tokyo, the Boston Consulting Group, and Stockholm School of Economics. He has pioneered industrial management applications in health care and cofounded the Institute of Healthcare Engineering, Management and Architecture (HEMA) at Aalto, Finland, and the Nordic Healthcare Group (NHG), a consultancy. He has published in the areas of health-care operations management, technology transfer, service quality, and process analysis. He teaches regularly at the Indian Institute of Technology, Kharagpur. e-mail: paul.lillrank@aalto.fi

Contributors

Sam Pitroda is an inventor, entrepreneur, and a thought leader. He is advisor to the prime minister of India on information infrastructure and innovations with the rank of cabinet minister. He is the chairman of the National Innovation Council and National Knowledge Commission of India. He holds over 100 international patents and is known as "The father of India's communication revolution." He has received many awards including the Padma Bhushan from the government of India.

Lord Nigel Crisp is an independent member of the House of Lords where he co-chairs the All Party Parliamentary Group on Global Health. He works extensively on health in low- and middle-income countries and was formerly the chief executive of the NHS and permanent secretary of the Department of Health in the United Kingdom. He has written and co-authored several influential books and reports on health globally.

Dr. Devi Shetty is a cardiac surgeon of repute and a strong advocate of "affordable and quality health care." He is chairman and senior consultant cardiac surgeon and heads NH. He is a luminary for his ingenious ideas in the health-care sector. His visionary leadership has drawn global recognition. Due to all its innovations, NH has been an interesting case study for Harvard. The *Wall Street Journal* has christened him as the Henry Ford of Heart Surgery.

Thulasiraj Ravilla, MBA, worked for a multinational company for 8 years before joining Aravind in 1981. Soon after, he spent a year at the University of Michigan as a visiting scholar. He has been a member of the initial leadership team that built Aravind over the years. In 1992, he was instrumental in establishing the Lions Aravind Institute of Community Ophthalmology that he continues to head.

Dr. R. D. Ravindran, on graduating as a doctor, went on to specialize in ophthalmology at Aravind and later at the Madurai Medical College. He then joined Aravind and was instrumental in the development of each of its large hospitals in Tirunelveli, Coimbatore, and Pondicherry. He now serves as the chairman of the entire Aravind Eye Care System.

Dr. Anne Snowdon is the academic chair of the Ivey International Centre for Health Innovation at Western University where she leads work to drive health system improvements. She is a professor at the Ivey Business School and a member of the Health Sciences faculty at Western University and is an associate professor of the School of Rehabilitation Therapy at Queen's University. A Fulbright Scholar, she holds a PhD in nursing from the University of Michigan.

Karin Schnarr is an instructor of strategy at the Ivey Business School at Western University and a research fellow at the Ivey International Centre for Health Innovation. Before academia, she served in senior roles in government including chief of staff at the Ontario Ministry of Health and Long-Term Care in Ontario, Canada. She also held positions as a senior strategy consultant to executive-level clients who spanned the private, public, and not-for-profit sectors in health care.

Dr. Charles Alessi is the Chairman of the National Association of Primary Care, a national membership organization in England. He is a senior advisor to Public Health England and the chairman of NHS Clinical Commissioners, an organization representing Clinical Commissioning Groups. He also holds roles at Western University, serving as an adjunct research professor at the Ivey Business School and in clinical neurosciences at the Schulich School of Medicine and Dentistry.

Marc S. Hafer is responsible for overseeing the strategic direction of Simpler Consulting, including the Simpler Healthcare^{SM} practice. Marc has coached the leadership of health-care clients in North America implementing guided discovery and involving client leadership in the health-care transformation process. He is a frequent conference speaker and volunteers in support of industry organizations including the Centre for Healthcare Value, the Joint Commission on Accreditation of Healthcare Organizations, and the Institute for Healthcare Improvement.

John Gallagher is coaching senior leadership at a large, multispecialty ambulatory care group practice in Boston, United States, on their journey to implementing a Lean organization focused on achieving the IHI Triple Aim through their Lean Transformation. He has over 20 years of Lean implementation experience in many industries including manufacturing, real estate, construction, and Health care and is now leading the Simpler Healthcare Innovation Strategy Development.

Adam Ward, after leveraging 12 years of direct experience using the Toyota Product Development System as a trained design engineer, has spent the past 7 years translating and applying those principles in the health-care environment—a combination of medical equipment, disease specialization, clinical application and facility design—to radically reduce cost and improve both patient outcome and satisfaction. Using this approach, he continually searches for ways to break paradigms and lead organizations to introduce performance disruptors.

Tan Ghim Meng brings with him more than 12 years of experience in quality improvement and organizational development. In his current position, he facilitates process improvement and standardization efforts in TTSH. A man with a knack for writing, he has, between 2010 and 2012, helped TTSH publish two books on its MyCare journey. He also played the editor's role for the hospital's monthly newsletter on MyCare from late 2011 to early 2014.

Professor Philip Choo has been a practicing geriatrician for over 20 years and is the Chief Executive Officer (CEO) of the National Healthcare Group (NHG). Prior to his current appointment, he was the CEO of TTSH. A persistent champion for building staff capabilities and grooming future leaders, and pioneered the MyCare program in TTSH in 2008—an improvement initiative drawing on Lean Management principles to provide faster, better, cheaper, and safer patient care.

Chris Lloyd has introduced Lean principles and practices to over 50 health-care organizations around the world over the past 10 years including the United Kingdom, the United States, the Netherlands, India, Singapore, and Malaysia. His focus has been on health-care innovation and developing the Simpler Lean Hospital Design System. He has applied Lean design techniques to the design of new hospitals and facilities to enhance the patient experience, reduce waiting time, and optimize operating costs.

Dr. S. K. Biswas, after a successful practice career spanning 11 years as a clinician, ventured into Healthcare Planning, Design & Management for the last 24 years. His experience in clinics and management has led to a Lean approach to functional processes. He is presently involved in a number of performance improvement initiatives at the Iris Hospital. He has an MPhil in Hospital and Health System Management.

Dr. Vandana Kumar is a medical professional and a public health specialist. In her public health career, she has worked on national and international health projects with governments, civil society organizations, international agencies, and corporate groups. She has been CEO of a not-for-profit health venture. She is a visiting faculty member at Faculty of Management Studies, Delhi. She is a gold medalist in health-care management.

Dr. Shiban Ganju has participated in over 100 health-care projects dealing with planning, policy, strategy, operations, and advocacy. He is the founder of Save a Mother, a health-care NGO working in over 1000 villages in Uttar Pradesh and Karnataka. He is the founder chairman of Atrimed Pharmaceutical and the chairman of Action for India, which encourages social entrepreneurship. He graduated from AIIMS, Delhi, and specializes in medicine and gastroenterology.

Ankur Pegu earned his B. Tech in computer science from Indian Institute of Technology (IIT), Bombay (1997–2001). At IIT, he worked with India's first campus startup. He then joined the advisory practice of KPMG in 2001 and worked with them for 7 years across different industry verticals such as development, insurance, health care, rural infrastructure, telecom, and information technology. He cofounded Swasth India (meaning *Healthy India*) in 2008 with the desire to implement rapidly scalable health systems.

Sundeep Kapila earned his BTech in computer science from IIT, Bombay (1997–2001). At IIT, he codeveloped the world's first *graph-database*, now a successful enterprise (www.neotechnology.com). Sundeep worked at McKinsey & Company (2001–2008), specializing in health care and development sectors. Subsequently, he completed 2 years of law studies (Mumbai University) and earned a diploma of associateship (Insurance Institute of India). He cofounded Swasth India in 2008 to build a scalable social enterprise with the vision *Health for All*.

Bahare Forotan currently leads an initiative involving country coordination and communication using an innovative social-business model pioneered by Novartis in 2007. The initiative sustainably serves the unmet health needs of the underserved poor in developing countries. A leading innovation in the sector, the initiative is now widely acknowledged by global thought leaders as a leading example of sustainable DFID, National AIDS Control Organization development at the bottom of pyramid. She has been working to innovate solutions that address health-care constraints in rural villages.

Anssi Mikola, Msc Eng, is a specialist on efficiency in health care and a serial entrepreneur. He has worked in academic research, consulting, and health-care production management. Mikola has spent hundreds of hours on the shop floor in different health-care organizations on detailed studies. He cofounded Megaklinikka.fi, an innovative dental care system, and Wellbookers.eu, a portal supporting patient choice; and served as director of business development at Nordic Healthcare Group.

Amir Dan Rubin serves as president and CEO of Standford Healthcare in Northern California. Across its growing health system, Stanford seeks to serve humanity through science and compassion, one patient at a time, through its commitment to care, education, and discovery. Before Stanford, he served as chief operating officer for the UCLA Health System in Southern California. He also currently sits on the board directors of several leading health-care quality consortiums.

Kavita Narayan, one of the youngest fellows of the American College of Healthcare Executives, is a health policy and management expert with 15 years of systems strategic planning and administrative leadership experience. Currently, she brings innovative policy and programmatic solutions to health system issues and PPP options in her leadership role at the Public Health Foundation of India and serves as a technical advisor to the Indian government on health human resources, especially allied health.

Sachin Gaur is a researcher of mobile applications and their applications in the health sector. He was in the top 10 innovators in India under the India Innovates Growth Programme 2013 by FICCI. Part of his field research is covered by broadcast and print media. He has a double MSc (tech) from Aalto University, Finland, and University of Tartu, Estonia. Also, he has multiple patents issued apart from contributing book chapters on topics of innovation.

Dr. Venkataramanaiah Saddikuti is a faculty member in operations management at the Indian Institute of Management, Lucknow, and Fulbright Visiting Scholar to Arizona State University, United States. He has around 22 years of teaching and research experience. He published around 70 articles in peer-reviewed journals and conferences. His current research interest includes health-care management, sustainable SCM, Sourcing and Supply Management, Excellence in Manufacturing, Sustainability of SMEs, and Cluster Development.

Dr. Mohan Gopalakrishnan is a research faculty member in the health-care supply chain consortium at the W. P. Carey School of Business in the Supply Chain Management Department at Arizona State University, United States. Mohan's research interests center on effectiveness and efficiency issues in operations and supply chain management, and his health-care focus has been in modeling and analyzing people, material, and innovation flow management at different layers of the health-care value chain (in global settings).

Dr. Saji Gopinath is the dean of academics and professor in operations management at Indian Institute of Management Kozhikode. He was the director of T. A. Pai Management Institute (TAPMI) Manipal during 2009–2011. He received the London Business School Aditya Birla Centre Award for best case study and knowledge economy fellowships from the British Council. He is very active in social development projects and has won national and international awards.

Atanu Chaudhuri is an assistant professor in Operations Management at Indian Institute of Management, Lucknow, and at the Centre for Industrial Production, Aalborg University. He has more than a decade of experience in the automotive industry, operations consulting, and research and teaching. His areas of interest are in New Product Development, Healthcare Operations, Supply Chain Risk Assessment, and Global Manufacturing Competitiveness. He has published in reputed international journals and obtained research funding from international funding agencies.

Dr. Satish Kr. Gupta is senior consultant of Cardiology and Medicine, J. Watumull Global Hospital & Research Centre, Mount Abu and its branch at Abu Road. He is a fellow of many institutions of repute, and was twice awarded a lifetime achievement award by the President of India; he has also been awarded by Russia, the United Nations, the United States, the United Kingdom, and many other organizations. He has many original breakthrough research articles on Soul, Mind, Body linkages causing lifestyle diseases.

Dr. Vishwas Mehta is from the Indian Administrative Service and has held several positions including managing director of the Rubber and Milk Marketing Federation, secretary of the Health & Family Welfare Kerala, and joint secretary and senior directing staff at the National Defence College, before joining the Ministry of Health & Family Welfare, government of India, as joint secretary. He has an MBA and PhD and has published several books. He has traveled abroad extensively and received several citations and awards.

Dr. Sandeep Bhalla earned a postgraduate degree in public health. He has worked with DFID, National AIDS Control Organization. Currently, he is working as a public health specialist in PHFI, Delhi, managing capacity building initiatives for training primary care physicians in NCDs. One of these programs received IDF recognition, www.ccebdm.org. He has trained more than 7000 doctors. He is a member of healthcare division of Quality Council of India and assessor for the National Accreditation Board of Hospitals and Healthcare Providers.

Nimisha Singh Verma earned an MBA and postgraduate degree in Hospital & Health Management, and her interest is in health-care quality management, IT, and innovation. She brings with her experience in various esteemed organizations; she was awarded best employee, and is currently working with a large tertiary care hospital. She is an assessor of the Healthcare Excellence Award based on the European Foundation Quality Model and is certified Bronze in Lean Healthcare, by Cardiff University, and trained in the JCI, NABH, and NABL quality models.

Dr. Preethi Pradhan is currently dean, Chitkara School of Health Sciences, a private university. She earned her PhD in health-care management with a focus on health-care HR from IIT Madras and masters from TISS, Mumbai. Before joining Chitkara University, she was with Aravind Eye Care System as head of training for capacity building of eye care health professionals. Her interest is in the areas of training, TQM, health literacy, and pedagogy in health care.

Keerti Pradhan is a health-care management professional with 25 years of experience in the developing world. His forte is providing strategic guidance to health-care leadership. He is also a health care and public health management teacher at various universities in India and Africa. At Chitkara University, he is an adviser in developing the health care HR teaching/training programs. He works to enhance sustainable health-care services for the needy by being an adviser to social enterprises.

1

Introduction

V. K. Singh and Paul Lillrank

CONTENTS

WHY THIS BOOK?

Health care is a troubled industry. It needs all the help it can get from innovations. There are four major types of health-care systems: (1) out-of-pocket, (2) the tax-financed Beveridge model, (3) the insurance-based Bismarck model, and (4) the national health insurance systems. In none of these are all stakeholders satisfied. Health care is perceived to be in a chronic state of crisis regardless of how money is paid out and how much is spent.

The dissatisfaction is different in different places. In poor countries and emerging economies, the problem is *affordability*, access to basic life- and limb-saving care. Health services cost too much or are not available at all. The clear-cut solutions are investments in capacity and improvement of productivity, getting more with less.

The rich world keeps spending and demanding more. Annual per capita spend in the United States is about US$8000, whereas the Organization for Economic Co-operation and Development (OECD) average is around 3250.[1] At a per capita spend of about US$1500 per year, the curve depicting the relation between resources consumption and public health outcomes flattens out. On the macrolevel, health care spending has already passed the point of diminishing returns; more is used to produce less. On the microlevel, many still feel they do not get the care they need. When the volume of resources ceases to be the primary problem, focus turns on *outcome* effectiveness. According to John Wenberg's research,[2] in the United States one-third of what doctors do is obvious or evidence based; one-third is based on preferences, patient choice, and negotiations; and the last third is supply driven, useless or in worst cases harmful to the patient.

On the societal level, the question is about equity in how resources are *allocated*. Are resources directed at those who would gain most, are some groups left out, or are easy early interventions neglected creating expensive emergencies later? The question is more complicated than lack of insurance coverage. In many rich countries with universal access, a person's socioeconomic status correlates significantly with health. Some people are deprived of care, not because of lack of overall economic means, but because of the lack of personal behavioral resources. The problems are associated with lifestyle issues, diet, intoxicants, and exercise, and also with access and ability to navigate in and negotiate with an increasingly complex, professionalized, and bureaucratic system. Recent advances in service research[3] have emphasized that services in general and health care in particular are not one-way streets where providers produce health and pour it into patients like receiving vessels. Rather, health is cocreated in complex relations that involve mutual rights and responsibilities that may be confusing both to providers and patients.

In such a context, it is apparent that health care needs innovations, not only in clinical methods, diagnostics, and pharmaceuticals, but also in how services are organized, financed, produced, delivered, and distributed. Innovation, like evolution, requires a large seeding bed of variety, from which best practices can be selected, nurtured, and developed. With globalization and information and communication technologies (ICT) comes the possibility to bring together a variety of ideas and innovations from different contexts, such as high and low resource endowments, large and small volumes, frugal and opulent service levels, and tight and loose regulatory regimes. This book builds on the observation that India has become a fertile ground for innovations, with legacy-free emerging organizations, high volumes, high variety, and technology leapfrogging, all with a backdrop of massive public health deficiencies and deprivations, against which innovations are bound to stick out with clarity.

WHAT IS INNOVATION?

The standard definition of innovation is that it is something novel, it can be replicated and repeated, and it produces value both to the innovator and users. Innovation is like Darwinian evolution, it requires variety,[*] repetition, and selection.

Novel varieties can come from a multitude of sources: creative genius, persistent experimentation, grand visions, perceived needs and opportunities, failures and desperation, scientific discoveries, new combinations of old technologies, unexpected interactions, or discovery of mutual beneficial cooperation.

A new variety is an invention. To turn it into an innovation it must be replicated. A unique happenstance or a freak event in a laboratory is not yet a scientific discovery. It needs to be repeated, verified, and peer reviewed. Technical innovations need to be formalized as blueprints and recipes, management innovations as processes and business models. In competitive markets, innovations spread rapidly, because rival firms cannot survive for long ignoring a new best practice. In nonmarket environments, the diffusion of innovations takes its time, because the incentives to replicate and the mechanisms of selection are weak or nonexistent.

The value an innovation brings to users and producers determines selection, survival, proliferation, and further development. Value, as an economic term, means the perceived difference between what you give and what you get. Perceptions can be backed up by evidence and reason, or distorted by fear and greed. In the end, however, value is subjective and cocreated by customers with the aid of producers. Economic value is determined by the sellers' and the buyers' surplus at a transaction; true value is created only if both parties are better off. If nobody or only one party benefits, innovations will not be sustained. For innovations, as for marketing campaigns, you can fool some people all the time, all people for some of the time, but not all people all the time.

An entrepreneur is not necessarily an innovator in the full meaning of the word. An entrepreneur can take old, true, and tested ideas to the marketplace to create value. For that to happen, an entrepreneur needs to be a management innovator.

---

[*]In management, variety is defined as a number of different ways to achieve similar objectives. Variation means deviations from a given target, errors, and defects that carry a cost of poor quality (CoPQ) (Lillrank 2003).

WHAT IS A MANAGEMENT INNOVATION?

Some innovations are technological. A newly discovered natural phenomenon, such as combustion or electromagnetism, is harnessed for some use. Some high-impact innovations have been based on rather humble technologies, such as the stirrup that created the medieval mounted knight and the crossbow that later became his unraveling. The cast iron sewage pipe is said to be the most important public health innovation ever. In medicine, innovations from antibiotics and vaccines to open heart surgery and artificial joints have contributed mightily to human well-being. This book, however, is not primarily about technological breakthroughs. We focus on innovations in management, how people come together, organize themselves, and cooperate to create value with the tools and technologies available to them.

The Industrial Revolution, starting in the eighteenth century and continuing through various stages and crises to present, has been an extraordinary period of innovations. Although technologies such as steam engines and moon rockets fill the public with awe, none of them would have been more than science fiction without corresponding advances in management such as how to accumulate capital and spread risk to finance investments; how to find out what can be marketed and sold; how to keep track of numerous transactions; how to recruit, train, reward, and develop people; how to integrate various technology elements in functioning products; and how to coordinate the multitude of tasks required to make credible offerings to customers. Some well-known management innovations are double-entry bookkeeping, commercial credit, division of labor, specialization, standardization, the limited liability corporation, the moving assembly line, the multidivisional organization, quality assurance, performance measurement, franchising, and supply chain management.

The practice of management is largely collecting, sorting, analyzing, understanding, and acting on information with the help of knowledge. To integrate several specialized skills and coordinate numerous tasks, information telling what each person is supposed to do in each situation is necessary. All technologies that expand capabilities to deal with information and create new knowledge have significant managerial implications. ICT is a great enabler, it makes a lot of things possible, but it does not cause them without a clear managerial purpose.

One of the most solid and applicable principles of management is you cannot manage what you cannot measure; you cannot measure what you cannot define. A mirror image is what is measured (and rewarded) gets done. Therefore, performance measurement is crucial in purposeful activities. If an organization strives at something, it should be able to tell to what extent it has succeeded or failed. The ability to measure outcomes is a necessary condition for experimentation and innovation. This is not to say that everything of value could be quantified. Play, social relations, and spiritual experiences are best left out. Performance measures can range from simple perceptions (Does it hurt? Are you comfortable?) to exact quantitative measurements of throughput times or clinical indicators. Because you tend to get what you measure, management innovations need to be accompanied with performance measures.

Some technical innovations cannot be easily anticipated. Market researchers were told people value the buttons on their phones and would see no benefits in touch screens. Only a few years later mechanical keyboards were fast becoming obsolete. Management innovations are easier to identify, because they are about finding better ways to do things, old or new. Therefore, measurement boils down to a few fundamental key performance indicators (KPI), such as cost, throughput time, quality, and flexible response. A management innovation must bring improvement in some or all of these KPIs.

The cost of production is a key element in making health care affordable and accessible. Costs are driven by the logic of technology, price of resources, and the task at hand. The necessary value-creating steps form a value stream. A surgical intervention requires, by necessity, a diagnosis and an idea of what to do, and that the patient is on the operating table, sedated, and incised. Each step in the stream requires resources that carry costs, personnel, consumables, equipment, and facilities. The value stream, however, is not all there is. There are other tasks and steps that together constitute the production process. Some steps, like transportation, do not add value to the patient, but are nevertheless necessary supports to the value chain. Some other steps like waiting due to administrative complications or poor scheduling are not adding value, but still cause costs and take time. Process innovations focus on reducing such nonvalue-adding activities, thereby cutting costs and shortening throughput time.

Quality, strictly speaking, means conformance to customer-appreciated requirements. Quality is measured as deviations from known targets. Deviations stem from common causes, that is, natural variation in a production process when it functions as planned, and from specific causes, such as unexpected external disturbances, equipment breakdown, poor judgment, or lack of required skills and attention. Quality-relevant management innovations are focused on quality assurance: error prevention through standardization and checklists, root cause analysis to identify sources of deviations, and statistical process control to monitor and improve processes. Because quality errors may cause costs and harm patients, quality improvement has the double benefit of reducing cost and increasing value.

Quality in a broad sense is associated with customer satisfaction. The requirements of each patient may not necessarily be fully known in advance. Some requirements can be met by various means, some others not at all. Therefore, flexibility and adaptability are needed, which, in turn, may run against the demands of standardization. This creates a perennial management dilemma: how to increase resource efficiency (cost reduction of resource use) while achieving good flow efficiency, where each flow unit (patient) gets the right type of care and attention in a swift, even flow. In this respect, management innovations are typically systemic: they need to be measured by more than one performance indicator.

Productive organizations, businesses, hospitals, and clinics are complex adaptive systems. Complexity means that there are several elements that interact in ways that cannot always be predicted. Individuals, teams, and organizations adapt to changes in their environment in ways that are not necessarily easy to identify. Therefore, an innovation in one part of a system can create imbalances and bottlenecks that may be detrimental to the performance of the system as a whole. For example, if a surgical team increases its throughput but the wards cannot receive all patients, a bottleneck is created. The pursuit of flexibility and customer satisfaction may increase costs and make the service unaffordable to a segment of the population; a pursuit of the best drives out the sufficiently good. A reduction in prices may increase demand but cut margins and starve a hospital for funds required for renewal. The idea of the business model has been created to deal with the systemic complexities of productive organizations by linking their offerings, resources, and customers. Business model innovations can, therefore, have a broad impact on several issues beyond the core production processes. These issues include demand management, how to segment, screen, filter, direct, and empower patients; supply management, how to acquire supplies, staff, skill-sets, equipment, and facilities; financial management, how to raise funds for investments; and strategic management, how to decide about objectives, priorities, and allocations.

Management innovations in health care should appear as measurable KPIs. They can be expected to be novel solutions to classical management problems, such as the resource versus flow efficiency dilemma, or the standardization–flexibility trade-off.

METHODOLOGY

Given the global interest in innovations, scholars, practitioners, and policy makers have been searching for ways to promote, accelerate, identify, and support innovations. A scientific discipline, Innovation Research, has turned the searchlight on the innovation process, the innovators' personalities, and supportive enablers in the hope that these could somehow be formalized and repeated. Then policy makers could learn how to promote innovations and create the next silicon whatever. However, decades of experimentation with innovation policy has a poor track record. It is, as Josh Lerner put it, "a boulevard of broken dreams."[4] It appears that innovations, like many other aspects of the human condition, such as love and happiness, are elusive; the harder you try, the farther they slip away. However, several necessary conditions can be identified. These are availability of capital, infrastructure, demand, academic research, legal protection of intellectual property, taxes, and critical mass. But there is no way of telling when and how such necessary conditions merge to become a sufficient condition. Some conditions may be elusive and impossible to manage. Deirdre McCloskey's study[5] on the Industrial Revolution identifies as the key elements of bourgeois dignity and freedom. Where regulators take away the freedom to explore and envy strips the innovator of his dignity and his rewards, be it in the name of equality and justice, there will be few, if any innovations. Only the most stubborn persist and the ensuing evolutional variety remains narrow. Innovations may be disruptive and bring creative destruction. Therefore innovators have enemies.

Inventions may originate in laboratories, innovations appear in the marketplace. Although many thinkers have made significant contributions, there are no management innovations that would have in full form been developed at universities. Management innovations typically emerge in companies and at production sites where people tinker, adapt, borrow, and steal ideas from various fields, experimenting and proceeding through trial and error often without knowing what they are doing. Henry Ford got the idea of the moving assembly line by observing slaughterhouses in Chicago, where animal carcasses were disassembled into their constituent parts. The bright idea was that this process could, if reversed, be applied to the assembly of manufactured products. The basic ideas of Japanese Lean production came from observing how shelves were stocked in American supermarkets.

Given these overall observations, we believe the proper role and task of innovation research in health care is to identify, observe, describe, model, explain, and communicate innovations to accelerate learning and adaptation, that is, make more variety available from which best practices can be developed and selected. The process of inquiry is as follows:

- Identify innovations based on the criteria of novelty, repeatability, and value, which for management innovations come in the shape of the fundamental KPIs: cost, throughput time, quality, and flexibility.
- Describe the innovations in terms of technologies employed and management methods used. Is it a solution to the resource versus flow efficiency dilemma? How does it deal with processes, coordination, control information, and quality assurance? What performance measures are used? How are offerings, resources, and patient needs combined in business models and operating logics?
- Create theory-backed models to explain how and why the innovation works.
- Find out if it can, or has been, repeated and transferred to different contexts.
- Communicate the results to enhance mutual learning and the circulation of innovations.

Although innovations can emerge in unexpected places, it stands to reason to look closely in areas where the necessary supporting conditions are about right. When it comes to innovations in services in general, and health care in particular, India is such a place. Economic growth and an expanding middle class create needs, articulated wants, and purchasing power that together constitute demand. Capital and labor are available, and technologies and ideas circulate freely, not the least due to the Indian diaspora coming home while maintaining its contacts to the Western world. The Indian central government's inability to take forceful and drastic measures, can, as Dretzé and Sen[6] have argued, be seen as the reason for the public health disaster that much of India still is, even compared to countries with similar income levels. India is definitely not a paragon of public health. However, for the purpose of this book, the point is that India is rich in variety. A weak government is not in a position to impose stifling regulations, restrict financing, or monopolize production and create the conditions that burden management innovations in countries with exemplary, but in the long run unaffordable health care.

Some variety enhancing conditions in India are, first, cost-constrained markets. The combination of immense needs, increasing awareness, and low purchasing power asks for frugal, low-cost solutions. Good enough is better than nothing. Such innovations, called *jugaad*,[7] are not necessarily appreciated by regulators and professionals in rich countries. However, frugal innovations can lead to discoveries that may find different applications elsewhere.

Second, patient volumes tend to be very high in India. The mechanisms of economies of scale in health care are not fully known. Studies on the effects of hospital size on productivity have not produced unanimous results. Big may, or may not be, better, depending on what is done with what kind of management. To meet demand and ease deprivation, some Indian service providers have built very large focused units with high volumes. To management research, such a facility is what the banana fly was to studies on hereditary traits. Large volumes and repetition create conditions where small changes in processes and methods can quickly be verified by statistical analysis. Repetition enables experimentation and standardization that is not possible in low-volume, unfocused, multipurpose organizations.

Third, India has a rich tradition of various types of organizations, the license Raj, Weberian bureaucracies, charities, religious and spiritual communities, merchant houses, and tribal communities, which come in multitudes of varieties in different parts of the subcontinent. Although the health insurance industry is growing rapidly, about half of the total spend is still out of pocket. With an affluent middle class, demand grows and becomes increasingly informed, and growing supply leads to competition. Thus India provides a case for studying how markets work in health care. Although markets in health care, by necessity, are far from perfect, third-party financing tends to disrupt how supply and demand meets, how patients choose when they pay from their own pockets, and how suppliers respond to paying patients. Therefore, the part of India where the middle class pays for health services out of pocket is the best known case of free market health care.

Fourth, in health care, as in many other industries, latecomers may leapfrog to the technology frontier and enjoy the benefit of a legacy-free environment without outdated but entrenched technologies, organizations, and vested interests. This is important in ICT and patient information systems, where rich countries have to struggle with legacy systems and sunken costs.

Having made the case that India is an interesting place to study, this book is a collection of cases contributed by several authors with first-hand experience in their respective fields.

REFERENCES

1. OECD: Health at a Glance, 2011. The numbers are for the year 2009, PPP US$.
2. Wenberg, J., 2010, *Tracking Medicine, A Researcher's Quest to Understand Health Care.* Oxford University Press, New York, NY.
3. Lusch, R.F. and S.L. Vargo (eds.), 2006, *The Service-Dominant Logic of Marketing.* E.M. Sharpe, Armonk, NY.
4. Lerner, J., 2009, *Boulevard of Broken Dreams. Why Public Efforts to Boost Entrepreneurship and Venture Capital Have Failed—And What to Do About It.* Princeton University Press, Princeton, NJ/Oxford, UK.
5. McCloskey, D., 2010, *Bourgeois Dignity: Why Economics Can't Explain the Modern World.* University of Chicago Press, Chicago, IL.
6. Drezè, J. and A. Sen, 2013, *An Uncertain Glory. India and Its Contradictions.* Penguin Books, London, UK.
7. Radjou, N., J. Prabhu, and S. Ahuja, 2012, *Jugaad Innovation: Think Frugal, Be Flexible, Generate Breakthrough Growth.* Jossey-Bass, San Francisco, CA.

2

Global Trends in Health-System Innovation

Anne Snowdon, Karin Schnarr, and Charles Alessi

CONTENTS

INTRODUCTION

When one thinks of health-care innovation, advances in pharmaceuticals and medical devices immediately come to mind. This is not wrong; there are incredible discoveries that are taking place every day, all around the world, that are transforming health services and procedures in ways that are revolutionizing patient care. As an example, ConforMis Inc., a medical device company based in Bedford, MA, engineers knee resurfacing implants for osteoarthritis patients that preserve more bone tissue than traditional knee replacement surgeries.[1] This kind of innovative medical device can improve care quality while saving costs on repeat procedures more common with current products and procedures. Although these types of technologies, and many other like them, hold tremendous promise both for patients and for the health system, health systems need to significantly evolve and adapt to properly embrace their potential. For example, new incentive and compensation models are needed, which reward the personalization of medical devices that will inevitably be more expensive on a per-unit basis. As a result, we adopt a health-system approach to global health innovation to examine growing trends that will facilitate the translation and acceptance of innovative products, services, and processes in a way that improves patient-care outcomes.

Health-care systems are large, complex arrangements of organizations, which often include competitors, cooperators, funders, and regulators. These systems are not uniform; they vary in how they are structured and organized. A highly effective and productive health-care system is one that is efficient in delivering high quality, accessible patient care services based on the strongest clinical evidence, and aided through the most appropriate technologies available with the goal of improving care outcomes in a cost-effective and sustainable manner.[2] In such a system, the health professional workforce embraces change, seeks opportunity for innovation in service delivery, eagerly tests and integrates promising new technologies into patient care processes, and interacts directly with patients and families as a seamless and highly skilled collaborative team. There is also integration across health sectors, including health-care institutions, such as hospitals, primary care services, long-term care facilities, pharmaceutical companies, medical devices companies, not-for-profit organizations (e.g., special health interest groups focused on specific health issues), and system-funding partners to promote the translation and adoption of new health-care innovations. Health-care clients are actively engaged and informed, displaying high levels of health literacy and using technologies to monitor and personalize their own care. Although this type of system may sound unattainable, we propose that it is possible for health systems to achieve this end; it can be done through the deliberate creation of cultures of innovation, health sector leadership that develops workforces that are trained, socialized, and empowered to create and adopt innovation, and knowledge dissemination led by senior management who create and participate in collaborative, multidisciplinary, multisector health-care networks.

As we consider trends across global health innovation, we ground our consideration on a few key principles. Any level of transformational change must begin and end with the patient in mind. Thus, quality of care and patient safety are the fundamental drivers by which health outcomes should be measured and innovation should be focused.[3] Further, an evidence-based approach to supporting innovation adoption should be the foundation on which a health system's transformation should occur.[4] Finally, leaders with the styles and competencies associated with innovation should be developed to successfully drive health system change management in a way that accepts values and promotes innovation.

The goal of this chapter is to present the overarching trends in innovation in global health systems as they move in different ways toward creating those aforementioned effective and productive health-care systems. We present the main questions framing these trends in Figure 2.1. Specifically, we consider the trends toward value-based health-system structure and design, consumer-driven influences on health systems, the growing trend of mobile health technologies, and electronic health systems, including big data and emerging health analytics. By highlighting these emerging global health innovation trends, health-care entrepreneurs and innovators, health practitioners, health-system policy makers, and health-system funders may consider the potential applications of these trends

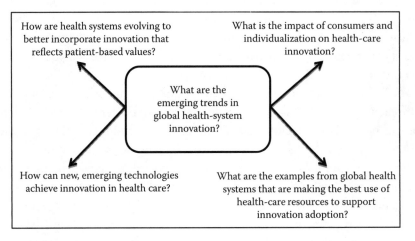

FIGURE 2.1
Questions framing emerging trends in global health-system innovation.

to accelerate innovation translation to achieve global health equity, accessibility, quality, and sustainability.

TREND TOWARD VALUE-BASED HEALTH-SYSTEM STRUCTURE AND DESIGN

There have been many reviews of health-care systems around the world that have predominately focused on health services that are funded on a *fee for service* basis. A number of these have generated substantial evidence describing the costs of health care, which has led to concerns regarding sustainability and affordability of health systems in future. However, health care is, at its core, about more than just numbers. The unique and highly personalized nature of the services involved can be emotionally charged for those receiving and providing health care, whether directly or indirectly.

Another way to examine global health systems through the lenses of structure and governance provide an important framework for exploring how these two elements influence health-system costs versus the values of health-system participants and stakeholders. There are a number of different types of health-system governance models around the world. Prevailing models include the *State as Guardian* model of health systems, which is prevalent in European countries, such as France, Germany, Switzerland, and the Netherlands, and the *State as Owner/Operator*, which is the more prescriptive model used in countries such as Canada, China, Australia, and the United Kingdom. There is a third, rapidly growing category that includes the growing dominance of the private sector as seen in countries such as the United States and India.

Given the different funding assumptions that underlie each of these three models, it may be more appropriate to shift the lens of health-system examination from one of costs to one of values, embracing the aspect of innovation that looks at existing items in new ways. This shift in perspective encompasses the growing trend toward the engagement of the consumer in health decisions. Much less work has been done to categorize health-care values and determine how well health-care systems are doing in achieving metrics linked to them. New theoretical health-system models are beginning to incorporate the concept of values as an important element in health-care delivery. An example is management scholar Michael Porter's value-driven health-care model. Porter and Teisburg have suggested health systems need to radically redefine competition, focusing on how to improve value (quality of health outcomes per dollar expended) at the disease and treatment level to better drive process and health quality improvement while fostering system innovation.[5]

By examining the values framework in health service organizations, there is an opportunity to determine where there has been a governance shift to incorporate the publicly articulated demands and desires of the populations who are receiving and delivering health-care services. A recent analysis of mission, vision, and value (MVV) statements for federal health organizations in Australia, Britain, Canada, France, Germany, the Netherlands, Switzerland, and the United States has uncovered gaps in value frameworks of those funding health-care systems, be it the public or private sector, those delivering the health services, and those receiving health services.[6] The components of the MVV statements for each of these countries focused on one of two central themes: health and wellness of the population and the viability and sustainability of the health system. Health and wellness subthemes included a strong focus on patient-centered care and viewing patients in a holistic way, achieved through better health and active living for people in those countries. The health and wellness theme also incorporated patient choice and equity, detailing a strong focus on impartial, fair, and effective health-care services. There was also a focus on the responsibilities of individuals to manage their own health and wellness, and ensure they have choice in accessing health-care services. The dominant focus of this theme was to ensure equity in access and availability of health services, evident in all of the comparator countries. Finally, a few countries stressed health literacy as important for making choices that would promote the sustainability of national health systems. Although this theme was less often described, it clearly has a strong fit with the dominant themes of health and wellness, patient choice, and patient engagement. Health literacy refers to the value placed on ensuring people have access to and awareness of health and wellness information to support decisions. Transparency is a subtheme of health literacy, whereby health systems offer transparency and access to information to support patient decision making. In addition, overarching values observed in France, Germany, and the United States included health-system goals and the quality of health care. This theme focused on quality (timely, evidence-based, inclusive), accountability, and system integration. Participation, collaboration, strategic clarity, and efficiency are all common values in the MVV statements.

Although national-level health-system values are shifting toward health and wellness, patient engagement and prioritization, and health-system quality, current measures of health-system performance focus primarily on access to care, and quality outcomes that identify hospital-related adverse events (e.g., hospital-acquired infections, mortality, falls, medication errors, and readmissions to hospital). There is very little evidence that the values of citizens are aligned with how performance is measured or evaluated in health systems. This misalignment is further evidenced by the way in which senior health-care managers are incentivized, largely focusing on the financial health of the organization and the prevention of adverse event.

Global Examples of Innovations Supporting the Shift to Value-Based Health Care

There are a number of global examples of how individuals, companies, organizations, and health systems are adopting innovative approaches to health-system reform and capacity building to create structures that empower and support consumers to achieve better individual and population-level health and wellness outcomes. Interesting projects are taking place right now in Britain where the primary focus of health-system innovation is to shift toward community-based management of chronic illness as a strategy for decreasing the reliance on hospital-based services. Hospital-based services are substantially more expensive and have a limited capacity for utilization. The individuals and organizations involved with reshaping the British health-care system are employing information technology in ways that enable consumers to manage their own health, both administratively and through health outcomes. British consumers can use technology systems that allow them to choose and book their own health appointments. The organizational impact of the *choose and book service* is related to reducing waiting times, minimizing the rate of no-shows, improving the speed of the referral process, and improving service delivery to patients.

Other British health services including telehealth provide quick and informed advice in real time to assist consumers in making health decisions. Mexico's Medicall Home program offers a similar telephone-based program, where for $5 a month (paid through the telephone bill) subscribers and their families can receive health-care advice and triage services. Over 1 million Mexicans and their families currently take advantage of this service, which is less expensive than a visit to a physician.[7] The results are impressive; 62% of calls are resolved over the phone by trained paramedics and physicians who staff the phone line 24 × 7. The remaining 38% of cases are referred at a discounted fee to a network of 6000 preapproved physicians or 3000 clinicians in 233 cities.[8] This type of service not only saves patients money (~US$300 for those who have their issues resolved over the phone), it also frees up capacity within the health-care system from nonurgent cases.

A more detailed example of how health-system innovation is currently being implemented in Britain can be seen in the *Unique Care Program,* a case-management program that integrates both social services and health services to support frail elderly and high-risk populations to maintain health and independence at home, while reducing the rate of hospitalization and emergency department admissions for this high-risk population. There are three elements to the Unique Care approach. First, all referrals are directed to a practice-based Unique Care team. The team manages all medical and social needs of the patient. Second, a hospital in-reach program is established, so that if a patient is admitted for an acute medical problem, the hospital informs the practice and the Unique Care team of the admission. During the patient's stay, a nurse and a social worker from the Unique Care team work with the hospital to coordinate care once the patient is discharged. Finally, practices identify potentially high-need patients, using information such as previous illness and hospital admissions before they are referred for assessment or experience an acute admission. This program is being implemented through pilot sites across Britain, with exceptional examples of cooperation and collaboration being witnessed across test communities, both between practitioner groups, and between practitioner groups and patients. A focus on care coordination also can be seen in Switzerland, where there is an initiative that involves the creation of physician networks to facilitate faster information sharing between care providers. The use of interdisciplinary teams is intended to enhance patient care through increased coordination. To further care coordination, a nationwide electronic patient file is currently being implemented and should provide each Swiss citizen with a personal e-patient file by 2015.

A second British innovation initiative is that of the *virtual ward,* designed to support the drive toward strengthening health-care services in communities as a strategy to reduce the demands on acute care services. This concept is designed to deliver community-based services to patients in their home to avoid hospitalization. A virtual ward is a group of patients receiving care similar to hospital ward care; however, they receive care in their homes. These patients live at home, but are high-risk for emergency admission to the hospital, and they tend to have long-term conditions with complex needs. Staffing includes a community matron, who is assigned to each ward and manages its logistics and operations. Each ward also has nurses, a pharmacist, a social worker, a physiotherapist, an occupational therapist, and a ward administrator. This model has been adopted in other communities, because there is a belief that patients would rather be in their home and hospital admissions can be dangerous and expensive. Virtual wards are expected to not only improve patient safety and care, but also reduce costs through reduced hospital admissions.

But are these types of health-system innovations that prioritize patient empowerment actually working? Using our Britain example, they have one of the lowest per capita rates of expenditure among Organization for Economic Co-operation and Development (OECD) nations, yet Britain also is one of the most active nations in the implementation of innovations in the health system. The substantial focus on mobilizing health services to keep patients at home, improving quality of health care in the community, and avoidance of hospitalization is distinct among the comparator countries. The use of telehealth and information technology solutions to engage consumers directly in managing their own health services is distinct from other countries such as Germany; however, in combination with the other initiatives such as the virtual ward and the Unique Care Program, there is evidence of capacity building and increased quality in the British system as a result of innovation.

TREND TOWARD HEALTH INFORMATION TECHNOLOGY INNOVATION AND ADOPTION

Every conceivable industry has been transformed by information technology. Information technologies have revolutionized banking, the travel industry, and entertainment. Manufacturers are connected with their suppliers and customers in a supply chain of incredible complexity, and even more amazing speed. The financial services industry moves trillions of dollars in nanoseconds and the variety of services offered to clients is only bounded by imagination. These services can be delivered from anywhere in the world, at any time of day or night. Yet, when we look at health care, we see a system still struggling with some of the basics of the information age. Health care is arguably the most information-intensive of industry sectors—perhaps rivaled only by financial services. As an example, in Canada, about 2000 health-related transactions happen every minute of every day according to Canada Health Infoway. The information recorded or transmitted contains everything from the mundane to the life-critical, and until recently in most developed countries, the vast majority of these hundreds of millions of health-related transactions involved handwritten records. Critical information was filed in hospitals, doctors' offices, and clinics with limited ability to retrieve the information when and where needed. This is starting to change, but change is happening slowly in many countries.

Health information has the potential to create seamless delivery of health-care services by digitizing basic health records, using electronic tracking of patient information through the health system, and improving digital communication among health professionals, patients, and their family members. In other words, health IT (HIT) has the ability to transform the foundations and interoperability of health systems and contribute greatly to its long-term effectiveness and sustainability. As such, there has been explosive growth in the number of online health information websites, portals, and databases.

Technology is also being used to revolutionize the categorization of health-care products, so that public and private health systems can communicate with each other using common codes as have been done in other industries such as grocery services in North America. This standardization of the international health-care supply chain is being implemented through the use of bar codes, global trade information numbers, and radio frequency identification (RFID) technologies, and is being led globally by organizations such as Global Standards 1 (GS1), the world's leading supply chain standards organization. Standardization in health-care supply chains is assisting in product traceability, important for recalls and adverse effects, and organizational interoperation ability. This drive toward supporting global standards across the entire health-care supply chain was supported in a recent report by McKinsey & Company titled "Strength in Unity: The Promise of Global Standards in Healthcare."[9] The report recognized the advantages of standardized identification and automated tracking of products such as reducing the time delay between recall notification and product removal.

Although HIT innovation is being broadly embraced for its ability to provide better data analytics for clinical and administrative decisions, improve patient safety, create efficiencies in health systems, and empower health consumers, not all health-care providers are confident about the quality of information being provided online.[10] As a result, some providers are taking an innovative approach to information quality while at the same time, directly involving patients. A perspective in the *New England Journal of Medicine* suggests that if the information in personal health records is secure, complete, and verifiable, it can play an important role in improving doctor–patient communication, quality of care, and the aversion of medical errors.[11] The Mayo Clinic in the United States has, therefore, taken the approach of establishing its own health information site and clinic health manager, through a partnership with an IT vendor that enables consumers to access accurate health information and create their own online personal health records. Working in tandem, their health information site (www.mayoclinic.com/health-information) serves consumers with easily accessible information about diseases and conditions, symptoms, drugs and supplements, tests and procedures, advice for healthy living, and links to expert blogs. The focus of the site is on the provision of reliable health information for consumers with the Mayo Clinic indicating that 3300 of their physicians, scientists, and researchers provide input into the site. The Mayo Clinic health manager enables consumers to create their own personalized electronic health record and share their health information with providers.

Other programs use technology to provide information to consumers to assist in making choices related to health care. Minnesota HealthScores (www.mnhealthscores.org) provides health consumers with information about treatment processes; comparative performance of providers (e.g., in caring for chronic conditions); and patient outcomes and experiences in Minnesota's individual medical clinics and physician practices, medical groups, and hospitals. The data are drawn from multiple sources including data from health-care plans (insurers), patient medical records, and surveys, which are used to calculate individual provider ratings and a state average. Key to the program's success has been their collaborative approach involving health-care providers, insurers, consumer representatives, and quality improvement organizations, all committed to the idea that greater transparency will lead to better health outcomes for the people of Minnesota. Physicians too are using the site and their scores to improve the care they deliver. As of 2010, approximately 90% of primary care sites in Minnesota were submitting quality information to Minnesota Community Measurement for use on the health scores website.

Personal Health Records

Another emerging trend in health information technology is the move to person health records (PHR). These PHR technologies—being delivered by companies as large as Microsoft and Google, and by startup innovators such an Indivo—hold great potential and are trends worth watching. These technologies allow consumers to import, store, and share standardized health records and offer patients the opportunity to achieve autonomy in managing their own health information.[12,13] The emergence of PHRs in the health sector presents both challenges and opportunities for the management of health information. In the current healthcare system, health information records are managed and controlled by the health-care system or provider (e.g., hospital-based medical records, primary care physician patient records, health maintenance organization [HMO] patient records). In the future, PHR hosts and the social networks they spawn may assume greater responsibility for housing and managing health information, whereby health consumers become responsible for managing and communicating their personal health information to various health-system stakeholders. So far, there are few studies examining the implications of PHR technologies on health information systems and processes.

Integration of PHR technologies into the health-care system to achieve productivity and efficiency and health-care delivery has not been described in the literature. Although the challenges associated with personal health records, such as privacy protection and accuracy, are a significant concern in this area, countries such as Germany have moved forward with IT strategies for managing health records using a *smart card*. Germany introduced health smart cards in 2006, consistent with their consumer-driven approach to innovation whereby consumers carry their personal health records electronically and share it with health providers or health-care agencies with a simple swipe of their smart card. In Germany, the smart card is a national project that implemented an electronic health card for both patients and health professionals. The health providers use the cards to access identifying information about patients and insurance information for all citizens. Additional voluntary features available for smart card users include e-prescribing and private electronic patient record management.

The card system requires patients to physically present the card for all health transactions and requires the use of a private PIN number before a health provider can access the information on the card. This design was intended to respond to concerns about privacy and accessibility of information among the general public. Although the concept of the smart card is very innovative, the uptake and adoption of the card system faces challenges including citizen confusion with its use. In addition, confidentiality and security features are currently undergoing review and there are limitations in the range and extent of health data available on the card.

Similar smart card projects are also underway in France and Taiwan. The Taiwan health-care smart card project is one of the largest healthcare smart card solutions in the world and the first of its kind in Taiwan, Republic of China. Introduced in 2006, the smart card replaced a papercard system administered by the Bureau of National Health Insurance (BNHI) in Taiwan.[14] Smart cards have been distributed to the entire Taiwanese population (around 22 million people). The card is a microcontroller-based card and has 32 kilobytes (KB) of memory, of which 22 KB will be used for four kinds of information: personal information; national health insurance (NHI)-related information including cardholder status, number of visits, and admissions; accumulated medical expenditure records and amount of cost-sharing; medical service information including drug allergy history, certain medical treatments, and long-term prescriptions; and public health information such as instructions for organ donation. Hospital and clinics upload electronic records daily to BHNI, and after every six patient visits, card information is uploaded online for data analysis. The electronic system allows for faster reimbursement, and BNHI has taken numerous steps to protect the safety and security of the health information.

Enabling Successful Health Information Technology Adoption

Health systems in many countries have already achieved an extensive record of successes in the use of health information technology with respect to health system efficiency and productivity. Involvement by health professionals in the design and development of health information technology can create win-win scenarios where health information technology can benefit patients, organizations, and clinicians without imposing additional work or loss of flexibility. Health professionals need to be involved early in the planning, testing, and execution of health information systems, given their role as critical members of the health team who can focus health information projects and solutions quickly and effectively with other members of the health-care team. Implementation of new systems takes time and needs to be performed in sequence for benefits and potential issues to be fully understood. Time is also required to appropriately engage stakeholders. Further, implementation of new health information technology must examine and reengineer all of the business and clinical processes the technology supports. This step-by-step approach corrects mistakes early and helps to avoid the catastrophic failure of *big bang* implementation. Health information technology implementation must also be linked to organizational incentives; for successful innovation adoption to occur, employees must be financially rewarded and recognized when they do engage in the development and integration of health information technology systems, because they are critical to the long-term success of technology adoption and use.

TREND TOWARD CONSUMER-DRIVEN INFLUENCES ON HEALTH SYSTEMS

Health consumers are becoming increasingly empowered to take control of their own health journey. Individuals are well informed, seek health information independently, and leverage this information to engage in collaborative discussions with health providers to make decisions on health goals and strategies to achieve specific health outcomes that are meaningful and important to them as they negotiate health services. This is easier in health systems where there is competition and consumers have a choice in providers, services, and health-care locations. In systems where there are constraints on health care access either due to service capitation, limited health practitioners, geography, or restrictions by system funders, citizens have fewer, if any choices available to them, making it more difficult to be part of a collaborate health-care team.

Health systems are being challenged to respond to the rise of discriminating health-care consumers who are demanding to be involved in decisions about treatment and empowered with choice in flexible, responsive, and patient-centered health-care services. This consumerism, or need for consumer engagement, is closely linked to rising levels of education and incomes. It is a consumer response to attempt to ration care and geographic limitations on providers and health-care institutions, and the use of legislative, regulatory, or service provider protocols to impose barriers to access, which over time characterized practices within both private mixed models (such as HMOs in the United States) and public and social insurance models.

Responding to the trend of consumerism in health care is challenging, because it has the potential to undermine the hegemony of the medical model of health, contrasting with established traditions of professional dominance and requiring that professional judgments of clinical *need* be reconciled with the *wants, preferences,* or *choices* of patients. However, it is increasingly being recognized that health-care consumerism is much less about responding to limitless consumer demand for services and technology and the prevalence of an entitlement mentality, and more about enabling patients to make informed treatment choices and set priorities for their own health-care agenda, providing the public with information about health and health-care quality, respecting rights to privacy, enhancing patient expertise, and with expert guidance from health-care professionals, helping patients understand what is necessary versus what may be discretionary, and ultimately finding ways to make them more responsible for their own health.

An example of an innovation that directly engages consumers at the individual, provincial, and system levels in the delivery of health services can be found in the Netherlands. *Dutch Personal Health Budgets* build on the existing structure of the social insurance health system that relies on market mechanisms of competition and consumer roles in purchasing and negotiating their own health-care services. This strategy strengthens the role of consumers further, whereby consumers manage their personal health budget to plan and negotiate their own personal health-care services. Consumer-directed (consumer-engaged) health care in the Dutch system means that consumers coordinate their own health services; they decide who will provide their care, and what price they are willing to pay. The innovation strategy in the Dutch system acknowledges the importance of leveraging consumer engagement to support patients managing their own health-care services and to take advantage of market competition to reduce costs and stimulate competitive approaches to health-care service delivery. Indeed, this consumer-driven coordination of care has been gaining attention as an alternative to the more common agency-directed care.[15]

Consumer Engagement in Managing Chronic Illness

For health-system models such as the one occurring in the Netherlands to be successful, there must be a more collaborative partnership between patients and providers, an evolution from the traditional prescriptive approaches to health services. In a collaborative system, consumers are seeking and insisting on a partnership approach with their health-care service providers where there is a balance of power, a *level playing field* where the health provider assumes a role as coach and mentor, supporting a person's decision to achieve health and wellness goals as well as dignity and quality of life.

To achieve such patient–provider collaborations, health systems are transforming models of care toward self-management and care closer to home, by employing collaborative and virtual technologies that support individuals in monitoring and tracking their health status in a way that allows them to engage in decisions to manage their health and wellness as a partner in care, rather than recipients of care. Most applications of IT intended to facilitate patient self-management have been implemented as pilot studies and demonstration projects. An example that illustrates the potential of HIT to activate patients in their own care and that provides useful guidance for future innovations is the Diabetes Connected Health (DCH) application developed by Centre for Connected Health in collaboration with the Partners Healthcare Network and Massachusetts General Hospital.* DCH is a remote blood glucose monitoring application that consists of a website designed to enhance the flow of information and collaboration between patients and providers and that also allows for patients to upload glucometer readings from commercially available glucometers. The readings are stored and then graphed by the application to all for trends to be viewed and discussed by patients and providers. Providers use the site to familiarize themselves with a patient's trends and overall habits, to send comments based on their assessment of the trends, and to recommend treatments without patients needing to make clinical visits. Results of trials have shown that patients were more motivated knowing that providers were monitoring their results or even just acknowledging their efforts in managing their disease.

Other countries have similar project innovations that focus on patient empowerment. A program in India called *Make Me Healthy* (www.makemehealthy.in) has a Health Risk Report, a wellness tool targeting chronic disease management in a country where millions of citizens

---

* Additional information about this program can be found at http://www.connected-health.org/programs/diabetes.aspx.

cannot afford preventative health services, saving their health care spending for catastrophic health events or treatments that are able to hold the highest levels of disease conditions at bay. Given that preventative health care for the middle class is not affordable or time-efficient, the Make Me Healthy program designed a 15-minute, at-home Health Risk Assessment tool that includes risk tests for diabetes, cardiovascular disorders, respiratory ailments, obesity, and stress. The equipment is approved by the Food and Drug Administration (FDA) in the United States and only requires a small puncture. The tests cover electrocardiograms (ECG), total cholesterol, triglycerides, blood pressure, pulse oximetry, spirometry, random blood sugar, and body composition (eight parameters). The report provided to consumers consists of scientific risk profiling, doctor's consultation, customized diet and fitness chart, and specialist referral and further testing advice. Not only does this program provide a necessary service for individuals in terms of helping them to prevent chronic diseases, it addresses a broader public policy issue for India given that the WHO estimates that between 2005 and 2014, diabetes, heart disease, and stroke together will cost $336.6 billion in India due to premature mortality.[16]

Prescriptive health systems focus on disease care that is based on the system's ability to deliver care, rather than the quality of life outcomes achieved for and with patients and families. A shift in performance management systems, including metrics that evaluate performance and cost, could be an important tool to drive change in how health systems are organized, what they are mandated to achieve (shift from disease management to health and wellness management), and how they are incentivized or reimbursed to support the shift from disease care to wellness care. Healthcare systems need to shift the culture away from disease-focused management in hospitals with a lot of expensive, high-tech equipment and move toward achieving/restoring quality of life whereby patients are part of the health-care team, working in partnership with health-care professionals to achieve quality of life through innovative tools and integrated services.

TREND TOWARD INCREASING HEALTH LITERACY ACROSS THE POPULATION

It is clear that health-system information technology is being used to organize health-system administration; gather, organize, and make available large data pools for health analytics; and provide tools for chronic disease management. However, the advent of the digital age through the rapid global spread of online and mobile tools and technologies has created numerous health opportunities including instant access to a very wide range of health information, the ability to create personalized health and wellness programs, and linkages to global online patient advocacy and social networking platforms. For those with access to online resources, this access to online health information has strengthened health literacy across populations, providing access to care in some instances where it has not been previously available. Health practitioner consultations through programs like *Skype* and other webcamera and videoconferencing tools are bringing care to individuals in remote and geographically inaccessible locations.

But the phenomenon of *Dr. Google* is more than just the availability of and access to online technology. The desire to take control of one's health and wellness through mobile technologies is a rapidly growing trend in the health sector, as witnessed in the explosion of health applications for mobile phones and computer tablets and technologies such as the iPad. Mobile health trends in developed economies have augmented existing health systems and had the effect of the *personalization* or virtualization of health care, whereby health services are tailored to meet the specific needs, motivations, and perspectives of individuals who seek mobile health-care services.

The drive toward health-care personalization has been supplemented by the explosion of health applications (apps) designed for mobile technologies. The figures related to usage of apps are staggering for a market that only debuted in 2008. By 2012, there were 44 million health apps downloaded, with that number predicted to grow to 142 million in 2016.[17] Currently, there are more than 97,000 mobile health applications, 42% of which are paid apps, listed on 62 fully catalogued app stores worldwide.[18] In 2012 alone, there was a 134% growth in mobile users viewing health content on their mobile devices, the highest of all content categories.[19] Global revenues for mobile health-care applications were predicted to reach $1.3 billion in 2012, up from $718 million in 2011, and are expected to reach $26 billion by 2017.[18]

There are two broad categories of health apps: (1) health and wellness (including fitness) and (2) medical. The majority of current applications are general health, wellness, and fitness apps that allow users to track health parameters and progress, or provide users with basic health and fitness-related information. According to a 2012 report by the Pew

Research Group of consumers in the United States, most *health-care* apps are used for these purposes with 38% tracking fitness, 31% tracking diet, and 12% tracking weight control.[20] This study further found that one in three cell phone owners (31%) had used their phone as a tool to look for health information and 19% of smartphone users had some kind of health app that assisted them in managing or tracking their health.

Health-care apps have also been categorized by user. User categorizations have been divided between apps for consumers or patients as compared to health professionals. It is predicted that 15% of global mobile health apps are designed for health-care professionals, not surprising given that 80% of physicians surveyed in the United States owned a mobile device with 30% of physicians reporting using a smartphone and/or tablet to treat patients as of 2012.[21] The types of apps targeted to health-care professionals include continuing medical education, remote monitoring, and health-care management applications.

Appeal of Health Apps

There are a number of immediate benefits to health apps, beyond just their convenience, ease of access, and often low cost for the consumer. Health apps and mobile technologies increase patient participation in health decision making, allowing for the real-time collection of data at (or close to) point of care. It becomes easier for patients to collect and store data, which could assist in filling in the gaps by providing information about a patient's health status outside of the clinical setting. Health apps also enable more personalized or tailored care, which could result in better health outcomes. For example, by tracking an individual patient's diet and activity level rather than relying on group norms (e.g., age and gender), a health practitioner could have a clearer picture of whether they need to educate their patient about better nutrition and lifestyle choices.

There is an administrative advantage as well for health systems. Health apps are increasingly being used to reduce the administrative burden on health-care support through the creation of automatic systems for scheduling appointments and sending reminders to patients. There can also be a reduction in administrative burden on the patient as some health apps have the ability to schedule appointments (ZocDoc), refill prescriptions (Walgreens app), and look up emergency room wait times (iTriage). These features provide an easy and immediate way for patients to perform tasks and get information without creating additional pressure on health-care systems or personnel.

Finally, health apps provide a way for people to engage in their health that is consistent with social norms. The average smartphone user checks their phone 127 times a day; given the norm associated with cell phone use, it becomes more discreet for patients to use mobile technologies to monitor health behavior as it conforms to the actions of the broader society. As an example, patients with diabetes have been found to prefer to use their smartphone to manage their condition rather than an insulin pump, because in checking a cell phone, they are doing something that everyone around them is doing.[22]

Challenges with Health Apps Adoption

It is important to recognize that there continues to be challenges with and barriers to the widespread adoption and impart of health apps. The most evident challenge continues to be around the privacy, security, and liability regarding the data that are inputted into health apps. Health information is often highly sensitive and private and it is sometimes unclear who is liable if that information is released, or if the app ceases to function properly due to technical issues. There are often not suitable protections placed around who is able to access the app from both a provider and consumer perspective. This also raises questions around the assessment and potential regulation of apps, particularly if they are being used in a clinical context. Currently, the FDA in the United States has released draft guidelines for industry and for FDA staff on the regulation of mobile medical applications, indicating some future mobile health apps will require FDA approval, specifically those that interact with currently regulated mobile devices.

It also has to be recognized that health apps and mobile technologies are still fairly new; as such, it is difficult to get evidence on the impact an app has on health outcomes, because the technology continues to change and evolve at such a rapid pace. A study published in the *Journal of Medical Internet Research* noted that outcomes of mobile health have barely been documented.[23] The study could not find a single scientific paper published through early 2012 that evaluated a smartphone app in general release through an app store, just a few pieces of software developed for research purposes.

Although the challenges surrounding health apps and the use of mobile technologies as health-care enablers must be addressed, it is clear that the advent of these tools in the health space have the opportunity to revolutionize health care globally. As the populations of more and more countries gain access to online resources, finding ways to ensure that they are accessible and understandable by as many people as possible should become a priority for nations, given their potential for providing health and wellness education that can assist in early preventative health measures. These technologies can serve alongside other web tools including telehealth and webcams to bring at least basic medical care and monitoring to geographically remote locations. By taking best practice health apps from one jurisdiction and supporting their translation to other nations in a way that reflects the differences in cultures, traditions, and practices, there can be a rapid dissemination of health innovation with the goal of improving patient outcomes, provider services, and system-level health accessibility.

SUMMARY

It is clear that there are exciting transformations taking place as a result of global health innovation at the system level. Although no single country has managed to completely transform their health system to achieve sustainability, a number of countries have made impressive strides in various areas to improve the quality of care delivered and health outcomes for the population. In every case, health care costs continue to outpace the growth of OECD nations as each one faces growing demands for health services from aging populations and rising rates of illness. Research has noted patterns and trends in countries relative to innovation as a strategy for health-system transformation including the distinct cultures of health systems, the integration of health services across the continuum of care, the emergence of value-driven health care, a growing accountability for health care in communities, the emerging role of consumers in engaging and managing their own health and wellness, the financial models that drive competition, and the increasing role of health information technologies and mobile technologies as tools for both individual health-care management and system-level operations.[24]

Although the momentum for health-care innovation is growing globally, as witnessed by the exciting health-based innovations being developed on a daily basis around the world, there is a strong need to continue to gather and share evidence on the impact of change of innovation approaches at the individual, practitioner, and health-system levels. Without empirical, irrefutable evidence, even those leaders inclined to seek out innovative solutions to serious problems will have little, if any, research that provides *best practice* approaches for the implementation of innovative solutions.[25] An evidence-based approach will provide greater certainty around the value-add of health-system innovations, leading to broader innovation translation and adoption globally as the return-on-investment in terms of clinical outcomes to country-level populations becomes more evident.

REFERENCES

1. ConforMIS, Inc. (2009). ConforMIS receives CE mark for the first and only personalized Bicompartmental Knee Resurfacing System. Hospital Business Week. Retrieved from http://ezproxy.uwindsor.ca/login?url=http://proquest.umi.com/pqd web?did=1773891081&Fmt=7&clientId=2241&RQT=309&VName=PQD.
2. Ferlie, E. and Shortell, S. (2001). Improving the quality of health care in the United Kingdom and the United States: A framework for change. *Milbank Quarterly*, Vol. 79. No 2, pp. 281–315.
3. Omachonu, V. and Einspruch, N. (2010). Innovation in healthcare delivery systems: A conceptual framework. *Innovation Journals: The Public Sector Innovation Journal*, Vol. 15. No 1, pp. 1–20.
4. Scott, K. (2009). The search for effective physician leaders: New strategies for new challenges. *Physician Executive*, Vol. 35. No 2, pp. 44–48.
5. Porter, M. and Teisburg, E. (2006). *Redefining Health Care*. Boston, MA: Harvard Business Press.
6. Snowdon, A., Schnarr, K., Hussein, A., and Alessi, C. (2012). *Measuring What Matters: The Costs vs. Values of Healthcare*. London, ON, Canada: Ivey International Centre for Health Innovation.
7. Ehrbeck, T., Henke, N., and Kibasi, T. (2010). The emerging market in health care innovation. Retrieved from: http://www.mckinsey.com/insights/health_systems_and_services/the_emerging_market_in_health_care_innovation. Accessed August 15, 2013.
8. Medicall Home. (2013). Think: The Innovation Knowledge Foundation. Retrieved from: http://www.thinkinnovation.org/location/medicall-home/. Accessed October 11, 2014.
9. McKinsey & Company. (2012). Strength in Unity: The Promise of Global Standards in Healthcare. Retrieved from: http://www.gs1.org/docs/healthcare/McKinsey_Healthcare_Report_Strength_in_Unity.pdf. Accessed October 3, 2013.
10. Eysenbach, G., Powell, J., Kuss, O., and Sa, E. (2002). Empirical studies assessing the quality of health information for consumers on the world wide web. *Journal of the American Medical Association*, Vol. 287. No 20, pp. 2691–2700.

11. Steinbrook, R. (2008). Personally controlled online health data: The next big thing in medical care? *New England Journal of Medicine*, Vol. 358. No 16, pp. 1653–1656.
12. Kaebler, D.C., Jha, A.K., Johnston, D., Middleton, B., and Bates, D.W. (2008). A research agenda for personal health records (PHRs). *Journal of the American Medical Informatics Association*, Vol. 15, pp. 729–736.
13. Kummervold, P.E., Chronaki, C.E., Lausen, B., Prokosch, H., Rasmussen, J., Santana, S. et al. (2008). E-health trends in Europe 2005–2007: A population-based survey. *Journal of Medical Internet Research*, Vol. 10, p. e42.
14. Smart Card Alliance. (2005). The Taiwan Health Care Smart Card Project. Retrieved from: http://www.smartcardalliance.org/resources/pdf/Taiwan_Health_Card_Profile.pdf. Accessed September 15, 2013.
15. Low, L., Yap, M., and Brodaty, H. (2011). A systematic review of different models of home and community care services for older persons. *BMC Health Services Research*, Vol. 11, p. 93.
16. Moondraa, R. Technology Enabled Proactive Healthcare. Retrieved from: http://www.articlesbase.com/health-articles/technology-enabled-proactive-healthcare-6112299.html. Accessed October 11, 2014.
17. Juniper Research. (2011). Mobile Healthcare Opportunities. Retrieved from: http://www.ihealthbeat.org/articles/2011/12/1/44m-mobile-health-apps-will-be-downloaded-in-2012-report-predicts. Accessed October 14, 2013.
18. Jahns, R. (2013). The Market for mHealth App Services Will Reach $26 Billion by 2017. Retrieved from: http://www.research2guidance.com/the-market-for-mhealth-app-services-will-reach-26-billion-by-2017/. Accessed October 20, 2013.
19. Comscore. (2012). U.S. Digital Future in Focus 2012. p. 24. Retrieved from: http://www.comscore.com/Insights/Presentations_and_Whitepapers/2012/2012_US_Digital_Future_in_Focus. Accessed October 20, 2013.
20. Fox, S. and Duggan, M. (2012). Mobile Health 2012. Retrieved from: http://www.pewinternet.org/Reports/2012/Mobile-Health/Main-Findings/Mobile-Health.aspx. Accessed August 30, 2013.
21. Oldenburg, J., Chase, D., Christensen, K., and Tritle, B. (2013). *Engage! Transforming Healthcare Through Digital Patient Engagement*. Chicago, IL: Health Information Management Systems Society.
22. Walsh, B. (2013). Mobile Health Has Opportunity in Addictive Nature of Smartphones. Clinical Innovation + Technology. Retrieved from: www.clinical-innovation.com/topics/mobile-telehealth/mobile-health-has-opportunity-addictive-nature-smart-phones. Accessed August 30, 2013.
23. Fiordelli, M., Diviani, N., and Schulz, P. (2013). Mapping mHealth research: A decade of innovation. *Journal of Medical Internet Research*. Vol. 15. No. 5, p. e95.
24. Snowdon, A. and Cohen, J. (2011). *Strengthening Health Systems Through Innovation: Lessons Learned*. London, ON, Canada: Ivey International Centre for Health Innovation.
25. Snowdon, A., Shell, J., and Leitch, K. (2010). *Innovation Takes Leadership: Opportunities and Challenges for Canada's Health Care System*. London, ON, Canada: Ivey Centre for Health Innovation and Leadership.

3

Learning from Industry: Innovating in Health-Care Operation

Paul Lillrank

CONTENTS

INTRODUCTION

This chapter discusses improvement methodologies available to health-care providers around the world. Most of them have their origins in manufacturing industries, where quality, cost efficiency, and flexibility have improved dramatically over the past half-century. Despite valiant efforts and several success stories, the overall performance of health service systems in relation to the resources spent has not improved at the same rate. Therefore, it is reasonable to assume that health service production exhibits some characteristics that make it different not only from manufacturing, but also from other service industries, such as travel and tourism, banking and finance, retailing, and wholesale. If this assumption is true, it follows that health-care needs improvement methodologies and innovation support based on the specific characteristics of health care.

VALUE IN HEALTH CARE

Lean management, an approach that will be discussed in the next chapters, strives to efficiency through the systematic elimination of "waste"—any step or activity that consumes resources but does not contribute value to the customer.* To do this, there must be a way to distinguish waste from value. In manufacturing this is reasonably straightforward: everything that moves the product toward completion contributes to value. In health care, however, it is not obvious how, say, another x-ray or a second opinion contributes to patients' health outcomes. It can be known only afterward.

In manufacturing, customers do not really care how something is made; internal process efficiency and quality assurance are the producer's problems. In services, value is created both by What is done and How it is done.

In health-care value creation can be divided into three separate aspects. First, what is done to a patient is the result of clinical decision making. It requires information about the patient's condition gathered through interviews, observations, and tests, a diagnosis identifying the nature of the problem and its probable causes, and a treatment plan including one or several clinical interventions. Second, once a treatment plan has been established, it needs to be executed following best-known practices to assure patient safety. Third, a patient going through a treatment process experiences it in various ways. Obviously, a correct diagnosis and safe execution are the core elements of the experience, but there are nonclinical issues, such as waiting times, information, and respect that contribute to the experience. Thus the value chain of clinical interventions, the process that makes them happen safely, and how they are experienced by patients are different, but interrelated things.

The All Indian Institute of Medical Science (AIIMS) in Delhi is known for having the best clinical quality in the country, although facilities are falling apart and queues snake all the way to the street. Still many people willingly trade the How for the What. In other cases people may prefer the most convenient to the best solution. The world view of manufacturing does not know such trade-offs; neither is it able to deal with the fact that a

---

* The basic text on Lean is Womack J.P., Jones D.T., and Roos D. (1990). *The Machine That Changed the World*. Rawson Associates, New York, NY. For healthcare applications, see, for example, Graban, Mark (2009). *Lean Hospitals: Improving Quality, Patient Safety, and Employee Satisfaction*. CRC Press, Boca Raton, FL.

significant part of quality problems in services are caused by the customers not doing their part.

Innovation is to change the value chain by adding, removing, or changing value creating activities, or the value itself. For example, the ulcer medication Losec was a major innovation, based on a breakthrough in understanding the causes of ulcer. For many patients it removed the need to go under the knife; they could take pills instead.* Both the What and the How changed dramatically.

When the waste surrounding a value stream is removed, it is assumed that it has no negative impact on clinical quality, and no risk for patients is involved. If it may, it is essential that medical expertise be closely involved. Tampering with the value stream in manufacturing may cause economic losses; in health care lives are at risk. Patient safety is one of the major concerns that makes health care different from manufacturing.

It cannot be known exactly how much of the total health spend is waste. Estimates range from 20% to 50%. However one looks at it, it is a lot and too much. Therefore, responsible and resourceful providers all around the world do not remain idle waiting for clinical, technical, organizational, or financial innovation to work the magic. The performance of health service operations can be improved right away as several methods are available.

MANAGING OPERATIONS

Operations Management (OM), also known as Industrial Management, is the scientific study of production systems with the explicit aim of increasing productivity and quality: to produce more and better with less. OM is distinct from product and production technologies. It does not define what customers may need or want, it is not about inventing new widgets or production machinery. Its task is to find out how they could be put to best use. Health care Operations Management (HOM) does not strive to get involved in clinical decision making or the administration of therapies, that is, the core value chain of health services. The focus is on how to organize resources and flows of materials, energy, tasks, and

---

* Major innovations in healthcare are described in Le Fanu, James (1999). *The Rise and Fall of Modern Medicine*. Abacus, London, UK.

skills so that given targets, cost, and clinical quality, as well as issues contributing to the patient experience, such as throughput and waiting time, number of visits per patient episode, responsiveness, courtesy, and other soft issues, can be achieved with the available resources. Technically speaking, the aim is to optimize resource efficiency (how well resources are employed to do their job) and flow efficiency (the swift, even flow of patients through the system). To this end, HOM is concerned with the organizational arrangements that support processes, workflows, networks, supply chains, quality assurance, integration, coordination, and incentives.[1]

Like most areas of science and technology, OM consists of the meat-and-potatoes basic theories, methods, and rules of inquiry. In OM such are staffing, scheduling, process control, planning, resource, capacity, and inventory management, supply chain management, and managerial accounting. Building on them, there are different schools of thought. The most common are Lean management, Agile, and Theory of Constraints (TOC). The schools of thought are often packaged into programs to make them easier for practitioners to grasp. With the packaging sometime follows simplifications, panaceas, and hype.

Lean Management

Lean management evolved in the post-World War II Japanese automobile industry. It has become the dominant paradigm of OM. It is supported by a large amount of research and it is described in all university-level textbooks. As the word "Lean" suggests, the objective is to create maximal customer value with minimal use of resources. The basic principles are to identify customer value, the value flow that produces it, and waste. The methods used are process standardization, statistical control of variation, and to move from batch production to flow production. Ultimately, the vision is a production system that works in perfect synchrony and is capable of swiftly correcting itself. Change management is based on the idea of all-employee involvement in continuous improvement through teamwork.

Total Quality Management (TQM) is a school that emerged from the Japanese industry before Lean. It puts focus on relentless reduction of quality problems through continuous improvement. A core methodology is Statistical Process Control (SPC), of which Six Sigma is an extension and elaboration. By and large, the TQM principles have been absorbed into

Lean. Many large companies have built and labeled their own programs based on a collection of principles, tools and techniques, together with a corporate culture or ethos. The best known is the Toyota Production System. Several hospitals, particularly those focusing on high volume elective surgery, have adopted similar approaches.

Agile Management

Although Lean was born in the world of mass production of consumer products and components, Agile arises from job shop environments, where mostly capital goods are built to individual customer specifications in single units or small volumes, such as ships or industrial machinery. As the word "Agile" suggests, the objective is to produce highly individualized solutions by organizing resources flexibly, using excess capacity when necessary. The principal methods are to build rapid response capability by multi-skilling, integrate design and production, organize for learning and iterations, and effectively use real-time information flows. In the world of Agile, keeping a resource idling in standby is not considered waste, as flexibility requires it. Agile and Lean do not necessary contradict each other, as they apply to different production environments. They can be combined (*Leanagility*),[2] for example, by building flexibility in complex diagnostics and standardization in routine therapies.

Theory of Constraints

The TOC was developed by Eliyahu Goldratt in his landmark book *The Goal*.[3,4] TOC is also known as the theory of bottlenecks, as it puts a great emphasis on finding and managing the constraints of production. Every process has a bottleneck, a step or resource that determines the total capacity of a process; a chain is as strong as its weakest link. Therefore, process improvement should focus on finding the bottleneck resource and managing it.

Lean and TOC contradict each other on some issues. Lean maintains that improvement in all aspects of production is always beneficial, whereas TOC claims that improving non-bottleneck resources only creates overproduction and waste. Lean strives at reducing variation to achieve an even flow, whereas TOC admits that variation is inevitable and needs to be managed through bottlenecks. Beyond that, however, both methodologies can be applied for their appropriate strengths.

HEALTH CARE IS DIFFERENT

All the major schools of thought have been developed in manufacturing, where each of them can point to a series of success stories. Their track record in services in general and health care in particular is more varied. Several hospital systems in the United States following Lean have reported dramatic improvements in quality, access, cost of care, reduction in unnecessary procedures, and elimination of various forms of waste inherent in the existing practice of medicine.

Nevertheless, OM methods have not been able to reproduce the overwhelming successes they reaped in manufacturing. The reasons can, obviously, lie in the lack of motivation or insufficient implementation. However, more profoundly, health care is a sector, where the logic of production, value creation, waste, demand, and finance are different. Moreover, health care might not even be an industry, like automobile manufacturing, with one logic of production. Rather it is a cluster of industries each posing very different challenges. To manage an emergency department is different from managing a clinic focused on prevention of lifestyle-based diseases. The task of HOM is to develop a set of theories and methods, that while applying what is universally known about production, would rise from the specifics of health care. Recent advances in Service Science may be of help.

Service Science or Service Research emerged around 2005 as a new wave of thinking.[5,6] Services account for up to three-quarters of modern economies. Still the bulk of service-related management research had been focusing on marketing and the identification of customer needs. How service producers might fulfill those needs was left with less concern. To fill the gap, Service Operations Management and Service Engineering have been developed. A basic tenet of Service Research is that the production of goods and services are founded on different logics. Goods-dominant logic (GDL) sees production and consumption as different spheres, connected through a distribution system. Building a product creates value and it resides in it until it is unleashed in consumption. Customers may place orders or express their views; otherwise they do not participate in production. Customers are like empty vessels to be satisfied by offering them something good.

Service-dominant logic (SDL) is founded on the idea that value is always cocreated. Production is the combination and integration of producers' and customers' resources. Customers essentially create value; producers can only sell value offerings and support customers' value-creating activities. The value of a car does not lie in its physical form, but the value it brings to a user. Using these ideas as a starting point, the major differences between manufacturing and health care can be elaborated.

Following the goods-dominant view, manufacturers can rely on the following assumptions.

- The market mechanism works, unless there are specific reasons why not, such as monopolies or regulation. Customers may not be fully rational, but a manufacturer can expect them to be able to identify the difference between good and bad, cheap and expensive. Improvement always pays, harming or disappointing customers is always punished.
- Customer value can be known; therefore, waste can be known.
- Customers may have a say through market research, otherwise they do not get involved in production.
- Processes are plannable tightly coupled dependent events. Production facilities can be controlled and external harmful influences, such as dust, vibration, or humidity, can be restricted.
- Capital resides chiefly in plants, equipment, technologies, designs, and brands. Human capital does not have an independent role.
- Each industry has a competitive logic that follows from the types of markets served, technologies used, amounts of capital required, and entry and exit conditions.

This is not the kind of environment where health services are produced.

Markets do not work in health care. In North Europe, the public sector takes care of both finance and most of production. In the private or mixed systems found in Central Europe and the United States, a third party collects and distributes most of the financial resources. This creates a patient–provider–payer triangle, where various incentive traps easily form. Insurance policies dictate what kinds of care are demanded and supplied. Regulators may prevent good enough frugal solutions.[7] In India, more than half of the total spent on health care is out of pocket. In theory, it should be an environment where the market mechanism balancing supply and demand could work. There is, however, little evidence to support such a conclusion.

Demand does not necessarily react to price, as most of health care is "essential goods"; desperate people pay whatever is asked. On the other hand, the value of additional care is difficult to establish, therefore the marginal utility mechanism (the perceived value of a third car is less than that of the first) does not automatically limit demand.

Patients cannot easily be seen as customers. They do not necessarily have the information and knowledge to choose, and in many cases, such as an emergency, their choice is limited.

Patient value is difficult to define precisely. Although it is obvious that people desire good health outcomes, little risk, minimum inconvenience, and no pain, sometimes any of these can form a trade-off with no obvious solution. The identity of the customer is not clear as it may include several stakeholders: the patient, the family, the payer, the employer, and the community.

Patients are not passive recipients of procedures. Ultimately, health value is produced by the patient's body and mind, with some assistance from service producers. Health services are built on the mutuality of providers and patients with specific roles and responsibilities.

Some processes are plannable (lab tests, elective surgery), while some others are not (emergencies, complex and iterative care, multi- and comorbidities). In the latter cases the industrial process logic is difficult to apply, except in some subroutines and supporting processes.

A hospital is not like a factory, where various activities are tightly linked. Rather it is like a shopping mall with a common infrastructure, on which several different merchants ply their trade to different customers.

Hospitals are not capital intensive; in advanced countries, the cost of building and equipping a brand new hospital equals the cost of running it for less than 2 years. Some areas require significant investments in capital equipment such as MRI imaging; whereas in many areas most important is human capital, the skillsets of practitioners that are deployed individually to individual patients. Indeed, in traditional analytic psychiatry the only equipment needed is a couch and a notepad. Despite all the high-technology gizmos, health-care production still to a large extent resembles more preindustrial craft production than mass manufacturing.

With such fundamental differences in the conceptions of value and value creation, it is not obvious that methods born in manufacturing could easily be applied in all aspects of health care. A possible way to deal with such issues would be to look at their applicability separately at different types of health services. For that, a typology or segmentation scheme is necessary.

SEGMENTATION IN HEALTH CARE

Historically the basic segmentation principles in health care have been urgency and severity. Organizations or units dealing with urgent and severe cases, such as massive trauma, must be organized differently from those that cater to nonurgent, nonlethal cases, such as diabetes. Although some hospitals are multispecialty and multipurpose, some have been organized to serve some specific population groups, such as women, children, elderly, or military personnel. Further, with advances in clinical medicine, segmentation follows specialties based on body systems (ophthalmology, cardiology, orthopedics, etc.), primary causes (trauma, infections, tumors, etc.), and principal methods (surgery, internal medicine, radiology, etc.). Such overlapping segmentation principles lead to complex organizations.

Recently, there have been attempts to develop complementary segmentation principles based on managerial issues. Christensen, Grossman, and Hwang, in their 2010 book *The Innovator's Prescription*, present a three-step model.[8] First, there is traditional intuitive medicine. As only about one-third of medical procedures are based on evidence, there is room for the clinician's intuition, experience, and focus on a single patient case in all its varieties. *Intuitive medicine* responds poorly to mass production–based methods, as it treats each patient as a unique individual. Second, advances in clinical medicine and diagnostics have given rise to *precision medicine*. It applies to cases where a precise diagnosis can be made and a precise therapy can be applied with known results. Examples are hernia, cataract, and joint replacement surgery. For such cases, highly efficient surgical factories can be established. Third, much of health care is a social and communal affair. Particularly for prevention and chronic conditions, *supported networks* can be established.

A more elaborated model is the demand-supply–based operating (DSO) logic.[9] It is based on the notion that different patients demand different things, but the supply side cannot do everything to everybody. It is constrained by economic (affordability), technical (every illness cannot be cured), and behavioral (patients must do their part) factors. From this, seven different health service types can be formulated. Each of them delivers different types of value to the patient; consequently the value chains, processes, and business models are different.

Prevention deals with situations, where a patient is not yet sick or injured but, if the current condition or lifestyle continues, there is a significant, predictable risk of getting ill in the future. The value that prevention may create is that something that could have happened does not happen. That means that value is a nonevent, from which it follows that revenue models are difficult to formulate (why pay for something that may not happen). Therefore, prevention resembles insurance and finance: precaution and investment now might generate a return later. The value chain chiefly consists of tasks that the patient has to perform. Service providers can offer facts, advise, support, and encouragement, but in the end, the doctor cannot stop smoking or hit the gym on behalf of the patient. The technologies employed are chiefly behavioral; the Hows are more important than the Whats.

Emergencies are medical conditions where there is a time window, within which something must be done to prevent death or permanent injury. Patient value is a saved life and a stabilized condition to make further care and recovery possible. Emergency departments (ED) and ambulatory services are organized for rapid and flexible response, following the Agile principles. The value chain needs to be configured specifically for each patient, and necessary resources should be mobilized. Prevention and emergencies are in many ways direct opposites. In prevention, patients often must be cajoled and motivated to undergo treatment; in emergencies a major task is triage, an assessment based on which patients whose condition is neither urgent nor severe must be turned away. In emergencies the Whats override the Hows.

One-visit refers to situations where a medical condition is neither urgent, nor severe, and requires no more than one brief intervention, such as stitching a wound, having a tooth cavity filled, or writing a prescription for common antibiotics. Patient value consists of the intervention as such and convenience of access. Things that can be done during one visit should not unnecessarily be split into two. One-visit clinics resemble in many ways retailing, fast food, and other high-volume services: without easy access there would be no or little demand. The Whats and the Hows are of equal importance.

Electives are procedures to treat problems that may be severe, but not urgent. They are typically based on precise diagnostics and well understood processes. The intervention, such as a cardiac bypass, aims at creating a stepwise improvement in patients' conditions. The value chain consists of diagnosis, preparations, procedure, and recovery. As electives are plannable, they can be scheduled, and resources can be allocated accordingly in advance. From a management perspective, elective hospital departments are the area of health care that most resemble manufacturing plants. As electives are precisely known service products, they can be offered at fixed prices.

Cure means a set of procedures that, differing from electives, cannot be planned in advance from end to end, such as, complex cancer, where the value chain and supporting procedures can be planned only a few steps ahead. If a patient does not react to medication as anticipated, the process may have to go back to square one. Value for the patient resides in achieving the anticipated cure, and as the path there typically is long and complicated, the patient experience and the relation to caregivers is important. From a managerial perspective cure resembles new product development. The process is iterative and new findings need to be flexibly integrated into treatment plans. Because of the risks and uncertainties involved, cure processes cannot be assigned a price tag in advance. Cure processes, however, are initiated with the assumption that there will be a cure, and that the process has a desirable end point.

Care is a type where desirable end points cannot be defined, because the medical condition is chronic, incurable, or terminal, such as diabetes, dementia, and other frailties related to aging. The value of care is to help patients live with their condition, manage risks, and arrest decline. The value chain consists of a regular rhythm of therapies, examinations, and monitoring of conditions. In care-supported networks, self-service and community involvement are important.

Projects, finally, relate to situations where a patient's condition is unknown, extremely complex, costly, or involves several stakeholders. No ready set processes exist for rare cases. Therefore, each patient case should be managed as a project, with an assigned project manager, who orchestrates various resources and sees to it that they are integrated and coordinated. The primary value to a patient comes from the synergic combinations of various resources, as no single medical specialty can provide the solution to a patient who is a project.

The seven DSO types could be considered single industries within the health-care cluster. In some instances, specific organizations can be developed to deal with one type. Such are health and wellness clubs for prevention, ambulatory units for emergencies, health kiosks for one visit, or focused surgical hospitals for electives. An organization dealing with one DSO type is often innovative, as it can focus on only one managerial logic. Clinically speaking, pregnancy and hypertension, cataract and cardiac bypass, a split tooth and influenza are different, but they can be managed with similar processes. However, much of health care cannot be organized in single logic units. Patients may change from one type to another within one health episode. Some units include by necessity several types. For example, birthing and maternity care involves four: care of expectant mothers (prevention), normal deliveries (one-visit), planned sections (elective), and sudden crises (emergency). Rather it could be said that health care is a *virtual cluster*, a collection of different production logics that, most of the time, need to coexist, collaborate, and coordinate.

FOCUSED INNOVATIONS IN HEALTH CARE

The variety of patient value, value chains, processes, skill requirements, patient involvement, revenue logic, capital intensity, and demand conditions explain why there cannot be a single solution, one overriding principle to improve and innovate.

One possible route to innovations is to take one DSO, one patient or demand type, focus on it, and do it exceptionally well. There are several examples; some are discussed in this book.

- Prevention can be organized into meditation centers, with surroundings and facilities that do not convey the image of a hospital, and rather build on positive motivation.
- Elective procedures, such as standard cardiac bypasses, cataract, or artificial joint surgery can be organized into surgical factories, where resource and flow efficiency can be optimized.
- One-visits are well handled by conveniently located heath kiosks or drop-in clinics where patients can get the help they need in one session.
- Care can be managed in nursing homes and hospices with various service levels.
- The "each patient is a project" approach has been used in symptom-centric clinics that focus on pain or migraine, problems that can have several different or overlapping causes requiring well-orchestrated diagnostics.

Beyond such focused units, many health service organizations still need to incorporate and manage different logics. Therefore innovations could well focus on finding out better ways and routines to manage the inevitable difficulties that follow when one patient needs to move from one logic of production to another.

SUMMARY

Many important innovations are not new to the world. Rather they are new to the discipline, applications of something that has worked elsewhere. Using scarce resources to reinvent the wheel is waste. Health service producers are well advised to look beyond their own field and learn from others, not only the mighty manufacturers, but also the lowly retailers, chain stores, and kiosks, and also study how research and development is managed in high-technology startups. Given the complexity of the task, it pays to follow some general principles, adopt a vocabulary understandable to others, and use proven methods that come with the schools of thought and development programs such as Lean. In the end, every service provider should develop its own version and its corporate culture. Health care is, and will remain a people-to-people business; therefore, the soft aspects should not be neglected.

REFERENCES

1. Hopp W.J and Lovejoy W.S. (2013). *Hospital Operations—Principles of High Efficiency Health Care*. FT Press, Upper Saddle River, NJ.
2. Sabri E.S, and Salim N. (2010). *Lean and Agile Value Chain Management: A Guide to the Next Level of Improvement*. J. Ross Publishing, Fort Lauderdale, FL.
3. Goldratt E. and Cox J. (1982). *The Goal: A Process of Ongoing Improvement*. North River Press, Great Barrington, MA.
4. Ronen B. and Pliskin J.S. (2006). *Focused Operations Management for Health Service Organizations*. Wiley, New York, NY.
5. Vargo S.L. and Lusch R.F. (2004). Evolving to a new dominant logic for marketing. *Journal of Marketing*, Vol. 68, pp. 1–17.
6. Sampson S. and Froehle C. (2006). Foundations and implications of a proposed unified services theory. *Production and Operations Management*, Vol. 15, No 2, pp. 329–343.
7. Reid T. (2009). *The Healing of America: A Global Quest for Better, Cheaper, and Fairer Health Care*. The Penguin Press, London, UK.
8. Christensen C., Grossman J., and Hwang J. (2009). *The Innovator's Prescription—Disruptive Solutions for Healthcare*. McGraw-Hill, New York, NY.
9. Lillrank P., Groop J., and Malmström T. (2010). Demand and supply–based operating modes—A framework for analyzing health care service production. *Milbank Quarterly*, Vol. 88, No 4, pp. 595–615.

4

Lean and Innovation: "The Two Responsibilities"

Marc S. Hafer, John Gallagher, and Adam Ward

CONTENTS

INTRODUCTION

We will explore the two different improvement methodologies that are available to health-care providers around the world. We refer to them as the Two Responsibilities. The first is to run the business, providing safe and effective health care to their patients. Known quality assurance and improvement methodologies are applied to achieve this goal. We refer to this as *conversion* of a current state of affairs into a better one by following known principles aiming at industry best practices. The second responsibility is to fundamentally change the way care is provided to the customer. This approach involves new methods that may be disruptive to existing practices. We refer to this as *innovation*, the subject matter of this book. We will explore how the two responsibilities can be applied to address the global escalation of costs and the increasing pressure on resources within health care provision.

CALL TO ACTION

The global health-care industry is at a precarious point. Although this chapter leans toward the North American provider crisis, there is no debating that the global health-care economy is in tumult. Although there have been many initiatives to curb rising costs and improve quality, the industry faces a growing mismatch between demand and supply.

The need for a system change is not a new idea. Dr. Robert Ebert wrote back in 1967: "The existing deficiencies in healthcare cannot be corrected simply by supplying more personnel, more facilities and more money. These problems can only be solved by organizing the providers optimally for the health needs of the population."

In technology, *Moore's Law* predicts that every 2 years the cost of computing will fall by half. The health-care industry finds itself in the opposite position: the U.S. health care costs have *doubled* as a percentage of GDP every 13 years for the last half century.[1] What if health care was able to reverse the trend and reduce the cost of care by half every 13 years? What would a health-care system have to look like to achieve that audacious goal?

The current system is poorly suited to meet three major challenges: the aging population, the increase in chronic long-term conditions, and the shortage of skilled resources.

The U.S. national census shows an acceleration of the over-65 and over-85 population in the next 40 years. The baby boom generation is in many ways healthier than the previous generations who suffered from wars and shortages. However, in developed countries up to 80% of an individual's total life-cycle cost of care is spent during the last years of life. As the number of people approaching this stage increases, health-care organizations will have to absorb additional costs to provide a similar level of care compared to today. Advances in clinical medicine and pharmaceuticals have succeeded in reducing mortality. However, many conditions that a generation ago would have been fatal are now turned into long-term chronic conditions requiring continuous care.

Even though rich countries could afford the needed care, for example, by liquidating the assets of elderly people, the availability of skilled labor becomes a bottleneck. The Institute of Medicine predicts a shortage of 130,000 physicians by 2025. They foresee that there will only be one primary care physician for every 10,000 people. There is already pressure to increase the number of patients served by a physician to above 5000. As new physicians who want a better work–life balance replace the current hardworking baby boomer clinicians, and fewer new graduates enter primary care, a labor supply crisis will evolve.

The system crisis of health care appears overwhelming. There is no top-down silver bullet solution in sight. However, responsible and resourceful providers all around the world are working to improve their performance. One of the most successful techniques is Lean management.

BRIEF HISTORY OF LEAN MANAGEMENT IN HEALTH CARE

The principles and practices of Lean management evolved in the post–World War II Japanese automobile industry. It has become the dominant paradigm of industrial management; therefore, it can no longer be described as a fad. Recently, it has found many applications in the services sector. As the word "Lean" suggests, the objective is to create maximal customer value with minimal use of resources. The basic principles are identification of customer value and the value flow that produces it, standardization of processes, reduction of waste, involvement of people, and continuous improvement.

In the United States, health-care providers were experimenting with Lean principles in the 1990s. In the following decade, more Lean thinkers joined the movement in pursuit of the Institute of Health Care Improvement's Triple Aim in health care. The *Triple Aim* is a framework for optimizing health system performance by the following:

- Improving the patient experience of care (including quality and satisfaction)
- Improving the health of populations
- Reducing the per capita cost of health care

By 2004, several U.S. hospital systems proved that Lean principles could dramatically improve quality, increase access, reduce unnecessary procedures, and lower the cost of care. Most of these early successes were the result of applying Lean principles to identify and eliminate various forms of waste inherent in the existing practice of medicine. It was shown that Lean principles work in all aspects of medicine and clinical care, as well as in administrative areas that support clinicians. The early Lean adopters made compelling cases that Lean is not just for manufacturing; when pared back to the essential principles, beliefs, and practices, Lean management can deliver on the Triple Aim.

In retrospect, such early innovations easily won successes simply by the application of Lean tools and techniques to existing processes, improving within the margins but essentially being nondisruptive in the main. Existing processes were filled with variation and waste, presenting a low hurdle for the implementation of Lean to convert batch processes to flow processes, eliminate the wastes of waiting and overproduction, and reduce variation through the implementation of standardized work. In 2004–2006, Institute for Healthcare Improvement's (IHI's) 100,000 Lives Campaign was the best example of improvements driven by conversion to best known standards of practice, reducing or eliminating altogether common health-care system flaws such as ventilator-associated pneumonia (VAP), central line infections, deaths from adverse drug effects, and deaths from acute myocardial infarction (AMI).

The government's ambition is to achieve health care outcomes that are among the best in the world. This can only be realized by involving patients fully in their own care, with decisions made in partnership with clinicians, rather than by clinicians alone: no decision about me, without me.

Shared Decision Making is a process in which patients, when they reach a decision crossroads in their health care, can review the treatment options available to them. With current clinical information, relevant to their particular condition, patients will be helped to work through any questions they may have, explore the options available, and take a treatment route that best suits their needs and expectations.

To achieve this we need to encourage patients, carers, and the public to work alongside, in equal partnership, with clinicians and managers. This puts Shared Decision Making not only at the care level but also at the strategic and commissioning level with patients involved in the codesign, co-commissioning, and indeed coproduction of health care. Without this change we will not get the required transformational culture change of Shared Decision Making.

Shared Decision Making provides a new paradigm for managing the inexorable demand for health care where demand is managed by informed and empowered patients making rational health-care decisions.

A3 THINKING: A SCIENTIFIC APPROACH TO PROCESS INNOVATION

A systematic Lean approach is used to define an opportunity and develop and implement solutions in a scientific manner. This is referred to as "A3 Thinking," named after the A3-sized paper and related formatting that prescribes a logic pathway for problem solving. Although various forms of problem solving exist, the nine-step approach described in Table 4.1 is

TABLE 4.1

The A3 Problem Solving Steps

Step 1	Define the reason for action: what are the compelling reasons for this project; what is the scope?
Step 2	Detail the initial state: fact-based description and anecdotal evidence that defines the current process and its performance outcomes
Step 3	Detail the target state: performance goals and description of desired future state
Step 4	Gap analysis: the differences (deltas) between initial and target states, including root causes, prioritization, and estimated impact of resolving gaps
Step 5	Solution approach: the design of a solution and the series of major events, projects, and actions that will deliver the target state
Step 6	Rapid experiments: prove or disprove the hypotheses that form the basis of the solution approach
Step 7	Completion plan: detailed action steps with responsibilities and delivery dates
Step 8	Confirmed state: proof of progress toward Step 3 target state goals
Step 9	Insights: lessons learned to inform stakeholders and to build into future innovation projects

frequently used and these steps are placed in nine boxes on A3 paper to tell a story on one page that is easy to comprehend and monitor.

LEAN PRINCIPLES: TRANSFORMATIVE BELIEFS FOR INNOVATION

Lean is based on the scientific method including data collection, experimentation, analysis, rational reasoning, verification of results, and standardization of best practices. However, successful, enduring Lean practitioners need to develop their business systems and organizational cultures based on fundamental Lean beliefs, principles, and habits that apply wherever work is done. Table 4.2 shows a sample of beliefs that are particularly applicable in health care improvement and innovation.

TABLE 4.2

Lean Beliefs Applicable in Health Care

Lean Belief/Principle	Application to Health-Care Innovation
Takt time, the rate at which customers demand a product or service, drives performance.	Innovation in service design must enhance the providers' ability and agility to achieve takt time under different demands and time constraints.
In health care, practitioners will assert that all patients are different. At a fundamental level this is true, yet when demand data is analyzed properly, sufficient evidence can be brought forward to determine an overall rhythmic cadence of demand, to which resources can be properly allocated.	
Customers define value	Innovation is built on facts gathered regarding patients, their families, physicians, clinicians and other caregivers, and the environments for each. This includes both qualitative outputs and experiential. Patients are increasingly knowledgeable about their treatment options and able to exercise choice.
Creativity before capital	Lean innovation makes the most of existing technology, infrastructure, and human resources. Creativity must be exhausted before capital will be spent on potential wastes.

Lean Belief/Principle	Application to Health-Care Innovation
Create horizontal flow	Innovation will remove impediments to the flow of patients, information, decisions and other value-adding steps by removing obstacles, such as production batches, islands of excellence, extreme specialization, and departmental boundaries to achieve flow of defect-free services on demand at the lowest cost.
Standard work is liberating	Far from being an inhibitor of creativity, standard work enables physicians and clinicians to operate at the top of their licenses; focus on diagnosis and care delivery.
Quality and productivity are not mutually exclusive concepts	Both zero defects and lowest costs can be achieved concurrently, reinforcing the belief that time saved in health-care services drives higher quality outcomes, and consequently lower costs and higher patient and staff satisfaction.

"TWO RESPONSIBILITIES"

Many health-care practitioners are asking how to accelerate the results they are achieving with Lean. This is where the evolution between the Two Responsibilities, conversion and innovation, come into application.

The improvements described in the preceding sections worked on existing processes through rigorous application of Lean principles and techniques. Processes were standardized and stabilized to eliminate errors and wasteful practices. As a result, the processes worked in the way most people can agree they should, without the downside of quality problems and confusion.

Small improvements can accumulate into innovations that change the way an organization produces value. A classic example comes from the Japanese automobile industry. Car bodies are assembled from a number of parts stamped out of sheet metal by huge press machines in long series. When a machine is to produce a different type of part, the stamping die must be exchanged for another. This used to take more than a day of work. Although necessary, this work did not produce value to the customer. Through a long series of small improvements the time to exchange a die could be reduced to less than 10 minutes. Efficiency was improved and wasteful use of time was reduced. There was, however, an unintended consequence. As the time and cost of changing production from one part to another was reduced, the optimal batch size was reduced. When previously a stamping press had to produce a huge number of parts to be stored for future use, it could now produce only the amount needed. From this followed, through several steps, the possibility to produce small series of different automobiles that more precisely satisfy the need of customers. This was a breakthrough, known as mass customization: the possibility to use a standard process to produce a huge range of variety.

In health care a similar development has been observed. If the time and cost of routine diagnostic examinations, such as x-rays and blood tests, can be significantly reduced, it becomes possible for an outpatient clinic to send all patients in a given triage category to diagnostics immediately before seeing a doctor. Thus the confusion and paperwork associated with laboratory referrals can be eliminated and the doctor can see the patient with the necessary test results at hand. Such a major improvement, however, requires several small improvements in the diagnostics process, and an understanding of how such improvements may accumulate and create possibilities to redesign the whole patient process. When this culture transformation occurs, then, and only then, do the improvements result in long-term sustained results improvements.

In summary, the first responsibility is to improve existing processes based on existing views of patient value by eliminating quality errors, unnecessary steps, and waiting. After all, it can be safely assumed that every patient prefers an error-free and swift process to the opposite. The second responsibility, innovation in how patient value is created, is a much larger challenge. Returning to the automobile example, before the advent of mass customization, a manufacturer could safely assume that customers want affordable error-free cars. When product variety became possible, it became apparent that the customer wanted cars that fit their individual tastes in terms of performance, styling, colors, and options as well as the quality and performance. In a similar vein within health care, when basic quality and cost efficiency are assured, innovation needs to focus on health outcomes and patient experiences.

APPLYING THE INNOVATION APPROACH

Lean health-care innovation Innovation is about developing solutions that the customers are not currently offered and providing that solution better than anyone else. Although the aim for Lean improvements is to eliminate waste, the aim for innovation is to increase value in the eyes of the customer. Facebook did not crunch Myspace by simply eliminating wasteful experiences that the customer did not want; it offered a better experience. Google beat a host of other search providers by developing a better algorithm, not just eliminating waste. When introducing something new, the market decision should be a simple one to make, a clear choice over incumbent offerings. The way to ensure this is to have a true understanding of the market and the customer.

Innovations can, as described, evolve out of accumulating improvements. However, innovations in the creation of patient value expands the scope from the core clinical process to consider a wide array of issues, including patient preferences, technological possibilities, financial arrangements, and integrated patient journeys. Therefore, many service providers take a proactive, systematic approach to innovation and create the necessary organizational structures. Typically innovations are pursued with specific projects and they need to have a number of basic components:

Correct resources—The first requirement is for appropriate resources including a dedicated cross-functional project team. This team should be composed of all required functions necessary to deliver the new service. Changing team members at various stages impedes the continuity and project speed. Each team member should expect to invest a minimum of 20% (ideal state would be 50%) of their time to this activity. In health care, the team members could be from all facets of the organization: physicians, advanced practice clinicians (APCs), nursing staff, medical secretaries, and medical assistants. Supporting areas of the business such as information technology, finance, human resources, and marketing should be available on an ad hoc basis. Patients are not included in the project, at this stage, but their voice is critical and they will be involved at various times.

The project team is led by the product/project leader. The other team members do not necessarily work directly for this person, but their activities are facilitated and directed.

Funding—Although this is an obvious need, any delay in receiving funding will have a critical if not catastrophic impact on the project success. During a major redesign project for an Asian center for infectious diseases, we learned that the mortality and financial impacts during an infectious disease outbreak were directly impacted by the timeliness of funds to finance the research to determine the disease. The organization should be committed to the overall completion and prioritization of the project and funding is one way to confirm that commitment.

Operating system (mission control)—Simple transparency is very important. The project should have a dedicated space to visually manage the project progress. The space becomes the hub of information including competitive information and project tracking. This space, sometimes referred to as an *OBEYA*, is also about creativity, internal and competitive insight, and providing a workspace where the team can collaborate and create new unique solutions. The illustration in Figure 6.8 in Chapter 6 shows a typical mission control room.

Regular review—The team needs to get together on a weekly basis, at a minimum, to review and report out on completion plan responsibilities. Each individual should schedule personal time in the mission control room for reflection and regular work. Formal team reviews with a coach providing external perspective should be completed at least quarterly. The mission control room becomes the hub of the project team providing continuity and knowledge sharing.

THREE PHASES OF THE INNOVATION DELIVERY MODEL

The innovation approach consists of three phases as in Figure 4.1.

- Research
- Exploration
- Execution

Phase I: Research

The trigger for the research phase is an idea. This idea usually comes from an executive and must be directly tied to the organization's strategic goals. The project team must understand what is going on in the market and the foundation of the idea is validated during the research phase. During this phase, the team will gather in the mission control room and make lists of what they believe to be true.

FIGURE 4.1
The three phases of innovation.

Armed with an idea, research then takes the form of one-on-one interviews with key stakeholders. These interviews can provide further hypotheses that can be expanded in focus groups. The insights collected from the focus groups can be validated across the population by surveys. Clinicians, business leaders, and the patients are all stakeholders that need to be researched in this phase. As data from interviews and surveys reflect peoples' perceptions and opinions, such data may have to be corroborated with survey results, demographic studies, and a true understanding of the current operations. Also, hard, measurable data on issues such as production volumes, resource consumption, and elapsed time should be well understood. It is during this time that the Project Leader in combination with the Executive Leader can set project level targets for the new service. These should include performance in all the critical business metrics of quality, cost, delivery, and growth. The output of the research phase is a business case clearly explaining the reason for the project, current market requirements, and the projected outcomes. In A3 thinking, this would be referred to as the first three boxes outlining the case for action, current state, and target state.

At the close of this phase, a go-no-go decision would be made to fund the project into Phase 2. It is important to note that in a traditional environment, executive teams typically demand hard numbers, assured returns, and definitive dates. The project plan should accommodate this by setting team targets for performance and should include the best estimates of expected outcomes.

Getting through the research phase can be a challenge for health-care executive teams as the lag can give the impression of being too lengthy between the research phase and the cash-in date. Using a health-care analogy, a quick diagnosis and treatment plan is what is desired. With a *known* disease state and its accompanying symptoms that would be fairly straightforward. However, with many projects, the "disease state" is *unknown* and the symptoms are typically masked, very much like an infectious disease outbreak.

Phase 2: Exploration

During the exploration phase, the actual feasibility of the project proposal can be tested. Armed with a hypothesis of what the project should achieve and a deep understanding of all stakeholders' true needs, the solutions can drive forward progress. This feasibility is actually the process of answering a series of unknown questions. These unknowns primarily come from two areas we just mentioned: true needs and related solutions.

Prior to developing a work plan, the true needs need to be prioritized. We must remember that the project does not have an unlimited budget and the new design must ensure that the individual stakeholder requests do not make some caregivers or patient experience better at the expense of another. To avoid this outcome, the needs are ordered by rank or weighted by importance. During the exploration phase, there should be direct input from the customer (patient in most cases) and not just the project team operating in a vacuum. Once a weighted ranking is established, the team will be able to focus their effort on the highest ranked of the prioritized needs.

For example, a true need might be identified as "Convenient Access." What is the target for achieving this? If robust questioning was completed during the research phase, the correct target may have been determined that patients want to be seen between 6:30 and 8:00 AM Monday to Friday. This requirement would become the new target for fulfilling the need.

To successfully satisfy that need, it is necessary to design the proper feature or solution. For example, an easy-to-imagine solution may be to just open the clinic earlier. However, as it is uncertain whether or not this solution could be offered, a series of questions must be asked to find out if that solution is feasible. For instance:

- Which staff members or grades would be required at the clinic for it to open?
- Is the support staff willing to be there?
- What is the impact on pay or weekly hours?
- Will coverage for normal hours be affected at all?

If the above questions are not satisfactorily resolved, deeper probing may be required

- What is the daily demand?
- What type of appointments should we see?
- How many clinicians are available?

When these questions are answered, a proposal can be created for the need and its corresponding solution. During this time it is important to involve all stakeholders in the feasibility study. The project leader must be able to facilitate tough decisions when the team members' opinions are not in complete alignment, always keeping the patient at the front of the decision-making process. Through the exploration phase, the team will be faced with making trade-offs between features and solutions. If morning access is the primary issue with patients and the physicians actually do not want to come to the clinic until 9 AM, then a tough decision has to be made.

A series of small questions for each big question must be made, whether it is an unknown need target, an unknown solution, or an unknown solution target. Each big question with the associated small questions requiring research should be placed in sequential order. The sequence should be in the order that results in the longest lead time impact or the most impact on the project if the stage is required to be repeated. The purpose of sequencing in this proper order minimizes the risk of rework the project would have to undertake when answered sequentially. As with Lean, we are trying to establish decision flow; however, the flow here is the knowledge, not a product.

Ultimately, these decisions must be made in the proper sequential order. Few health-care providers have the luxury of unlimited resources; therefore, identification and validation of features in advance can have a significant impact on the timeline for completion.

The flow of decisions in this phase is critical. The amount of cost associated with reworking a project is exponentially correlated to how long a project goes before the defect is identified. As such, there is a specific sequence in which decisions should be made. In traditional design work, teams want to answer the easiest questions right away. There is a push to answer as many questions as quickly as possible and arrive at a solution. The paradox here is that the proper innovative approach is to delay decisions as long as possible. Answer the longest lead time questions first and the shortest lead time items later. This allows the team to suspend the decision on the ultimate solution and minimize future rework. Our approach is a series of questions, or a decision flow that guides the efforts and activities of the team members. Each question may require varying input from each of the team members. With the Decision Flow tool the team takes responsibility for the individual learning and the progression of the flow. Not only are the questions being answered in the right order but the team members who have subject matter expertise are guiding the answer through their discovery work. This not only ensures best quality but significantly reduces the amount of potential rework.

Another technique used during this phase is multiple option analysis. In the Lean world, this is referred to as Set-Based Concurrent Engineering. Instead of determining an endpoint solution and working toward it, the process focuses on what must be solved today. It could be one of the small questions feeding a big question in the Decision Flow. Using that one question, multiple alternative solutions could be studied simultaneously. This allows a thorough study of which alternatives best fit the true targets. It also allows the evaluation of technical solutions that may or may not be available yet.

A note of caution: The project plan cannot be dependent on future technology development. Many teams have attempted to do this and have failed to meet the output standard, on-time completion was late, and approved cost was overrun resulting in the cancellation of the project. Technology solutions should be proven to be feasible during the research phase or early exploration phase. This includes health portals, EMR plug-ins, smartphone apps, imaging equipment, and so on.

The exploration phase comes to a close when the unknowns have all been answered. Feasible known solutions are chosen to achieve targets. The project team has calculated the time, effort, and cost associated to implement. It also means that the teams are confident that the features are of high enough quality so that rework upon implementation is unnecessary. A robust method used to validate the feature selection is the Failure Modes and Effects Analysis (FMEA) tool. At this point a release date of the project can be established and the features, costs, and targets are all set.

Phase 3: Execution

During the execution phase, the detailed design of the solution is specified and documented. Pilots or prototypes are created and tested during this phase. An overall systems approach to ensure the components work together in unity is also critical. During the execution phase, bugs, mistakes, and errors in the design are found, countermeasures are developed, and the new design is verified to ensure that the product or service delivered is correct on day one. Once the prototype or pilot is verified and countermeasures have been implemented, the project is ready for pre-launch and validation in a real working environment.

During this phase, formal ownership of the new product/service transfers from the development team to the delivery team. Final issues are worked out in time for the market launch. The market launch marks the end of the execution phase and the beginning of delivery. This is when the product/service is formally available for the patient and can be fully marketed and used.

FOUR LEVELS OF INNOVATION

Not all innovation ideas are created equal. There are four different levels of innovation that we refer to when developing projects. Each level of innovation is differentiated by the impact of the innovation idea in terms of return on investment, and the resources that will be required to bring that idea to fruition. The level of effort required increases with each level, however, the overall results realized must increase incrementally as well. The four levels of innovation are the following:

Application of a New Technology

This could be something as simple as a smartphone or tablet app to be used by patients or health-care staff, or the installation of a new PET/CT suite. Most view this as a simple plug and play when the reality is it is anything but that. Just ask anyone who has recently implemented an EMR (Electronic Medical Record) system. The key initial consideration therefore is "has the solution been determined before the project has been through a proper research and exploration phase?" Information technology or original equipment manufacturer vendors love to peddle their solutions as infinitely updateable, perfect drop-in fits when in reality they tend to be overpriced, over featured behemoths that do much more than is frequently required and take much more effort once up and running than anyone imagined.

Technology is an enabler. Available technology should be evaluated to determine if and how it supports the ability to meet customer demand, enhance flow, increase productivity, improve safety, increase patient and provider satisfaction, and lower cost. The selection of technology options to drive innovation should be rigorous. Simpler have developed a process known as "3P" to develop right-sized technology and processes. The 3P process (Production, Process, Preparation) has been used in a number of health-care process design projects, a variant of which (2P) is described in Chapter 6 that appears later in this book.

Design of a New Service Line

Oncology, cardiovascular, and orthopedics are examples of service lines that would benefit from an innovation approach. Instead of simply looking at the processes that could be enhanced, this level takes a ground up approach to how the service line could be *reimagined* to improve care and make a quantum leap in performance and results, including business and patient outcomes.

Design of a New Care Model

This could be for a segment of your population (women, pediatrics, elderly, etc.) or for a diagnosis population (diabetes, obesity, congestive heart failure, etc.). The added difficulty above Level 2 comes from the merging of different service lines and specialties to create unique solutions for the specific care model in question. Expanding the scope allows the performance to be nonlinear in its improvement results.

Design of a New Business Model

This looks at the fundamental way business is done, for example, moving toward population health management. The model could require the establishment of a true patient-centered medical home. It could be becoming an Accountable Care Organization[2] with shared savings. This fourth level of innovation takes a key element portion of the Level 3 innovation and adds the complexity of shifting the entire organization, including its cost and revenue structure, resources, and partners, to align around a new care delivery model.

To achieve such innovations, an organization might choose to implement an innovation center, developing a core group with competencies focused on tackling and running innovation projects. This internal team is fully funded and staffed to generate new innovation ideas on the first four levels. An innovation center is akin to the research and development centers found in many industries. An innovation center shows a significant commitment to preparing for the future and recreating health-care delivery to achieve the triple aim. Kaizer Permanente in California, United States has invested in such a center.

TYPICAL FAILURE MODES OF INNOVATION IN HEALTH CARE

The health-care system is not integrated in purpose and/or objectives. Its three subsystems, provider, payer, and supplier, tend to act as opposing forces rather than in harmony. Providers focus on fee for service income with payment models that are rarely outcome based. The payers are focused on reducing reimbursements for services and not optimizing the systems. Suppliers provide ever more complex equipment and the providers are lured into purchasing so as not to be seen by the market as falling behind. If these three subsystems are not properly aligned, there is a risk that innovations fail. Figure 4.2 identifies dysfunctional combinations of two subsystems aligning against the third, and the innovation sweet spot where the interests of all three may meet.

- When providers are lined up with suppliers ignoring the payers, this results in technology investment that cannot be recovered through fees. Multimillion dollar robots can perform surgeries but the outcomes cannot be shown to be better than those performed by a competent surgeon.
- When providers are lined up with payers and the suppliers are not involved, you end up with a health management organization that does not leverage the expertise of the supplier base. A typical example is the antiquated approach to inventory management in many hospitals where many clinical hours are lost taking care of supplies.
- When payers are lined up with suppliers and the providers are not involved, the result is a tendency to utilize technology that may not be patient centered.

True reform occurs in the sweet spot when providers, payers, and suppliers are lined up to achieve the same goals.

Other failure modes limiting innovations include the following:

- Small-scale thinking. The industry is risk averse and does not want to stretch. Leaders are not leading from the front, not investing enough, and not protecting emerging innovations.

FIGURE 4.2
The innovation "sweet spot."

- Blind faith in the newest "silver-bullet" technology without due attention to organizational culture and incentives.
- Lack of a systems approach to design. Too often, the industry jumps to the first solution before they know the root cause of the problem that can be exposed in the research and exploration phases described earlier.
- Time to results feels like it takes too long. Generally, the industry is patient for scientific solutions, such as new drugs. Yet, the pressure on financial results of process improvements requiring 9 months or more is high as this is seen as a long time and funding is often cut just prior to the realization of improvements.

HEALTH-CARE INNOVATION CASE STUDIES

ThedaCare's Collaborative Care Model

ThedaCare in Appleton, Wisconsin, United States was an early adopter of Lean in health care. Among the many recent recognitions they have received include the Consumer Reports no 1 Quality Performance in 2013 in their Physician's Group, and they had the lowest cost per Medicare beneficiary of 32 pioneer accountable care organizations organizations.

In 2007, ThedaCare opened its first collaborative care hospital unit after using both conversion and a few of the innovation tools and techniques to design the model. They opened their second unit in 2009, the third in 2010, and, as of 2013, have converted all eight of their medical–surgical units to this new model. This is a further example of the well-founded innovation principle that for a new process to be considered innovative, the process or practice must be replicable.

Collaborative care is team-based care at the bedside, replacing the fragmented and delayed decision making done in traditional hospital ward rounding. The team consists of a physician, nurse, pharmacist, and discharge planner collaborating together at the bedside, often including the family or caretaker of the patient as well, to determine the optimal plan of care for the patient (standard work) and projected discharge date. This approach minimizes duplicative efforts (waste) and helps to ensure that the strengths of each team member are leveraged (operating at the top of their license).

Figure 4.3 shows a comparison to ThedaCare's previous model of delivery of care.

Key attribute	Traditional model	Collaborative care model
Patient experience	Often disjointed, confusing, even contradictory.	Single plan of care developed with and visible to patient. Continuously updated with patient-driven schedule and goals.
Clinical quality	Generally good but considerable variation in clinical protocols and uneven reliability. Nurses spending time managing errors.	Reliable, standard work, using evidence-based quality and real-time problem solving to prevent errors.
Physician role	Hierarchical.	Partner in care team. Exposes thinking to professional team.
Nursing role	Task oriented. Too much time spent running for supplies and equipment.	Care manager. Expanded and empowered role in decision making and patient-care progression. Bedside management of quality measures.
Pharmacist role	Dispensing medication from pharmacy.	Bedside presence. More involved in patient contact/education. Teacher to patient and team.
Discharge planner role	Evaluates and recommends discharge needs through chart review.	Active member of the care team: facilitates patient's transition from hospital.
Environment	Semi-private, dated.	Private. Designed for patient/staff safety and to support collaborative processes.

FIGURE 4.3
The collaborative care model compared to traditional health care model. (From Simpler Process Preparation and Rapid Improvement.)

The results from this approach have been a dramatic improvement as shown in Figure 4.4.

Lean health care begins with the principle that the patient defines the value in the process, therefore, a near 50% improvement in patient satisfaction truly shows that the innovative collaborative care model had the greatest impact on patient satisfaction. Achieving a 45% improvement in quality outcomes while reducing costs by 15% shows that the innovation approach improves quality free of charge.

ThedaCare has learned several lessons in this journey that they have applied to future innovation projects including the following:

- Follow a methodology
- Start from scratch (In this case, they did not use their current delivery model as the baseline to improve, but started anew.)
- Provide infrastructure

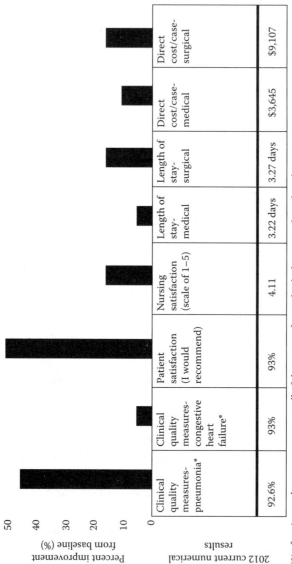

	Clinical quality measures-pneumonia*	Clinical quality measures-congestive heart failure*	Patient satisfaction (I would recommend)	Nursing satisfaction (scale of 1–5)	Length of stay-medical	Length of stay-surgical	Direct cost/case-medical	Direct cost/case-surgical
2012 current numerical results	92.6%	93%	93%	4.11	3.22 days	3.27 days	$3,645	$9,107

*% of patients whose treatment met all of the centres for medical of services clinical quality measures.

Methodology:
The baseline measurements were captured prior to implementing collaborative care. Post-implementation performance was measured monthly through a combination of data extraction, observation and surveys. Approximately 20% of patients were surveyed monthly. The outcomes measured align with the purpose of the collaborative care model to improve the safety, efficiency, and effectiveness of inpatient care.

FIGURE 4.4
ThedaCare collaborative care results. (From Simpler Rapid Improvement Events.)

Readers who to wish to learn more about this extraordinary story can log onto: http://blogs.hbr.org/2013/09/redefining-the-patient-experience with-collaborative-care/.

Bolton NHS Trust in the northwest of England, an early pioneer in integrated community and acute care studied the early experiments in ThedaCare and developed their local version known as patient gateways. To date, the efficiency and patient outcome improvements have been significant, further evidence that innovation should be replicable both within the experimenting organization and in other health-care providers in many countries.

Boulder Community Hospital's Patient-Centered Medical Home

Building on our earlier observation of the increasing burden of caring for the elderly and the need for alternative approaches that are cost-effective and patient centric, Simpler has been working with health-care providers to develop the Patient-Centered Medical Home (PCMH) model. The concept of PCMH is not a new concept to the health-care industry in North America. The National Centre for Quality Assurance (NCQA) defined the PCMH as a model of care that emphasizes care coordination and communication to transform primary care into "what patients want it to be." NCQA has been certifying practices to their definitions since 2008 and today, there are over 6000 practices with this certification.

From an innovation standpoint, though, Boulder Community Hospital (BCH) in Colorado wanted to go beyond "checking the box" to gain certification and fundamentally change the way they provided care. BCH used an innovation approach to design their PCMH model and a Lean innovation project plan to achieve successful certification. A Quality Functional Deployment (QFD) matrix, an innovation tool used to identify critical factors in the design, was used in the system design. It identified several key patient needs including reduced waiting time for labs, improved billing accuracy, and educational tools. (The QFD matrix is explored more fully in Chapter 6.)

The outputs of this innovation were not just the PCMH certification, but improved team design, roles, and standard work for each of those roles. There was also a better understanding of panel size for each physician, and the team implemented huddles to work collaboratively to solve problems. As a result of this work, BCH was able to gain PCMH certification, improve access to urgent appointments, and optimize panel size to ensure best care for the patient.

SUMMARY

The time is right for a breakthrough in health care across the globe. We are moving away from a system that is supply-driven organized around physicians to a patient-centered system organized around patients' requirement to be healthy. Under severe pressure to reduce costs dramatically while improving the quality of life of the patient and not overworking the staff to get there, industry leaders must become much bolder in their approach to improvement.

This chapter has outlined two approaches:

- Conversion—Continue to run the business and make sustainable improvements by implementing waste elimination techniques such as Lean
- Innovation—A breakthrough, systems approach driven by bold target setting and a dramatically different mindset as to what is possible in the creation of value to patients

Conversion and innovation are purposeful accomplishments. Both approaches require, in their own ways, commitment and deep personal involvement from top leadership, a systematic approach, breakthrough thinking, dedicated resources, and transparency.

REFERENCES

1. OECD. (2011). *Health at a Glance 2011: OECD Indicators*. OECD Publishing, p. 12. Retrieved from http://dx.doi.org/10.1787/health_glance-2011-en; accessed April 10, 2014.
2. Managing Innovation. (2009). *Managing Innovation*. Case studies: Aravind Eye Clinics, pp. 1–3. Retrieved from http://www.managing-innovation.com/case_studies/Aravind%20Eye%20Clinics.pdf; accessed April 10, 2014.

5

Cultivating an Innovative Culture through Lean

Tan Ghim Meng and Philip Choo

CONTENTS

INTRODUCTION

The practice of Lean involves the continual exercise of the following five principles:[1]

- Specify value from the customer's perspective
- Map the value stream of activities and minimize those that do not create value
- Manage the process flow of remaining activities so that they occur in a tight sequence
- Use the principle of "pull" to trigger production only on customer request
- Strive for perfection through continuous cycles of improvement using systematic methods

These principles were first practiced in the manufacturing sector. Thus health-care institutions need to consider how they could adapt these principles in their own context.

Lean Management strives for efficiency through the systematic elimination of "waste"—any step or activity that consumes resources but does not deliver value to the customer. In health care the definition of value and waste is more complicated than in manufacturing. However, current health-care practices include a lot of activities that quite obviously can be identified as waste. Some examples are given in Table 5.1.

Waste can be identified and eliminated through various means. The Lean literature provides many examples of systematic improvement methods, such as problem identification, process analysis, the five whys, error-proofing, and statistical analysis. Improvements should result in new work practices codified in quality assurance systems. In the end, such improved practices need to be implemented and maintained on a daily basis by every member of an organization. A quality system is effective only if people are following it. Therefore, Lean needs to be deeply embedded in the organizational culture and the values that support it.

This chapter will present the practice of Lean in Tan Tock Seng Hospital (TTSH), belonging to the National Healthcare Group (NHG), Singapore. Lean has proven to be applicable in improving efficiency, as well as building an innovative culture.

TABLE 5.1

Categories and Examples of Waste

Category of Waste	Example in Health Care
Defects	Patient is given an incorrect dose of medication.
Overproduction	Staff prints 20 patient labels, though only three are required.
Waiting	Patients wait to make payment.
Not utilizing resources effectively	A nurse does patient registration at the counter, though counter registration staff is available.
Transportation	Case notes for consultation are brought to the clinic's utility room, before being moved to the consultation room.
Inventory	Stock of gauzes stored in a ward takes up an excessive storage area.
Motion	A doctor walks to many wards to locate all his patients.
Extra processing	Health-care assistant and nurse separately take a patient's temperature within 10 minutes.

NECESSITY: THE MOTHER OF INNOVATION

The Lean implementation journey at TTSH was started in 2007 with strong management support and a compelling reason. The reason was not economic—the hospital was financially sound. It had little to do with starting a quality culture either—TTSH had already been active in clinical and service quality improvement work many years prior. Rather, this journey was started as a platform to prepare the hospital for the future.

Singapore's population is aging. There will be significantly greater demand for health-care services. As capacity and cost cannot be increased infinitely, the only way to meet this future demand is to fundamentally change the way health-care institutions operate. To thrive in the new environment, TTSH has to transform itself, by taking up the challenge to continually improve its processes and outcomes end to end. It must also equip its entire workforce with the skills, tools, and mindset for continual change, and sustain them in the long run. Against this background, TTSH knew that its clinical and service quality improvement programs, although good, would be inadequate to cope with the pace, intensity, and scope of changes. The practice of Lean Management seemed to provide a way to do so, if it could be contextualized.

Getting Ready for Change

Though TTSH found the reasons compelling, there were several major hurdles standing in the way. First, the hospital required a core group of trained and dedicated personnel to start and sustain this journey. They would be full-time Lean Facilitators, charged with the key responsibilities of guiding process owners with their improvement projects, as well as training all staff on Lean principles and tools.

However, in 2007, TTSH had no such pool of people possessing such capabilities. A pressing issue was to quickly recruit good and suitable staff. Rather than rely solely on consultants and external recruitment, TTSH developed a secondment scheme. In late 2007 and early 2008, Professor Philip Choo, in his capacity as Chairman of the Medical Board of TTSH, identified and spoke to several managerial staff with excellent performance and potential, trying to convince them to be seconded to the newly set up Kaizen Office as Lean Facilitators. Those who were keen were offered a 2-year secondment stint as part of their career advancement.

This scheme brings about several benefits and it is still in effect today. The people seconded are familiar with TTSH's workings and culture, which shortens their learning curves. It also offers a platform to develop these staff professionally. In addition, it progressively builds a pool of strong Lean advocates within the hospital. On completing their stints, these individuals will return to their respective departments and spread their knowledge.

Second, the application of Lean principles in the health-care industry was an unfamiliar idea in Singapore at that time (2006–2007). Although several hospitals in the United Kingdom and United States had successfully implemented Lean principles, their circumstances, operating environments, and reasons for practicing Lean were different from TTSH's. Many of them implemented Lean as a means to improve their bottom line. It was perceived then that the U.S. hospitals had a relatively more comfortable staff-to-patient ratio. Hence, TTSH had to conscientiously address any potential misconception about Lean, by working with the clinician leadership to explore ways of using Lean principles to cut waste. Thereafter, TTSH spent much time and effort to assure its staff that it was not embarking on this journey to reduce staffing or impose unreasonable demands, stressing that the practice of Lean would ultimately improve care delivery.

Birth of "MyCare"

TTSH realized early in this journey the importance of developing a framework to guide its communication and implementation approach. It must be acceptable to the health-care workforce—doctors, nurses, allied health professionals, and administrators—and must also be sufficiently simple so all staff can understand.

To do so, TTSH first distilled key Lean principles it had learned from visits and literature. These principles include staff empowerment, *genchi genbutsu* (or go-and-see), understanding and delivering value from the customer's perspective, facilitating pull and flow, as well as striving for perfection through continuous improvement. The tricky part was to link the principles and express them in a language accepted by health-care workers. In TTSH, the ideas of good patient care and patient safety resonate well with the employees. TTSH staff had also regularly heard Dr. Lim Suet Wun, then Cluster CEO of NHG and CEO of TTSH, stressing the need to provide "Faster, Better, Cheaper and Safer" (FBCS) care. Hence, weaving the Lean principles into the context of providing FBCS care could provide a simple, yet compelling message.

By early 2008, the aforementioned ideas culminated in a framework that met all the stated requirements as in Figure 5.1. As several other NHG institutions were also starting their Lean implementation at that time, this framework was shared and quickly adopted within NHG.

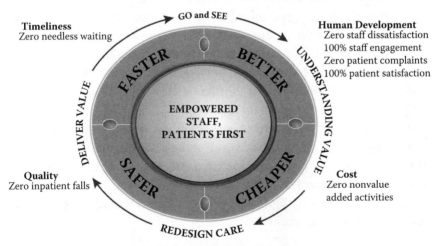

FIGURE 5.1
MyCare framework.

After undergoing some refinements, the core of the framework today states "Empowered Staff, Patients First." This espouses the ideal to proactively empower and involve all staff on this journey so that they can deliver patient-centric care. The four dimensions in the ring surrounding the core—Faster, Better, Cheaper, and Safer—embody what is of value to the hospital's patients.

The outer ring in Figure 5.1 signifies TTSH's approach in using Lean principles to bring about FBCS care:

- *Go-and-see:* TTSH will build and reinforce a mindset for going on site to observe so as to understand what actually takes place and what the issues are.
- *Understanding value:* By practicing "go-and-see," TTSH seeks to understand what is of value to patients and staff (internal customers).
- *Redesign care:* With an understanding of what patients and staff value, TTSH will cut nonvalue adding steps and activities (waste) so as to simplify and streamline its processes.
- *Delivering value:* Through rapid experiments, TTSH will test the feasibility of any changes, before it implements and standardizes them to deliver better value to patients.

These four elements collectively form an unbroken ring, illustrating TTSH's commitment to continuous improvement.

To guide TTSH's progress in delivering FBCS care, stretch targets are set for selected indicators in the areas of Timeliness, Human Development, Cost, and Quality. These targets and indicators, called "True-North Metrics," act as beacons to guide continuous improvement efforts. Although it is very difficult to reach the targets set for these metrics, they constantly remind staff that there is always room for improvement. They also challenge staff to think through their improvement initiatives thoroughly, as an initiative that can improve TTSH's performance in all of these metrics must have changed the staff's mindset, improved the system or process, as well as influenced the operating environment.

The framework's base signifies the fundamentals that enable changes to take root, such as the following:

- Developing leadership in TTSH's people
- Building systems and teams to enhance skills and capabilities in staff
- Providing appropriate support to staff, such as in areas of manpower, IT, and facilities

This framework has proven to be effective. Today, it is communicated at TTSH's onboarding program for new hires, as well as during in-house Lean training programs.

It was also recognized that the Lean movement needs a name to rally its efforts. This gave rise to the name "MyCare." Within TTSH, it is synchronous with a line in the hospital's mission statement, which states, "Doing our best to serve, care and heal." This name also conveys two key beliefs behind TTSH's Lean efforts: everyone can play a part and everyone can be a problem-solver.

The development of "MyCare"—the name and the framework—helps to facilitate TTSH's subsequent work on changing its culture. Without either, it would have been difficult for TTSH to communicate a compelling message for change, and culture change would have been hampered.

TAKING THE LEAP FORWARD

At the start of the journey, TTSH's leadership realized that the key to MyCare's success goes beyond mastering a set of tools; it lies in building the desired culture for improvement. However, culture is an entity that is difficult to define, much less manage and monitor.

Importance of Culture Building

To guide its culture-building efforts, TTSH adapted the use of the Kirkpatrick Four Levels of Learning Evaluation. This model was originally developed to evaluate the effectiveness of training programs on the following levels:[2]

- *Reaction:* Participants' satisfaction (i.e., positive reaction) with the program
- *Learning:* The increase in participants' competency on the subject, in terms of their knowledge, skills, and change in attitudes
- *Behavior:* Post-training application of the participants' newly acquired competencies at the workplace through changes in job behavior
- *Results:* Impact on performance or occurrence of desired outcomes due to the participants' attendance of the program

TTSH adapted this model in the following way:

- *Awareness:* Awareness and positive reaction enable culture change to take root. As a hospital-wide culture change will take place over several years, efforts and activities carried out at this level have to be ongoing and varied.
- *Learning:* To change culture, it is essential to first train and equip the hospital's staff with the right competencies. Furthermore, doing so puts into practice the notion of empowering every staff to deliver value to patients, as presented in the MyCare framework.
- *Behavior:* Culture changes when staff promptly put their learning into practice at their workplaces. It is thus critical that the hospital provides platforms to get staff involved in improvement work.
- *Results:* The results of TTSH's culture change are tracked. At the project level, each team is challenged to identify and monitor their measures and impact. At the divisional and hospital levels, the use of performance dashboards and scorecards help to track performances. Staff perceptions on MyCare are also tracked via a biennial Employee Climate Survey at the hospital, divisional, and departmental levels.

Some Platforms to Raise Awareness

TTSH uses several platforms to raise staff awareness of MyCare.

MyCare Lunchtime Talks

This platform was started in 2009 as a way to blend two ingredients to facilitate culture change—knowledge sharing and a sense of ownership. It was believed then that having regular talks, where TTSH staff could share their insights on MyCare improvements, could accomplish this objective. Today this talk is held quarterly. In late 2009, after the initial three runs, TTSH found that staff was not yet prepared to openly share their insights at a hospital-wide forum. However, they were interested in attending regular talks dedicated to improvement. To cater to these needs, the MyCare lunchtime talks are now open to both internal and external speakers, who may cover a variety of topics that are applicable to improvement work, such as design thinking and coaching.

Roadshows

Held annually, roadshows are informal and interactive ways to reinforce staff understanding of Lean principles or tools. Most times, this is done through a game booth at TTSH's Quality Day.

Newsletters

Started in May 2008, the monthly TTSH MyCare newsletter is still the mainstay of the hospital's approach for raising awareness on MyCare. The newsletter is currently published in electronic and print versions. The former is disseminated to staff via the electronic mail system, whereas the latter is printed on paper and a copy is distributed to each department. Copies of the print version are also placed on the notice boards inside selected elevators to reach staff without e-mail access. TTSH goes to such lengths to propagate information with the greater objective of staff engagement. Over the years, the sense of pride among staff in seeing their efforts featured is increasingly palpable. This sense of pride and ownership can facilitate the desired culture change.

Portal

The MyCare portal is the latest addition to this suite of platforms, launched in July 2013. It seeks to address one of the greatest constraints of the newsletter—the ability to connect people to exchange insights. In addition, as information is stored online, this platform allows people to pull the information they require on demand.

Equipping Every Staff with the Appropriate Skills

For the notion of staff empowerment to be realized, it is essential that every staff is trained and equipped appropriately. In TTSH's context, the size of its workforce poses a huge challenge. Early in its Lean journey (in 2008), TTSH employed about 4000 staff; 5 years later the staff count was more than 7000. The typical profile and educational qualification of this workforce differ across the hierarchy and professional groups.

Given these conditions, a one-size-fits-all training program would be unwise. It would also be unviable to rely on external training vendors in the long run. To work around its constraints, TTSH gets a core group of staff to acquire knowledge first and then customize it into the hospital's context. This is how TTSH's current four-tier MyCare training approach came about. With this approach, MyCare training programs can be pitched appropriately, so that each staff gains the competencies relevant to his or her work environment and context.

The four tiers in this approach are the following:

- MyCare Overview: Introduction to MyCare

This is a short but formal platform to build awareness and teach basic Lean concepts to new hires. It is a 30-minute presentation incorporated into the hospital's Company Induction Program, which is mandatory for every new staff.

- MyCare Basic: Program for all levels

To build ownership for simple changes and improvements, this program teaches staff the following three essential items:

- Basic Lean principles
- Application of the 6S methodology (detailed later in this chapter) to systematically reorganize and improve their workplaces
- Importance of frequently proposing and implementing simple but practical suggestions to improve workflow

The training approach for this program is decentralized, with the trainers recruited from the line divisions. This came about when the program was launched in 2008, as it had to be taught to more than 95% of TTSH's workforce within 3 years. As the line-trainers also have to be good role models, candidates for this role must have good work performance and be passionate about improvement. They must then pass a strict training and assessment regime. This approach has expedited the rollout of the program to large divisions in TTSH.

- MyCare Intermediate: Supervisory-level program

For culture change to occur, it is essential to also equip and involve supervisory staff. They have to ensure that their staff members are properly instructed, support their managers for improvement efforts, as well as keep morale strong despite difficult changes.

For this reason, the MyCare Intermediate program was developed in 2008 to equip supervisors with the skills to (1) conscientiously teach their staff to perform a job, (2) lead their teams to improve job methods systematically, (3) establish post-improvement standardization to lock in the benefits gained, and (4) lead teams effectively by building good job relations.

Ideas for this program were adapted from the Training Within Industry (TWI) program—an initiative that supported the United States' production of war supplies during World War II, as well as Toyota's success in driving continual improvement and sustaining them through standardization.[3]

- MyCare Advanced: Managerial-level program

The MyCare Advanced program was started in September 2007 with the intention of equipping managerial staff with the tools and competencies to lead improvements of value streams. TTSH has since conducted more than 18 runs of this program. Its content and structure have also been refined several times to improve participants' understanding of the subjects covered. For example, a key change made right after the first run was to make the program more experiential, so that participants could learn and retain their knowledge better. This has since been a hallmark of this program.

This program now spans 4 days. Participants learn various Lean principles and tools, including cause-and-effect analysis and value stream analysis, and how to apply them. To keep the program hands-on and experiential, various instructional techniques, such as lectures, group exercises, and a simulation activity, are used.

Making Involvement Prevalent

Based on TTSH's adaptation of the Kirkpatrick Model, post-training behavior change is integral to cultural change. Through the training programs, each staff member is equipped with the tools and competencies that will enable them to be involved in improvement work. Involving staff continually post-training will then get them to adopt new behaviors and habits, which will change the culture over time. Hence, TTSH adopts an approach similar to Toyota's as in Figure 5.2, which allows many people to concurrently identify and solve different problems. It differs from the traditional approach, where only some people (usually managers) come together to attempt to solve the problems identified.

By adopting this approach, TTSH tries to emulate Toyota's extraordinary buzz of having many people solving many problems; many people engaging in improvement and innovation, as represented by the numerous colored circles seen in Figure 5.2. However, the hospital has to regularly remind itself on a subtle lesson that lies therein: Lean Management is about culture building.

The aforementioned approach deploys a variety of Lean tools that will be briefly presented in the following pages. For this book, we will only present those tools used in TTSH that have brought about innovations. Each tool

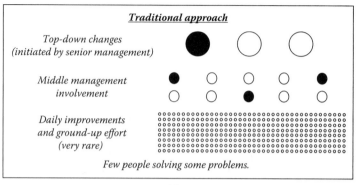

(a)

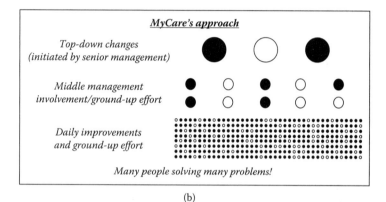

(b)

FIGURE 5.2
Approaches to problem-solving.

has its unique characteristics and strengths that empower its user. As such, opportunities for improvement and innovation are now within the reach of every staff member, as each person can now initiate and carry out changes.

DAILY IMPROVEMENTS

Suggested and implemented by staff, Daily Improvements (DIs) are small and simple solutions to improve their work areas. These solutions do not require expensive technological investments; they can be easily implemented and need not await lengthy approvals. Many of these solutions can be innovative. Given its simplicity and ease of use, DIs provide an avenue for employees to be involved in *kaizens* (small, incremental continual improvements), and help to build a culture of innovation and empowerment.

To reinforce the importance of DIs, TTSH uses a simple tool called the "Daily Improvement Board" (or DIB) to help staff suggest DIs. The DIB is a lightweight suggestion and communications board. Easily mounted, it has been rolled out to every department. On spotting a *kaizen* opportunity within his or her work area, any staff can post a suggested solution on the DIB. The staff's manager must then promptly evaluate the suggestion's feasibility, assess whether it addresses the root cause of the issue, and communicate his or her decision to the staff. If the manager rejects the suggestion, he or she must also explain the rationale to the staff, so as to maintain staff enthusiasm over the long run.

Many people may be surprised to learn that the manual DIB replaces an electronic Staff Suggestion System that TTSH used in the past. This seemingly counterintuitive move helped to bring TTSH's suggestions to a higher level. This is because the DIB addresses the key weakness of the previous Staff Suggestion System: the inability to visually present the promptness of the manager's evaluation, and the quality of each suggestion.

INNOVATIVE DAILY IMPROVEMENT AT POSTANESTHESIA CARE UNIT

Area for Improvement

Postanesthesia care unit (PACU) staff had difficulties communicating with deaf/mute patients, especially when they had postoperative anxiety (e.g., after spinal anesthesia). To communicate with these patients, PACU staff had to write or draw on blank papers.

Solution

Develop flash cards with pictures and descriptors in Singapore's four main languages. The cards can aid communication with these patients.

Benefits

(1) Paper usage cut, (2) more patient contact time, due to less time spent searching for blank papers, (3) patients feel more secure as anxiety is reduced.

Key Learning Point by Team

These cards can also be used as a medium for language translation, between PACU staff and nondeaf/mute patients.

6S PROJECTS

The 6S methodology uses a systematic process, simple problem-solving tools, and visual management to create and sustain a safe, clean, organized, and efficient workplace. Its concepts are simple and results can be seen right away. Thus, many TTSH staff use 6S projects to initiate and effect improvements. TTSH's 6S methodology is adapted from the proven 5S methodology—the key difference being TTSH has explicitly stated basic safety as a component. To reap its benefits, 6S is practiced in the following sequence:

1. Safety: The team begins with safety in mind to eliminate hazards. It ensures that (1) personal protective equipment is available, visible, in working condition, and within reach, especially when handling hazardous material, (2) waste is segregated and appropriately disposed, (3) confidential documents are properly stored, and (4) items are stored in a way that minimizes the chances for errors. The team also takes steps to reduce cross-contamination and the spread of infections.

2. Sort: The team distinguishes items that are needed from those that are not. This is because it must get rid of "unneeded items" to create space and capacity. In general, "needed items" are those that the staff needs to perform the job in question. In contrast, "unneeded items" are those that are obsolete or faulty, and thus are unused. Excessive inventory of items are also "unneeded items."

3. Straighten: The team designates a place for each needed item and takes steps to ensure each item is returned to its designated place after use. When deciding the location for an item, the team considers three interrelated factors: (1) the unit's workflow, (2) frequency of usage for that item, and (3) quantity to be stored. Frequently used items (e.g., those used daily) will be placed at the staff's work area. Those used less frequently (e.g., once a month) will be placed at a specific location further away, such as a predetermined shelf in the unit's storeroom. Doing so minimizes unnecessary staff movement and time spent searching for items. To help the staff quickly locate each item and know its remaining quantity, various types of visual aids, such as line demarcations, labels, the outline of each item's shape, and color codes, can be used.

4. Shine: The team's members need to understand their colleagues' work habits, as old habits can soon create "filth" in the form of clutter and disorganization. This will negate the benefits brought about by the earlier steps and render the effort unsustainable. To address this, the team sets the criteria for "cleanliness," that is, the state of the work area being organized and clutter-free. It will also use root-cause analysis to identify the root causes behind the "filth." If the "filth" cannot be eliminated, team members will work with their colleagues to schedule "cleaning," depending on how frequently the "filth" returns.

5. Standardize: The team creates routines and standards for everyone's practice, so as to improve the chances of the effort's sustainability. The team will usually try to illustrate these in pictorial form, so that they are easy to learn and understand.

6. Sustain: This final step gets the department or unit to keep up their efforts over the long run, especially those under "Shine" and "Standardize." This is usually done through regular audits using a 6S scorecard.

INNOVATING THROUGH 6S

Context

In TTSH's experience, 6S has proven to be versatile and supportive of innovation. Though it is primarily used to encourage ground-up involvement, it can also support innovative improvements within large, complex value streams, as presented in this story.

Background

A value stream analysis (VSA) event for hip fracture, done at TTSH in April 2008, showed that staff spent a lot of time searching for items at the wards on Level 12 (which care for orthopedic patients). It was suggested that the use of 6S might improve the situation and contribute to the improvement of the hip fracture value stream. Hence, the nurses working in these wards came together to study what their colleagues commonly searched for and how much time they spent doing so.

These nurses found that each staff member spent on average 30–45 minutes daily, walking all over the wards to look for surgical supplies, medical equipment, case notes, and stationery. Nurses from these wards then brainstormed and piloted ideas. Calling their project "Burnout Searching," they sought to cut by 30% the time spent searching for these items.

Solutions

Two innovative ideas utilizing 6S principles were piloted in September 2008.

1. The team built a prototype for a cubicle-based trolley to house frequently used items. These items included clerking toolkits, patient case notes, as well as pre- and postoperation care supplies. Placement of these items in the trolley would be standardized. A magnetic lock installed on the trolley would safeguard the confidentiality of patient case notes. With this trolley deployed at each cubicle, time and movement spent searching for items could be minimized. This would result in more patient contact time.
2. Through the use of visual aid and floor demarcation, the team standardized the home locations of various medical equipment. That way, each staff member would know the spot where they should retrieve and return the equipment. This cut unnecessary movement and time spent searching for equipment.

Impact

Information gathered during the pilot period showed an 80% cut in the time taken, as well as the distance walked by the staff to locate and retrieve items/equipment. The cubicle-based trolley was then refined and spread to other wards in TTSH, as the gains from this idea could translate to more time spent on direct patient care. The impact of this idea did not stop there. TTSH is currently in the midst of refurbishing its wards, so as to streamline its inpatient workflow and facilitate cubicle-based nursing care. The key elements behind the cubicle-based trolley idea—having all necessary items within easy reach and storing all items in a standardized location and consistent manner—support the practice of cubicle-based nursing. They are now weaved into the new design for the ward layout.

VALUE STREAM ANALYSIS/RAPID
IMPROVEMENT EVENT

TTSH learned to use this tool from three sources. It first picked up this tool from a Lean Management course conducted by the University of Michigan. Next, TTSH's pioneering group of Lean Facilitators learned to use this tool during their attachments to various National Health Services (NHS) hospitals in the United Kingdom that had implemented Lean Management. TTSH also learnt from Simpler Healthcare in 2008. After several rounds of learning and relearning, TTSH adapted the best of these methods into its context. Today, VSA and a rapid improvement events (RIEs) in TTSH typically span 2–4 days in a stretch. They involve the process owners, as well as the upstream and downstream stakeholders. For VSAs, "fresh eyes"—staff who are not part of the process and have no vested interest in the improvement effort—are involved too. Usually, a value stream earmarked for improvements will undergo a VSA first, followed by RIEs.

At a VSA event, the team will map the current state of the value stream, identify the key problems, and determine their root causes. They will then map the desired future state of the value stream and draw up an action plan to reach the future state. The rationale for involving stakeholders stems from the fact that nobody knows every process and issue in its entirety. To improve the value stream end to end, it is critical to rally every party involved to collectively understand the issues and develop the action plan. The "fresh eyes" are ideal for introducing fresh perspectives and challenging existing paradigms.

Within the action plan, some items can be executed quickly, whereas others may require a series of experiments to assess their feasibility. For the latter, the process owners and stakeholders of the value stream will proceed to carry out RIEs. The nature and requirements of each RIE depends on its scope and complexity. In TTSH's experience, some could be as simple as testing the use of communication scripts, whereas others could be as complex as piloting an acute stroke unit within a ward over 3 months.

Although the execution of a VSA/RIE is geared toward achieving better efficiency, it can be used to bring about innovations. The key to doing so lies in how the team members develop and refine their solutions, as well as spread their insights post-improvement.

IMPROVING THE QUALITY OF CARE
FOR HIP FRACTURE PATIENTS

Background

A common injury among the elderly, hip fracture is a frequent reason for admission to an acute orthopedic ward. Among the hip fracture patients that TTSH admits, many can be treated surgically. These patients are comanaged by orthopedics and geriatrics doctors, together with a dedicated case manager. Selected patients undergoing this surgery have to do preoperative cardiac tests, as patients with preexisting heart conditions have an increased risk of a cardiac event, or even death postsurgery. As these tests take time, they must be done quickly. Hip fracture patients tend to suffer more pain and are less mobile, which increases their chances of developing urinary tract infection (UTI) and urinary retention. These patients seen by TTSH are mostly elderly with multiple medical, functional, and social problems. They tend to stay longer and require more coordination of care between health-care workers, caregivers, and rehabilitation centers.

Before this improvement effort began in April 2008, the average length of stay (ALOS) for hip fracture patients treated surgically was 11.8 days. Of these patients, only 29% had their surgery done promptly within 48 hours. The average waiting time for the presurgery cardiac tests was 4.6 days and the complication rate due to UTI was 17%.

Root Causes

The following contributed to the high ALOS and complication rate.

- Delay in obtaining consent for surgery, due to the lack of standard information on treatment options and inability to hold family conferences early
- Long wait for presurgery cardiac tests due to lack of (1) a clear algorithm to guide junior doctors requiring cardiac referral and (2) priority for hip fracture patients
- High hospital-acquired UTI rate due to the lack of bladder/bowel protocol for early intervention
- Delays and differing standards in care delivery, as patients were not grouped into a dedicated ward

- Delays in referral and transfer for early rehabilitation due to the absence of (1) "fast-tracking" arrangement between TTSH and its offsite rehabilitation wards and (2) a system to update the TTSH team on the availability of beds at the rehabilitation facility and community hospitals

Solutions and Experiments

The team involved worked on the following solutions:

- Facilitated prompt decision making by patients/families on treatment options and postsurgery care, by providing an information booklet and arranging a family conference within 24 hours of admission.
- Incorporated cardiology referral guidelines to expedite administration of presurgery cardiac tests. That way, junior doctors are empowered to list patients for relevant tests to detect heart abnormalities. A team also successfully piloted the feasibility of building a mobile two-dimensional (2D) echo machine to administer this test in the ward.
- Reduced UTI rates by designing a standard bladder and bowel protocol, and then training and empowering nurses to use it. That way, trained nurses can initiate the protocol promptly without having to wait for a doctor's order.
- Facilitated early rehabilitation by establishing arrangements with community hospitals and TTSH's offsite rehabilitation wards to "fast-track" suitable patients.
- Grouped patients into a dedicated ward to facilitate the execution of the aforementioned solutions, as well as enable a more consistent level of care delivery.

Impact

This effort brought about the following results as at December 2008:

Outcome	Measures	Pre	Post
Faster decisions	Average time to consent	3.6 days	2.1 days
	Average wait time for presurgery cardiac test	4.6 days	2.3 days
Better clinical outcomes	ALOS	11.8 days	8.6 days
	UTI rate	17%	2%

In addition, faster rehabilitation was achieved. About 61% of patients were discharged to step-down care facilities for short-term rehabilitation within 2 days of referral.

The impact of this team's efforts went beyond this initiative. A reflection of this effort resulted in the sharing of the following key learning points and insights:

- Use of standardized work to empower nurses to initiate pre-defined protocols or workflows: This was adopted in a subsequent VSA/RIE in mid-2008 that strengthened TTSH's discharge process.
- Two ideas—(1) grouping patients into a dedicated ward to facilitate faster and more consistent care delivery and (2) use of standard information packages to expedite decision making by patients and their families—were adopted in a subsequent VSA/RIE in April 2009 to improve the care delivery process for stroke patients.

The sharing of one's reflections enabled the teams working on subsequent initiatives to start with a greater wealth of knowledge, as well as shortened their learning curves.

PRODUCTION AND PROCESS PREPARATION

TTSH also uses a tool called "Production & Process Preparation" (3P in short), which it learned from Simpler Healthcare in 2008 and subsequently adapted to suit its context. Today, 3P is done as a part of any facility renovation or building plan that involves the introduction of new services or the relocation of an existing service. Used in conjunction with VSA, 3P taps on Lean principles to systematically improve processes and the patient's experience, by designing facilities that optimize space usage and facilitate an efficient flow. Usually spanning 4–5 days, a 3P event gets a multidisciplinary team to do the following:

- Perform a VSA to thoroughly understand the workflow in question
- Map the seven flows—patients, staff, equipment, medical/surgical supplies, instructions, data and other items—to see how people and items flow through the site as work is done

- Brainstorm and design facility layouts that support the seven flows
- Conduct a "beauty contest" to select the best layouts (usually best two)
- Create a hybrid layout by combining the best features from the layouts selected
- Simulate the hybrid layout to determine its feasibility
- Codevelop the action plan and implementation timelines

In TTSH's context, the use of 3P has innovated the way space planning is done. To determine the benchmarks on a facility's floor area (e.g., an operating theatre or a clinic consultation room) previously, a team would visit and learn from other health-care organizations. They would then return to discuss with the stakeholders and try to fit the benchmarks and practices seen into TTSH's context. Sometimes, these may not fit optimally. In addition, the workflow for that facility was usually only ironed out after it had been renovated and set up.

With 3P, the workflow determines how the facility should be set up. Renovations only take place after this. In addition, the best benchmark for the facility's floor area can now be easily determined by carrying out a simulation during the 3P event. This simulation can be done by using stationery to build a simple three-dimensional model of the facility so as to see the flow through the entire site. The simulation can also be done by using tape, cardboard, and paper to build a simplistic life-size mock-up of a selected area within that facility (e.g., consultation room) so as to test the feasibility of the proposed setup and floor area.

CHARTING THE WAY FORWARD

It might be worthwhile at this point to consider TTSH's critical success factors and key challenges, so as to gain richer insights into the hospital's journey.

Critical Success Factors

There are essentially three critical success factors in TTSH's experience. First, the importance of the senior management team's strong will and commitment cannot be overstated. MyCare is in fact an undertaking without any precedent. Though there were many hospitals worldwide that implemented Lean Management before TTSH, none did so with the hospital's intent, scope, and intensity. At many points in TTSH's journey, the hospital had to quickly learn and adapt to move ahead. Usually, investments in resources had to be made at these points. Without this commitment, TTSH could never have achieved so much in such a short time.

The second critical success factor is the hospital's commitment to learn from others, not just at the start of its journey, but also continually thereafter. Doing this enables TTSH to always advance with the best knowledge and evidence on hand. This posture is essential for any innovative culture to take root.

Third, TTSH's MyCare journey has shown some early successes because the hospital chose to tackle some of the most difficult issues that it faced. This presents a good lesson for future innovative efforts—although taking such a stand is inconvenient, it ensures that the innovation/change meets the needs of all stakeholders. That way, the change becomes meaningful to the staff and the improvement will be of value to the user.

Challenges and Next Steps

The following paragraphs will highlight three perennial challenges that TTSH has to tackle to this day.

First, the issue of finding time to get involved in MyCare has surfaced many times in staff feedback. A common point made at these instances had been the lack of dedicated time for staff to get involved in improvement efforts. Providing this dedicated time would have meant taking those involved off their work commitments. With tight operational conditions, TTSH cannot afford to do this across the board. Moving forth, the hospital must explore ways to better weave innovation and improvement efforts into the staff's daily work.

The second challenge is to raise the level of doctor involvement in MyCare. Although most senior doctors in TTSH have accepted MyCare and even took part in some improvement events/efforts, involvement by the junior doctors is less prevalent. To make some inroads, TTSH is exploring ways to raise the awareness of MyCare among young doctors.

Third, most TTSH staff now know what MyCare is and what it does. But it is doubtful if they understand that MyCare is not about projects per se, but about continually weaving a new way of life into the hospital's cultural fabric through regular changes and innovation. Recognizing that good engagement between staff and managers is critical for tackling this challenge, TTSH has already started some work in this area.

SUMMARY

From TTSH's experience, it can be seen that Lean Management is applicable in a health-care setting, although some contextualization must be made in the way Lean principles are applied. It also seems that the use of Lean tools can indeed bring about various forms of innovations. Regardless of the tool used, some of the keys to doing so include rigorous reflections of each improvement effort, as well as precise distillation and prompt sharing of critical insights.

As for building an innovative culture, TTSH still has much to work on. At this point, most TTSH staff accept MyCare as an improvement philosophy in the hospital and embrace the fact that MyCare brings about benefits to patients and staff. However, to have an innovative culture, the hospital's staff must embrace frequent changes as a way of life. As TTSH continues to build this culture, nobody can tell for certain if its efforts will succeed. But there is one thing that everyone can be sure of. In all aspects, as long as TTSH continues to maintain a hunger for improvement, the humility to learn from others, and the fortitude to stay the course, the best is yet to be.

REFERENCES

1. Womack J.P. and Jones D.T. (2003). *Lean Thinking: Banish Waste and Create Wealth in Your Corporation* (2003 Edition). Free Press, New York, NY.
2. Kirkpatrick D.L. and Kirkpatrick J.D. (2006). *Evaluating Training Programs: The Four Levels* (Third Edition). Berrett-Koehler Publishers, San Francisco, CA.
3. TWI Institute. History. Retrieved from http://twi-institute.com/training-within-industry/about-twi/history; accessed November 28, 2013.

6

Innovative Approaches to Build Health-Care Facilities

Chris Lloyd

CONTENTS

INTRODUCTION

Simpler's Lean Transformation Practice has been operating in health care for over 10 years. We have developed Lean health-care processes in hundreds of facilities from Boston to Bangalore. Our starting point is always that the customer defines the value in all processes. Yet in nearly every facility we work in we find that the current design does not follow the principles of patient flow. Certainly the floors are shinier than ever, the walls are colorful, and there are more signs than at any highway intersection. Still the question remains, has the patient really benefitted in any other way than spending even more time in a nicer seat?

This author had a recent experience in a newly renovated hospital in the North of England. The fracture clinic was well placed on the ground floor with an adjacent x-ray suite, but the ultrasound was on the second floor and was not directly connected by the same elevator. It was a painful experience for this writer and a total waste of time for the nursing escort. The designers clearly did not take the unhindered flow of the patient into account.

We have the saying "the designer casts the longest shadow." The decisions taken in the design of products, processes, services, and buildings have a lifetime impact on the cost of ownership. Over 5 years ago we asked the question, "Why can't the same principles that build customer value into the design of products and services also be applied in health facility design?" This chapter describes how we made the principles work.

INNOVATIVE DESIGN PROCESS PRINCIPLES: LEAN HOSPITAL DESIGN

Lean hospital design is based on a concept of engaging the skills and knowledge of all the key players to develop hospitals that provide maximum patient value. This means

- Respect the patients, staff, architects, and engineers; combine their knowledge for the best outcome.
- Design waste-free processes first, THEN the facility.
- Do it fast and collaboratively.

We have worked with many hospital designers and architects and have the utmost respect and sympathy for them. We have seen them face some significant challenges like the following:

- The design process is heavily focused on the input of the physician.
- There is frequently a false staff engagement creating high expectations that cannot be realized.

- Hospital leaders are often unprepared for the significant distraction resulting from the project. The National Health Service (NHS) England Financial Regulator concluded several years ago that one of the three primary causes of NHS Hospitals experiencing financial and operational problems was new build programs.
- The impact of both cost and time overruns can have a catastrophic impact on the organization's finances.
- Constant change to the program resulting from well-meaning enthusiasm to build the best hospital.

All before We Have Used the Hospital!

Lean hospital design provides a methodology that focuses first and foremost on patient flows; engages the staff, patients, and stakeholders; is fast and effective; and ensures robust, repeatable, and sustainable operational concepts. Figure 6.1 shows the Lean hospital design process that has been successfully applied to many projects. Let us explore the five phases in the process.

Define the Customer Needs: Voice of the Customer

The Lean hospital design process begins with the Voice of the Customer (VOC) stage. With a health-care facility there are many customers to

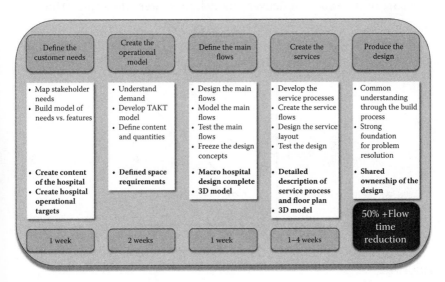

FIGURE 6.1
The Lean hospital design model.

consider, such as the patients, their families and carers, the staff, the hospital financiers, and regulatory authorities. Failure to capture and then differentiate between wants and needs can have a significant adverse impact on stakeholder satisfaction.

VOC begins with a methodology known as the Kano model. It was developed in the 1980s by Professor Noriaki Kano. Customer preferences are classified into three categories:

- Basic attributes—typically service elements that are taken for granted but when absent cause complaints or adverse publicity
- Specified needs—usually given in a contract or service level agreement
- Delighters—contain a feature that the customer never anticipated

The model uses a simple graphic with customer satisfaction represented on the vertical axis and the absence/presence of a feature on the horizontal axis, as illustrated in Figure 6.2.

This technique captures multiple customer inputs and enables a dialog about what a real customer needs and not an uninformed want, the result of an undefined problem and perceived resolution.

To give an example, we ran VOC exercises in a Specialist Outpatient Clinic, where patients were accustomed to 2–3 hour waits. They asked for a large waiting area with WiFi, drinks, and soft seats. Because waiting was part of the expected delivery model, these were the wants. However,

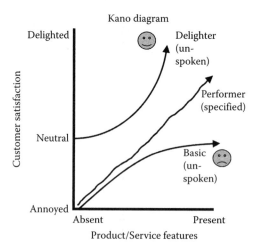

FIGURE 6.2
The Kano model.

the need was to reduce waiting, particularly for health advice, booking the next appointment, or payment advice, aspects that typically occur at the end of the visit when the patients just wanted to go home. VOC would establish that the real need is not the content of the waiting room but the length of wait. If it can be ensured that every minute of patient's time in the clinic adds value, there is little need for a VIP waiting room.

A team of nurses, physicians, and managers working on the new design during a Simpler innovation workshop built a VOC model in just 30 minutes and significantly influenced their design approach.

Create the Operational Model

TAKT Time

The first step in the design of the new operational model is to determine the TAKT time for varying patient demands. TAKT time is the rate that patients should progress through a pathway to avoid queuing. This tool is one of the most invaluable in the Lean toolbox. It can be used to correctly size a facility, and determine how many consulting rooms how many staff are needed. Failing to design the operating model around TAKT inevitably leads to facilities that are too big, too small, have significant delays, cost more to run, and lead to negative patient feedback.

The formula is simple. Define a period long enough to provide representative demand. Divide the available process time with demand. The available time should represent the actual time that the service is available to the patient. Within a pharmacy, for example, the opening hours may be 9 hours. If 200 patients visit the pharmacy the TAKT time is 9 hours (540 minutes) divided by 200 patients = 2.7 minutes. This means the pharmacy must dispense a prescription every 2.7 minutes to avoid queues.

Demand

Over- or understating demand will result in a facility that is either too large or too small. Annual and seasonal demand needs to be studied. If there are significant variations in demand, multiple TAKT times may be calculated and flexibility built into the facility design.

The consultant head of the Emergency Department (ED) at Singapore's National University Hospital studied the variation in ED demand and designed his ED processes with the variation in mind. He curtained off five ED bays that were only opened when TAKT time throughput reached the set level. This provided a simple visual trigger to alert physicians of rising demand.

Space

The TAKT time calculations and time per visit can be used to calculate the facilities required by dividing the cycle time (visit time) by the TAKT time. The example in Figure 6.3 now shows the rooms, counter positions, and waiting chairs required.

Developing Patient Flow First

The most common failure in hospital design is that the buildings are designed to be esthetic, optimize staff and materials flow, and then finally consider patient flow. This usually results in long traveling times within the facility, often causing bottlenecks in elevators/escalators and overburdening porters. An optimum patient flow should be designed first, then the supporting flows.

	TAKT time = available time divided by demand				# resources = cycle time/TAKT
		Number of rooms			
Resource calculations	TAKT time	Consult	Nurse	Pts @ counter	# waiting
Primary consult (simple)	3.2	6.2	0.0	3.1	14.0
Diagnostics - blood test	4.5	0.0	1.1	0.0	13.3
Diagnostics - CUBT	72.0	0.0	0.2	0.0	0.2
Diagnostics - fibroscan	120.0	0.0	0.3	0.0	0.0
Diagnostics - ICG	120.0	0.1	0.3	0.0	0.0
Diagnostics - plain x-ray	36.0	0.0	0.0	0.0	0.0
Same day referral and elective surgery	36.0	0.8	0.4	0.3	1.3
Same day scope (clinical + financial counseling)	0.0	0.0	0.0	0.0	0.0
Same day scan (CT/MRI/)	36.0	0.3	0.0	0.3	0.4
Same day joint consult	90.0	0.3	0.0	0.1	0.0
Total resources		**7.8**	**2.2**	**3.8**	**29.3**
		rooms	rooms	spaces	**58.6**

FIGURE 6.3

Example of resource calculation from TAKT time.

Optimizing Working Efficiency

The Simpler 2P (Process Preparation) process design methodology develops patient flow through the identification of the core value-adding process steps. It leads to what is known as the process backbone. It is developed by the staff that performs the tasks daily.

Each process step has a number of enablers, such as data, equipment, and supplies. These are provided by the supporting flows, as illustrated in Figure 6.4.

- The data flow includes the required patient information, such as diagnosis, care plan, medication, and observations made at previous stems.
- The staff flow should identify the skills qualifications required for each step.
- The information required to efficiently complete each step, including relevant quality standards, is identified and is available on demand without delay.
- Equipment flow ensures that the correct functional equipment is available at each step. The total equipment requirement can also be calculated from this model thereby avoiding equipment shortage or surplus.
- Facilities flow ensures that environmental and structural needs are built into the process such as light, ventilation, and access.
- The supplies flow identifies all supplies required for each step to avoid nurse or physician time lost looking for stuff.

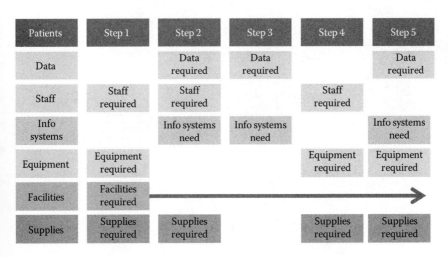

FIGURE 6.4
The 2P process backbone construct.

Try before You Buy: Try Storming

A two-dimensional (2D) desktop model is satisfactory for a virtual design hypothesis. This must be tested before architectural resources are deployed thereby avoiding prolonged trial and error. Many organizations develop extensive computer simulations, which require considerable development time and are difficult to understand.

In a major hospital redesign project in Southeast Asia, a colleague and I developed a simulation exercise overnight, which we then tested in just 3 hours with the design team. We could do this because we knew that the flow model always produces two optimum results. The simulation had to identify and quantify the flow stoppers after which we could design solutions.

The exercise was to test the flow of patients from infection outbreak detection to outpatient screening, from there to inpatient admission, and then to discharge or holding.

Team members undertook roles akin to their actual responsibilities, for example, outpatient clinic manager and ward sister. They led patients through the system as a simulated outbreak developed. The diagram in Figure 6.5 shows the 2D model with defined capacity for each resource and prescribed paths for each patient to follow.

Routing cards were developed for a number of alternative routings for a varying range of patients. The card was designed to show the path that

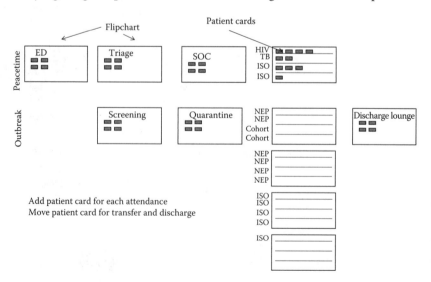

FIGURE 6.5
The simulation exercise used to test design.

the patient needed to follow. Several different routes were used to create a realistic scenario designed from reflections of staff who had served during the SARS epidemic.

Four scenarios were designed and contained the required information for the simulation, including the number of patients, inpatient length of stay, admission rate, discharge rate, and escalation gradient (speed of ramp-up) varying from single patient arrivals to 200+ in a single episode.

Following the completion of the simulation the teams identified the bottlenecks and flow stoppers and developed solutions that included

- Determining the number of wards and inpatient beds
- Setting up a temporary command center to control patient flow and optimize resource utilization
- Optimizing flow resources so that the peak utilization point for each service should not be loaded over 85% for a prolonged period

Design Freeze

My hospital planning architectural colleagues frequently inform me that their project deadlines, cost budgets, and margins are regularly not achieved due to constant design changes and new ideas introduced by their client. The team-based hospital design process avoids this by engaging the key decision makers in the design process.

- At the beginning of the design workshop, the leadership briefs the team with the objectives and vision.
- The leading physicians, nurses, and managers participate in short, sharp, and engaging workshops.
- At the briefing at the end of the workshop, the senior leadership approves the output.

Develop the Services

Having tested the improvement hypothesis in the "try storming phase" the service design is completed. The process cycle time is calculated and the resource model calculated from TAKT time is verified. This phase has three primary elements such as the following:

Service Design

Standard work for each step on the process backbone is created. This involves recording the value-adding steps with the process and assessing the optimum time for completion. This describes a standard repeatable process that staff can be trained to follow. Figure 6.6 shows a typical standard work document for an urgent care center designed in the United Kingdom.

Service Flow

Having developed the service process, the design workshops develop up to seven options of area layout and staff, material, and equipment flows around the optimum patient movements. We refer to this as the Macro model.

Service Layout

Having determined the optimum Macro model for patient flow, the next step is to develop the internal layout for each room to optimize efficient workflow for the staff. This design step, known as the Micro model, now focuses on staff efficiency as the patient is now in the right physical location at each step in their pathway. The micro layout determines the locations of fixed points such as power, gas, and IT. It is vital that these services are in the optimum location at this stage to avoid retrofitting in the future.

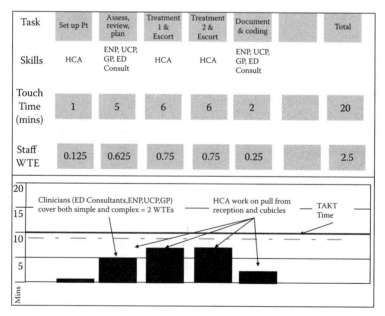

FIGURE 6.6
Example of standard work cycle times chart.

Produce the Design

Having developed, tested, and detailed the preferred final design, the architect can now take the drawings, principles, and processes and produce the detailed design for the facility. This avoids constant review, rework, and redesign loops that typify many health-care facility projects. Having produced their own layouts and simple 3D models the staff can relate their input and ideas more closely to the architects' output.

Shared Ownership

Through briefing their ideas and models to the leadership, the team has the responsibility for the new design. The pride and ownership is carried forward to the commissioning phase.

INNOVATIVE DESIGN PROCESS PRINCIPLES: INNOVATIVE APPROACH TO PROJECT MANAGEMENT

Many organizations have taken advantage of applying Toyota's manufacturing techniques to improve their services and processes in recurring or repetitive environments. Toyota has also developed principles for project management, of which the Simpler Project Management is developed for hospitals.

Lean Project Management Phases

There are the following four phases in the lean project management process:

- Preplanning—the unknowns are explored, needs and capabilities are identified, and the focus for solutions is identified.
- Program planning—multiple outline solutions are developed and then matched to the ranked needs to identify the best solution or combination thereof.
- Detailed design—detailed solutions are created from the top-ranked outline solution.
- Production—the final solution design is implemented and commissioned.

The first two phases are known as the exploration steps and the final ones as execution.

The promise point occurs where the outline design has been evaluated and feasibility tested with a high degree of confidence thus ensuring that the detailed design effort is focused on the best solution and avoiding future rework.

Simpler Project Management: The Process

There are three primary processes within Simpler Project Management: Decision Flow, Lean Project Management (Vertical Value Stream), and Daily Management. We explore each process in some more detail below.

Decision Flow

The first process within the exploration phase is decision flow. Here the process concentrates on the identification of the customer's primary needs. Decision flow differs significantly from conventional project management. It starts from the output and then works back to the decisions that must be taken linking to the knowledge required to make those decisions. Knowledge gaps are identified, and learning requirements are defined and filled. At the integration point, the project team is satisfied that the correct knowledge has been acquired to make the decisions, which are then frozen. The structure of the decision flow is shown in Figure 6.7.

Vertical Value Stream Map

The vertical value stream map (VVSM) is a team-based tool developed in the precomputer era. It can be used to manage a program by the many rather than the privileged few with access to Microsoft Project. Constructed from butcher paper and sticky notes, the map is typically 2–3 m tall and follows the timeline from top to bottom rather than left to right. The top row denotes the key personnel responsible for the completion of project steps, review, and agreement at integration points. The integration point is determined by a review, which has given inputs and outputs. If these criteria are not met, the review is postponed until they are satisfied. A detailed plan is developed only to the next integration point.

Daily Management

Weekly targets are created from the VVSM identifying what should be completed at the end of the week. The project teams then plan their

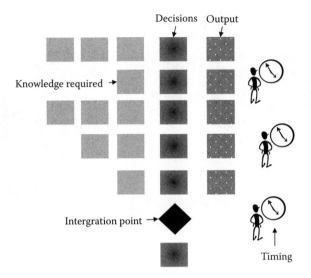

FIGURE 6.7
Decision flow structure.

activities for that period. Problems are identified much earlier and the whole team is engaged in their resolution. The daily review is a stand-up meeting of only 15 minutes around the daily planning board. This short daily process is more productive than long project reviews that require significant preparation and communication.

Obeya: Project Space Where the Team Work Together

The photograph in Figure 6.8 shows a typical Lean Program control room known as an "Obeya" or large room. The VVSM, decision flow, and daily team management board as well as other key visual management aids are located in the Obeya. The picture shows the visual management principles.

Benefits

Our studies show that by focusing on the project flow, organizations achieve

- A 30% to 50% reduction in project lead time
- Closer satisfaction of customer needs
- Better morale in project teams
- A 20% to 40% reduction in labor time spent on a project
- Improvement of the right first time quality of the project

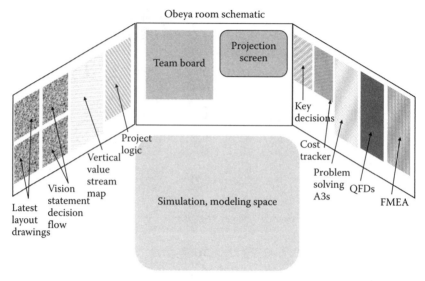

FIGURE 6.8
Example of an Obeya.

Some of these tools and techniques are up to 70 years old but have rarely been applied to the development of hospitals and health-care facilities.

SUMMARY

The basic principles of health-care facility design can be summarized as follows:

- Listen to the voice of the customer—get the needs not the wants!
- Patient flow trumps everything else. The shortest end-to-end time in the pathway will result in the best patient experience and higher real efficiency.
- Form follows function—design the optimum processes, then the facility around them.
- If the staff designs the process, the patient flow and efficient work will be owned by the many, not the few.
- Leadership provides the vision, staff the details.

Lean application at the hospital design stage using the above principles would not only make hospitals efficient but even reduce the operational cost.

7

Hospital Planning and Design Innovation for Lean Operation

S. K. Biswas and V. K. Singh

CONTENTS

INTRODUCTION

Hospital design and planning concepts have been evolving rapidly in the last few decades. Earlier it was "Functions follow design": hospital facilities were created in any existing building such as an old barracks or a jail. This was followed by "Design follows functions": facilities were designed as per needs of hospital functions and functionaries, but patients' concerns were not taken on account. More recently, the concept "Design follows first patients, then functions" has been adopted. The emphasis now is on integrating the needs of patients, hospital functions, and functionaries. New tools and technologies, such as information and communication technology (ICT), evidence-based planning (EBP), Lean process thinking, and innovation and life-cycle cost analysis are being used. This chapter discusses how such concepts can be integrated at the planning and designing stages, and how they were applied at Iris Hospital in Kolkata, the first Indian hospital that has been planned by us using these newer concepts.

INNOVATION, LEAN PLANNING, AND DESIGN

Important premises are

- Most of the operating costs of a hospital are affected by decisions taken at the planning stage. Inflexible physical structures such as walls, elevators, and shafts may become impediments for progress in the future.
- Technologies such as real-time data, ICT, bar codes, radio frequency identification devices (RFID), and modular design allow for creative solutions.

Innovation is a process of translating an idea into goods or services that create value for which the customer is ready to pay. An innovation is to be replicable and its selling price must be lower than its perceived value. Innovation involves deliberate application of information, imagination, and initiative in deriving greater or different values from available resources. It includes all processes by which new ideas are generated and converted into useful products. Innovations have two broad categories: (1) evolutionary innovations (continuous or dynamic evolutionary innovation) and (2) revolutionary innovations (discontinuous or radical innovations),[1] which are often disruptive. According to Lean thinking, many small- and low-risk improvements in processes, behavior, or culture may through an evolutionary process accumulate into radical transformations. Improvement and innovation are two sides of same coin.[2] Because innovation results in something new, be it a technology, product, service, or business model, it implies risk-taking.

Process improvements seek to remove waste to reduce cost and simultaneously improve outcomes. For an innovation to be radical, it must produce world-class quality; achieve a significant price reduction in relation to performance; be scalable to quickly build volume; and be adaptable to various environments, such as rural and urban. For an innovation to have maximum impact, it must be affordable by all, regardless of income. Innovation has to be market driven, so that waste reduction benefits both patients and providers. Waste gets accumulated because of ignorance as nobody benefits from it.

Health innovation has two components, operations and infrastructure. Both are applied in hospital planning and design. Flow and functional diagrams are made before infrastructure design to have minimal movements of patients, staff, and supplies. Technology allows collection of reliable real-time data; analysis and collation can reveal problems and help testing solutions.

Iris Hospital has developed local ICT solutions instead of customizing existing packages. Bar codes and RFID tags are used to track the movements of patients, staff, and supplies and various other activities in clinical areas. Various mobile devices have been integrated at all levels.

EVIDENCE-BASED HOSPITAL PLANNING AND DESIGN

Evidence-based design (EBD) is a field of study that emphasizes the use of credible evidence to influence the design process. The approach has become popular in health-care architecture in an effort to improve patient and staff well-being, patient healing, stress reduction, and safety. EBD is a relatively new field of study that borrows terminology and ideas from several disciplines, such as environmental psychology, architecture, neuroscience, and behavioral economics. The overall objective is to create a healing environment as detailed in Figure 7.1.

Zimring et al.[3] have identified the following 10 strategies for EBD:

1. Start with known problems, such as hospital-acquired infections, patient satisfaction, and staff performance, and envision new solutions.
2. Use a multidisciplinary approach, but ensure that senior leaders demonstrate the support necessary to achieve change.
3. Include patients and families.
4. Seek cost efficiencies.
5. Use decision-making tools to keep the process on track.
6. Establish quantitative criteria linked to incentives.
7. Use strategic partnerships to accelerate innovation.
8. Support and demand simulation and testing throughout the process.

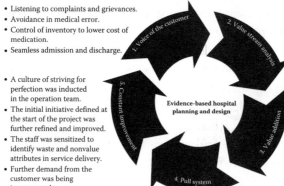

EBD approach at Iris Hospital during planning and design phase

• Listening to complaints and grievances.
• Avoidance in medical error.
• Control of inventory to lower cost of medication.
• Seamless admission and discharge.

• A culture of striving for perfection was inducted in the operation team.
• The initial initiative defined at the start of the project was further refined and improved.
• The staff was sensitized to identify waste and nonvalue attributes in service delivery.
• Further demand from the customer was being incorporated.

1. Voice of the customer
2. Value stream analysis
3. Value addition
4. Pull system
5. Constant improvement

Evidence-based hospital planning and design

• The requirement of the customer formed the basis of the value stream analysis (VSA).
• The design team, consisting of various stakeholders, analyzed the purpose, the concept, and the constraints, during VSA.
• Further, the possible process flow and improved design concepts were visualized for each of the issues during VSA.
• Following the exercise for VSA, further details were incorporated from the perspective of service detail, detail engineering, detail fabrication and logistics, processes involved, space requirements, rationalizing the staff numbers, and other logistics.

• Following testing of the IT software and training of the hospital staff, the continuous integration phase started.
• Each of the points mentioned in the *voice of the customer* was incorporated to ensure a pull rather than a push system.
• Such systems included
  • Medication management system.
  • Automated billing and discharge system.

• Prime objective was to avoid waste of resources by leveraging information technology (IT) and empowering and training them to add value for the customer.

FIGURE 7.1
Evidence-based hospital planning and design.

9. Use a 30- to 50-year cycle perspective to determine the return on investment.
10. Communicate frequently with all stakeholders about the desired outcomes and potential benefits.

The EBD principles are closely related to Lean Management:[4]

- Identify the outcome value and the activities that produce or contribute to it.
- Identify the wasteful activities that do not create value.
- Identify the stream of value-creating activities and organize them into processes.
- Apply tools and automation to achieve just-in-time flows.
- Codify best practices into standards and foolproof practices.

Iris Hospital is a 180-bed multispecialty hospital. It was built as a part of the diversification plan of a group of local entrepreneurs, who desired to enter the vibrant health-care domain with a green field project. The brief given to the design and execution team was to address various shortcomings, which were apparent at the existing public and private hospitals. The ethos of the brief was to bring forth a hospital that differentiates its services by leveraging information technology (IT), and to organize a team of well-trained employees who follow standardized protocols and processes and avoid wasting resources while delivering service to the patients. The brief also included a system of data collection, which would enable decision support.

The design and the project team kept the five cardinal principles of Lean as follows:

1. Listen to the voice of the customer (patients and other stakeholders).
2. Undertake a value stream analysis to get a direction for planning and operating the hospital.
3. Identify the value addition attributes and eliminate the nonvalue addition (waste), thereby improving process flow.
4. Put in place processes based on demand-pull from the patients rather than push from centralized planning.
5. Constantly strive for improvement and perfection.

Iris Hospital was planned keeping these Lean principles in mind. By leveraging IT, evidence-based hospital planning and design was followed.

The various process flows were incorporated in the physical layout, keeping IT as its backbone. This was to ensure that processes standardized at the design stage were followed by the staff, using the forms, reports, and tools within the software.

Software to fit Iris Hospital's process flow did not exist in the local market. The cost of customizing existing packages would have been very high. A strategic decision was taken to mobilize an in-house team. It ensured that at the startup of the hospital, the software and the various IT tools would be developed to work seamlessly.

The team undertook a value stream analysis in the areas of stakeholders' desires. Value is what a patient is ready to pay for, nonvalue activities are waste. By value stream analysis, a process is broken down to its component parts to identify and remove those that do not add value.

In this chapter, we describe how these principles were applied in the four areas illustrated in Figure 7.2.

- Value outcomes were identified and tracked through a patient feedback system.
- Waste in the medication management system (MMS) was cut out.
- *Just-in-time* was applied in the inventory management system.
- The value stream was improved in the decentralized billing system.
- A standard methodology was designed for the discharge system.

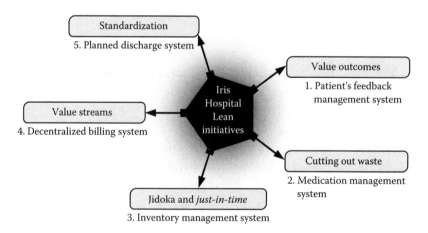

FIGURE 7.2
Lean principles applied for designing processes.

VALUE OUTCOME

Patient's feedback management system

- Feedback from the user on the quality of key attributes in the service being provided is an important tool for management.
- As part of quality assurance, the hospital implemented a data-driven feedback system, which measures the gap between the expected service and what the patients perceive during their stay.
- Measuring the gap between expectations and perceptions helps management to evaluate the outcome of the initiatives taken on quality of services and to take appropriate measures.

Value

Background on the Lean Approach for the Patient's Feedback Management System

Stakeholder satisfaction is the key to success in health care. Doctors influence patients to choose a hospital best suited to them. Hospital management needs to convince doctors that their hospital is the most appropriate to satisfy the requirements and expectations of the patients. Both management and doctors thus need to have an accurate and timely understanding of how they succeed in making patients satisfied. As the public is increasingly sensitive to error-prone hospital services, this is of utmost importance.

Value Stream Analysis

The considerations here were

- Could an evaluation process be designed to assess patient satisfaction during their stay in the hospital?
- Could the evaluations be compared over time?
- Could these evaluations be made before and after changes to provide evidence for their efficacy?

The focus on increased assessment and accountability has been called the third health care revolution by Kohn et al. The first revolution was the rapid expansion in medicine and technology; the second was cost containment. Health-care providers are now required to become more responsive to patients' needs and work within a clearly established framework for determining clinical and nonclinical performance.

Professor Mike Hart[5] has stated that "it is increasingly recognized that patients and the health delivery system should be given a voice in the assessment of the quality of the provision of services that are offered to them within the NHS (National Health Service), UK. The method of eliciting patient satisfaction is by a questionnaire, typically administered after inpatient treatment in a hospital but not after other episodes of treatment."

The well-known SERVQUAL methodology, developed by Zeithaml et al.[6] has been applied to the evaluation of service quality in health care.

> Servqual is an instrument for measuring service quality, which begins with the assumption that service quality is determined by the difference between customers' expectations of a service and their perceptions of the service actually delivered. Confirmation of expectations leads to customer satisfaction and disconfirmation to dissatisfaction.[6]

There have been a number of successful applications of the SERVQUAL model. The practical use of this technique was found in reports on SERVQUAL analysis of samples of outpatients in the United Kingdom.[5] Professor Hart in his report suggested this as the most appropriate methodology to assess the effect of process change with the end users.

At Iris Hospital, the ten original attributes for evaluation of service quality were combined into five: *tangibles, reliability, responsiveness, assurance,* and *empathy.* The perceptions–expectations (P–E) gap in service quality is measured across these five attributes by the application of an adaptable 10-item survey using a Likert scale, where three will be good or excellent, two acceptable, and one not up to standard. The intention was to produce a reliable tool that could be applied comparatively in different services.

Challenges to Implement a Patient's Feedback Management System

The challenges were how to formulate a concise and easily understood questionnaire, which could address the relevant service attributes. When the data have been collected, they need to be digitized and analyzed. Results should be reported through a dashboard, which would be available to the management for taking improvement initiatives. Finally, the methodology needs to be evaluated to ensure the attributes are comparable over time, and that appropriate measures are taken at the earliest to address the causes of dissatisfaction.

How Iris Hospital Tackled All the Issues Related to Patient Feedback Management System

Survey

A questionnaire was developed to measure patients' and relatives' perceptions of service on the following attributes.

- *Tangibility* is defined as any deliverables that patients' sensory system could pick up, such as ambience; taste of food; cleanliness of the bed, toilet, and the surrounding environment; or excess noise. These are important considerations for patient recovery and positive impression. It was brought out by questions such as "During this hospital visit, was the area around your room/area kept clean, quiet and comfortable? During this hospital stay, did you feel safe from fire?"
- *Reliability* from the patient's perspective is that requirements are met. This is the accuracy of test reports, patient data, and filing of patient's records. It is brought out by a question such as "Would you recommend this hospital to your friends and family in terms of reliability of service?"
- *Responsiveness* translates to the readiness and willingness of employees of the hospital to help patients or their relatives in providing prompt and timely services. Attending to a call for the nurses, or setting up appointments for the doctors quickly and effectively are the criteria by which responsiveness is evaluated. A measure of responsiveness is keeping the patient and their relatives informed in a language they are able to understand, and providing pertinent answers to their questions on the service and its cost. Questions included in the survey included the following: "During this hospital visit/stay, how well did the staff explain procedures and instructions to you that you could understand? Were your requests for assistance (e.g., nurse call) answered in a reasonable amount of time?"
- *Assurance* is the promise that the hospital offers required skills and professionalism to perform the service necessary for the patient. This reflects on the way the service to the patient is effectively delivered. The

patients have to feel assured and reassured that the hospital has their best interest in heart and will follow the correct processes. Questions included the following: "During this hospital visit, how well did the doctor/staff explain details about your illness, related procedures and medications that you could understand? Was the check-in/check-out process conducted professionally and within a reasonable amount of time?"

- *Empathy* is manifested with a clean and neat appearance of hospital personnel and whether they are polite, respectful, and friendly. Empathy relates to fulfilling the patient's individual needs, and providing individualized attention. As an example, simply recognizing the patient and relatives when they arrive would delight them. A simple question like "Did you find the staff members responsive to your personal request?" will reassure them about sincerity of the hospital's management.

Data Collection

Following collection of the data with the questionnaire, an effective method of transcribing or digitizing and analyzing the results was developed in the Hospital Information System (HIS).

- The gap between perceived and expected service will be iterated by the HIS including the statistical mean from the response to the questions.
- It can be assumed that expectations will be higher than perceptions.

Software

A program was built in the HIS software, as a flexible questionnaire that reflects the patient's view as well as management's initiative taken on quality of service.

A dashboard is available to the management for taking initiatives to improve the quality of service and therefore the patient satisfaction in Figure 7.3.

Evaluation

The attributes are comparable over time, to recognize the various failure points during the delivery of service to each admitted patient. This ensures that appropriate measures are taken at the earliest to address the system or the process. This will serve as a catalyst for improvement of quality of service.

	Stratified SERVQUAL Score Card		82/1 Raja Subodh Chandra Mullick Road, Kolkata 700047, Phone - 6609 - 6000
HOSPITAL			

Date : 01-JAN-13 TO Date : 28-OCT-13			N = 260

Attributes	Weight	Perception (P)	Expectation (E)	Gap (P – E)
Responsiveness	0.25	2.03	2.27	–0.25
Tangibles	0.25	2.36	2.50	–0.14
Assurance	0.25	0.90	1.02	–0.12
Reliability	0.25	2.08	2.25	–0.17
Average:	1.00	1.84	2.01	–0.17

FIGURE 7. 3
A sample result from the SERVQUAL survey undertaken.

In the survey conducted between January 13, 2013 and October 28, 2013, in Figure 7.3, the management noted that the tangibles was slipping. This was due to lackadaisical approach of the housekeeping personnel. On analyzing the cause, it was found that the agency supplying housekeeping personnel had not properly trained these personnel as per the housekeeping protocols, which Iris Hospital had standardized and contracted out to them. The effect was apparent in the dashboard, where the average scoring was poor as underlined in Figure 7.3.

The management, being sensitive to the importance of patient perception, put in place an action plan, with the collaboration of the external agency, to address the issue. This action ensured that better surveillance was put in place, so as to expect better outcomes and positive value for future surveys.

CUTTING OUT WASTE

Medication management system

- The task is to deliver the right medicine to the right patient at the right time in the right dose.
- Errors should be reported, resolved, and prevented in all steps.
- Billing should be transparent and accurate.
- Management should have effective control on inventory to avoid out-of-stock situations while reducing inventory levels and accompanying costs.

Value

A study "Reduction in medication errors in hospitals due to adoption of computerized provider order entry systems (CPOE)," by Radley et al.,[7] concluded that processing a prescription drug order through a CPOE system decreases the likelihood of error by 48%. Given this effect size, and the degree of CPOE adoption in 2008 in the United States, it has been estimated that a 12.5% reduction in medication errors cut $17.4 million in error costs in 1 year. CPOE, an instigated part of MMS, helps to avoid errors in medication by ensuring the right medicine is given to the right patient, in the right dose, and in the right frequency and duration. The data entered through CPOE are mined from the software and used to generate various forms and reports.

The Institute of Medicine[8] estimates that at least a quarter of all medication-related injuries are preventable. It recommends electronic prescribing (e-prescribing) through a CPOE system to reduce medication errors and harm to patients.

By definition, a medication error can occur in the event of

1. Errors in ordering
2. Transcribing
3. Dispensing
4. Administrating
5. Monitoring
6. Billing

An article by Amy Buttell,[8] "The Payoff: Preventing Errors in Medication Management," refers to a case where a patient had been prescribed two cholesterol-lowering medicines at the same time—Lipitor while under treatment at the hospital, and Zocor at discharge. During a follow-up, it was discovered that the patient was on the same class of drugs twice over. The CPOE system is used to prevent this type of errors.

As described in the same article, a 50% reduction in medical errors was achieved at Piedmont Health in Atlanta, after it adopted its end-to-end MMS in 2005. John Hilliard, vice president and chief information officer of the two-hospital, 600-bed health system, describes the challenge as a "hugely complex internal effort to develop interfaces that work safely." However, it paled in comparison with the cultural shift: "The system of managing medication by paper movement and duplication was so firmly entrenched that it was incredibly difficult to change," he says. "So it wasn't as much about fine-tuning; we had to completely redo the process."

Value Stream Analysis

Challenges to Ensure the Implementation of Medication Management System

At the onset of the design phase of Iris Hospital, it was clear to us that we had to address all the statutory issues from the Drug & Cosmetics Act of 1940.[9] We also needed to ensure that the process of delivering medicines to the patients was done effectively. We identified and improved the information flow for medical management, as well as the physical flows and space requirements, and tackled the culture change issues.

The issues before us were

- Analysis of the current process and the problems
- Designing of a more effective process
- Culture change and training
- Identifying issues to look out for

How Iris Hospital Tackled All of the Issues Related to Medication Management System

Analysis of the Current Process and the Problems

The first step was to define the process by which the medicine is prescribed by a physician and how it will be documented in the relevant treatment file of the patient. All patients are allocated a unique Patient ID (PID) number on admission and this will be represented through a bar code system.

Next, the manual prescription will need to be transcribed in the software against the bar coded PID. At the point of supply from the pharmacy, the bar coded PID will be checked, from the software, to ensure that no error has occurred in terms of the drug indented, and the quantity supplied.

Further, at the point of delivery of the medicine, the right quantity will be chosen from the stock and delivered at the correct time in an efficient way. The right dose will be administered to the patient by the nurse and documented. Should any adverse drug reaction occur, the appropriate physician should be informed. All this will be recorded and represented automatically in the patient's final bill.

Where manual documentation or partial use of a computer is involved, the process flow is as depicted in Figure 7.4.

From the perspective of Lean management, the objective is to eliminate waste, by reducing or eliminating:

Defects	Transportation
Overproduction	Inventory
Waiting	Motion
Nonutilization of staff	Excess processing

The conventional process as in Figure 7.4 points toward a simultaneous lack of transparency, inefficiency, and too much documentation. Effective nursing hours are wasted on paperwork, slowing the flow of patients from admission to discharge. Iris Hospital's decision to use integrated software based on Lean lead to the process described in Figure 7.5.

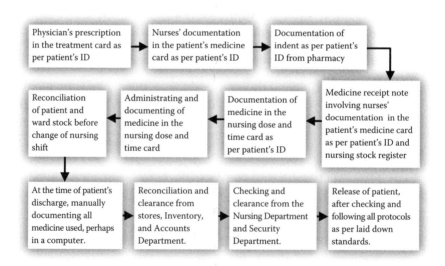

FIGURE 7.4
Process of a manual medication management system.

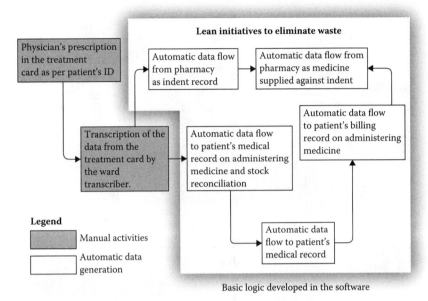

FIGURE 7.5

Process of an automated medication management system.

Designing of a More Effective Process

A crucial element is to define the physical space requirement as the system will deal with tangible items (medicines) as shown in Figure 7.6.

The goal will be to ensure an efficient supply from source (pharmacy) to destination (patient). This will involve the positioning of nursing stations in relation to receipt of supply (from source) and the way in which the nursing staff shall be informed about the prescribed medication and its subsequent administration to the patient (destination). Finally it will address the issue of administering the correct dose and any report of adverse reaction. Only after all these stages will the details be ready for posting medicine in the patient's bill.

The Lean process of operation necessitated a redefinition of physical space as in Figure 7.6. A pneumatic transport system allowed a reduction in manpower, which in turn helped reduce waste from unnecessary physical movement and increase staff utilization. Further waste reduction was achieved by ensuring that all input and output of information related to medication and inventory control were done through computers, or handheld tablets to and from the HIS.

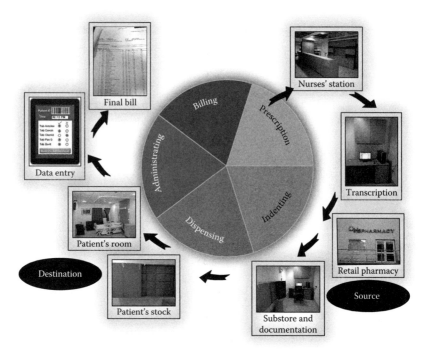

FIGURE 7.6
Physical space for automated medication management system.

CULTURE CHANGE AND TRAINING

CPOE systems, an essential part of MMS, are used in only a few hospitals in India. A challenging task is to explain the concept behind MMS to all who will be using it.

The attitude toward the use of computers by all staff members need to change to ensure that CPOE and MMS will become an operational reality and effectively implemented.

Any new process and system will involve initial resistance unless the costs and the benefits are explained clearly. The costs are direct investments in equipment, software, and floor space; running costs in personnel and consumables, such as plastic packages used in the PTS; the management efforts in planning, persuasion, training, and communication; and the discomfort to staff that comes from new ways of working. On the benefit side, there are issues, such as automated, just-in-time supply capability reducing inventory levels; reduction of medication errors; data transparency that enables internal and external audits, and shorter discharge times; and less use of manpower transporting supplies and documents back and forth.

In any quality hospital, the patients have the right to know everything about their medication and also to be assured of safe administration of medicine. It involves their basic rights as well as safety. No hospital will be certified by any accrediting body unless these processes are adopted. So software needs to be in place to mine all data related to rights and safety issues from the HIS.

Value

"Whoever can deliver care at the highest quality and lowest cost will be the winner," says Richard Grundling,[10] vice president of the Healthcare Financial Management Association.

The supply chain of medicines and other consumable items needed for running the hospital account for 25%–40% of the operative expenditure. A possible course of action is to control the hospital's inventory through Jidoka (automation). It should address the following issues:

- Establish minimum and critical stock levels for each type of item in stock.
- Ensure that the vendors supply items in the shortest time to maintain minimum and critical level of stock and to reduce inventory levels.

JIDOKA AND JUST-IN-TIME

Inventory management system

- A large inventory of consumables must be maintained in a hospital. This accounts for more than 25% of the gross revenue.
- It is a significant task for any management to maintain effective control over inventories.
- A process that traces from the beginning, the point of raising the indent, the order release to the vendor, recording the receipt of the items, consumption, and finally ending with billing the patient. This would be an ideal process.
- A system that takes care of all the above stages and results in the effective management of consumables and inventory could be the goal of a hospital.

- Remove redundant items.
- Manage product expiration and analyze consumption trends.
- Ensure that adding and restocking tasks makes a difference in waste reduction.
- Ensure time spent on physical stock checking and tracking is kept to a minimum.
- Implement inventory tracking tools operating in real time.
- Generate reports on the value of on-hand stock, the value of supplies on orders indented, product expiration, physician utilization, and so on.
- Lower the on-hand inventory value.
- Automatically generate lists of items in stock to the dashboard using the ABC-VED matrix. ABC denotes a ranking of the items by price. It follows the 80–20 rule: 20% of the items (A) in stock account for 80% of the stock value. Managing the A's efficiently reduces inventory costs. VED classifies items in the order of importance into vital, essential, and desirable. As an example, atropine sulfate is a low-cost, life-saving drug, that is, a C and V category in the ABC-VED strata. Such items should never be out of stock, whereas an A and D category item can be ordered as needed.
- Ensure educating physicians about practice patterns and supply costs that will promote and address the budget constraints of hospitals.
- Use data for decision making about item standardization and eliminating redundancies.
- Ensure automatic expiration notices to prevent item wastage, and exchange of older items for new stock with the vendor.
- Mine data on consumption patterns to help negotiate more favorable pricing and consignment arrangements from the vendors.
- Secure additional discounts with vendors for the future indent.
- Ensure that the HIS system automatically generates an order and e-mails it to the vendor.

How Iris Hospital Tackled All of the Issues Related to Medication Management System

Given the challenges as above, a Lean approach was taken. The basic plan for developing the software and the process flow was drawn out as in Figure 7.7.

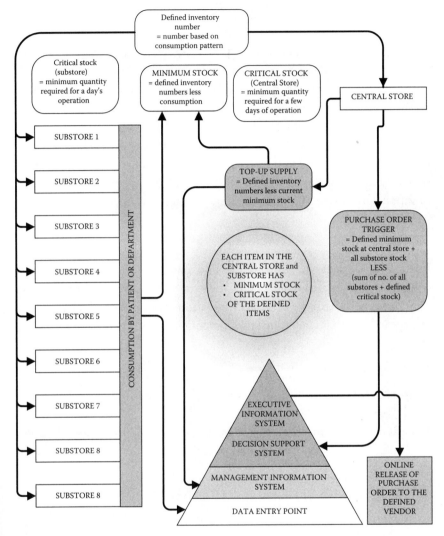

FIGURE 7.7
Inventory management process flow.

Although implementing the system, the minimum and critical stock levels were identified against each item in the stock. As the goods arrived, it was taken into the central store and registered in the HIS software. As an indent for supply was raised, based on the primary physician or resident medical officer, this data were entered by the transcriber into the HIS against the patient's unique ID, and the supply reduced the stock in hand by the proportional number. This process carried on till the minimum stock in hand for the given item kicks in at the central store as in Figure 7.7. At the midpoint between minimum and critical stock, the HIS triggers an automated purchase order. On vetting from the appropriate manager, the order is e-mailed to the defined vendor. The physical supply is usually within 24–48 hours of consumption. The goods are received through the HIS and the cycle continues.

The complete data set is then mined to generate certain predefined informative and statistical reports as part of the executive information system.

The entire inventory management system at Iris Hospital is being run by a team of four pharmacists and one manager. There is the backup of a PTS, from where the indent from the central store is supplied to the nursing station, operation theater, and other destinations. At times, porters are used to supply larger-sized items to the required destination.

Value

In Kolkata, even at the best-managed hospital, the average time taken to complete the formalities of discharging a patient is between 2 and 4 hours. The process of discharge is the accumulation of a number of activities and tasks that have to be taken up simultaneously.

Value Stream Analysis

The discharge goal includes

- Records of condition of patient at admission, and available documentation of history of illness.

VALUE STREAM AND STANDARDIZATION

Decentralized billing and discharge system

- A vital parameter for patient satisfaction in any hospital is the convenience of clearing the hospital's outstanding and the facility to receive fast and comprehensive information of any pertinent detail regarding the patient's stay in the hospital.
- Using the HIS, a patient can be discharged at any nursing station. Queries raised by a patient can be answered and resolved instantaneously by the floor manager.
- For the sake of transparency, details of every transaction could be classified under various heads, and presented for records.

- Documentation and collection of reports of all investigations in an orderly manner kept ready for handing over to the patient at the time of discharge.
- Documentation and collection of all investigation reports, doctor's findings, and prescriptions for medical records.
- Cross-checks with stores and inventory for bill clearance.
- Cross-checks with various other departments on issues related to billing.
- Appropriate transcriptions in case of a surgical procedure.
- A transcription of the discharge summary.

How Iris Hospital Tackled All of the Issues Related to Medication Management System

The number of hospital staff and departments involved in producing the documentation for a discharge is large and the work is tedious and time consuming as seen in Figure 7.8. This increases the possibility of human error and wasteful repetitions and corrections. Lean management will go a long way to avoid these shortcomings if, during the patient's stay in the hospital, details of each stage are reported in the HIS.

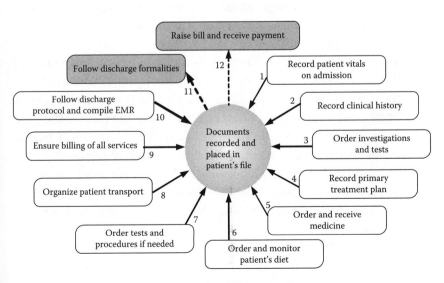

FIGURE 7.8
Some of the tasks in the process flow of delivering service.

Discharge on a standardized template, as defined by the Joint Commission International (JCI) under section Access, Assessment, and Continuity of Care (AAC) 3.2 of the "Joint Commission International Accreditation Standards for Hospitals," requires that all the relevant outputs must be represented in the discharge summary.

The HIS can be used to collect all details through various input data forms available in the system. These are to be filled by trained staff or transcribers during the various stages of the patient's treatment as in Figure 7.8, including the manual form that the resident doctors currently submit, and advice on diet, medications, and further investigations submitted by the resident medical officer or the primary physician treating the patient.

Value Addition

The HIS software designed in-house enabled reducing waste of resources, based on Lean principles. Repetitive, mundane, inefficient, and ineffective tasks in service delivery were analyzed and avoided. The HIS software helped develop a standard flow in various modules, from which the system automatically mines the data and incorporates it into the discharge summary. Some of the features are as follows:

- The food and beverage department knows the type of diet to be delivered to the patient at the appropriate meal time. This is through the *diet module* in the HIS.
- The pharmacy knows the type of medicine indented and consumed for the treatment of the patient. This is through the *MMS module* in the HIS. These data are mined and iterated for the final patient's bill.
- Further, as soon as the dose is administered to the patient, the posting will be placed in the patient's bill in the *accounts and finance module*, through the hospital's wireless network system.
- The diagnostic department records the requirements and concurs on timing and collection of the test or the timing in which the diagnostic procedure will take place. This is through the *diagnostic test module* in the HIS.
- At the point of discharge, the data from the various fields are automatically mined and put into the discharge summary report. The report is editable in the event the primary physician feels any of the information needs to be altered. All the information collected

during the life cycle of the patient's stay in the hospital remains in the hospital's database, and is available at a click of an icon in the HIS. The discharge summary is ready for printing and the discharge process ends.

For the convenience of the patient, the entire process of printing the bill and discharge summary is done at the nursing station of the floor in which the patient is admitted. The final bill settlement is also done from the nursing station of that floor of the hospital. The process allows any query raised by a patient to be answered and resolved instantaneously by the floor manager or the shift in charge of nursing.

To validate the discharge and billing process, an internal study showed that the average time taken was 20 minutes. This is also reflected in the patient satisfaction survey.

SUMMARY

Iris was a green field hospital project. Evidence-based Lean design could be developed right from the start. Nonvalue activities have been removed at the planning and development stage.

Iris Hospital is an example of designing an HIS based on Lean thinking, and using the system to implement Lean processes. The information system defines a structure for tasks, thereby improving compliance to best practices.

At Iris, the HIS was developed in-house, from the ground up. This ensured flexibility in the design and its implementation. There is, however, an ongoing debate on the relative merits of in-house versus off-the-shelf IT solutions. Building from the ground up ensures a start from a clean table free of the legacies of a past system. On the other hand, this software very much defines the current processes, which, over the years, will turn into a legacy. Further process improvements will require changes and upgrades in the software, which might be expensive. Vendors serving several clients with a standard package are typically better situated to continuous upgrades and dissemination of new best practices. In the case of Iris, however, no suitable packages were available that would have suited our purposes. The tailor-made systems developed by us achieved the desired performance.

There has been an increase in the value perceived by the patients, and in the quality of service rendered. Fewer errors in medication management have been observed. A substantial saving in inventory carrying cost has been achieved. The faster discharge of patients has become a key positive differentiator for the hospital. The reduction of waste and increasing value reflects a planning success for this approach tried for the first time in India.

REFERENCES

1. Retrieved from: http://www.businessdictionary.com/definition/revolutionary-innovation.html.
2. Singh, V.K. 2013. Innovating for good health. Express Healthcare, May 6, 2013. Retrieved from: http://healthcare.financialexpress.com/sections/strategy/1550-innovating-for-good-health.
3. Zimring, C.M., Augenbroe, G.L., Malone, E.B. and Sadler, B.L. 2008. Implementing healthcare excellence: the vital role of the CEO in evidence based design. White Paper Series 3/5, Evidence-Based Design Resources for Healthcare Executives, Center for Health Design, September 2008.
4. Spoerl, B. 2012. How to Get Hospitals to Think 'Lean': 5 Key Principles. Retrieved from: http://www.beckershospitalreview.com/strategic-planning/how-to-get-hospitals-to-think-lean-5-key-principles.html.
5. Hart, M. 2003. Quantification of Patent Satisfaction. Retrieved from: www.mikehart.org.uk /qps3.doc
6. Zeithaml, V., Parasuraman, A., and Berry, L.L. 1990. *Delivering Service Quality: Balancing Customer Perception and Expectation*. Macmillan, London.
7. Radley, et al. 2013. Reduction in medication errors in hospitals due to adoption of computerized provider order entry systems. Retrieved from: http://jamia.bmj.com/cpntent/early/2013/13/01/amiajni-2012–001241.full
8. Burttell, A. 2007. The payoff: Preventing Errors Medication Management. Retrieved from: http://www.hhnmag.com/hhnmag/jsp/articledisplay.jsp?dcrpath=HHNMAG/Article/data/10OCT2007/0710HHN_FEA_ClinicalMgt&domain=HHNMAG.
9. Malik, V. 1996. *Drug and Cosmetics Act, 1940*, 9th Edition. Eastern Book Company, Lucknow, India.
10. Grundling, R. and Jarousse, L.A. 2011. Key Steps to Strategic Supply Chain Management. Retrieved from: http://www.hhnmag.com/display/HHN-news-article.dhtml?dcrPath=/templatedata/HF_Common/NewsArticle/data/HHN/Magazine/2011/Dec/1211HHN_Feature_Gatefold

8

Public Health Innovations

Vandana Kumar

CONTENTS

INTRODUCTION

Public health innovations are equitable, applicable to all in a population, cost-effective, and may address health determinants in the nonhealth sector of society.[1]

This chapter profiles two public health innovations from India. Mobile Kunji is an audiovisual job aid that the frontline health workers can use during counseling sessions with rural families. SughaVazhvu Healthcare functions at the interface of technology and human resource innovation to provide evidence-based primary health care to rural Indian populations. The first innovation focuses on maternal and child health, the second covers a basket of common primary care conditions, including pregnancy and cardiovascular diseases. A common feature between the two initiatives is the innovative use of technology—mobile phones as audiovisual job aids for the use of frontline health workers during counseling sessions with rural families and an Android application for population enrollment and risk assessment.

Both innovations are being implemented by not-for-profit organizations. The two innovations are at different scales of operations—one is being implemented in one state, where it has been included as a core component of the common minimum package of solutions by the state government, and the other is operational in one district of a state.

Various aspects of each of the two innovations are described in detail below: the need for innovation; its inception; originators/implementers of the initiative; features of the innovation—design and key processes; coverage; challenges faced during implementation of the innovation and future plans; and potential for scale-up across geographic and functional areas. Impact and cost-effectiveness of these solutions has also been discussed to an extent.

MOBILE KUNJI

Background

The starting point for any innovation is a question. And so it was with Mobile Kunji—the audiovisual job aid created for the frontline health workers by BBC Media Action as part of the Shaping Demand and Practices project in Bihar. There were, in fact, a series of questions to be addressed: Can a job aid for the frontline health workers be created that will deliver hundreds of lifesaving health messages? That can be carried at all times? That does not require reams of paper or expensive equipment? That excites and motivates the frontline health workers and the families they visit?

It is widely recognized that the availability of timely, accessible, accurate, and relevant information plays a key role in shaping knowledge and attitudes, which in turn serves as a driver of health-related changes. Information also influences social norms and culture by increasing awareness about what other people are doing. And information can create demand for health products and services. The more trusted and credible a source of information is, and the more relevant and resonant it is made to its target audience, the greater its potential is to influence behavior. Many studies have suggested that combining mass media with interpersonal communication or other communication activities has a greater impact than any one intervention alone.

The development paradigm on innovation for communication reaffirms the diffusion of innovations theory. Professor Everett M. Rogers, a communication scholar, sociologist, writer, and teacher, defined diffusion as a social process through which a new idea or product is communicated through certain channels over a period to individuals, communities, and society. This is translated as "the systematic utilization of appropriate communication and techniques to increase peoples' participation in development and to inform, motivate, and train rural population, mainly at the grass-root level."[2]

Being one of the fastest growing technologies in history, mobile telephony provides a fresh set of opportunities for those working to improve health outcomes in the developing world. With around 6 billion mobile phone subscriptions (and counting), global mobile penetration stands at 86%. In the developing world, mobile penetration is only slightly lower, at 79% (which means there are 79 active mobile subscriptions, or SIM cards, per 100 people).[3]

Maternal and child health indicators in the State of Bihar have remained poor even though there are a large number of evidence-based and cost-effective interventions that have shown to reduce maternal, neonatal, infant, and child mortality, and improve reproductive health and nutritional outcomes. Bihar also ranks high as one of the most rapidly expanding mobile markets. Thus, in a region where mobile phones outnumber basic amenities, such as water taps and toilets, they naturally emerge as a simple, high-impact solution for improving the survival chances of mothers and babies. An mHealth service to equip and train the frontline health workers to communicate lifesaving health information seemed to be a promising solution. That was the genesis of Mobile Kunji—a combination of a deck of cards with an interactive voice response (IVR) service.

In May 2010, the government of Bihar and the Bill & Melinda Gates Foundation signed a memorandum of cooperation to develop, test, and scale up innovative solutions to improve the health and development of Bihar's families. The partnership aims to help the government of Bihar build on its recent successes and meet its goal of reducing mortality rates for mothers, newborns, infants, and children under five by as much as

40% by 2015. This effort is being implemented in partnership with several Indian and international nongovernment organizations, and is called *Ananya*, a word meaning *unique* and *boundless* in Sanskrit. BBC Media Action leads the Shaping Demand and Practices project under the Ananya initiative. Under this project, BBC Media Action aims to help increase the demand for family health services by enhancing knowledge, changing attitudes, shifting norms, and improving risk perception using a combination of mass media, information communication technology (ICT), community mobilization, and interpersonal communication. The project has been implemented in eight priority districts in Bihar since 2011 and is currently also being scaled up to eight additional districts.

To deliver the project, BBC Media Action leads a consortium comprising Pathfinder International, which supports the delivery of interpersonal communication activities; Madison Media Plus, which supports media planning, buying, and rural marketing projects; and the GSMA Development Fund, which provides strategic, technical, and operational guidance to the project and shares best practices on health and women initiatives. The project intends to impact the 33-month critical period from the time a woman gets pregnant until the time the child is 2 years old. The following nine behavioral areas are targeted through the intervention:

- Institutional delivery
- Safe delivery at home with skilled birth attendant
- Preventive postnatal care
- Skin-to-skin/kangaroo care
- Early and exclusive breastfeeding
- Age-appropriate complementary feeding
- Postpartum family planning
- Immunization compliance
- Hand washing at critical times

The project identified specific primary and secondary participants for change as in Figure 8.1, based on an analysis of decision-making processes and the determinants of and barriers to behavior change. The primary participants for change are people who have a direct role in changing their own behavior or play a very direct role in the behavioral decision making of others. Secondary participants for change are people who either play an influential role in the decision making or hold the resources that may be required for adoption of behaviors.

Primary target of change	Secondary target of change
• Women—currently pregnant women, women with children up to 2 years • Husbands • Mothers-in-law • Front-line health workers	• Community leaders • Government • Community groups • Village health and sanitation committees

FIGURE 8.1
Targets of change.

Inception of Mobile Kunji

Shaping Demand and Practices is rooted in theoretical and practical evidence that integrated and sustainable multichannel communication and social mobilization strategies can support increased demand for and use of family health services and the adoption of recommended family health practices. In addition to the theoretical constructs of behavior change, the efforts are guided by the development of a thorough understanding of the target groups' needs, desires, aspirations, and fears, and aligning these with goals of the communication program. This people-centric approach ensures that communication activities resonate with the populations, who can actively engage in the communication to improve their knowledge, attitudes, social norms, and self-efficacy—thereby achieving sustainable behavior change. The project has adopted a 360° integrated approach as shown in Figure 8.2 to reach and surround target audiences with communication outputs.

The 360° approach implies surrounding the consumer through the use of multiple, distinct, yet complementary channels of communication that work in synergy to create a whole, that is, greater than the sum of individual parts. This implies use of multiple change agents, differing levels of engagement with various channels, and a judicious balance of intensity and reach, among target groups whose current knowledge, attitudes, norms, and self-efficacy need to be aligned with the proposed behaviors.

The communication framework for the Mobile Kunji as in Figure 8.3 was arrived at after many strategic processes, discussions, and field-testing. Keeping the target audience at the core, the behavioral objectives and communication objectives were developed around it. Only a thorough analysis and understanding of the barriers and triggers for each behavior can help in reaching the target audience. The communication objectives focus on

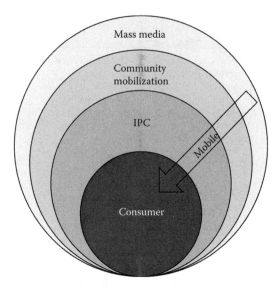

FIGURE 8.2
360° approach for communication.

knowledge—informing target audiences and making them aware, so that knowledge could then evolve or translate into simple doable actions.

The Reproductive, Maternal, Newborn, Child, and Adolescent Health (RMNCH+A) report of the Ministry of Health and Family Welfare explains that household or community education contributes to preventing health complications, quality care provided at the community level helps avoid the need for hospitalization, and sound referral systems at the primary care level support early identification of risks and better treatment for acute and complicated conditions. Hence, the essential interventions to improve the health of women and children need to take into account social determinants, such as early marriage, birth spacing, and literacy levels, both in the rural and urban settings, while including the socially disadvantaged groups. It also needs to be undertaken at all levels in the health system, that is, from the home to the community level and through all the health facilities. Also, a significant proportion of maternal, neonatal, and child deaths can be prevented by adopting key health-care practices.[4]

To improve communication education, it is therefore essential to enhance the interpersonal communication skills of the frontline health workers. This is considered critical in delivering correct and complete information with suitable arguments to convince families about simple doable actions that can lead to adoption of healthy behaviors. Lack of uniform

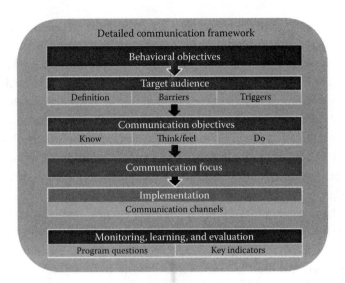

FIGURE 8.3
Detailed communication framework.

and standardized tools/job aids for conducting quality interpersonal communication by the frontline health workers was identified as an important factor to be addressed. Alongside, it was also important to motivate the frontline health workers by enhancing their recognition at the community level and providing opportunities for recognition at different platforms.

In line with the project objectives to affect knowledge, attitudes, and practices, the behaviors were further defined to address self-efficacy action, normative action, and behavior action. On the basis of the behavior, mass media, ICT, interpersonal communication, and community mobilization were used to affect the action.

Mobile Kunji: How It Works

Mobile Kunji—Kunji means a *guide* or *key* in Hindi—is an audiovisual job aid that the frontline health workers can use during counseling sessions with rural families. It seeks to build support for healthy practices within families and communities. The job aid's content aims to redress long-standing misconceptions and negative social norms around health-related maternal and child behaviors. For example, when mothers were asked why they did not follow the advice to breastfeed exclusively for the first 6 months, many said: "People in my community will think I am keeping my child hungry if I only breastfeed."

This job aid includes both an IVR-based mobile service and a printed deck of 40 illustrated cards on a ring as shown in Figure 8.4, which communicate essential information on pregnancy and newborn health. The deck of cards is designed to be portable and durable. Each card carries a short code—a unique, seven-digit number that can be dialed on the frontline health worker's mobile phone. The frontline health worker dials the short code and puts her phone on speaker mode, so that both she and the family can hear the audio content, or simply hands the phone to the pregnant woman or mother to listen. The content, which is delivered in the authoritative yet sympathetic voice of a woman doctor character, is deliberately designed to be both engaging and conversational and to reinforce the health message illustrated on the card. For example, one of the leading causes of maternal death is severe bleeding. One card encourages women to involve their husbands in decisions around planning for birth, so that families will identify their nearest hospital, make arrangements

FIGURE 8.4
Job aid.

for emergency transportation, ensure that they have their health worker's phone number handy, and save money to cover costs in case of complications during labor and delivery.

Mobile Kunji is a toll-free service that can be accessed by any health worker in Bihar from any mobile handset, across five of the largest mobile networks in India—Airtel, Vodafone, Reliance, Idea, and Tata. These operators account for approximately 80% of all mobile subscribers in Bihar. This service is based on existing contracts between BBC Media Action and the mobile network operators. Calls to Mobile Kunji can be made from any mobile handset and do not require any special or bespoke software or applications. Calls are toll-free for the frontline health workers and cost an average of 40 paisa (0.01 cents) per minute. This is more than a 90% reduction on the standard tariffs charged for a normal value-added service offered by any mobile network operator. In Bihar, these call costs are currently paid by the project but are intended to be paid by the government of Bihar.

> Now that I have Mobile Kunji, every time a woman asks me for information regarding a particular behaviour, I look at the index card of the Mobile Kunji deck of cards and choose an appropriate message. All I have to do is explain the information provided on the card and dial the number provided—I can answer all the questions the women have with ease and confidence.
>
> **Reba Rani, ASHA Health Worker, Bihar**

The Kunji was developed keeping in mind the communication framework and the final cards are the result of testing by multiple users. Each card has six elements as in Figure 8.5:

Conversation starter: It helps the frontline health workers begin talking with the woman/family about a particular health practice.

Picture/illustration: It helps give the woman/family an idea about the health practice.

Connecting sentence: It provides the gist of the message about the health practice.

Phone number: This is the number to dial directly into the audio using the mobile phone. This is where views of a woman doctor character, Dr. Anita, can be heard about the health practice and why it is important. The number can be used when the health workers are getting stuck in their conversation with the woman/family. It can also be used to validate the message by Dr. Anita.

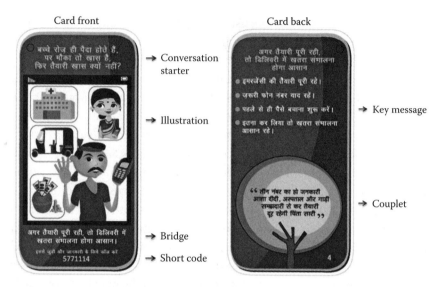

FIGURE 8.5
Kunji layout and design.

Main message: This provides the main information about the health practice that must be communicated to the woman/family.

Couplet: This summarizes the information about the health practice in one short and memorable rhyme.

I have learnt how to explain things in simple and easy language. Many times, people do not listen to us … but when they hear this mobile job aid, they respect us more.

Health Worker, Bihar

Key Processes

A mobile landscaping study was undertaken to understand the mobile ownership and usage pattern in the households of Bihar. It also provided an assessment for using mobile as a platform to share the maternal and child health messages. Overall, study results found that mobile phones offered potential for use to reach the target population on maternal and child health issues. Some of the other important observations include:

- Mobile phones alone contribute close to 20% of incremental reach over TV and radio.
- More than half the users own a mobile phone personally.

- A reasonably high proportion (60%) is also favorable toward receiving information on maternal and child health issues.
- Mobile phones are used for the most obvious purpose of communication with relatives, spouse, and friends, primarily through voice calls.
- Audiences are not very familiar with using other services/technology, so the services to be offered need to be simple in design and will require rigorous orientation.
- Average spend per month on top-up is INR 111 (US$1.85) and the majority of people perceive it to be reasonable, which suggests that users might stretch a little if the service offered and its cost are in line with their expectations.

User tests were an essential component of the innovation; field observations were utilized to make revisions in the illustrations and cards. The user experiences of health workers and beneficiaries were an important component of developing the Mobile Kunji.

Usability testing was conducted with the frontline health workers in a controlled laboratory environment for duration of 2–3 hours. Interactions of the frontline health workers with the job aid as well as conversations with the researchers were recorded both in video and audio formats. The objectives of the usability testing were to

- Understand the level of the frontline health workers' comprehension of language and content of the job aid.
- Understand the frontline health workers' ability to navigate through the job aid.
- Understand the perception toward creative content (use of couplets, phrases, etc.) and presentation of the job aid.
- Identify the need for additional content, if any, for the frontline health workers to effectively counsel beneficiaries and its nature.
- Identify effective ways of promoting the service.

Field-testing of the job aid was conducted by the research team in a live environment with the frontline health workers and beneficiaries. The objectives of field-testing were to

- Understand the usability of the job aid in context of its usage at primary health centers, Anganwadi centers, and beneficiaries' homes. (The word Anganwadi means *courtyard shelter* in Hindi. These centers were started by the Indian government in 1975 as part of the Integrated Child Development Services [ICDS] program to combat child hunger and malnutrition. A typical Anganwadi center also provides basic health care in Indian villages.)

- Understand the perceived value and usefulness of the job aid by the frontline health workers during their day-to-day work.
- Understand the reactions, responses, and level of understanding of the beneficiaries toward the content of the job aid.
- Understand the trust levels of beneficiaries toward the frontline health workers and other information sources.
- A 3-day training course was designed with content focusing on improving the interpersonal and negotiation skills of the frontline health workers. This training introduced the concept of interpersonal communication through a sales cycle approach as in Figure 8.6, wherein the frontline health workers were trained to use each contact with households/families as a sales opportunity for promoting *simple doable actions* at the household level. Using this approach, each contact between the frontline health worker and the family is presented as an opportunity to identify needs, formulate solutions, and follow up on next steps. Critical next steps must be agreed on that persuade women and their families to adopt and sustain lifesaving behaviors.

In close association with the State Health Society, Bihar and Directorate of ICDS, Department of Social Welfare, BBC Media Action, and Pathfinder

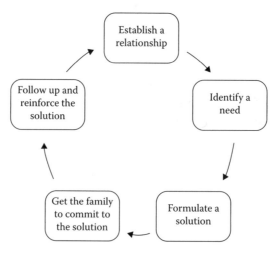

FIGURE 8.6
Sales cycle approach used for training.

International have jointly delivered this 3-day training course to 38,512 Accredited Social Health Activists (ASHAs) and Anganwadi workers ("She is a health worker chosen from the community and trained in health, nutrition and child-care. She is in charge of an Anganwadi which covers a population of 1000") over a period of 5½ months in 8 priority districts. To carry out this training, 75 master trainers were hired and trained, who in turn trained the frontline health workers across the 8 districts.

This training was planned and implemented in consultation and close coordination with the National Rural Health Mission (NRHM) and ICDS functionaries at state, district, and block levels. To conduct this training, necessary approvals on content and training modules were obtained from the State Health Society and Directorate of ICDS. Subsequently, detailed micro-plans were developed in consultation with block-level NRHM and ICDS functionaries.

"Mobile Kunji has made my job much easier," says Anganwadi worker Renu Devi from Bihar. "Without Kunji, I feel it would be almost pointless to try and convince people in my community."

Because of the inception of the Mobile Kunji, ICT log data are being recorded to understand the extent of use of the IVR services. All registered frontline health workers are monitored based on the use of number of minutes and the most dialed short codes. This also helps to identify the behavior that is most dialed for, to assess the relationship.

In May 2012 through December 2013, Mobile Kunji had 146,208 unique users, which included 31,548 frontline health workers from 8 districts of Bihar. Audio content of 5.26 million minutes had been accessed via mobile, indicating that it had been well received.

A structured analysis of this trend revealed that the interpersonal communication training of the frontline health workers significantly drove the Mobile Kunji usage—the training created a buzz in each district and played a catalytic role in initiating the Kunji usage. Currently, these trends are being analyzed to reach out to the medium and low users and encourage them to maximize Kunji usage.

Impact Evaluation and Cost-Effectiveness

Research studies are being planned to generate empirical evidence for the impact and cost-effectiveness of the Mobile Kunji. The quality of Mobile Kunji was given a lot of importance when the product was being designed. It was necessary to ensure durability and a long stay for the material used. This was kept in mind with the wear and tear possible in the working conditions of Bihar. The initial cost of the Mobile Kunji was INR 450 (US$7), including the deck of cards with a handy pouch. In response to the interest indicated by NRHM for mass production of the Mobile Kunji, a more cost-effective Kunji has been procured, which costs 40% less than the original cost. This will be priced at INR 286 (US$4.5). The new card material is equally durable, lighter, and of similar quality.

Challenges

It cannot be denied that any new product does face challenges at the outset. One of the emerging challenges has been related to the frontline health workers' inability to use the IVR service. This is due to the lack of battery charge on their mobile phones. It is also sometimes difficult to ensure that the frontline health worker uses the Mobile Kunji at every home visit.

Through various activities and promotions, Kunji usage is being furthered. The evaluation study hopefully will provide effective results on mapping the density of the use of Mobile Kunji.

Way Forward

It is expected that the low-cost Kunji will be scaled up to the remaining districts of Bihar, as it has been included as a core component of a common minimum package of solutions proposed by the government of Bihar. Support for cost of production has been sought by the government, thus helping the innovation to be adopted at a mass scale.

The innovativeness of the Mobile Kunji has attracted the attention of governments from different States and many international organizations. The compact size and easy access to information through a deck of cards and the IVR has been appreciated by everyone.

Currently, BBC Media Action is collaborating with Sector Wide Approach to Strengthen Health (SWASTH) to support the overall efforts of the government of Bihar by scaling up interpersonal communication skill enhancement for the frontline health workers in additional districts. BBC Media Action is supporting the training of independent master trainers with the Bihar Technical Assistance Support Team (BTAST) and Nutrition Management Unit (NMU) on Mobile Kunji in nine additional districts. In a recent partnership with ICDS, new cards on growth monitoring, malnutrition symptoms, and micronutrient deficiencies are being added to the deck of cards to be used by the Anganwadi workers.

The Mobile Kunji training is also being integrated with the 5-day ASHA training module conducted by the ASHA resource center. Pilot initiatives are being undertaken for effective integration of the Mobile Kunji training.

The Mobile Kunji is planned to be rolled out within a few months in other States like Uttar Pradesh and Orissa. The Kunji will be adapted to the regional language in both the States.

The success of Mobile Kunji is evident from its popularity and demand.

> Mobile Kunji became a handy tool in the art of persuasion for Renu Devi, a front line health worker from the Patna. Initially Renu Devi did not find much success counseling families. But things started looking up as Renu Devi attended the BBC Media Action training on interpersonal communication and job aid—Mobile Kunji. Impressed and convinced by the simple, doable things taught in the training and the audio component of the job aid, she decided to use it while counselling families. She would refer to her job aid while conversing with families and it supported her with the required logic. In one particular instance, the family who had been very averse to Family Planning initially, not only adopted it, but has also been urging their neighbours to opt for Family Planning.

SUGHAVAZHVU HEALTHCARE

Background

There is a significant disparity in access to basic health care in India. Although 70% of Indian population resides in rural areas, over 70% of India's medical infrastructure is concentrated in urban areas. The health-care expenditure in India is around INR 2500 (US$50) per capita on health care with the government spending limited to only INR 500 (US$10) per capita. Over 70% of health-care expenditure in India is out-of-pocket, two-thirds of which is on primary care. An additional 20 million people in India are driven below the poverty line every year due to catastrophic health expenditure. The inadequate supply of qualified health-care practitioners in modern medicine in rural geographies leaves the health of rural populations largely in the hands of unqualified and unlicensed practitioners, who constitute the sizeable unorganized primary health-care market in India.[5]

The IKP Centre for Technologies in Public Health (ICTPH) is working on devising innovative solutions to tackle the challenges in the provision of health care to the rural populations. ICTPH is a fully owned subsidiary of

IKP Trust and is a company under Section 25 of the Companies Act (1956). It is currently funded entirely by the IKP Trust. IKP Trust's mission is to enable the use of advanced scientific knowledge for the progress of society. In particular, it seeks to focus on the intersection of information technology and life sciences and incubates organizations that explore different facets of this intersection in a manner that adds value to society. ICTPH aims to demonstrate sustainable and scalable models of health-care delivery for rural Indian populations. The central objective of the research work at ICTPH is to develop frameworks that address the challenges of human resources and limited finances, so that both the public sector as well as the private sector that is interested in these issues can ensure the delivery of high quality health care even to the remotest of rural Indian populations.

The framework developed by ICTPH seeks to deliver health outcomes at the population level through a combination of community-level monitoring and the provision of continuous care at the local level. SughaVazhvu Healthcare functions at the interface of technology and human resource innovation to ensure evidence-based primary health care is provided to rural Indian populations. With a strong focus on early risk assessment, community-based, technology-enabled strategies implemented through mobile phones ensure community-based and community-driven disease mapping and surveillance. In their innovative approach, which is focused on rural India, a community-based, physician-staffed health-care center, assisted by a village-based health extension worker, providing the broadest possible range of health-care services (including dental fillings and scaling, cervical cancer screening, vision screening and dispensation of glasses, and management of chronic diseases) at the primary level, sits at the core of a sustainable model of *proactive* health-care delivery. ICTPH in collaboration with SughaVazhvu Healthcare, a local health-care provider in Tamil Nadu, has rolled out its health-care delivery model to field-test it and to eventually demonstrate its effectiveness in the rural Indian context.

SughaVazhvu Healthcare was featured in *Express Healthcare* (one of the leading health-care magazines in India) as one of the *13 Game Changer Ideas* within the Indian health-care landscape.

SughaVazhvu Healthcare: How It Works

Before the launch of a rural clinic, the entire catchment population of 8,000–10,000 people (2,500 households) are enrolled and issued bar coded identity cards to create the seed database for the rural clinic. The enrollment exercise is accomplished using Android mobile phones, compatible with field enrollment software developed by a Bangalore-based company—Artoo Technologies. The enrollment exercise is accomplished for a new site in a week's time, using 6–8 local village residents, trained for 2 days. The enrollment exercise captures the name, age, and gender of each family member residing in a given household, along with latitude and longitude (GPS coordinates) of the household. Each individual is promised a free health check-up at the center, which interestingly costs the organization itself a paltry amount of INR 5 (US$0.08).[6]

The cumulative population database from the enrollment exercise allows for continuous patient management and also aids landscape epidemiology, providing intelligence into utilization of specific services, geographical distribution of diseases, and surveillance of outbreaks.

After the launch of a rural clinic, another community-based intervention called the *Rapid Risk Assessment* is launched within the catchment area. The objective of this assessment is to identify high-risk subpopulations as target groups for specific interventions. The Android mobile phone–based exercise captures marital status; pregnancy; blood pressure; anthropometric measures—weight, height, waist, hip circumference, and personal history—diabetes and blood pressure, and tobacco consumption. All adult individuals identified at risk, primarily for cardiovascular disease and pregnancy, are given diagnostic vouchers for aiding confirmatory assessment such as plasma glucose and cholesterol values.

A typical rural clinic is a 500 square foot rented facility in the village common place. The space is refurbished to suit the requirements of a primary healthcare center. Each rural clinic primarily has three sections:

1. Patient waiting area: This includes space for the health extension worker to screen patients. This space is equipped with necessary screening devices, such as a Snellen chart, weighing machine, stature meter, sample display of vision glasses for myopia and hyperopia, Internet-enabled laptop, and printer.
2. Physician consultation room (almost 50%–60% of space): This is equipped with an examination bed; pharmacy unit; blood collection unit including centrifuge, refrigerator, and strip-based diagnostic tests, such as blood glucose and hemoglobin; emergency management unit for basic dressing and suturing; vision assessment unit (trial lens set, ophthalmoscope, and retinoscope); autoclave unit; and Internet-enabled laptop.
3. Cervical screening room: This is equipped with a cervical screening bed and necessary equipment such as speculums and so on.

The ICTPH Essential Drug List consists of 11 broad categories: (1) endocrine system, (2) cardiovascular system, (3) nonsteroidal anti-inflammatory drugs, (4) respiratory system, (5) gastrointestinal tract, (6) immune system, (7) anti-infective, (8) nutritional, (9) vaccines, (10) local anesthetics, and (11) skin. A total of 43 single formulation drugs (barring a few exceptions) are available as a part of the standard rural clinic pharmacy.

As developed by ICTPH, their Health Management Information System (HMIS) is the first-of-its-kind primary health-care management tool in India. Other than capturing patient–physician interaction, the web-based, open source HMIS has fully functional units for supply chain management and human resource management, inclusive of training and integration with Android-based mobile platforms for data integration. Modules such as monitoring and evaluation, clinical audit, clinical data analysis, and community disease mapping aided by geovisualization are also under development.

Each rural clinic is staffed by a locally hired physician assisted by a locally hired health extension worker. The physician typically holds an undergraduate degree in the Ayurveda or Siddha systems of medicine, and is certified by ICTPH as a primary care practitioner, after successful completion of their 3-month long bridge training program. This training enables the practitioners to practice disease management protocols of ICTPH that govern the assessment and management of 82 common primary care conditions that primarily include management of infectious diseases and noncommunicable diseases, eye examination for refractive error correction, cataract detection, basic fundus examination, eye infections aided by prescription and dispensing glasses, and cervical screening including cervical cancer.

One of the rural clinics operates a referral laboratory, where trained personnel perform hematology, blood biochemistry, and simple strip-based tests to manage disease burden among village residents. Advanced diagnostic capability will be made available at all rural clinics. All rural clinics will facilitate blood collection, and sample preparation of either whole blood or blood serum for transportation to the SughaVazhvu diagnostic hub for processing and evaluation. Most significantly, hematology and biochemical parameters, such as blood glucose, lipid profile, and so on, will be made available through the entire rural clinic network with a turnaround of 24 hours.

SughaVazhvu Healthcare follows a user fee-driven model. The patient pays INR 15 (US$0.25) per consultation. All tests at the clinic are priced at

INR 30–150 (US$0.5–2.5), which is 30%–40% less than the average market rates. A cross-subsidization approach is used for providing these services free of cost to patients who cannot afford to pay. A total of 30%–40% of patients at the clinics fall in this category.

The core management team at SughaVazhvu Healthcare is responsible for appropriate site selection based on criteria such as accessibility, connectivity, and private and public health-care provider landscape followed by establishing the rural clinic. The locations of the SughaVazhvu rural micro-health centers (RMHCs) are chosen to ensure exclusivity as compared to other health-care providers in the geography. As part of general management and rural clinic network maintenance, the core team is responsible for

- Physician and health extension worker training and continuous medical education
- Pharmacy management across the rural clinic network
- Daily blood movement from rural clinics to diagnostics laboratory
- Audit, compliance, and performance management
- Patient satisfaction
- General network upkeep and maintenance
- Technology (HMIS) management and data analytics
- Outcome evaluation research

Coverage

As a village-based rural primary care provider, SughaVazhvu today is a network of seven clinics in rural Thanjavur, district of Tamil Nadu, and has served more than 30,000 patient visits. On an average, SughaVazhvu Healthcare serves 2000–2500 patient visits each month across its network.

Challenges

Providing health care in rural settings has its own set of challenges. On the supply side, finding the right human resources, training them, and retaining them long enough to have them imbibe principles of the organization has been the biggest challenge. On the demand side, adoption of the services has been challenging. It has been an enormous task to make the communities believe in the scientific approach followed at the clinics vis-à-vis the village quacks they have been visiting who make them feel much better *just with one injection*. SughaVazhvu Healthcare has been focusing very sharply on community engagement, which is crucial for uptake of primary health-care services. The organization has been actively engaging with champion leaders, panchayats, self-help groups, and schools to increase the participation of communities in the initiative.

Way Forward

ICTPH along with SughaVazhvu Healthcare will double its rural clinic network from 7 to 14 in 2014. They also plan to set up semiurban clinics, which will have a catchment of around 10 villages. Compared to 8–10 patients visiting a clinic in a day at present, 40–50 patients are expected to visit the new clinics in a day. This will strengthen the business model of SughaVazhvu Healthcare. ICTPH is also working with an established tertiary care hospital to replicate a network of seven clinics to establish India's first integrated care delivery model for rural Indian populations. ICTPH is planning to work with governments too through public–private partnerships for implementing integrated health-care model in public health delivery system. ICTPH's Centre of Excellence in collaboration with the University of Pennsylvania will launch the joint certificate program for alternate practitioners in evidence-based primary care.

Going forward, the organization plans to work with multiple field partners across the country including States such as Orissa and Uttarakhand. ICTPH and SughaVazhvu are also collaborating to develop a full *Managed Care* program for rural populations, building on their unique primary care delivery model to offer a full-service model of health care and financial protection.

The success of this initiative is resounded by Amrithavalli S. who visited the newly inaugurated health center in her village four times. Earlier, she used to spend INR 40 (US$0.67) traveling 2–3 hours to the government hospital nearest to her Andipatti village in Thanjavur, district of Tamil Nadu. Now, she and her family have health check-ups done and their ailments treated at the clinic. It is a big relief for them. "This centre is closer to my place. I can just walk it," Amrithavalli says. "Here, they take really good care of your health."[6]

SUMMARY

The two initiatives described earlier are designed to improve the health status of the populations through innovative approaches. Mobile Kunji seeks to build support for healthy practices within families and communities by redressing long-standing misconceptions and negative social norms around health-related maternal and child behaviors, by means of a unique audiovisual job aid that includes both an IVR-based mobile service and a printed deck of 40 illustrated cards, which communicate essential information on pregnancy and newborn health. The frontline health workers are trained to use this job aid during counseling sessions with rural families.

SughaVazhvu Healthcare functions at the interface of technology and human resource innovation to ensure provision of evidence-based primary health care to rural Indian populations. Their model uniquely hinges on proactive care delivery vis-à-vis reactive care delivery. With a strong focus on early risk assessment, community-based, technology-enabled strategies implemented through mobile phones ensure community-based and community-driven disease mapping and surveillance.

In both cases, information technology is an important component of the innovation. Similar systems have been used in developed economies for some time. It is encouraging to see the use of ICT-based tools in high-volume primary care in rural areas of India. This also involves technology leapfrogging to some extent as some of the systems are directly using mobile devices.

Mobile Kunji has been endorsed by the State government of Bihar and is also receiving interest from other State governments. Going forward, it has potential for a nationwide rollout. SughaVazhvu Healthcare, although currently operating at a relatively smaller scale, has plans to ramp up its operations in the near future and also work with State governments.

What remains to be seen is how much each of the innovations at its current and potential scale contributes to improvement of public health indicators. Robust and systematic studies will need to be undertaken to evaluate the impact of these innovations on relevant health indicators of the concerned populations. This evidence will strengthen the case for replicability and scalability of these solutions and also expedite the diffusion of innovations, which otherwise are known to disseminate slowly—if at all.

ACKNOWLEDGMENTS

The generous contribution of BBC Media Action and SughaVazhvu Healthcare in form of discussions, materials, and feedback is sincerely appreciated.

REFERENCES

1. Fung, M., Simpson, S. and Packer, C. (2010). Identification of innovation in public health. *Journal of Public Health*, 33(1): 123–130.
2. UNICEF. (2005). Strategic communication for behaviour and social change in South Asia. Working Paper.
3. MacPherson, Y. and Chamberlain, S. (2013). Health on the Move: Can Mobile Phones Save Lives? BBC Media Action Policy Briefing # 7.
4. Ministry of Health and Family Welfare, Government of India. (2013). A Strategic Approach to Reproductive, Maternal, Newborn, Child and Adolescent Health (RMNCH+A) in India.
5. Planning Commission of India. (2011). High Level Expert Group Report on Universal Health Coverage for India.
6. Sivaramakrishnan, V. (2011). Healthcare @ INR 5. *Outlook Business*. 62–63.

9

Behavior Changes, the Last Mile in Health Care

Shiban Ganju

CONTENTS

The success of health service distribution depends on the last mile, where adequate supply matches demand from enlightened customers. The prevailing model of health-care delivery in rural India focuses more on the supply of health care through public and private providers. There is little emphasis on demand generation, which depends on the individual's ability to access and afford health care. In traditional societies, demand is not only a matter of individual choices, but values, attitudes, and norms held by local communities. Creating community demand could reduce preventable diseases, which form a significant portion of the total disease burden[1,2] and morbidity rate of India.[3]

The poor need two instruments to be active participants in health care: financial tools such as insurance to purchase health care and health literacy to seek health. Affordability is the relation between cost of care and purchasing power. Access, however, is more complex. It involves structural issues such as availability or distance and cognitive issues such as understanding of symptoms and the ability to articulate needs. Health literacy empowers people to overcome structural barriers to care and improves community health outcomes at a low cost.

Save A Mother (SAM), an NGO working in Uttar Pradesh (UP) and Karnataka in India, has been working on demand generation by spreading health literacy through social behavior change communication (SBCC). SAM is driven by a mission to develop health-care solutions for the poor. Since 2008, the NGO has worked among over 2 million people in over 1000 villages in 6 districts of UP and Karnataka. This population provides a platform to innovate and validate models for health-care solutions with the participation of communities. The solutions are flexible and modular for each problem to facilitate adoption by other communities. The design is kept simple, sustainable, and scalable with speed.

SAM trains community volunteers as health leaders who serve as a conduit for delivery of knowledge to the community. SAM has trained over 3500 volunteer village health activists, over 5½ years through December 2013, and continues to train more every month. The process is a nonstop campaign with no preset end point.

On the basis of SAM experience, this chapter describes some innovations in SBCC and the impact on maternal-neonatal mortality reduction and detection of tuberculosis.

BACKGROUND

Health literacy is a process of health promotion through health education and communication activities. Ownership of the new knowledge by the community, perpetuated through a visible and tangible benefit, is the end goal. Acceptance of behavior change in health care by a community takes a long time because of slow visible effects, obstacles of local culture, and complexity of solutions. For acceptance of a new idea, it should have a demonstrable advantage over the old idea and be compatible with the existing social norms.[4,5]

Various successful practices of SBCC have theoretical foundations. Social cognitive theory describes how environmental and personal factors affect each other. Learning should be done by observation and reinforcements.[6] The theory of diffusion of innovations emphasizes that a new idea disseminates in a society through stages of innovation, evolution of communication channels, and social networks.[7] Community organization theory believes that a community's strength can be developed by building community capacity over a key issue and community participation raises critical awareness.[8] Theories of planned behavior and reasoned action dwell on attitudes and social acceptance of behavior based on reasoned action or perceived behavioral control,[9] which leads to a modified behavior. The theory of stages of change asserts that an individual goes through stages of precontemplation, contemplation, preparation, action, and maintenance to induce a change based on reasoned action.[10]

SAVE A MOTHER INNOVATION

Relying on the vast experience of others and employing proven methods of communication, SAM has included four innovative elements in its SBCC program.

Responsibility-Based Approach

SAM believes that maintaining health is as much a responsibility as it is a right. Emphasizing a pure rights-based approach transfers the burden of the solution to an external agency. It creates dependency and the solution is likely to last as long as the agency responds. For a sustainable effect, a community should take responsibility of its health of a health-care program.

Voluntary Health Activism

The responsibility approach implies that health maintenance should be voluntary. Any monetary compensation makes health maintenance a profit-driven activity and will last as long as profit can be made; absence of disease by itself should serve as a reward. SAM trains village volunteers to perpetuate the message of health, which is likely to produce motivated leaders to assume responsibility for their communities and make preventive health care affordable.

Songs and Slogans with Cultural Context

SAM simplifies complex knowledge into a few essential messages. Communities convert these messages into songs and slogans. A community develops its own original song for each health issue such as maternal health, population stabilization, and immunization. SAM hopes that the songs and slogans will become part of the community culture that is transmitted through generations.

Repetition

SAM engages in continual message delivery without an end point. Repetition of a message seems to have a lasting transforming effect as we have known from the experience of religious organizations.

SAVE A MOTHER MODEL

SAM has developed a replicable tool, Effective Social Persuasion Platform (SAM-ESP), to decrease disease burden. It is a low-cost training platform, which uses principles of SBCC for a community to modify its health-seeking behavior to prevent disease.

SAM-ESP is based on three assumptions. First, health literacy is an inexpensive way to decrease burden of diseases. If people are aware of simple preventive measures, many diseases will not even manifest and thus the expenditure on treatment will be avoided. Second, health is an individual and community responsibility. Ownership of responsibility sustains the change beyond the initial project time and empowers a community to demand health care. Third, a sustained, repetitive, and intense campaign to push health information can persuade a community to modify behavior.

METHOD

SAM-ESP uses seven steps to develop a modular SBCC solution for a health-care issue.

The following describes the SBCC steps in detail as in Figure 9.1.

Organize the Structure and Build Capacity

Each district constitutes a unit for dissemination of health literacy. A program manager, trainers, and supervisors are selected from the local population. They receive intensive training on health issues, motivational techniques, and leadership for SBCC. The organization is lean on the top and heavy at the bottom; there are more volunteers than supervisors as in Figure 9.2.

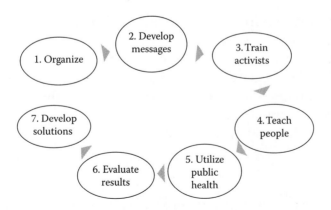

FIGURE 9.1
Program steps.

FIGURE 9.2
Manpower organization structure for one district.

Develop Messages for Health Literacy

SAM uses local community talent to create flip charts, slogans, songs, and stories. A good message is simple and focuses on only one issue; it is short for easy recall; it has clarity for easy comprehension; and it is structured as a story, song, or a slogan and evokes emotions about an unmet need. The community is encouraged to own the message by participating in developing the message.

Train Health Activists

Master trainers impart health education to volunteer health activists over a 3-day period on one health topic. Each topic of health care has a separate training module. Examples are child and maternal health, tuberculosis (TB) eradication, and population stabilization. Repeat refresher training for ½–1 day is given once a month. Volunteer health activists are encouraged to own responsibility for village health.

The staff performs the following functions:

Teach People

SAM organizes a village into an interactive health-care community. Master trainers and health activists meet with the villagers every week to discuss health issues and best practices to promote health and prevent

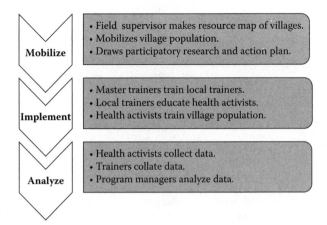

FIGURE 9.3
Functions of staff.

disease. Health behavior modification messages are delivered repeatedly at these meetings. Repetitive SBCC, education campaigns, and training of health volunteers are essential elements of the program. Between 2008 and 2011, SAM held multiple training sessions for the volunteers, who in turn held weekly SBCC discussion groups at the village level. Tables 9.1 and 9.2 illustrate that the training sessions are repetitive and intense with no preset end point. Figure 9.3 summarizes the functions of the staff.

Cooperate with Public Health Workers

Utilizing all available public health resources is the essential component of the program. Public health workers are invited to all meetings to establish linkages with the local public health system. The linkages create awareness, which leads to increased demand and encourages accountability of the health system.

TABLE 9.1

Number of Social Behavior Change Communication Sessions, Villages, and Volunteers from May 2008 to June 2011

Number of SBCC sessions	994
Villages covered	854
Village volunteers trained	Over 2000

TABLE 9.2

Frequency and Duration of Social Behavior Change Communication Training and Village Sessions

Activity	First Year	Second Year	Third Year	Duration
Training of trainers	First month	First month		4 days
Induction training for village volunteers	Five per month	Nine per month		3 days
Refresher training volunteers	Two per month	Six per month	Seven per month	1 day
Sensitization of health officials	One per month	One per month	One per month	½ day

Evaluate and Improve

All programs are monitored and course correction applied based on the learning from the field. Modifications to training are done by participatory research action and community involvement as shown in Figure 9.4.

Develop Solutions and Replicate

The field experience helps SAM to innovate modular solutions for the health care of the rural poor. SAM develops these solutions in an innovation zone of approximately 2 million people in about 800 villages in UP. The solutions are further validated and modified in over 300 villages in three districts in northern Karnataka. The solutions are kept simple, sustainable, and scalable. SAM, in partnership with other institutions, replicates the solution in other districts.

IMPACT OF SAM-ESP (SBCC) ON MATERNAL-NEONATAL MORTALITY

SAM started the health literacy program in May 2008. After over 3 years by June 2011, SAM was working in 854 villages. SAM collected baseline data before the program from 1550 pregnancies in 256 villages and compared it with 7719 pregnancies from 854 villages after 36 months of the

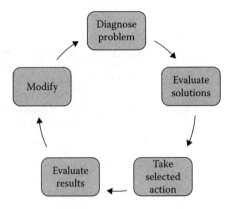

FIGURE 9.4
Evaluation and program improvement.

program. After 5 years, the impact of the program was reevaluated again up to December 2013.

Qualitative Impact

Women had better awareness of government-sponsored programs. Community support for public health workers increased. The sense of responsibility improved among government functionaries. Data collection improved. Community members internalized best practices in health care. Health-seeking behavior improved.

Quantitative Impact

SAM successfully used SAM-ESP to decrease maternal mortality by 92% and neonatal mortality by 57% in about 854 villages in UP after about 3 years of the program. The annual cost was less than Rs. 10,000 per village with an average population of 2000. The effect seems sustainable after 5 years. In an evaluation done in January 2014, there were zero maternal deaths in a sample of 1503 child births, which consisted of about 10% of total deliveries in the district as in Table 9.3.

In 2011, SAM replicated the maternal health program in the Gadag, Dharwad, and Hospet districts in Karnataka. After 18 months of the program, an evaluation in January 2013 indicated that the trend in maternal and neonatal mortality reduction was similar to that in UP.

The reduction in maternal mortality can partly be attributed to the National Rural Health Mission (NRHM). But the SAM program amplified

TABLE 9.3

Impact of Save A Mother Program on Mortality

Events	Baseline Data for 256 Villages for 6 Months before the Program	Impact in 854 Villages after 36 Months of Program	Reduction in Expected Deaths after 36 Months (%)	Evaluation in 309 Villages from March 13 to January 14 5 Years after the Program
Number of children delivered	1550	7719		1503
Maternal deaths	10	4	92	0
Neonatal deaths	63	43	57	9

the impact. A comparison was done in the Gadag district between 107 villages where SAM worked along with NRHM and 97 adjacent villages where NRHM worked without SAM presence. Tetanus immunization rates were 20% higher and neonatal mortality was 78% lower in the combined program (Table 9.4).

EXTERNAL VALIDATION OF MATERNAL MORTALITY PROGRAM

SAM invited a research team from the International Institute of Health Management Research, Delhi, to study the impact of SAM program. They evaluated "Save A Mother—Effective Persuasion Platform" in selected blocks of Shahgarh, Sangrampur, Gauriganj, and Musafir Khana in UP. They surveyed women in the reproductive age group through focus group discussions and interviews with key informants. They evaluated outcomes of behavior change, resource mobilization by the community for maternal health, health-seeking behavior, hygiene practices, and coordination among different health workers. The key findings were health volunteers were a major source for dissemination of information on health issues, which resulted in improved health and hygiene practices. Initiatives increased institutional deliveries, immunizations, utilization of health facilities, access to transport, and finances. A close-knit working

TABLE 9.4

Save A Mother Amplifies the Impact of National Rural Health Mission

Gadag, Karnataka	Maternal Mortality Rate	Neonatal Mortality Rate	Tetanus Immunization Rate (%)
SAM + NRHM in 107 villages	186	8.6	79
NRHM alone in 97 villages	199	39	59

relationship existed between public health workers and SAM health volunteers. Enhanced awareness on health, increased participation in decision making, and acceptance by men with due recognition to women brought a remarkable change in health status and development of villages. A working relationship with local self-help groups improved financial security. Women's health correlated with social development.

They concluded that a strong need exists to recognize the importance of volunteers in behavior change communication and their crucial role in tracking women's health status. They recommended that the voices of SAM health volunteers should be heard by policy makers to bring a change at the program level with improved resource allocation.

SAVE A MOTHER TUBERCULOSIS CONTROL PROGRAM

SAM has successfully applied its experience in maternal health to other major health-care issues, namely tuberculosis control, population stabilization, and water-borne diseases. Preliminary results are available for TB control program while the other programs are in the early stages at the time of this writing.

In April 2012, a pilot program for tuberculosis control was started in 24 villages with a total population of over 74,000. Repeated SBCC for population mobilization and health literacy campaigns were conducted for 15 months until July 2013. People with symptoms suggestive of TB were encouraged to get their sputum tested. All those with TB bacilli in sputum were enrolled in the treatment program with public health facilities.

Out of 4734 people with symptoms who attended the first SBCC sessions, 2322 went for the sputum test. Of 869 people who attended a second or third session, all went for a sputum test. 1543 people who attended only one session did not go for the sputum test (Table 9.5).

Lessons from the Tuberculosis Program

Behavior change communication helped detect 10 times more new cases of active TB. Prior to the launch of the pilot program, there were only 19 sputum positive patients under treatment in these villages. The SAM-ESP program detected 192 new cases through behavior change communication. All of them went for DOTS treatment; 185 recovered, four died, one migrated, one dropped out of treatment, and one stayed sputum positive after treatment.

Repetitive communication sessions were more effective. All (100%) who attended more than one session went for the sputum test while only 49% of those who attended one session went for the sputum test. In July 2013, SAM replicated this program with a new block of 44 villages and applied lessons from the pilot program to emphasize early detection and work in close partnership with the local public health TB control personnel. The results are awaited from this ongoing program.

TABLE 9.5

Effect of Social Behavior Change Communication for Tuberculosis Detection and Control

	Number of People	**Percent**	**Sputum Positive for TB**
People with symptoms who attended one community session	4734		
People who went for sputum test after one session	2322	0.49	172
People who went for sputum test after two sessions	869	0.184	20
People who did not go for sputum test after two sessions	1543	0.326	

AFFORDABILITY OF SAM-ESP

The per capita annual cost for the program has been INR 5 or approximately 8 cents, which may rise up to 16 cents as the program expands. Use of health volunteers, locally recruited staff, lean top management, and a culture of frugal innovation minimizes the expenditure.

SUMMARY

Health literacy is probably the least expensive way to reduce disease burden. SBCC for better health should have two objectives: changing the mind-set to a new option and sustaining it through social acceptance and empowerment. Mere transfer of information, however, to a community is not enough; the community must exercise ownership over this knowledge. Others have used the foundation of behavior theory to create many successful methods of communication. The public health model[11] consists of defining the problem, identifying the risk, developing strategies, testing, and dissemination. The precede and proceed[12] approach considers social, epidemiological, environmental, and educational factors to make policies. The health belief[13] model considers individual response based on perceived threat of disease and benefit of changing behavior. The health promotion model[14] includes health literacy to enhance awareness to encourage healthy lifestyles. The ecological/social factors model[9] focuses on surrounding environmental and sociological influences, which modify a person's behavior.

Although utilizing the vast experience of others, SAM added a few innovations: community responsibility, volunteerism, and repetitive simple messaging. The innovations ensure that SBCC is replicable, sustainable, and affordable. Early experience validates that the model is replicable in different geographical locations and can also be used for different healthcare problems. Sustainability is ensured by keeping the ownership with the community and not transferring it to an external agency as in a rights-based approach. Volunteerism keeps the program affordable.

These low-cost innovations seem to have had the desired impact in less than 3 years, as measured by an over 92% decrease in maternal deaths, 57% decrease in neonatal mortality, and 10-fold increase in detection of TB. The success has not only sustained but also enhanced further over 5 years. Whether these innovations will translate into long-term sustainability will be known only after a few years. SBCC, however, seems to be a valid tool to accomplish the social transformation in health-seeking behavior.

REFERENCES

1. National Health Profile (2010): www.cbhidghs.nic.in.
2. Indira Gandhi Institute of Development Research, Mumbai (March 2008): http://www.igidr.ac.in/pdf/publication/WP-2008-007.pdf.
3. Government of India (2006A). Morbidity, healthcare and the condition of the aged, NSS 60th Round (January–June 2004) NSS Report No 507, National Sample Survey Organization, New Delhi.
4. Goldman, K.D. and Schmalz, K.J. (2001). Theoretically speaking: Overview and summary of key health theories. *Health Promotion Practice* 2(4): 277–281.
5. United Nations Children Fund, UNICEF (2005). Strategic communication for behaviour and social change in South Asia, working paper, Regional office South Asia.
6. Bandura, A (2004). Health promotion by social cognitive means: *Health Education & Behaviur* 31(2): 143–164.
7. Grrenhalgh, T, Macfarlane, F, Bate, P, and Kyriakidu, O. (2004). Diffusion of innovations in service organizations; systemic review and recommendations. *Milbank Quarterly* 82(4): 581–629.
8. Weiner, BJ. (2009). Using organization theory to understand the determinants of health, http://her:oxfordjournals.org/content/24/2/292.full.pdf.
9. Green, LW and Kreuther, MW (2005). *Health Program: An Educational and Ecological Approach*; 4th edition, New York: Mcgraw-Hill.
10. National Cancer Institute (2005). *Theory at a Glance: A Guide for Health Promotion Practice*, U.S. Department of health and human services: National Institutes of Health.
11. Glanz, K, Rimer, B.K., and Vishwanath, K. (2008). *Health Behavior and Health Education, Theory, Research and Practice*, San Francisco: Jossey-Bass.
12. Ying Li, Jia Cao, Hui Lin, Yang Wang, and Jia he (2009). Community needs assessment with precede-proceed model: a mixed method study, http://biomedicentral.com/1472-6963/9/181.
13. Eisen, M, Zellman, G.L., and McAlister, A.L. (1992). A health belief model; social learning theory approach to adolescents' fertility control: Findings from a controlled field trial. *Health Education Quarterly* 19(2): 249–262.
14. Stokols, D. (1996). Translating social ecological theory into guidelines for community health promotion. *American Journal of Health promotion* 10(4): 282–298.

10

Cost-Effective, Scalable, and Sustainable Model for Primary Health Care

Ankur Pegu and Sundeep Kapila

CONTENTS

INTRODUCTION

This is a turning point in human history. For the first time ever, the majority of the world's population is living in cities, and this proportion continues to grow. In India, more than half of the urban population is estimated to live in slums characterized by overcrowding, poor hygiene and sanitation, and the absence of civic services.[1] In this context, the health needs of urban poor in India need to be addressed, as depicted in Figure 10.1.

WHO and UN Habitat have clearly established the direct link between economic inequity and health inequity.[2] The urban poor face a significantly higher disease burden compared to their rural counterparts driven by higher risk factors such as air pollution, water pollution, poor sanitation, stress, unhealthy diet, and lack of sleep. These risk factors expose them to the triple threat to their health—infections, noncommunicable diseases, and injuries. Urban Indian poor are also vulnerable to further impoverishment and missed growth opportunities, due to high out-of-pocket health spending, which in India stands for 86%[3] of total private expenditure of health. Health shocks are the single biggest cause of impoverishment in India, pushing between 32 and 63 million Indians below the poverty line each year as per varying estimates.[4,5] The situation will get worse with migration and a rapidly increasing population of urban poor living in slums.

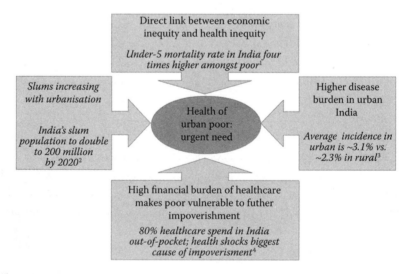

FIGURE 10.1

Why the health of urban Indian poor is an urgent need.

[1]UN-Habitat and WHO report. Hidden cities: Unmasking and overcoming health inequities in urban setting

[2]UN-Habitat

[3]National Family Survey (NFHS)-3 Data (India)

[4]WHO

UNCOVERING THE LEVER FOR CHANGE

In 2008, a social enterprise, Swasth India, was founded to address impoverishment due to health shocks. After 3 years of extensive grassroots work impacting 220,000 lives across urban and rural India, Swasth's team uncovered the key lever for change, primary preventive care, often overlooked by stakeholders. Affordable, quality primary preventive care could reduce health shocks by half. This, in turn, could reduce total system costs and improve health outcomes. Further, primary care provisioning could improve renewal rates of health financing schemes by two to three times. Recent studies[4] have reached similar conclusions. A total of 5.1% of Indian households incur catastrophic health expenditure each year. Research[4] has shown that if in-patient (IP) health-care facilities are available for no payment, the percentage of these households goes down to 4.2%. However, removing outpatient (OP) payments is five times more effective, and brings down the percentage of Indian households suffering catastrophic health expenditures to only 0.8%.

CURRENT PRIMARY HEALTH-CARE PROVIDER CONTEXT

Urban poor have three key needs for primary health care: affordability, convenience, and quality. Primary health-care provisioning efforts should focus on providing an optimal mix of these three needs. None of the existing service providers are able to fulfill them, as depicted in Figure 10.2.

Public provisioning in India is affordable as most treatment is free, but inadequate, due to an extremely low network density in urban areas. Further, it suffers from nonavailability of infrastructure and staff, long queues, and lack of respect for the poor. Similarly, charitable clinics are affordable, but lack scale and service quality guarantees due to their individual centric nature. Consequently, the urban, below the poverty line (BPL) population, is forced to resort to a largely unregulated private sector, which accounts for over 80% of health-care spending.[6] Private sector provisioning is expensive, causing out-of-pocket expenditure on private providers to constitute 15% of household income of urban BPL.[7] Further, malpractice is rampant due to incentives being aligned to financial gain rather than health outcomes.

L Low M Medium H High	Affordability	Quality	Convenience	Remarks
Public-/ govt.- sponsored	H	L	L	• Most treatment free • Very low network density • Multiple quality challenges: unavailability of staff and infrastructure, long queues
Charitable clinics	M	M	L	• Lack quality guarantee/ professional methodology • Small network as clinics individual-centric
Private clinics	L	M	M	• Price ~2x of other options • Doctor incentive: financial gain, not health outcomes • Dense network, but need to travel to multiple providers (clinic, pharmacy, lab)
Optimal value proposition	M	H	H	One-stop-shop for all needs • 50% savings on OOP • Quality and process control

FIGURE 10.2

Primary care needs of urban poor—an optimal mix of convenience, affordability, and quality.

THE MODEL

Swasth has set up a dense network of Swasth Health Centers (SHCs) providing one-stop access to high-quality health-care services at half the market rates. The model has four key components:

- Centres to provide all primary care services—doctor consultation, diagnostics, drugs, day care, and dental services, as shown in Figure 10.3. Swasth has developed its own electronic medical records (EMR), available at each clinic for the doctor to refer to patient history. The data are also accessible to the patients on the cloud as well at any of Swasth's centers.
- A network of secondary and tertiary care centers for referring patients from primary health centers.
- Community outreach expands the reach of preventive–promotive care through health education, disease detection camps, follow-up for treatment compliance, and school health as shown in Figure 10.4.
- The streamlined back-end consists of a low-cost drug supply chain, pathology laboratory, an in-house integrated IT platform for electronic health records, and enterprise resource planning.

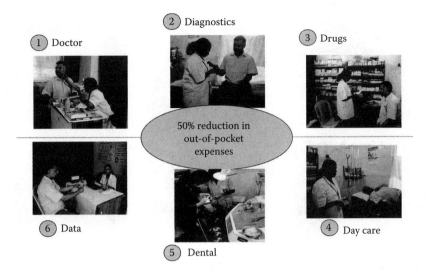

FIGURE 10.3
The 6 D's available at a Swasth Health Center, a 250 square foot facility.

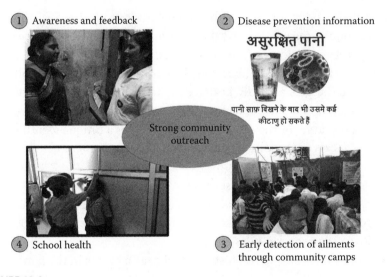

FIGURE 10.4
Swasth's community outreach program.

PATIENT PROCESS

Figure 10.5 depicts the typical flow of a patient interaction, designed for both efficiency and effectiveness.

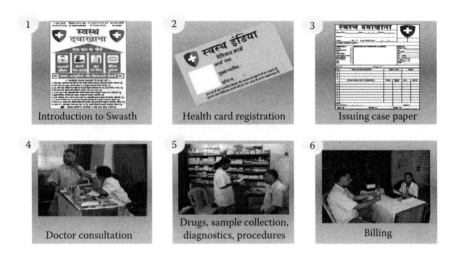

FIGURE 10.5
Steps of patient interaction at a Swasth Health Center.

Step 1—Introduction to Swasth: All new patients visiting Swasth get an introduction to Swasth, so that they can make an informed choice about whether they want to enroll for its services.

Step 2—Health card registration: If a patient chooses to enroll with Swasth, he/she gets a family health card as in Figure 10.6 for providing basic demographic and contact information. The registration is free and there is no charge for the same. The card serves as a unique identifier and provides access to the following benefits to the family members:

- All primary health-care services at half the market rates
- Consultation with specialists, radiology tests, and in-patient treatment through a network of hospitals/nursing homes at 20%–40% lower than market rates
- EMR and access to full history of all health events in the family

Step 3—Issuing case paper: After registration, the patient is issued a case paper in duplicate at the reception. In the case of follow-up of a previous illness, information about past visits can be retrieved and shared with the doctor.

Step 4—Doctor consultation: Key information is captured on the case paper as shown in Figure 10.7—vitals, history of chronic illnesses and

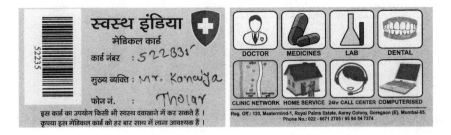

FIGURE 10.6
Swasth's family health card with unique identifier number.

present condition, diagnosis, diagnostics conducted, and prescriptions. This information is subsequently digitized and available to doctors as an input for decision making.

Step 5—Drugs, sample collection, diagnostics, and procedures: A nurse dispenses medicines and conducts procedures or strip tests prescribed by the doctor. If other diagnostic tests are required, a blood sample is collected, and sent subsequently to Swasth's Central Laboratory, for processing and reporting the same day.

Step 6—Billing: Billing is done through the in-house IT system; a copy of the case paper is made available to patients for their referral, and a copy is retained for records.

BACK-END

Low-Cost-Drug Supply Chain

Swasth has a drug distributor's license, and a lean team manages the space-efficient, IT-enabled central facility.

- The warehouse is a 400 square foot facility with four sections: receipt, barcoding, storage, and output.
- About 800 stock-keeping units (SKU) are stocked across 12 varieties: tablets, capsules, syrups, suspensions, ointments, drops, injectable, infusions, consumables, surgical material, dental equipment, and dental consumables.

स्वस्थ दवाखाना

Card No.:_____ Date : ___/___/_____ Time:____:____

Name : _____

Age :_____ M / F   Last Visit Date : _____/_____/_____

CHIEF COMPLAINT :-   CODE :

CHRONIC :		**HISTORY OF PRESENT ILLNESS:**	**VITALS**
HTN	☐		TEMP (F);_____
DIABETES	☐		BP: _____
TB	☐		PULSE: _____
ASTHMA	☐		RR: _____
CHOLESTROL	☐		Wt. (kgs): _____
EPILEPSY	☐		Ht. (cms): _____
THYROID	☐		Pregnanat: Y /N
OA	☐		Lactating: Y / N
RA	☐		LMP: _____

DIAGNOSIS : _____   **CODE :**

S.No.	Name of test	Date & Time	Result
1			
2			
3			

	DRUG-FORM, SALT, STRENGTH	FREQ	No. of Days	QTY.	CODE
1					
2					
3					
4					
5					
6					
7					

END TIME:	टोटल ₹-	Doctor Signature	CC Signature

FIGURE 10.7
Case paper designed to succinctly capture medical information of patient.

- The warehouse is managed by a team of three people.
- The entire process is managed through an IT platform; every SKU is bar-coded and its location is traced.

Pathology Laboratory

- Basic diagnostics are conducted at the centers through strip-based tests, such as malaria and pregnancy. For other tests, blood and urine samples are collected at the centers and tested at the 100 square foot central laboratory. It is managed by a team of a pathologist and a lab technician.
- The laboratory has a cell counter/hematology analyzer, a semiautomatic bio chemistry analyzer, microscope, and other equipment. The laboratory is equipped to conduct all hematology and biochemistry tests. Specialized tests such as vitamin levels, hormones, and so on are outsourced to more advanced labs.
- Reports are entered at the lab and available at the centers over the cloud-based EMR.

In-House Integrated IT Platform

Swasth Live is a cloud-based technology developed in-house, and capable of functioning in a resource-constrained environment with intermittent Internet, as is often the case on field. It has the following modules:

- Member enrollment and identification—For registration of consumers (both at the individual and family level) and searching for members based on card number, phone number, name, geography, and so on.
- EMR—For documenting the history of disease and care on a per-person basis. All records related to diagnosis of illness, outpatient/inpatient visits (i.e., treatment is sought in doctor clinics or hospitals), medication given, and lab tests referred are recorded/stored and subsequently tracked.
- Supply chain and inventory management—For tracking the procurement, stock levels, and distribution of drugs, consumables and material at the central and each health center level.
- Cash management—For tracking the billing of patients, movement of money from the point-of-sale (i.e., clinic, lab, hospitals) to central facility, from central facility to the bank, and routine expenses at the point-of-sale.

- Technology assistance for operations personnel—For assisting the field staff in being more effective in their outreach into the consumer pool (e.g., messaging system, task management, leave management, salaries, and expenses).

As of December 2013, in addition to Swasth India's own operations, Swasth Live was being used on more than 250,000 health records across two other organizations for their core business, and is being used by another two organizations and in the process of being adopted by others.

DEVELOPMENTAL IMPACT

A single unit of operations covers a catchment of 100,000 people. Figure 10.8 illustrates how, at steady state, each unit reaches about half of the catchment and delivers two types of impact: financial savings and improvement in health outcomes.

One of the root causes of health inequity is economic inequity. Swasth addresses this through a 50% reduction in out-of-pocket expenses. Average expenditure per health episode at Swasth Health Centers is US\$1.83 against US\$4.3 at other urban private providers.[8] Focus on health outcomes is ensured through several design choices: focusing consumer messaging on "health promotion" instead of "health-care marketing," incentivizing staff on patient satisfaction instead of revenue, and targeted interventions to address high-prevalence chronic conditions such as anemia, diabetes, and hypertension.

Cost-Effectiveness

The model demonstrates that a 50% reduction in out-of-pocket expense for patients is possible through innovations for cost-effectiveness on all aspects of the health-care delivery chain, as depicted in Figure 10.9.

- One-stop-shop delivery format: The primary health-care value chain consists of multiple players (doctors, dentists, chemists, laboratories, nursing homes), leading to inefficient resource use at a system level. By colocating all services, functionality is maximized in a minimal footprint. Typically, a patient seeking primary health-care services

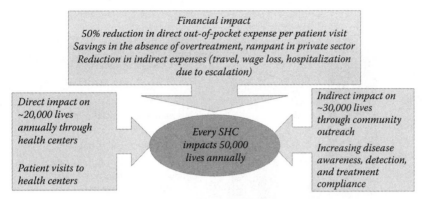

FIGURE 10.8
Developmental impact delivered by model.

would need to visit multiple providers—doctor, laboratory, chemist, and dentist. All these facilities put together would employ 5–10 personnel, housed within to 500–1000 square feet. However, at Swasth Health Centers 3–5 personnel in a space of 250 square feet provide the same facilities. Colocating these various facilities reduces rentals, staff salaries, and other operating costs.

• Vertical integration of supply chain: Swasth has vertically integrated supply chains for medicines and the pathology lab. Setting up a low-cost supply chain entailed getting a drug license, conversations with pharmaceutical companies to procure drugs by bypassing distributors and stockists, and having the doctor on Swasth's payroll to limit the choice of brand for the same salt to what is available in-house. Similarly, Swasth has also set up its own central laboratory to analyze samples collected from its various clinics.

• Promotion: Direct consumer access through a Community Outreach and School Program by health workers from communities (home visits, diagnostic camps, health talks) is cost-effective compared to the prevailing practice of commissions to access consumers via doctors who determine prescriptions/referrals.

• Staff incentives and governance: Focusing on sustainability and health, instead of profits, also leads to cost-effectiveness. By influencing doctor prescriptions through the back-end (controlled drug

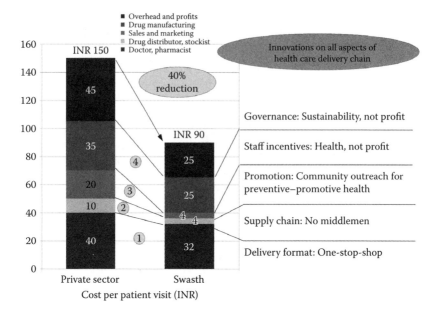

FIGURE 10.9
The levers that make Swasth cost-effective in comparison to private providers.

inventory) and incentivizing staff on health outcomes, overtreatment or prescription of specific expensive drugs is avoided.

• Self-sustainability: The total requirement to fund setup and operating losses of every replicable unit of operations (SHC) is US$20,000. It starts breaking even at 40 footfalls per day, around the 12th month of operation. Beyond this point, the SHC would generate cash to pay for its operations and be self-sustaining. At steady state, an SHC would deliver US$50,000 of direct savings to patients, annually.

Scalability

Three key factors make the model scalable within and outside India:

• Low-investment requirement per center to fund setup, operating losses, cost of shared services, and overheads until operational break-even.

- Staffing needs (one doctor, one dentist, and two to four field staff per SHC) can be met at scale. Health workers and doctor assistants are semiskilled women hired from communities and trained in-house.
- The operating model, including facilities, staffing, patient process, logistics, and quality control can be standardized and replicated in new locations with minimal adjustment through the in-house IT platform.

As market-based social innovation, the model can achieve widespread scale without long-run donor support.

OUTCOMES UNTIL DATE AND FUTURE PLANS

This model has been in place since June 2011, in the Mumbai metropolitan region (MMR) that was chosen as the pilot geography. A population of approximately 21 million[9] (equivalent to the population of Australia) with more than half residing in slums[10] makes the MMR one of the largest concentrations of low-income households in the world. In addition, high disease incidence due to pollution, poor sanitation, and high stress-levels make MMR a high-need target geography.

Post-operationalization with a pilot of three SHCs, the model has been scaled in stages. In this time, numerous changes have been made based on feedback from patients, field staff, and external evaluators. As of December 31, 2013, 16 units[11] (health centers and dental centers) had been launched, servicing 110,000+ patient visits at less than 50% of market rate with 92% patient satisfaction. Three-fourths of the operational SHCs were self-sustainable and others on track. Standard operating procedures had been documented for scale-up.

In December 2013, a third-party assessment of Swasth's model was conducted by Prof. Krithi and Prof. Arnab, faculty at the Centre for Urban Science and Engineering (CUSE), IIT, Bombay. The assessment[12] validates the ability of Swasth's model to service beneficiary needs more effectively than alternatives. Across all survey questions (e.g., cost of treatment, travel time, and cost, provider availability), satisfaction of SHC "members," was 35%–46% points higher than "nonmembers." Ninety-two percent of members were satisfied with Swasth, compared to 52% nonmembers with their current health provider.

Phase 1

In the next 3 years, Swasth aims to scale the model across the city of Mumbai. This is to demonstrate that this model can work across a city and serve the population of an entire city. In terms of effort, this means taking the network strength up to 70 SHCs with a catchment area of approximately 10 million low-income lives. This network will service approximately 1 million patient visits a year. During this scale up, they shall also conduct rigorous impact assessment with our partner, CUSE from IIT, Bombay (http://cuse.iitb.ac.in). A successful city-wide model will provide a blueprint for similar efforts in urban India, and globally. The expansion has been kick-started on January 1, 2014, fueled by an investment from Sir Ratan Tata.

Phase II

Once the model is proven at a city level, Swasth plans to roll it out across all cities in India. The company plans to raise capital and scale it on its own. Swasth aims to build a network of 500 SHCs, impacting 25 million people annually by 2020. However, to increase impact, Swasth would like to explore other models such as working with local municipal/state governments in a public–private partnership (PPP) to operate the government centers and with local entrepreneurs to franchise the model in different cities.

Swasth has been selected as part of a select group of international social enterprises by two forums—SEAD (Social Enterprise Accelerator at Duke) and IPIHD (International Partnership for Innovative Healthcare Delivery). The goal of these groups is to enable early stage social enterprises with a proven track record to scale their impact. With their support during a 3-year program, Swasth will get access to a range of practitioners, investors, policymakers, faculty, staff, and students to scale its solution first to Mumbai, and then across India.

SUMMARY

Swasth India has demonstrated that the primary health care needs of urban poor can be met through a cost-effective, scalable, and self-sustaining model. Operations since 2011 have demonstrated both a social and financial impact.

The primary social impact is the 50%+ reduction in out-of-pocket expenses of our customers, while maintaining a 90% customer satisfaction rating. We define social return as the quantum of saving for every rupee invested. Our internal rate or return (IRR) is a social return of 800%. This is computed as the present value of the infinite series of the year-on-year reduction in out-of-pocket expenses of the customers as a proportion of the invested capital.

Further, as a market-based innovation with significant social impact, the model can achieve widespread adoption without long-run donor support. This is especially relevant in today's context—a rapidly urbanizing world with increasing urban poverty. Instead of setting up new infrastructure to meet the primary health care needs of urban Indian poor, the Indian government can adopt this model through PPP, to improve existing urban public health infrastructure.

This has the potential to revolutionize primary health-care delivery to urban poor population, and ultimately lead to attainment of the vision "Health for All."

REFERENCES

1. UN HABITAT (2010). Retrieved from: http://www.unhabitat.org/documents/media _centre /APMC/ Slum%20trends%20in%20Asia.pdf. Accessed March 20, 2014.
2. WHO and UN Habitat (2010). *Hidden Cities: Unmasking and Overcoming Health Inequities in Urban Settings.* Chapter 4. pp. 39–56.
3. WHO (2013). World Health Statistics. Retrieved from: http://data.worldbank.org /indicator/ SH.XPD.OOPC.ZS. Accessed March 12, 2014.
4. R. Shahrawat and K. Rao (2012). Insured yet vulnerable: out-of-pocket payments and India's poor. *Health Policy and Planning,* 27: 213–221.
5. L. Berman, P. Bhandari, and R. Ahuja (2010). The impoverishing effect of health-care payments in India: New methodology and findings. *Economic & Political Weekly* XLV(16): 1.
6. WHO (2013). World Health Statistics.
7. S. Chowdhury (2009). Health Shocks and the Urban Poor: A Case Study of Slums in Delhi. Table 11, p. 21. Retrieved from: http://www.isid.ac.in/~pu/conference /dec_09_conf/Papers/SamikChowdhury.pdf. Accessed March 12, 2014.
8. SSO 60th Round (January–June 2004). Morbidity, Health Care and Condition of the Aged. Table 44, p. A-201. Retrieved from: http://mospi.gov.in/national_data _bank /pdf/NSS%2060th%20Round-507.pdf. Accessed March 12, 2014.
9. Mumbai (Greater Mumbai) City Census (2011). Retrieved from: http://www .census2011.co.in/census/city/365-mumbai.html. Accessed March 12, 2014.
10. World Bank (2006). Retrieved from: http://infochangeindia.org/poverty/news/54-of-mumbai-lives-in-slums-world-bank.html. Accessed March 12, 2014.

11. SwasthLive—A web-based Health Information Management System (2014). Live* Status—Health Centres, Dental Centres and Chakra. Retrieved from: http://www .swasthindia.in/impact/measure/status/. Accessed March 12, 2014.

12. K. Ramamritham and A. Jana (2013). Report on the Performance of the Swasth India Healthcare Facilities (Swasth Dawakhana) and Satisfaction of the People Availing Healthcare Facilities. Retrieved from: http://www.swasthindia.in/wp-content /uploads/2013/12/Third-Party-Assessment-Dec-2013.pdf. Accessed March 12, 2014.

11

Doing Community Good
Is Good for Business

Bahare Forotan

CONTENTS

INTRODUCTION

One of the most pressing global health issues is the lack of access to essential and life-saving medicines, especially for those residing in rural or remote areas in developing countries. The World Health Organization (WHO) estimates that one-third of the world's population is without access to the most basic essential medicines.[1]

According to the WHO's *Procurement Process Resource Guide*,[2] it is also equally important to ensure that medicines are of appropriate quality, and are delivered safely, reliably, and cost-effectively. Patients are often faced with informal vendors who sell counterfeit drugs. With the little money that is available to them, they sometimes spend it on fake or substandard medicines that might worsen their conditions and even lead to death.

Other major issues in remote areas include logistics (delivery of medicines), shortages of doctors and other health professionals, limited education and health awareness, strong cultural beliefs, and relying on traditional healers.

The consequences of this inadequacy include an enormous loss of life from preventable or treatable diseases; 6.9 million children under 5 years of age die each year mainly due to pneumonia, diarrhea, and birth complications.[3] The UN Millennium Project highlights that most illnesses, especially infectious diseases, are either preventable or to some extent treatable with a relatively small number of medicines. Combined with appropriate public health interventions, appropriately prescribed essential medicines and vaccines could massively reduce the impact of disease on communities. Illness is a major reason that the nearly poor slide into profound poverty. It also decreases people's ability to work, leaves many children orphaned, and prevents them from getting the education they need.[4] Therefore, improving and solving the access to medicines is a crucial task and cannot be solved by nongovernmental organizations (NGOs) or governments alone.

At Novartis, it is believed that pharmaceutical companies can play a major role in helping to solve some of the pressing health-care issues. In search for solutions and new innovative models, top management was inspired by C.K. Prahalad, a distinguished professor of corporate strategy who authored the book *The Fortune at the Bottom of the Pyramid.*[5] He argues that "if we stop thinking of the poor as victims or as a burden and start recognizing them as resilient and creative entrepreneurs as well as value-conscious consumers, a whole new world of opportunity will open up."

Professor Prahalad also challenges the convention that charity is the only way to help the poor by saying: "charity might feel good, but it rarely solves the problem in a scalable and sustainable fashion." With this new, radical approach to poverty, Novartis wanted to create commercial innovation whereby more people could be reached. As a result, Arogya Parivar (meaning Healthy Family in Hindi) was established in 2007 as a novel for-profit social business to improve access to health care for those living at the base of the pyramid in rural India earning US$2-4 a day. Novartis was one of the first health-care companies to employ a social business model to address the unmet health-care needs of the underserved millions at the bottom of the pyramid, and has set a goal of developing a sustainable and scalable business.

AROGYA PARIVAR: A NOVEL FOR-PROFIT SOCIAL BUSINESS HELPS TACKLE HEALTH-CARE NEEDS

The initiative tackles public health needs and therefore offers education on various diseases and basic health issues such as hygiene; it provides treatment options and prevention through improving access to affordable medicines. Arogya Parivar has proven that it is possible to build a sustainable business by making affordable high-quality medicines accessible to people at the bottom of the economic pyramid. The company strives to reach more patients through business models that can empower patients to take their health into their own hands. By treating people in low-income bands as individuals with a certain level of purchasing power and by increasing their level of health awareness through a market-based approach, companies can better meet their needs, prevent harm, increase their productivity and incomes, and empower their entry into the formal economy.

India's rural population of more than 800 million people represents one of the biggest health-care challenges in the world. There is little information about common diseases and even less access to professional advice or treatment. Health is a low priority for mostly illiterate villagers, who consider pain and suffering to be part of life. Given the low purchasing power of these populations, combined with special needs and necessary adaptations to products, efforts by companies to offer medicines and services at the bottom of the pyramid have been limited. These issues are compounded by the fact that companies concentrate on areas with a developed health-care infrastructure—the urban market.

With Arogya Parivar, a new approach to meet rural health-care challenges was created. From the outset, the guiding principles have been local knowledge, entrepreneurial creativity, and a bottom-up dynamic. Field operations are structured into cells (a cell is a market of 25- to 35-km radius, that serves about 80–100 villages) in 10 states across India. For every cell, two local villagers are appointed: a health educator and a cell supervisor. Health educators teach in local communities about basic health-care issues, hygiene, safe water, and nutrition while focusing on prevention. Cell supervisors serve as the initiative's local sales force, interacting with local pharmacies and collaborating with doctors to organize health camps where villagers can receive screening, treatment, and preventive care.

FOUR A'S OF COMPREHENSIVE RURAL HEALTH CARE

The program was designed based on four pillars to ensure long-running impact and the availability of comprehensive rural health care.

Awareness

Poverty-stricken villagers with low literacy levels have limited knowledge of how to prevent and treat disease. Raising awareness about health care, hygiene, and nutrition has been an essential step in fostering health-seeking behavior. The common messages are prevention, disease awareness, and the importance of seeking treatment in the event of illness—particularly to avoid loss of income because of ill health. Arogya Parivar also provides education to physicians through knowledge sharing and medical detailing.

Accessibility

With the help of physicians, the program ensures consistent availability of medicines and health care in rural settings. It is also critical to ensure that medicines are available at pharmacies; in many cases this has meant setting up distribution networks capable of supplying even the most distant locations. Arogya Parivar works with nearby city-based distributors to supply essential medicines to over 28,000 rural pharmacies. To reach deeper more efficiently, Arogya Parivar is appointing direct distributors inside villages who are supplied medicines directly from the company warehouse. Direct distribution is currently about 25% of the network, with plans to expand to 35% in 2014. Through health camps, qualified doctors from the city come along to rural areas and provide screening, diagnosis, treatment, and preventive care.

Affordability

Having services and essential medicines available close to home eliminates cost of travel and saves time for the villagers who are often field workers and earn just a few dollars per day. Generic medicines in the portfolio cater to price points of these markets and also include a range of essential medicines that are affordable.

Adaptability

All communications, some product packaging, and training are adapted to local conditions. The product portfolio is also customized per the local disease burden and includes products from across divisions including over-the-counter products, generic medicines from Sandoz as well as pharmaceuticals, and vaccines addressing 11 prevalent disease areas. Arogya Parivar recruits the field force from the communities where it operates to adapt to local dialects and culture, and to build trust within the communities.

OUTCOME, LEARNING, AND IMPACT

Since 2010, Arogya Parivar has conducted more than 300,000 health education meetings on 11 disease areas for more than 10 million villagers. Through a referral card system, it has been measured that 300,000 patients went to see a doctor for timely treatments. Another 450,000 people got direct benefits through health camps by qualified doctors. The initiative broke even after 30 months and has been self-sustaining ever since.

Through Arogya Parivar, the company got a more refined understanding of what other activities are needed and can be provided to the communities through a market-based approach beyond just making medicines available. Limited health infrastructure and lack of awareness of health issues proved to be the largest challenges in reaching consumers along with ensuring the right medicines are used at the right time. Take the example of tuberculosis (TB); the WHO's Global Tuberculosis Report 2013[6] found that 3 million TB cases go undetected each year, and of all the people suffering from TB, 33% never receive treatment. India is the most vulnerable nation in the world, accounting for 26% (2–2.4 million cases) of total cases. A recent analysis[7] of the TB issues in India highlights social stigma among the key hurdles. Social stigma is pervasive in Indian society:

> When a person is caught with such disease, they are compelled to live in segregation and societal illiteracy surmounted by negligence creates annihilating atmosphere for them ... women are most prone to such unscientific temper and negligence of society. Indian women, mostly rural populace are more prone to harsh living and as soon as they are caught, they find innumerable alliances against them.

These are some of the reasons Arogya Parivar puts a strong focus on education and awareness among the villagers.

Arogya Parivar has been acknowledged by the UN Right to Health program and the WHO for social impact. It is acknowledged by Harvard Business School professors for creating shared value to business and society and has won various awards including GBCHealth (business action on health awards).

The success of Arogya Parivar has led to new similar social business models in Kenya (Familia Nawiri) and Vietnam (Cung Song Khoe) since 2012, and Indonesia (Keluarga Sehat) since late 2013. The model is being adapted in each country to suit local needs, conditions, and disease burden.

SUMMARY

Arogya Parivar reminds us that the poor are customers as well, but that a different approach is required to reach them. The right approach is well aligned with the following Chinese proverb: "Give a man a fish and you feed him for a day. Teach a man to fish and you feed him for a lifetime." Last but not least, business solutions to poverty are longer lasting and more scalable than philanthropy, but both models are needed as they target different groups. However, charity alone is insufficient to reach the 4 billion people at the bottom of the economic pyramid. And therefore, more market-based solutions with a clear sense for the social impact that needs to be achieved have to come in to play to improve the situation for the billions suffering from lack of access to medicines.

REFERENCES

1. WHO. (2014). Access to Medicines. Retrieved from: http://www.who.int/trade/glossary/story002/en. Accessed March 25, 2014.
2. WHO. (2011). *Procurement Process Resource Guide*, WHO Medical Device Technical Series. pp. 10–11. Retrieved from: http://whqlibdoc.who.int/publication/2011/9789241501378_eng.pdf. Accessed April 7, 2014.
3. Unicef. (2014). Millennium Development Goals. Goal: Reduce Child Mortality. Retrieved from: http://www.unicef.org/mdg/index_childmortality.htm. Accessed April 7, 2014.
4. Leach, B. and Paluzzi, J.E. (2005). UN Millennium Project. Task force on HIV/AIDS, Malaria, TB, and Access to Essential Medicines. Working Group on Access to Essential Medicines. Retrieved from: http://www.unmillenniumproject.org/reports/tf_essentialmedecines.htm. Accessed March 25, 2014.
5. Prahalad, C.K. (2004). *The Fortune at the Bottom of the Pyramid: Eradicating Poverty through Profits*. Upper Saddle River, NJ: Wharton School Publishing.
6. WHO. (2013). Global Tuberculosis Report. Retrieved from: http://www.who.int/tb/publications/global_report/en/. Accessed April 17, 2014.
7. Ahmad, T. (2014). Tuberculosis in India – Multidimensional Analysis. Retrieved from: http://insightsonindia.com/tag/tuberculosis/. Accessed March 25, 2014.

12

Process Efficiency by Innovation

Anssi Mikola and Paul Lillrank

CONTENTS

INTRODUCTION

Aravind Eye Clinic is one of the best-known health-care innovations in terms of procedures, management, and business models. It has received a lot of positive publicity globally. C. K. Prahalad gives it as a prime example of frugal innovation in his landmark book *Fortune at the Bottom of the Pyramid*.[1] Pavithra Mehta and Sushitra Shenoy vividly describe its history in *Infinite Vision: How Aravind Became the World's Greatest Case for Business Compassion*.[2] Aravind combines a charity-type mission, "eliminating needless blindness by providing eye care to all," with a self-sustaining business model. Poor patients will receive care for free, whereas those better off pay according to their ability. To fulfill its mission, Aravind needs to grow and expand its reach. For this, it needs to be profitable.

To make all this happen, Aravind has developed a production system for cataract surgery. This chapter describes that system in terms of health-care operations management. It is based on the first author's extensive field-work at Aravind and research on cataract surgery in Europe. A service production system can be described by looking at its constituent parts: selecting and sorting demand, the flow of a patient through the system (flow efficiency), the use of resources (resource efficiency), quality assurance, and improvement.

Cataract as a disease is well-known and in its basic forms relatively easy to diagnose. Most cataract patients can be treated with a standard procedure. The more severe cases need a more complex, individualized procedure. The standard procedure takes less than 10 minutes to perform. Thereby, cataract is a prime example of precision medicine: an exact diagnosis is followed by a standard procedure with predictable outcome.[3] Because cataract is not an emergency condition, procedures can be scheduled in advance. Within health care, cataract surgery is as close as you can get to manufacturing management.

SERVICE PROCESS MANAGEMENT

The fundamental characteristics of a service are described by the intangible, heterogeneous, inseparable, perishable (IHIP) model:[1]

- Immaterial: a change in a state of affairs that is valuable to the customer, such as cannot see/can see.
- Heterogeneous: each service is produced for a customer, who may have varying needs, conditions, and situations.
- Inseparable: a customer needs to be present or otherwise interact with a producer.
- Perishable: services cannot be produced for inventories; therefore, if a customer is not present, the producer's production capacity will perish.

From this follows that the core of a service production system is demand, capacity, flow, and quality management.

Demand is the combination of need, want, purchasing power, and presence. A cataract patient needs to get his or her eyesight restored; wants to undergo surgery; has the means to afford the procedure through some financial arrangement, be it out of pocket, insurance, or reliance on taxes or charitable contributions; and must be able to get to the service location with reasonable effort at a certain time.

Capacity means the maximum output a given resource can produce under normal conditions. It is measured by the capacity utilization rate (CUR): what percentage of the maximum capacity is utilized for value-creating tasks in a given time. In services, maximal CUR is seldom achieved, as there are scheduled and nonscheduled breaks, setup times between customers, and variation in the incoming customer flow. CUR is important, as it determines resource efficiency, measurable as unit cost: total cost of the capacity divided by the number of treated cases.

Flow means the path of a *flow unit*, in this case a patient's journey through the service production system. Flow efficiency depicts the production system from a patient's perspective. It can be measured by total flow time (throughput time) from beginning to end of a health episode, the amount of time spent waiting within the system, and the number of steps or visits required for one health episode. For the patient, time can be translated into money if treatment requires absence from work, or costs of travel and accommodation.

Quality, in a narrow sense, refers to the clinical quality of a procedure: was it performed according to standards or best practices, or were there deviations that may harm the patient, such as infections or complications? Quality in the broad sense refers to the patient's overall experience of the journey.

In a service production system these basic issues are interlinked. Demand needs to be selected, sorted, and prepared to create a smooth flow of incoming cases, so that resources can be utilized efficiently. Resources need to be arranged so that the CUR of the most expensive or rare resources is maximal. Flow and resource efficiency need to be balanced, and quality must be assured to eliminate unnecessary steps.

DEMAND MANAGEMENT

Aravind manages demand through two types of inbound logistics: (1) the patients who show up at its facilities and (2) those approached by its outreach program. In both cases, demand is carefully screened and sorted into homogeneous groups.

The outreach program seeks to approach those who have problems traveling to the clinic, or can ill afford to be absent from work. A local partner invites those people to come to a local facility, where Aravind staff arrives on a Sunday by bus. The prospective patients are screened by ophthalmic technicians measuring sight, refraction, eye pressure, and so on and finally by a doctor. Those in need of treatment are then taken to the hospital on the same bus that the staff came on. This immediate transition has been found to greatly increase the number of diagnosed patients actually being operated on. If patients are left to decide when they would come to surgery, a large portion will fail to come because of feeling not able to take a day off work.

The outreach patients thus pose a managerial challenge as flow must be efficient to minimize patients' absence from work and other costs, resource efficiency must be maximized as most of these patients do not pay for their care, and quality must be assured to prevent complications and delays.

PRODUCTION PROCESS AT THE HOSPITAL

A production process at a surgical hospital typically includes the steps of diagnosis, decision to operate, patient preparation, the surgical procedure, recovery, and discharge.

Diagnostic Process

When a doctor meets a patient at Aravind, all necessary information is at hand. This is to reduce iterations, going back and forth between the doctor's office and a diagnostic unit, and other disturbances to the flow. If it is determined that cataract is present and a surgical procedure is needed, the patient goes to a counselor, who explains what will be done and what alternatives there are, for example, different lenses can be chosen.

The diagnostic process sorts patients into preset categories. There typically are cases where there are warning signs of a standard process not being applicable, such as cases where the pupil will not dilate due to previous medication or the cataract has proceeded so far that the removal of the original lens will take an excessively long time using standard phacoemulsification instruments. These patients are moved to a nonstandard queue.

Preparation Process

Regardless of which diagnostic process the patients have gone through, the operating process is the same.

The outreach patients undergo surgery on Mondays. On the basis of their diagnostics patients are ordered, so that first come the standard, predictable cases, then the more complex patients, some of which may have to wait till Tuesday.

Patients wait, seated in a room adjacent to the surgery. About 20–30 patients line up on the left side of the room, a similar number on the right. To the former, the left eye is operated on, to the latter the right. As patients are called in, the waiting patients move closer to the surgery, seat by seat.

Although waiting, patients get eye drops that enlarge the pupil, which is needed for the surgery. If the pupil is not large enough, the patient is moved to the end of the queue, to wait for another hour or so. With this arrangement disturbances in the patient flow are prevented as a patient with a pupil not wide enough will not enter the operating room (OR). The enlargement could, indeed, be done in the OR, but it would disrupt the flow.

According to our measurements, the setup time between patients at Aravind is 22 seconds. In Europe it is about 18 minutes.

Surgical Standard Process

The most experienced surgeons perform the high-volume standard surgery.

In the OR, there are two operating tables, one to the left for left eyes and one to the right for right eyes. A microscope, which the surgeon uses to look at an eye while operating, is attached to a moving arm located between the two tables, so that it can easily be moved from one to the other.

While the previous patient is operated on, a scrub nurse receives the next patient, covers him or her with blankets, and applies a disinfectant. When the surgeon is done with the previous patient, he or she moves the microscope to the other bed and focuses it on the eye that is to be operated on.

As the patient flow is sorted and standardized, the required instruments are always the same and come in the same sequence. When the surgical process is repeated several times over, the flow smoothens, to the extent that the surgeon does not have to lift his or her eyes from the microscope to receive a new set of instruments. When a subprocedure is completed, the surgeon lifts the instruments just a bit over the patient's eye so that they are still visible in the microscope. The nurse sees this and picks them up and puts the next instruments in the surgeon's waiting hands. This speeds up the process, as the surgeon does not need to refocus his eyes back and forth between the microscope and plain eyes. When the surgery is finished, the surgeon lifts up the instruments, the nurse receives them, and the surgeon turns around to the other table for the next patient. With such a process, a team can do up to 100 patients per day compared with 6–15 operations per day in the benchmarked European units.

Postoperative Recovery

When the procedure is completed, the patient is taken out of the OR. Eye drops are administered to prevent infections and drying of the eye. A shield is placed on top of the eye to prevent contact. After some rest, the patient goes home or is transported back to the community center.

The process could be even more efficient, if both eyes would be done (bilateral) at the same time. This, however, is not usually done, because the recovery after a bilateral procedure is longer. Poor patients cannot afford to be absent for the time it takes. With one eye at its prior condition, the patient can go back to work with the help of one eye.

Surgical Nonstandard Process

The patients from whose condition might not allow the application of the standard process are operated upon on Tuesdays. The schedule is not so tight and thereby resilient to more variation in the length of the operation.

On Wednesdays to Fridays, drop-in patients and those with appointments are treated. The pace is slower, as the patient flow is more diverse. Less experienced surgeons will be trained, and experienced surgeons both teach the less experienced as well as engage in research activities.

SUMMARY

The Aravind Eye Clinic cataract surgery process is a textbook example of the classical productivity drivers, explained by Adam Smith in his 1776 book *The Wealth of Nations:*[5] division of labor, specialization, and standardization. All of the more recent production philosophies, including Lean and the Toyota production system, build and expand on these principles.

Division of labor means that work is divided into different parts that require different tools, skills, and competencies. The more complex the task, the more difficult it is for one individual to be a master of all. Some tasks are more difficult to learn than others, and can therefore command a higher price. Therefore, rare and expensive resources should not be wasted on tasks that can be done sufficiently well by appropriately skilled people. Because eye surgeons are rare, they should concentrate on diagnosis and surgery, not on routine tests, administration, counseling, and other such things.

Specialization means that one individual concentrates on a subtask, and keeps repeating it several times over. Repeated performance of a task reveals its inner logic to the human mind more easily than randomly changing tasks. The best-known way of performing a task can be standardized and repeated in a similar way each time. A standardized process allows systematic experimentation: if I try a different way, how will results differ from the previous iteration? By observing the cause-effect connections in a production, best practices can be discovered, developed, and further standardized. Concentrating on incremental parts of the process makes it possible for new employees to become productive within weeks with little prior education.

In all production, the key is the value chain. It constitutes the steps that are necessary and sufficient to produce the expected value to the customer. In cataract surgery, the value chain consists of the sequence of diagnosis; preparation; the surgical procedure of removing the old lens and inserting a new one; the postoperative tasks of applying eye drops and a shield; and finally recovery. If some of these are lacking, or the sequence is disturbed, value is not created. In health care, the value chain is determined by clinical medicine and available technologies. The cataract surgery value chain is basically similar all over the world.

A value chain, however, cannot exist in a vacuum. It needs to be supported by a process that includes sorting and selection of demand, staffing, scheduling, preparations of facilities, and instruments. Supporting processes are needed to make the value chain possible, but they do not create customer value. For a surgical intervention, the patient needs to be present and ready in the OR. The process that takes her there can be long or short, complicated or simple. As long as it does what it is supposed to do, the way it is organized does not add to the value chain, it only adds cost. Thus, while the value chain can be improved through technical advancements, new diagnostics, medicines, and tools, the supporting process can be streamlined and simplified by various managerial initiatives that improve both resource and flow efficiency.

Within health care, cataract surgery is a special case of precision medicine. Most surgical interventions are more complex and may not, with current technology, allow a similar level of standardization. However, as diagnostics and clinical intervention technologies improve, the general trend in medicine is to move toward precision medicine and standardized procedures.

REFERENCES

1. Prahalad C.K. (2006). *Fortune at the Bottom of the Pyramid: Eradicating Poverty through Profits*. New Delhi, India: Dorling Kindersley.
2. Mehta P. and Shenoy S. (2011). *Infinite Vision: How Aravind Became the World's Greatest Case for Business Compassion*. Oakland, CA: Berrett-Koehler.
3. Christensen C., Grossman J., and Hwang J. (2009). *The Innovator's Prescription: Disruptive Solutions for Healthcare*. New York, NY: McGraw-Hill.
4. Fitzsimmons J. and Fitzsimmons M. (2006). *Service Management. Operations, Strategy, Information Technology*. 5th edition. New York, NY: McGraw-Hill.
5. Smith A. (1776). *The Wealth of Nations*. London, United Kingdom: W. Strahan and T. Cadell.

13

Stanford Operating System: Aligning Purpose with People and Performance

Amir Dan Rubin

CONTENTS

INTRODUCTION

Stanford Health Care (SHC or Stanford herein) has a bold vision to heal humanity through science and compassion, one patient at a time. As part of its mission to care, educate, and discover, the medical center has made groundbreaking health-care impacts.

Indeed, Stanford is a place of firsts—the first adult human heart transplant in the United States, the first successful heart–lung transplant in the world, the first use of radiation therapy for cancer treatment, and the invention of the CyberKnife, which delivers focused radiotherapy to treat brain and body tumors.

Preeminent scientists, physicians, and interdisciplinary researchers are drawn to Stanford because of this reputation for innovation. In fact, two Stanford medicine researchers were awarded Nobel Prizes in 2013 and another received the prize in 2012, underscoring the immense impact of discoveries made here for patients everywhere. Currently, 22 Nobel laureates are members of the overall Stanford community. In addition, SHC is the recipient of numerous awards and recognitions, and is consistently ranked as one of the United States' top hospitals by *US News & World Report*, and performs at the highest levels on quality and patient satisfaction metrics.

OVERVIEW OF THE STANFORD OPERATING SYSTEM

To continue to innovate and excel, SHC has deployed a management approach it calls the *Stanford Operating System* or *SOS*. The SOS helps Stanford align its purpose with its people and performance management. On the basis of Lean thinking or Toyota Production System philosophies, the SOS is SHC's approach to strategic deployment, value stream improvement, and active daily management.

Strategic Deployment

Strategic deployment involves the development and assessment of annual strategic and operational objectives. The process involves a review of corporate mission, vision, strategy, and competencies, as well as an assessment of market, technology, and competitive factors. With these factors in mind, the organization then develops strategic case statements called strategic A3s, as they are put down on A3-sized paper. These strategic A3s lay out current issues, a high-level current state assessment, key objectives and goals, and high-level countermeasures or actions to be undertaken.

These strategic A3s are developed for key strategic domains across Stanford's health system, including:

- Complex care (involving inpatient care and key clinical service lines, such as cancer, cardiac, and neuroscience services)
- Network care (including regional outpatient centers, clinics, and medical offices)
- Virtual care (approaches for online and connected health through the Stanford Health cloud)
- Population care (including goals for Stanford's health insurance plan and its approaches to maintain the health and well-being of patients and members before they become acutely ill)

In addition to laying out high-level goals for these strategic domains, strategic A3s and goals are developed for a balanced scorecard of performance dimensions. These include excellence in

- People
- Patient experience/service
- Quality/safety/clinical effectiveness
- Operations performance and reliability
- Strategic growth/innovation
- Financial performance/value

Together, these strategic A3s provide high-level guidance and direction for all entities and departments across SHC's broader health system. With these strategic A3s in mind, each organizational area and department develops detailed operations improvement plans, called strategic operating plans (SOPs). These plans lay out specific performance goals to be improved, specific initiatives to be undertaken to improve performance, targets for improvement, and managerial accountabilities for achieving outcomes. These SOPs are also accompanied by performance dashboards highlighting key metrics. These plans also link to annual financial incentives for key management and physician leadership. The SOPs and dashboards are then displayed on visual walls in each department and are regularly reviewed in leadership meetings and in regular leadership visits to each department, called Gemba rounds. Gemba, in Japanese Lean parlance, refers to the *factory floor.*

Value Stream Improvement

Although specifying high-level strategic aims and translating those goals into specific strategic operations plans are critical, aligning operations with strategic intent is an essential next step to execute plans. Stanford refers to the design and improvement of operations as *value stream improvement*, building off Lean concepts of engaging team members to improve processes that truly deliver value to customers.

Value stream improvement efforts involve engaging key stakeholders—including physicians, managers, staff, and patients—to fundamentally examine processes, remove waste, and design operations to increase effectiveness and reduce the likelihood of errors. A philosophy of respect for people and continuous improvement underlies Stanford's improvement efforts. Many "Plan-Do-Check-Act" improvement cycles are simultaneously occurring throughout the organization.

Improvement work may take advantage of an array of approaches including organization of the workplace (referred to as 5S in Lean parlance), mapping out processes (referred to as value stream mapping), root cause analyses, and waste assessments.

Active Daily Management

Although defining strategies/operational goals and then designing operational value streams to achieve these goals are critical to Stanford's pursuit of excellence, day-to-day performance is how actual results are delivered. To support performance execution and to increase the likelihood that improvement efforts are sustained into the future, Stanford deploys what it calls *active daily management*. Active daily management involves a set of regular activities Stanford leaders should undertake to manage operations and sustain improvements.

Active daily management begins by considering how new employees are recruited, trained, and retrained. It also focuses on assuring that there are standard approaches for carrying out work—called standard work in Lean parlance. Visual walls or whiteboards with goals and standards are displayed in departments, and daily huddles or brief meetings are conducted around the visual walls to reinforce standards and engage the team. Managers and leaders conduct regular Gemba or work-site rounds to directly observe performance against standards, help coach team members, and identify areas for improvement. Staff members are regularly recognized during rounds and key metrics are tracked on a daily basis.

STANFORD OPERATING SYSTEM IN ACTION

Strategic Deployment

The SOS and SHC's annual planning cycle are driven by Stanford's vision of healing humanity through science and compassion one patient at a time. Stanford pursues this vision through its mission to care, educate, and discover. This vision and mission are translated into a strategy referred to as Leading Edge and Coordinated Care.

Stanford not only develops strategy through the lens of the organization but leverages design thinking approaches of empathy mapping and extreme customer engagement to better understand how the organization can provide true solutions to the complex problems patients are experiencing. This approach answers the clear call from our patients to "apply the leading edge" and then "know me," "show me," and "coordinate for me."

- *Apply the leading edge.* In everything we do at SHC, we seek to give our patients the absolute best in care—diagnosing conditions sooner, providing treatments in more minimally invasive ways, reducing pain, and offering the best opportunities for outstanding outcomes. The best care also takes advantage of state-of-the-art facilities, including the new Stanford hospital as well as premier regional outpatient centers and clinics in our growing network of care.
- *Know me.* We strive to deeply know our patients, providing personalized and customized solutions in all aspects of care, from breakthrough Clinical Genomics to outstanding service based on our patient-first, C-I-CARE philosophy.
- *Show me.* We look to partner with our patients to help them understand and evaluate diagnostic and treatment options, assess the best personalized care plans, and determine the most convenient Stanford locations to receive their care.
- *Coordinate for me.* At Stanford, we are committed to owning the complexity of health-care delivery and to being a trusted health-care advisor and coordinator for our patients. As patients and families engage with Stanford physicians, nurses, care navigators, and our online tools, we want them to know that we are on their side, by their side.

Across our health system, we are committed to delivering this *Stanford Edge* for each and every patient we are privileged to serve.

Value Stream Improvement

SHC's value stream improvements include initiatives to increase accessibility and throughput. For example, over the past 3 years, SHC has grown its outpatient volume by almost 100% while reducing the wait times to appointment by over 50%.

In one improvement example, a team of physicians, nurses, medical assistants, and staff gathered to help develop an improvement A3 or project plan for their clinic. The problem statement or improvement goal for this clinic sought to reduce appointment duration for patients, increase clinic capacity with no additional resources, and reduce the nonvalue-added work for staff and physicians. At baseline, it took the clinic about 60 minutes to complete a patient visit, with 50% of the staff members' work identified as nonvalue-added. Moreover, physicians found themselves batching a lot of their electronic medical record documentation at the end of the day, taking over 60 minutes every evening after seeing patients all day.

The team mapped out the clinic value stream and identified a number of areas for improvement. For example, the team found that physicians were spending time collecting information that the front desk could collect or that the patient could complete online in advance of the visit. The team also identified that the physician, nurse, and medical assistant were geographically dispersed throughout the day and worked in isolation from each other, as opposed to working side-by-side during the day. Accordingly, the team members could not easily hand off tasks to each other and maximize their respective capabilities.

Therefore the team redesigned their approaches and developed standard work for each role, taking full advantage of each team member's capabilities. Moreover, the team began working in triads of a physician, nurse, and physician assistant. In this manner, for example, at the end of an examination the nurse could complete discharge instructions, whereas the physician could move on to the next exam room.

These efforts delivered outstanding results. The duration of a patient visit—referred to as lead time—was reduced by over 33%. Another way of phrasing this is that capacity was increased by 1/3 with no additional resources. The nonvalue-added work was reduced by 50% for the staff. Finally, physician time at the end of the day documenting in the electronic record dropped from 60 to 15 minutes.

Active Daily Management

Although SHC has always excelled as one of the world's leading centers for excellence and quality, its focus on customer service and the patient experience often took a backseat. This is no longer true, as now Stanford is recognized among the very best in patient experience in the entire United

States. This success is due in part to Stanford's use of active daily management, as reflected in Stanford's C-I-CARE patient experience philosophy.

C-I-CARE at its basic level represents standard work that is practiced by all staff and physicians at SHC. The letters within C-I-CARE represent an abbreviation to remind team members of best practices in engaging with patients, family members, and fellow coworkers.

C—Connect with patients/people by calling them by their proper name or the name they prefer (e.g., Mr., Ms.).

I—Introduce yourself and your role.

C—Communicate what you are going to do, how long it will take, and how it will impact the patient.

A—Ask permission before entering a room, examining a patient, or undertaking an activity.

R—Respond to patient's questions or requests promptly and anticipate needs.

E—Exit courteously with an explanation of what will come next and ask if there is anything else you can do for the patient.

Each department throughout the organization then took this basic C-I-CARE template and developed detailed standard work templates for key team members in their departments, for example, specific best practices for nurses, physicians, housekeepers, technologists, and so on.

With a standard developed, SHC then built C-I-CARE into the hiring process. All new recruits are assessed for their commitment and inclination toward C-I-CARE. Of course technical competencies are also assessed, but no new team member is brought on board without their agreement to abiding by the C-I-CARE standards.

Each new team member is then provided orientation and training in C-I-CARE. Understanding that a *one-and-done* training is not likely to stick, each team member receives annual C-I-CARE training.

Moreover, in daily huddles, C-I-CARE is reinforced and reviewed. Staff members observed preforming excellent C-I-CARE receive recognitions during huddles, and often are given tokens of appreciation (e.g., complementary coupons for the cafeteria).

Each manager is then required to conduct observations—called C-I-CARE Gemba rounds—to review how staff members directly engage with patients and family members in the actual course of care. Such rounds allow the manager to regularly coach team members, so that they continuously improve.

Senior leadership members conduct rounds with managers, observing how the managers observe and coach their managers—an approach Stanford calls *Linked Check-Ins*.

Through these and other efforts, Stanford Hospital now performs at the 95th percentile in patient satisfaction among all hospitals in the United States.

SUMMARY

SHC aligns its purpose with its people and its performance management through its Lean-based SOS. Components of the SOS include strategic deployment, value stream improvement, and active daily management. Through this management system, Stanford has been able to continue to develop innovative care delivery approaches, translate these approaches into high-value operations, and actively execute at high levels of performance for every patient, every time.

14

Managing Stakeholders and Patient Experiences to Achieve Better Outcome

Kavita Narayan

CONTENTS

INTRODUCTION

The main aim of public health is to make affordable, high-quality care available and accessible to all citizens. The measure of a health system does not lie in resources employed, such as the number of staff trained, beds added, doctors employed, or drugs distributed, but the overall health outcomes of its target population. There is a need to change from a resource-driven mind-set toward one that encourages health-care systems to be designed, delivered, and measured based on outcomes.

Globally, health-care outcomes are defined in several ways.[1-8] In summary, outcomes are the consequence of some action, typically a medical, professional intervention, but could also be something else, such as community support or changes in health behavior. Outcome measures what happens to a patient's medical condition, rather than what was done. Outcomes are measured through tests of observable health status and inquiries of perceived, subjective status. Measures are collected on an individual level, but can be aggregated to describe populations as the typical indicators of public health, such as life expectancy, morbidity, and mortality.

DRIVERS OF HEALTH-CARE OUTCOMES

Health outcomes at the population level are affected by several factors, as illustrated in Figure 14.1. Obviously, changes in health needs and morbidity impact outcomes. These in turn are affected by demographic changes and lifestyles. In the United States, as the baby boomers enter their senior years, about 25% of them are obese, 20% have diabetes, and more than 70% suffer from a heart disease. Although baby boomers are living longer than their parents did, their quality of life has declined, thanks to the public health consequences of the obesity epidemic.[9]

Within the youth segment of the Indian population, there has been an alarming increase in noncommunicable diseases such as diabetes, hypertension, and depression, apparently because of sedentary lifestyles, excessive food intake, and constant stress on the job.

Innovations that lead to good health outcomes do not necessarily have to be medical, if they reduce risks of illness. For example, a technical innovation in water purification has the potential of improving health for millions.

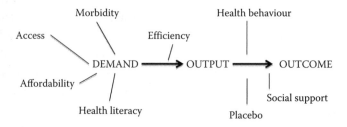

FIGURE 14.1
Drivers of health outcomes.

Demand for health services is a combination of what is needed and what is available. Therefore, improvements in health literacy, access, and afford-ability increase demand, which may lead to more service output, hopefully with improved outcomes. Efficiency in using available resources obviously increases the output volume.

The core issue in an outcome-based approach is that the link from out-puts to outcomes is not simple and straightforward. In a situation of total deprivation with no services at all, any service is an improvement. In sit-uations where services exist in sufficient volumes, it is not obvious that more is better. Outcomes are generated not only by clinical interventions, but also by changes in health behavior, placebo effects, and social support. A focus on outcomes opens the possibility to look at innovations in these areas.[10-12]

SAFETY AND EXPERIENCE

For a discussion on outcomes to be relevant, there has to be planned activ-ities to influence the health status of individuals and communities. These activities have three aspects:

1. Clinical decision-making must result in a diagnosis and a care plan.
2. Clinical interventions that occur following the care plan may be evaluated by checking whether services were performed as intended, following accepted norms and best practices. Clinical quality may thus be considered as a proxy indicator for patient safety and mea-sured as the absence of adverse events.
3. As the patient goes through the *care journey* of a series of interven-tions and treatments, he or she experiences them in various ways. These experiences are broadly based on how to get to the point of care, what is done, how long it takes, what happens, and what it costs. They are significantly affected by subjective perceptions on respect and dignity, and compared to the experiences of others.

Innovations in clinical decision making, patient safety, and patient experience are of different character. It is difficult to determine exactly how patient experience affects health outcomes. However, there is ample evidence that placebo effects play a significant role. Healing environments and spiritual support have always been used as nonmedical ways to enhance good outcomes. It stands to reason that patient experience can be used to improve outcomes.

INNOVATIONS IN SERVICE EXPERIENCE: DOING IT THE DISNEY WAY

In the past few years, more than 3000 health workers have visited the Disney Institute to study leadership, management, and service strategies. The courses offer solutions based on examples from within their business and are grounded in the time-tested insights from the Walt Disney Company. Its management principles are based on Walt Disney's definition of leadership: the ability to establish and manage a creative climate where people and teams are self-motivated to the successful achievement of long-term goals in an environment of mutual respect and trust. These are summarized as Disney's 10 Management Principles of Guestology:

1. Make Everyone's Dreams Come True
2. You Better Believe It
3. Never a Customer, Always a Guest
4. All for One and One for All
5. Share the Spotlight
6. Dare to Dare
7. Practice, Practice, Practice
8. Make Your Elephant Fly
9. Capture the Magic with Storyboards
10. Give Details Top Billing

Using common sense, the Disney Institute helps translate these into usable strategies for management in any field.

"It's all about making a guest feel welcome," Chris Caracci, Disney Institute consultant and a former hospital manager, explained to participants of a conference organized by Siemens Healthcare. "If we do it here, isn't it even more important to do it to a child, or a patient in a wheelchair?" Laura L. Shapiro, then a senior director at Siemens admitted, "Healthcare has been notoriously behind the times when it comes to customer service. As the industry gets more technologically advanced, patient satisfaction has suffered. Too often a hospital patient may be known only as 'The kidney in Room 305.'" The lesson they learned from Disney is that "high-tech has to be accompanied by high-touch."[13]

The East Jefferson General Hospital in New Orleans, LA, was one of the first health institutions to discover the relevance of the Disney experience. The CEO Peter Betts asked himself: Would it not be nice if everyone that left our hospitals would have the same feeling of a positive experience as when leaving a Disney theme park? Betts first visited Disney to study its service and people management strategies and explore how those strategies could produce a better health-care operation. The hospital then brought Disney officers to New Orleans to train its 1500 employees in the Disney methods of creating happiness. The East Jefferson team focused on providing care and comfort, and demonstrating courtesy and respect, thus creating a satisfying experience for each patient and family member.

Disney has identified 74 *magic moments* when a guest has contacts with Disney employees. It needs to ensure that every second of these encounters create a favorable impression. Similarly, East Jefferson has attempted to create a *service cycle*. The hospital manages the magic moment as soon as the guest enters, and they continue to monitor each and every contact point until the end of the stay. The hospital continues to make contact with the guest long after he/she leaves to encourage the hospital guest to return if he/she or a family member is ever in need of health care.[14]

The Disney concept of *guestology* encompasses every possible element of the guest experience. Everything matters and no concern is too small. For example, a hospital in Virginia found that introducing television in every room significantly reduced frustrations of patients. Even simple items such as extra pillows and blankets, juice, and ice led to high levels of overall satisfaction.

Some years ago, Dr. Lloyd Nazareth, then chief operating officer, Wockhardt Hospitals Group, said in an interview to *Express Healthcare*, "In the Disney model, poor service to a customer who expects so much is termed 'stepping on people's dreams.' If that happens there needs to be a service recovery team to convert tragic moments into magic moments."

Wockhardt has developed five key rules:[15]

1. Finish strong. The last, not the first impressions stay in customers' memories. Customers remember the end of their encounter more vividly than the beginning.
2. Get over bad experiences early. Questions that are likely to make patients uncomfortable, such as current pain levels, smoking habits,

eating patterns, and alcohol consumption, are moved to the beginning of an episode.

3. Segment pleasure and combine pain. Break pleasant experiences into multiple stages and blend unpleasant ones into a single stage.

4. Build customer commitment by giving them choice. A patient feels in command and, therefore, is happier if she feels like she is not being ordered around. It could be something as simple as meal selection or which arm to give blood from for a test. Nurses are instructed to preface any listing to the customer with: "You have a choice. Let me give you some options."

5. Stick to ritual and let customers maintain their habits. People find comfort with repetitive and familiar activities. This is particularly relevant for patients who need to make major lifestyle changes—allow them some familiar habits.

Although staff at Wockhardt may not call their patients *guests*, as Disney calls its customers, the group has asked its employees to treat them as guests.

RICH TRADITION OF AYURVEDA IN INDIA

The Vaidyaratnam nursing home is one of the oldest and most respected Ayurvedic treatment facilities and research centers. Located in Ollur, Kerala, a very different type of service excellence constitutes part of the culture. Having been a patient myself for a chronic spinal disc fusion-related pain, I can vouch for the absolutely impeccable clinical care pathways and service delivery processes that have been institutionalized there. Over 30% of the patients are international. The caregivers are most comfortable conversing in Malayalam, the local language of the state of Kerala, although they speak locally accented English pretty fluently. The main treatment modes include the *panchakarma*, which consists of five specific, specialized treatments using a mix of medicated oils, herbs, and potions, internal cleansing and detoxification using herbal enemas, and a well-balanced vegetarian diet that prepares the body to accept this holistic body-mind-spirit intervention.

The experience at *Vaidyaratnam* differs from the average ayurvedic hospital in many ways. There is the incredible mix of high-quality research-backed clinical protocols, streamlined and standardized care processes, a customized individual treatment regimen designed by the physicians that undergoes everyday monitoring and tweaking, a squeaky clean, modest yet comfortable patient environment, an idyllic tropical setting, and most of all, a highly compassionate and empathetic crew of caregivers (physicians and therapists) who each embody this institution's mission and values.

The result of this kind of dedication to the patient experience almost always results in patients describing their state at discharge as "feeling so much better, lighter, fitter, happier and with a healthy glow." *Vaidyaratnam* seldom uses a standardized method to evaluate outcomes such as a pain scale, vital statistics, or blood tests. In the ayurvedic philosophy, disease and health are both ultimately a reflection of the harmony/disharmony between body, mind, and spirit. When these are harmonized by deliberate retuning of the system to bring it to their natural state, disease or ill-health ceases to exist. If overall or *better than before* well-being is used as an outcome indicator, this institution and its methods will positively receive a perfect score. And is not that what we want all health-care facilities to be able to achieve?[16]

STAKEHOLDERS AND THE PROCESS OF INNOVATION

There is an ongoing debate on what comes first—innovation or need? The question, however, is misplaced, in the same way as the proverbial question: did the chicken or the egg come first? The chicken and the egg form a reproductive system. There is no chicken without an egg and vice versa. The components cannot be meaningfully separated in a before–after sequence. The relevant question would be which came first, the bird egg or the mammal-live born reproductive system?

In the health context, the basic needs are survival, functionality (lack of disability), avoidance of pain, and minimal discomfort. These can be fulfilled in innumerable ways. When a new solution to any of these needs appears, latent needs turn into active wants. Most innovations originate where wants and possibilities interact, that is, at the stakeholder interface.

Stakeholders were first defined in 1963 in an internal memorandum at the Stanford Research Institute as "those groups without whose support the organization would cease to exist." Simply put, it is those people who have the most interest (or stake) in a particular product, organization, or issue. Another way to define stakeholders would be "as an individual or a group that holds a legitimate interest in, and a possibility to influence an issue." (A burglar may be able to influence you properly, but is not legitimate. The United Nations is legitimate, but may have no influence.) Stakeholders can have both recognized and official claims as well as hidden agendas.

In health care, the first and foremost stakeholder must be the patient; for without a patient or a care-seeking individual, there is no role for the service or the service provider. The role of a patient in most instances implies that the person has a medical problem that is not consciously self-inflicted, and that the patient wishes to get well and restore functionality.

Most patients have a group of *significant others, family, relatives, and friends*, who in most cases are concerned and willing to help. For patients who work, *the employer is* an important stakeholder that wishes that the patient returns to work, and does not cause too much costs. Therefore, employers contribute to health insurance and provide occupational health services.

Professional caregivers have typically the interest to help sufferers, gain a good professional reputation, and earn an income. *Care organizations* have the interest to cut costs and/or increase revenues, and increase volumes, reputation, and stature. *Caregivers' labor unions* have an interest in protecting their members, including from abuse from patients and their families. *Suppliers* of devices, pharmaceuticals, and facilities have an interest in making a good business by providing value to their customers.

Health policy makers and regulators have an interest in promoting public health. Although an individual's health is his own business, health in aggregate, public health, is a national issue, an infrastructure and a positive externality that impacts the economy and national security. Regulators, however, have an interest in maintaining and expanding their power and position. In many countries health care is a major issue, into which *politicians* have significant stakes.

Given the large number of stakeholders and their often conflicting interests, it is no wonder that the innovation environment becomes complex and new ideas face many obstacles. It is therefore critical to clearly map out and define the extent of the influencing role/s that each of the key stakeholders would play before embarking on a health-care service or delivery innovation.

CASE IN POINT: TOTAL KNEE REPLACEMENT

Let us walk through the example of a new orthopedic service line that we launched at one of the hospitals in Atlanta where I served as the chief operating officer. The classic total knee replacement (TKR) surgery that has become commonplace the world over involves several of the stakeholders listed above. Unlike most life-saving surgeries, this is clearly one intended to improve the lifestyle and reduce pain for patients suffering from osteoarthritis or other debilitating pain in the knee joints. For optimal outcomes with TKRs, every stakeholder in the group must play the proper role.

Let us start with the *orthopedic surgeon,* who is the lead actor in the movie, besides the *patient* who could be described as a war hero. Typically, patients almost always choose the surgeon first after having done their online referral research and having somewhat decided (although still nervous in most cases) to undertake the surgery. It is now the surgeon's role to assess the patient, ethically and clinically, for true need for the procedure. This is particularly important because when a good joint is unnecessarily subject to replacement, the clinical outcomes are far worse than before, negatively impacting all the stakeholders. The surgeon's skill also lies in explaining this complicated clinical technicality as simply and accurately as possible, including all risks and the extensive postsurgical rehabilitation involved, and removing all fears from the patient's mind to put them at ease to proceed with the procedure.

Once the patient has been admitted to a facility, the *hospital's* role in ensuring that every step of the process is well designed and executed by high-quality nursing and other personnel is paramount, from admission to presurgical testing, anesthesia, operating room safety and efficiency, effective pain management, postsurgical infection prevention and care, inpatient rehabilitation, and, finally, hand over at discharge to the next set of caregivers—the family or immediate support network of the patient.

The role of the *device or implant manufacturer* is critical as well. New implants reach the market each day and because the surgeons make the final selection, they are constantly bombarded with product marketing. Those device manufacturers that have worked closely with surgeons in designing the devices and also in patient education have a definite market advantage over those that have tried to make the product fit the customer, the knee in place of the proverbial shoe.

Who pays the bill? If it is *insurance*, then the time and extent of paper-work, and what is and not allowed in terms of procedures will involve the patient, the surgeon, the hospital, and the insurance provider. If it is a self-paying patient, typically, family members may be involved in the decision depending on the extent of financial support provided by them.

Physical therapists are the group of professionals that work magic on the patients after surgery. Without a talented rehab team that constantly monitors, coaches, modifies, and manages the patient and his/her reha-bilitation protocols for several weeks following the surgery, all of the above ingredients may very well fail to achieve the intended outcome, that of pain relief, easy movement, and improved joint function.

Finally, the emotional and moral support provided by the *patient's fam-ily* or immediate support group is invaluable to the healing process. The pain experienced immediately after surgery for several patients is intense enough to make them question their decision to have undergone the pro-cedure in the first place. This could also make them very averse to the therapy and exercise that would be rather painful for several days. It takes a strong and persistent show of support and strength by the family of TKR patients as well as praise for every step taken, literally, to augment and enhance the recovery process.

Every stakeholder is important in this case. Each of them has a linked relationship to the other that directly or indirectly influences the indi-vidual stakeholder's desired outcome. In Figure 14.2, the internal circle denotes the immediate influencers while the external circle denotes those that have a lesser degree of direct influence on the patient.

LINKING THE CONCEPTS TO THE PRIMARY HEALTH-CARE SERVICE MODEL IN INDIA

The pyramid illustrated below indicates the various levels of the primary health-care system in India along with the expected level of service at each step. Figure 14.3 describes ascending levels of care from a subcenter, followed by a primary health center (PHC), a community health center (CHC), a subdistrict hospital (SDH), and finally a district hospital (DH). Medical colleges sit on top of this pyramid. To put it simply, the higher the level of the pyramid, the higher the complexity of the service delivered and the larger the population base served. Consequently, with increasing

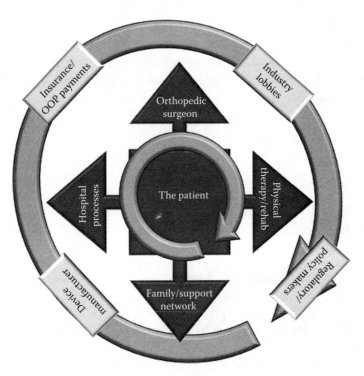

FIGURE 14.2
Interplay of stakeholders for a typical total knee replacement patient.

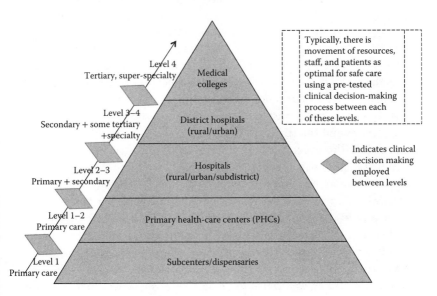

FIGURE 14.3
Public health system in India: organization by level of services.

patient movements between levels, the greater is the complexity of referral networks. In cases where patients move from one layer to another, the patient journey will include handovers from one caregiver to another.

There exist several challenges in strengthening the primary health-care system in India today.[17,18] Keeping aside the system's weaknesses for a minute, I have tried to provide a picture of what the service might look like, if everything worked perfectly.

An Ideal Scenario

Image an ideal scenario for childbirth as follows:

> A young woman living in the hilly areas of Northern India is ready to go into labor. Her family calls for an ambulance via dialing a three-digit number on their mobile phone. Within 15 minutes, the ambulance reaches her doorstep equipped with all basic life-saving facilities and a skilled emergency medical technician. He checks her BP and pulse rate and ensures that she is calm and breathing right. They reach the Primary Healthcare Centre (PHC) in about 20 minutes from being picked up.
>
> A thoughtful security guard pulls up a wheelchair to the ambulance and wheels the patient to the emergency waiting area, from where a transporter takes over. A cheerful hostess takes the husband over to the registration area for filling out vital demographics while also ensuring that another family member can accompany the patient to the birthing area. The husband hands over his family's health entitlement card, a government-issued ID that ensures free primary care services for citizens. Merely by scanning the card, the vital information of all family members automatically populates the registrar's screen, including the number of antenatal visits, general health history, previous conditions including a past surgical procedure, etc. The registrar clicks against the woman's field to indicate the patient receiving services and thereby ensures that all levels of the health system now know about this expectant woman from X village, district, and state.
>
> While skilled birth attendants are helping the woman, she is also offered the choice of an epidural or natural birth. She chooses the latter. In the meanwhile, a trained phlebotomist has skillfully drawn a blood sample to be sent to the lab for testing. The OBGYN has been informed and is on her way. In the meanwhile, an attendant is also seating the rest of the family members and asking them if they can be offered any refreshments, tea or coffee. He also indicates that there is a designated area for prayers/ meditation if they would like to do so. There is a general sense of calm and happy anticipation. Although nervous about having her first baby, the knowledge that her family is right by her side and that she is cared for by

professionals committed to her care and well-being makes her feel good. She cooperates with every instruction given by the nurses and SBAs and right in time for her final few pushes, the OB/GYN arrives to cut the cord and deliver a healthy baby girl. After letting the mother hold the baby for a minute, she is immediately handed over to the paediatric nurse who checks the baby and performs all the vital tests while an understudy notes each of these on the system. The baby is now successfully added as a family member to the family's health card.

All quality and safety procedures are followed, detailed instructions given at every step of the process, and most of all, fears allayed at every stage and the patient and her family treated with the utmost care and consideration. When the woman leaves the PHC within 48 hours to go home, she leaves happy and confident in her new role. She knows that help is only a phone call or a text message away. A lactation-trained nurse will visit her every alternate day for the next two weeks or until she is able to breastfeed successfully. This nurse will also remind her of the vaccination schedule for the baby that has been handed to the family, teach her about baby handling and infection prevention for herself and the baby, and record vital statistics for mom and baby each time.

Let us imagine a slightly different scenario; one in which the expectant mother developed further complications while in active labor at the PHC. In the ideal world where referral linkages are well developed between each of the service levels, a phone call would quickly alert the operating room at the CHC and an ambulance fully equipped with life-saving medical technology and well trained paramedics would be on board and transport this woman safely and in a timely fashion to the CHC. The emergency team on standby would wheel her in on a stretcher that was positioned in the receiving area, the surgical team would have scrubbed and be ready for an emergency C-section, and after completing the surgical safety checklist including verifying right patient and right site, the OB/GYN would proceed to deftly perform the C-section.

However, the patient ends up losing much blood in the process and her vital signs are looking dangerous. The baby is showing signs of distress and needs immediate neonatal care. While the family is awaiting news anxiously outside the OT, a hospitality aide checks with them for refreshments and assures them that all will be well. The physician's assistant has come out of the OT to apprise the family of the situation while continuing to assure them that the team is doing its best. In the meanwhile, the blood bank has already dispatched the required bags to the OT using the pneumatic tube transportation system. The baby has been momentarily stabilized with oxygen and is being transported to the neonatal ICU at the district hospital in a mobile neonatal warmer where the neonatologist awaits the little one with trained neonatal nurses and respiratory therapists.

The story ends with the mother being stabilized and discharged over the next three days while the baby had to undergo a longer stint in the NICU but came out safe and strong nonetheless. The new mom was encouraged to express colostrum as well as breast milk for the baby that was then transported twice a day to the DH NICU for the little one. The use of affordable technologies, strong communication links between the facilities, well-trained and thoughtful nursing and ancillary staff, and most of all, well-designed service process flows including robust standard operating procedures between all levels of care, made the difference between life and death in the second scenario. More importantly, being in the loop and kept informed of the situation helped the family stay calm and cooperative through the process.

This is particularly relevant given the dynamic nature of healthcare service delivery; there are several different scenarios that must be anticipated and planned for, in terms of clinical outcomes. The stress caused to the system actors and the patient and their family during one such complex scenario cannot be understated. Each situation will demand a completely different set of action protocols and procedures, necessitating controlled yet consistent information flow between all the levels. One could visualize a similar situation for various other specialties and other health conditions but the concept of assured service excellence remains at the core of the change and is essentially the system innovation.

SUMMARY

India today is a powerhouse of affordable innovations in all sectors, and health care is no different. The design and delivery of quality, affordable, accessible health care for India requires the active engagement of multiple stakeholders. It calls for innovations in concepts, products, and processes to get outcomes that ensure quality and stakeholder satisfaction.

"The idea of actively engaging with stakeholders in designing high-quality service experiences for patients to therefore get to a better outcome" is an innovation that needs to be further explored. Managing stakeholders will influence patient experiences at all points of the care continuum that in turn affect outcomes.

One can use several lessons learned in different parts of the world and even in completely different spaces such as entertainment to string together memorable patient experiences. The patient testimonials for Ayurveda in India or institutions that focused on the patient experience more than others demonstrate the need to invest in more focused research toward quantifying clinical outcomes based on stakeholder satisfaction and patient experiences.

ACKNOWLEDGMENTS

This chapter includes editing contributions from Ms. Aruna Dasgupta, independent editor, and Ms. Natasha D'Lima, program coordinator at Public Health Foundation of India, New Delhi.

REFERENCES

1. Krousel-Wood M.A. Outcomes assessment and performance improvement: Measurements and methodologies that matter in mental healthcare. In: Rodenhauser P. (ed.) *Mental Health Care Administration: A Guide For Practitioners.* Ann Arbor, MI: University of Michigan Press, 1999.
2. Gordis L. *Epidemiology Philadelphia.* Philadelphia, PA: W.B. Saunders Company, 1996.
3. Outcomes. Canadian Institute for Health Information. Available at: http://www .cihi.ca/CIHIextportal/internet/EN/tabbedcontent/health+system+performance /quality+of+care+and+outcomes/outcomes/cihi010651.
4. World Health Organization. Health Impact Assessment (HIA). Available at: http:// www.who.int/hia/about/glos/en/index1.html.
5. World Health Organization. *Health Promotion Glossary.* Geneva, Switzerland: WHO, 1998. Available at: http://www.who.int/healthpromotion/about/HPR%20 Glossary%201998.pdf.
6. Definition of wellness. Available at: http://definitionofwellness.com/wellness-dictionary /health-outcomes/.
7. Krousel-Wood M.A. Practical considerations in the measurement of outcomes in healthcare. *Ochsner J* 1999; 1(4): 187–194. Available at: http://www.ncbi.nlm.nih.gov /pmc/articles/PMC3145439/pdf/i1524-5012-1-4-187.pdf.
8. Segen J.C. *McGraw-Hill Concise Dictionary of Modern Medicine.* New York, NY: McGraw-Hill Companies, 2002.
9. Culp-Ressler T. As Baby Boomers Age, There's a Health Care Crisis on the Horizon for American Seniors. *Think Progress,* 2013. Available at: http://thinkprogress. org/ health/2013/05/29/2072011/baby-boomers-looming-health-crisis/.
10. Hight G. Elephant in the Room: Barriers to Innovation in Health Care. *McCombs Today,* 2010. Available at: http://www.today.mccombs.utexas.edu/2010/07/elephant -in-the-room-barriers-to-innovation-in-health-care.
11. Omachonu V.K. and Einspruch N.G. Innovation in healthcare delivery systems: A conceptual framework. *Innovation Journal: The Public Sector Innovation Journal* 2010; 15(1), Article 2. Available at: http://apsredes.org/site2012/wp-content/uploads /2012/06/InnovationPHC1.pdf.

12. Akenroye T.O. Factors influencing innovation in healthcare: A conceptual synthesis. *Innovation Journal: The Public Sector Innovation Journal* 2010; 15(1), Article 3. Available at: http://www.innovation.cc/scholarly-style/akenroye_concept_framework _force_drive_innovate_health_sector_v17i2a3.pdf.

13. The Disney Institute. Case Study: Siemens Medical Systems. Available at: http://www .trainingindustry.com/media/3381470/disney%20siemens%20medical%20cs.pdf.

14. Putting the Magic of Disney into Healthcare. Available at http://www.neilbaum.net /putting-the-magic-of-disney-into-healthcare.html.

15. DeVine J. and Gilson K. Using Behavioral Science to Improve the Customer Experience. Available at: McKinsey Quarterly. http://www.mckinsey.com/insights/operations /using_behavioral_science_to_improve_the_customer_experience.

16. The Vaidyaratnam Oushadshaala. Available at: http://www.vaidyaratnammooss .com/.

17. Report of the National Commission on Macroeconomics and Health. Available at: http://www.who.int/macrohealth/action/Report%20of%20the%20National%20 Commission.

18. National Health Mission. Available at: http://www.nrhm.gov.in.

15

Leapfrog through mHealth

Sachin Gaur

CONTENTS

INTRODUCTION

Today, in India, various estimates put Internet connectivity at nearly 16% of the population.[1] It is predicted to grow two- to three-fold in the coming years. Mobile phones have been another big growth trend. India has currently some 900 million plus mobile phones. The 1 billion mark will be crossed shortly.[2] A total of 20%–25% of the new phones will have Internet connection.

These trends have influenced all spheres of life in Indian society over the last two decades. This chapter tries to imagine the near-future impact of the integration of various digital interventions in the health-care sector. The umbrella term for all these is *Connected Health*[3] as illustrated in Figure 15.1.

TECHNOLOGY CONNECTS

Connected Health is a health-care delivery model that uses technology to provide services remotely. It aims at easing the constraints of

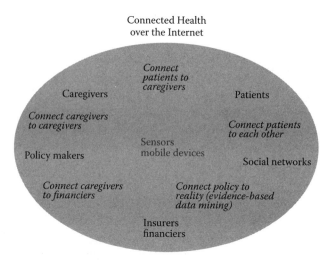

FIGURE 15.1
Connected Health.

location and time. The former means that patients do not have to travel to the location of the doctor in cases where the specialist's contribution is judgment and advice that can be delivered electronically. The latter means that the patient and the provider do not have to communicate synchronously in real time, when it is not necessary. Asynchronous media, such as SMS and e-mail, makes it possible for both parties to engage at times most suitable for them. For example, doctors can use small intervals between patient visits to do consultations by e-mail, thereby using their time more flexibly. Connected Health aims to maximize health-care resources and provide increased, flexible opportunities for consumers to engage with clinicians. Further, it puts more emphasis on self-managed care and underlines that health value is cocreated as a joint accomplishment of providers and patients. Connected Health enables denser communication with patients and their significant others and supports the formation of networks between people with similar problems. It builds bridges between caregivers, who can connect with experts possessing narrow and deep knowledge. As Connected Health generates massive amounts of data on real events, regulators can use data mining and analysis to formulate better policies.

Connected Health uses available technology—often leveraging affordable consumer technologies and existing cellular networks—to deliver patient care outside of physical service provision points, the hospital or doctor's office. As such, Connected Health illuminates the megatrend from point-to-point services to networked models of health provision ecosystems with a variety of interacting players. Connected Health encompasses programs in telehealth, remote care/home care, and disease and lifestyle management, where social networks play a significant role.[4]

The effects of the Internet on Indian society are immense. New Internet startups pop up every day adding to positive growth trends. However, India is different from Western countries in the way Indians connect to the Internet. Although broadband still dominates in many countries, in India mobile Internet is the key. Mobile devices have smaller screens and limited computation. However, with cloud computing and powerful sensors they can be added with superior capabilities compared to the personal computer. We will explore some of the global trends that are impacting health care and relevant Indian examples to gain a deeper insight about the future of Connected Health in India.

HYPER-CONNECTED NETWORKS OF CAREGIVERS

Social media has taken center stage in the United States in connecting medical practitioners. Such initiatives are led by various hospitals like the Mayo Clinic.[5] Hospitals and medical practitioners in the United States are heavily collaborating using new media tools like organized Twitter chats. These are digitizing tacit knowledge, which might be later useful to the medical community. Projects like symplur.com are initiating and managing such conversations.

In India mobile leads the way. WhatsApp is a mobile messaging application that can be easily installed on a smartphone; it identifies a user on the network just with their mobile number. Because the design and usage of mobile messaging is simple and cheap, it is gaining mass adoption with already millions of users on the platform.[6]

Doctors are, for good reasons, suspicious of new media and open platforms where patient privacy could be compromised. On generic platforms, such as WhatsApp, discussions are carried on in ad hoc groups that anybody can join, remaining identifiable only through a number. However, new tools can make doctors securely hyper-connected.

MixORG, an Indian company, has associated with a group of doctors to build a custom mobile messaging application to discuss orthopedic cases within a group of registered medical practitioners.[7] The application offers two unique advantages over third-party tools such as WhatsApp. First, it is built to discuss medical cases and designed to evolve best practices, beyond being just a chatting platform like WhatsApp. Second, it ensures patient privacy by hosting the application on a private and secured network limiting the access to registered practitioners.

USING MOBILE SOLUTIONS FOR PUBLIC HEALTH PROGRAMS

The National Health Portal (NHP) is an initiative by the Ministry of Health and Family Welfare to leverage new media to provide preventive health-care information in India.[8,9] The NHP will provide a single point of access for authenticated health information for citizens, students, professionals, and researchers, housing various digital initiatives. However, it will still take few more years to digitize and catalogue the health knowledge that the initiative can source from various stakeholders in the country.

India's huge illiterate population poses a challenge not found in advanced countries. The Internet is a read/write medium not accessible to a person who cannot read and write. NHP partnered with a mobile application company, Mobile Harvest, to create an application that provides preventive health-care information using audio and video health content, making the approach literacy neutral.[10] A screenshot of the application is shown in Figure 15.2. It uses visual icons for the user interface (symbol of ear and loudspeaker) instead of a textual interface.

The Gujarat and Bihar state governments have used a similar literacy-neutral approach, equipping community health workers (CHWs) with relevant mobile solutions.[11,12]

FIGURE 15.2
Literacy-neutral mobile interface.

MOBILE DIAGNOSTIC TESTS

An Indian company, BioSense, has developed several mobile-based diagnostic solutions to check blood and urine sugar and other critical indicators. The BioSense solution has three components: (1) a dipstick, (2) a portable testing kit, and (3) a smartphone. The person responsible for conducting tests is expected to dip the stick in the collected urine sample and after the specified period, place the dipstick in the testing kit. The smartphone with the mobile application is connected to the portable testing kit. The smartphone camera scans the dipstick visually and based on the color changes on it determines the test results.

Such diagnostic tests are cheaper than traditional methods. They do not require a lab, but can be conducted in the field. They allow the test data to be recorded in real time and backed up securely on cloud-based storages for analytics and archival purposes.[13,14] Lifestyle diseases like diabetes and cardiovascular conditions are on the rise in the country and creating demand for affordable and accessible testing and monitoring solutions. Several Indian companies are working on providing solutions built around mobile devices and sensors.[15]

GLIMPSES INTO THE FUTURE

Information and communication technology (ICT)-based interventions are coming from all possible touch points bringing improved efficiencies to the health-care system. Figure 15.3 illustrates a possible set of outcomes.

Technology alone is not enough. For innovations to spread and take hold, financial incentives must be aligned. Currently that is not the case. For example, hospitals and allied partners (diagnostic labs) in India make money when the patient is in hospital, whereas insurance companies lose money as they have to pay for inpatient care. With wearable technologies enabling health monitoring, it is possible to develop revenue models that make it possible for a hospital to make money and the insurance company to save money when the patient is not in a hospital. Hence, they would be incentivized to move the care from curative toward preventive. Such a model would be less abusive to patients as well.

Early experiments in this direction have already started.[16] Financially robust models of preventive health-care systems built on ICT can create new value and several possibilities to capture it in terms of better health, increasing revenues, new jobs, and further applications of technology. India is, and will increasingly be, a hotbed for such experimentation. Innovation is not only about figuring out something new but also about how to deal with the disruption it brings to existing practices. India has more than its fair share of health and social problems and deep pockets of deprivation. The sunny side of this is that there are underserved and legacy-free areas, where the alternative to an innovative service is no service at all. Such areas provide an opportunity for innovators to generate experience and volume, before they enter the mainstream.

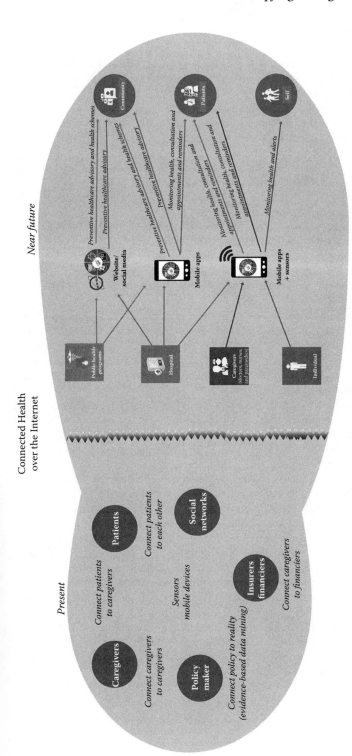

FIGURE 15.3
Possible evolution of information and communication technology-based services in the near future.

REFERENCES

1. *Time of India.* (2013). With 243 Million Users by 2014, India to Beat US in Internet Reach: Study. Retrieved from: http://articles.timesofindia.indiatimes.com/2013-11 -14/internet/44073307_1_internet-and-mobile-association-internet-penetration -rural-india, accessed on November 14, 2013.

2. Wikipedia. (2014). List of Countries by Number of Mobile Phones in Use. Retrieved from: http://en.wikipedia.org/wiki/List_of_countries_by_number_of_mobile_phones _in_use, accessed on April 14, 2014.

3. Ranck, J. (2012). *Connected Health: How Mobile Phones, Cloud and Big Data will Reinvent Healthcare.* San Francisco, CA: GigaOM Books.

4. Wikipedia. (2014). Connected Health: Definition. Retrieved from: http://en.wikipedia .org/Wiki/Connected_health, accessed on April 14, 2014.

5. Aase, L., Bierbaum, B., Armstrong, K., Boyer, C., Bunker, R., Dunlop, D., Detora, G., Haney, T., Gothard, A., and Gould, M. (2011). *The Thought Leaders Project: Hospital Marketing.* Minneapolis, MN: Bierbaum Publishing.

6. *Mumbai Mirror.* (2013). Docs Use Whatsapp to Save Heart Patients. Retrieved from: http://www.mumbaimirror.com/mumbai/others/Docs-use-WhatsApp-to -save-heart-patients/articleshow/27252815.cms, accessed on April 14, 2014.

7. MixORG Youtube Channel. (2014). Uttar Pradesh Orthopaedic Association Mobile Application Demo Video. Retrieved from: https://www.youtube.com/watch?v=pm3 -IGoZKWU, accessed on April 14, 2014.

8. Digital Medicine. (2013). The Inside Story of National Health Portal of India. Retrieved from: http://blog.digmed.in/2013/08/10/the-inside-story-of-national-health-portal -of-india/, accessed on April 14, 2014.

9. National Health Portal of India. (2013). National Health Portal Link. Retrieved from: http://www.nhp.gov.in, accessed on April 14, 2014.

10. Google Play Store. (2013). Android Mobile Application of National Health Portal of India. Retrieved from: https://play.google.com/store/apps/details?id=com .MobileHarvest.NHP, accessed on April 14, 2014.

11. BBC Media Action. (2013). Mobile Kunji Project. Retrieved from: http://www .rethink1000days.org/programme-outputs/mobile-kunji/, accessed on April 14, 2014.

12. DeshGujarat. (2014). CM Dedicates Development Works Worth Crores in North Gujarat. Retrieved from: http://deshgujarat.com/2014/01/25/chief-minister-dedicates -development-works-worth-crores-in-north-gujarat/, accessed on April 14, 2014.

13. Mail Online. (2013). The iPhone App for When You Take a Call… of Nature. Retrieved from: http://www.dailymail.co.uk/sciencetech/article-2285226/uCheck -iPhone-app-instant-health-check-picture-urine.html, accessed on April 14, 2014.

14. *Hindu.* (2014). Purse-Friendly Diabetic Testing Kits Launched. Retrieved from: http://www.thehindu.com/sci-tech/health/medicine-and-research/pursefriendly -diabetic-testing-kits-launched/article5575433.ece, accessed on April 14, 2014.

15. Product Nation. (2014). Sanket—A Disruptive Health/Wellness Product to Monitor Health Ailments. Retrieved from: http://pn.ispirt.in/sanket-a-disruptive-healthwellness -product-to-monitor-health-ailments/, accessed on April 14, 2014.

16. GoQii Life. (2014). GoQii Life: A Wearable Tech Gadget Promoting Healthier Lifestyle. Retrieved from: http://www.goqii.com, accessed on April 14, 2014.

16

Innovation Excellence: Learning from Emerging and Developed Economies

V. K. Singh

CONTENTS

INTRODUCTION

Innovation is an ancient concept. The capability to innovate is one of the most profound characteristics of human beings. Still, certain periods and places in history have exhibited more innovations than others. Aryabhatta, an Indian mathematician, 3600 years back innovated a thing called Shunya (zero).[1] Zero has different connotations. If used singly, it means nothing; if put to the right of another figure it increases many folds such as 10, 100, 1000 until infinity. Zero can be understanding or ignorance. In Indian religious books such as Vedas and Geeta, the universe is conceptualized as made out of nothing. To grasp it through meditation requires an empty mind, thinking of nothing. In Lean health care, zero can be applied such as zero waste, zero defects, zero medication errors, zero waiting, and zero infection rate. Prevention is successful if nothing bad happens. In leadership, zero means an open mind as modern management teaches us. Indian frugal innovation means that around the core value there is zero waste. Thus, innovations can be envisioned as nothing and something: management or process innovations remove things that do not create value; technical and clinical innovations create new value. It stands to reason that in poor countries emphasis is on the former, whereas in rich countries it is on the latter.

INNOVATION ECOSYSTEM

Let us approach innovation through the concept of an ecosystem. An ecosystem includes, but is not limited to, networks. A network is a set of connected nodes. The connections can be mapped and managed by establishing communication protocols between nodes. A food chain—big fish eats little fish—is in this sense a sequence of a network. In addition to clearly linked nodes an ecosystem includes agents, constraints, and conditions that have no obvious links. Temperatures that are comfortable for the big fish may be devastating to the little fish, leading to the extinction of their predators. Conversely, a change in acidity may kill off the big fish leading to an exponential proliferation of the small fish. Neither would have any way to experience the root cause. Isaac Newton was active in the ecosystem of Cambridge University, Galileo Galilei in the North Italian renaissance. Had these gentlemen been born at different times in different places we might have never heard of their genius. In a similar vein, a corporate organization is a network of tasks and reporting relationships. A corporate culture is more akin to an ecosystem that covers the company as well as its partners, including numerous formal and informal influences. Innovations are created from opportunities. The more diversity in an ecosystem, the more there will be opportunities.

MANAGING INNOVATIONS

The ancient concept of innovation has got new actuality. With globalization simple industrial jobs producing mature products have moved to low-cost countries. In advanced countries, factory labor and its wages are under pressure. The middle class is shrinking. The obvious solution is to innovate new, high-value, high-technology products. But many consumer durables that at times created millions of jobs are based on mature technologies and concepts. For example, the refrigerator radically changed food logistics and household economics, produced undisputable value, led to high demand, and created an industry employing millions. It is difficult to envision an innovation that anytime soon could have a similar impact. At the technology frontier, innovation is difficult. In developing countries, innovations are driven by needs and deprivation. Technical solutions to infections, sanitation, food storage, or energy generation exist. Affordability and access call for innovative solutions in distribution.

As innovations are seen as the solution, the obvious question is, why cannot we have more of them? Isaac Newton saw finding "the philosopher's stone," a way to turn lead into gold, as his main challenge. We know his efforts were futile. In a similar vein, modern management scholars and policy makers are searching for a formula that would turn needs into solutions and opportunities to realized success. The Internet age provides many tools to speed up the process:

> Just about anyone can have an idea at breakfast, design it with online CAD software, produce a prototype on a 3D printer, receive financing and marketing analysis from a crowdfunding site, rent supercomputer time from Amazon, contract a manufacturer and be done by lunch without even leaving the table.[2]

Nevertheless, no "innovator's stone" has been found. If there is no silver bullet, a leaden bullet will have to do.

A central concept in innovation research is "the fuzzy front end." As the histories of successful innovations are traced, it often appears that the initial steps were not clear at all. The new idea might have sounded crazy and been rejected by every sensible person. There are lucky accidents, solutions looking for problems, sudden insights, and painstaking labor. However, as the basic concept takes form, the fuzziness diminishes and turns into product development, engineering, commercialization, marketing, and distribution. Many concepts, which aid innovations, are interrelated and manageable.

Creativity often requires thinking out of the box. However, to go outside the box there has to first be a box. There are several boxes, systems, principles, and thinking guides. Lean thinking prompts an innovator to carefully consider customer value, what kind of value chain is needed, and separate value from waste. The Theory of Constraints (TOC) is a management philosophy introduced by Eliyahu M. Goldratt. Also known as the Bottleneck theory, it calls attention to constraints and weak links in a process. TOC includes decision tools like thinking processes (TP) that help in laying out a problem and thinking beyond the obvious.[3] Both Lean thinking and TOC are catalysts to innovate.[4]

Innovation management can also draw on excellence models such as the Malcolm Baldrige National Quality Award (MBNQA) and the European Foundation Quality Model (EFQM).[5]

Excellence models such as the EFQM given in Figure 16.1 build on the concepts of enables and results, and provide a systematic way to evaluate the levels of excellence in the areas of leadership, people, policy and strategy, partnership and resources, process, people results, customer results, society results, and key performance results. Innovation and learning is integrated in all nine criterions of EFQM to bring innovations in every criterion to achieve innovation excellence.[6] Dr. Sanjib K. Dutta and I have developed the EFQM model specifically for health care in India.

We need to migrate from innovation to innovation excellence. As illustrated in Figure 16.2, every component of innovative excellence is to interlink effectively to make innovation sustainable. In practice, every health-care provider is to chart its own path. However, to take an idea from the fuzzy front end to the market and to be the first differentiator is a troublesome effort, which requires creative leadership and top management commitment. The model of innovative excellence provides a guideline.

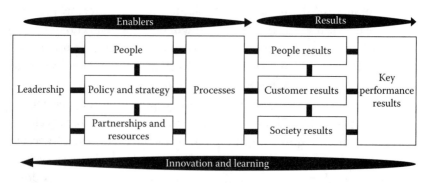

FIGURE 16.1
EFQM excellence model.

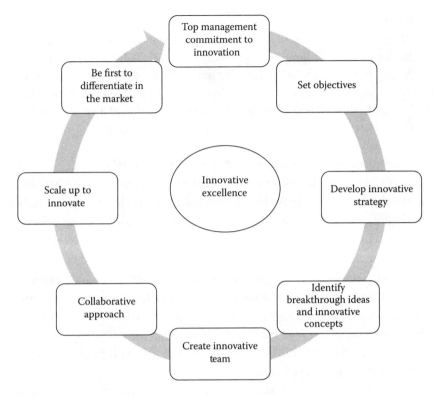

FIGURE 16.2
Innovative excellence.

Innovative excellence is to transform a health-care organization by using a variety of tools and concepts. It is scaling-up excellence for the whole organization. Strategy should precede structure. Organizations should not rely on a single innovation function but create a culture to encompass the entire organization.

INNOVATIVE LEARNING FROM EMERGING ECONOMIES

Emerging economies are deprived of all kind of resources and have many people to consume them. The challenge is to make more of the resources that exist through frugal innovation. India as an emerging economy is incubating many such frugal innovations. Alexander Blass, CEO of Innovation Institute of America and winner of Top Innovator of the Year award, says:

It is no secret that many of the world's top innovators come from India. Within the past few decades, India has embarked upon an incredible transformation from an agrarian-based society to a knowledge-based economy. Along with the population growth came survival instincts and the need to be different, better and unique. One can see innovation everywhere in India, whether in large game changing innovations that garner lots of publicity, or in less obvious yet important incremental fashions.[7]

Innovations of India such as the Aravind Eye hospital system, Narayana Health (NH), and Dabbawalas (Tiffin carrier service of Mumbai) have received a lot of publicity. Developed countries trying to apply Indian methodologies as a whole might find that they do not have the volumes, and that with such efficiencies half of their health-care providers would be redundant. Therefore, instead of copying, learning is recommended.

It is not possible to catalogue all innovations in emerging economies as there is no document where they could be found in one place. Some innovative projects in emerging economies such as India, Brazil, and Africa are discussed. These innovations might not be applicable in advanced countries as such, but with a little out-of-the-box thinking they could provide inspiration for other applications.

Saathi: A Harvard MBA student from India won the grand prize in the "Social Enterprise" category at the 18th Harvard Business School New Venture Competition on May 2, 2014 for her venture "Saathi." It provides affordable sanitary pads made from waste banana tree fiber for women in rural India. It is manufactured and sold by local entrepreneurial women at INR 2 or 3 cents per piece. The pad market is estimated to be US$940 million annually in India. US$15 billion is lost in productivity by women due to staying at home during their menstrual cycle.[8] This is due to lack of accessibility to affordable pads and lack of awareness about the use of sanitary pads. Some of the states are distributing pads free of cost to promote the usage. The new sanitary pads would be cheaper for individuals and state governments. Developed countries cannot comprehend such a thing and would not think of using sanitary pads made from banana tree fiber as they can afford branded products.

Forus Health has built 3nethra, which is an inexpensive device for the early detection of common eye ailments.

Zerodor is a waterless urinal technology patented by Indian Institute of Technology (IIT) Delhi in collaboration with UNICEF. It is one of the 200 high social impact projects exhibited by IIT in April 2014. A kit is attached to the urinal and saves 151,000 liters of water every year while separating a phosphorus mineral that India currently imports for farming. The kit is priced at INR 2500 and already in use at the IIT campus. When urine comes in contact with water, urine releases ammonia that gives out odor. With this system, flushing is not required hence it is odorless.[9]

Solar Ear is a low-cost, solar-powered hearing aid manufactured by a not-for-profit Brazilian company. The device contains solar chargeable batteries and a solar battery charger. The aid costs under US$100 and the rechargeable batteries cost approximately US$2 and last for 2–3 years. The company gets the product assembled by employees who are deaf.[10]

eRanger ambulance is a motorbike ambulance manufactured by eRanger company. It builds a high power motorbike with a sidecar that serves as a stretcher for the patient. The sidecar is cushion padded for the comfort of the patient and has a roll cage with safety belts for the safety of the patient. A rain cover can be attached to the roll cage in different weather conditions. There is also space for emergency on-site medical supplies. The bike has a good suspension system and suits all kinds of terrain. Motorbike ambulances have already been successfully used in Sudan, Zambia, and Malawi. The motorbike ambulances are stationed at health centers and health workers are trained to ride and maintain them. These motorbike ambulances are more cost-effective and simpler to maintain than car ambulances. The company also manufactures an eRanger immunization clinic that has a sidecar that folds out into a mini clinic with stainless steel work surfaces, refrigeration storage for vaccines, weighing scales, and a clean water unit.[11]

Basic medicines for free: India's new health minister is rolling out a new health-care initiative that will provide free access to 50 essential generic medicines. He states: "Fifty basic essential drugs address 75% of the healthcare needs of the majority, and we plan to make these available free to everyone, from birth to death. India's public hospitals and dispensaries will offer free medicine to treat pain, infections, hypertension, diabetes and many other diseases. The program which will be rolled out in phases will focus on efficient procurement, quality control and rational use—50% of medicines are wasted or overused, leading to complications and drug-resistance. A standard list of medicines will ensure that for the same amount of money, 35% more medicines of superior quality can be procured to meet the healthcare needs of the majority."[12] Many have a viewpoint that free distribution of medicine leads to misuse and corruption, and recipients also feel substandard drugs are being supplied. There are many studies to prove that anything provided free is not appreciated by people receiving it.

India has high death rates from amenable diseases and low immunization rates for infants. Out-of-pocket spending on health is pushing people below the poverty line. It seems obvious then that complimentary medicine will surely boost the country's health-care coverage. Similarly, but on a different level of spending, in the United States, a whopping US$8508 per person goes to medical care, more than double the amount spent in the United Kingdom. Still, in terms of public health, the United States ranks ninth among the top countries.[13] Part of the problem is astronomical prescription drug prices. *Bloomberg Businessweek* reports that "since October 2007 the cost of brand-name medicines has soared, with prices doubling for dozens of established drugs that target everything from multiple sclerosis to cancer, blood pressure, and even erectile dysfunction." In 2012, Americans spent a total of US$263 billion on prescription medicines. Steadily rising drug costs often forces American families into bankruptcy.

LEARNING FROM ADVANCED ECONOMIES

Developed economies have had two categories of innovations. The high end is based on research and advanced technologies resulting in expensive products that can be afforded only in rich countries. Later, when technologies mature and volumes drive prices down, they will be adopted by developing countries. Second, there are low-cost technologies that are developed basically for developing countries but not used in developed countries. This distinction is increasingly blurred. Many new technologies are cheap and portable, thus easily applied also in poor countries from the start.

Various Innovations by Developed Economies

Automated "lab-on-a-chip." A new computer programming language, created by a research team at the University of California, Riverside, will automate "laboratory-on-a-chip" technologies. It has the potential to reduce the costs of advanced diagnostics. The technology is used for DNA sequencing, virus detection, and drug discovery, among other biomedical applications. The device is only millimeters in size and allows for the automation and miniaturization of biochemical reactions, as reported by the school.

The language removes humans from the equation. In the past, the lab-on-a-chip used electronic sensors to enable health-care professionals to work with the device to analyze the sensor data. But with the data now being funneled into a computer that facilitates automated decision making, professionals do not need to interact with the data. Human interaction is minimized to "eliminate human error, cut costs, and speed up the entire process."

To create the new programming language, the team started with an existing one on bioprogramming, Bio Coder, developed by Microsoft's research office in India. The researchers used that code to process sensor feedback in real time. They then used a software simulator to mimic the behavior of a laboratory-on-a-chip.[14]

A *Smartphone* already contains sensors, an accelerometer that keeps track of our movement, a high-definition camera that can photograph external ailments and transmit them for analysis, and a global positioning system that knows where we have been. All of these devices can feed data into our smartphone and cloud-based personal lockers—turning this into a medical device. For example, *Enki*, created by NextServices, is a mobile electronic health record platform. *Wello*, launched by Azoi, a multinational company, is an iPhone case and application that tracks blood oxygen level, blood pressure, ECG, respiration, temperature, and has an attachment for reading lung functions. *Immune* uses a smartphone to create, access, and update the immunization records. People under the poverty line are enrolled under this program and are provided with a bracelet or a card with a unique QR code. The community health-care worker records the detail in the smartphone by scanning the QR code. This initiative is being supported by the U.S. National Science Foundation.[15]

There are more than 97,000 mobile health applications in the health, wellness, and medical category. 44 million health applications have been downloaded by 2012. It is expected to increase to 142 million by 2016.

Portable CD4 equipment was developed by Daktari Diagnostics. Globally, 35.3 million people were living with HIV at the end of 2012. Sub-Saharan Africa remains most severely affected, with nearly 1 in every 20 adults living with HIV and accounting for 71% of the people living with HIV worldwide.[16] Flow cytometry equipment that tests CD4 counts for HIV patients is expensive, large, and is not feasible for remote areas. This portable CD4 device processes CD4 counts within 8 minutes by placing a drop of blood into the assay chamber on a small plastic card, where antibodies grab onto CD4 cells while letting other white blood cells pass by. The process is known as microfluidic cell chromatography. This device helps clinicians perform a cheap, accurate, and quick CD4 test even in remote areas so that HIV-positive patients can be monitored regularly.[17]

VillageReach was founded in the United States and provides coverage in many developing countries, including Malawi, which has one of the highest maternal mortality rates and where there is 1 doctor for every 44,000 people. To address this, VillageReach came up with Chipatala Cha Pa Foni (CCPF) which is an accessible, cost-effective mHealth solution for maternal and child health. It provides information to trained health-care workers via a dedicated hotline and message service where the provider's intervention is not required. CCPF provides diagnosis and referral to the hospital, coordinates emergency transport, and educates mothers about prenatal and antenatal care. In 2011, CCPF was launched in one district of Malawi serving a population of more than 60,000 women and children. Now the program has reached to four districts.[18]

Do We Need Doctors?[19]

I had an opportunity to hear Silicon Valley investor Vinod Khosla at an international conference. He presented out-of-the-box extreme views questioning why doctors are required, and asking why they cannot be replaced by computers to do the work 24x7 with consistent quality. Many of us do not agree with his views: how can you replace the human touch of doctors to patients which is so reassuring to patients. However, part of his thinking is logical, doable, and adoptable.

As a patient you need to visit a clinic in person. You waste many hours to see a doctor for few minutes. "Doctor Algorithm," or "Dr. A" as named by Khosla, could replace 80% of doctors as you can do the checkup yourself with the aid of a computer.

Vital indicators can be measured by smartphone cameras. A skin scan measures risk of skin cancer from a photograph of a skin lesion. Cell phones that display vital signs and take ultrasound images of heart or abdomen are in the offing as well as genetic scans of malignant cells that match your cancer to the most effective treatment.

An electronic medical record (EMR) can pull out the history of a patient to make diagnosis easier. Genetics and metabolic pathways, of which there are a few thousand, impact our body in complex ways. These would be a perfect case for a computer to identify and track and give a differential diagnosis. In countries where there is shortage of physicians, computers can reduce the workload of middle level doctors serving patients that are capable and willing to do a part of the job themselves. Using computer or phone applications for primary care is like taking over-the-counter (OTC) drugs, and getting full information of the disease including possible complications and advice when one must visit a physician. The number of visits would be reduced but physicians would not be disposed of. I would call it aiding doctors and not replacing them. Technology can assist and innovate in optimization of resources but should not be the master of the humans who have created it.

Difficulty in Innovation Adoption

Innovations are difficult to adopt everywhere. Medical treatment has made appreciable advances but delivery often is inefficient, ineffective, and consumer unfriendly. For example, medical errors are the eighth leading cause of death in the United States. 48.6 million people (15.7% of population) had no health insurance in 2009 as per the U.S. Census Bureau.

> Despite this enormous investment in innovation and the magnitude of the opportunity for innovators to both do good and do well, all too many efforts fail, losing billions of investor dollars along the way. Some of the more conspicuous examples: the disastrous outcome of the managed care revolution, the US$40 billion lost by investors to biotech ventures, and the collapse of numerous businesses aimed at bringing economies of scale to fragmented physician practices.[20]
>
> Innovation is by definition about creating something new. Everything that is new includes a risk. Innovations are applied in ecosystems, where every possible interaction, constraint and unintended consequence can't be known in advance. Some innovations are disruptive, threating to drive incumbents out of business and creating heavy resistance from vested interests. Innovations are bound to produce waste, dead-ends, failed initiatives, adverse effects, and rejects by the public. An economy that can't afford, or tolerate such waste, will not innovate. Developed countries have the advantage of adopting innovations that have already been tested and evolved into

best practices. Countries that catch up can grow rapidly. When at the technology frontier, innovations and growth tend to slow down.

While innovative waste is inevitable, the question is, can it be reduced by applying Lean thinking or models of innovation excellence? There are various ecosystems in the world. Some are more receptive to certain innovations than others. For example, the above-mentioned Doctor A reducing the number of patient visits and doctors would be resisted in an ecosystem with an abundant supply of doctors, competing fiercely for patient fees. In an ecosystem with a scarcity of doctors, it would be welcomed as a solution to a problem. For an innovation to be successful, it needs to be integrated into a sustainable business model.

Hospital Corporation of America has successfully put in place an innovation in business model that consolidated the management of dozens of facilities and realized economies of scale in the fragmented healthcare industry. It currently has 190 hospitals and 200 outpatient centers and succeeded. In other cases innovations have been barred. For example, Duke University Medical Center's specialized congestive heart failure program reduced the average cost of treating patients by US$8,600, or about 40%, by improving their outcomes and therefore their hospital admission rates. The facility was penalized by insurers, which pay for care of the sick and not for improving people's health status. The healthier its patients were, the more money Duke lost.[20]

MedCath is a North Carolina–based for-profit chain of hospitals specializing in cardiac surgical procedures. In each of the 12 markets where it opened in the late 1990s and early 2000s, the company faced resistance from general-purpose hospitals. They argued that instead of offering cheaper care and better outcomes because of its specialized focus (as the company claimed), MedCath was simply skimming the profitable patients. In some cases, local hospitals strong-armed commercial insurers into excluding MedCath from their lists of approved providers, threatening to cut their own ties with the insurers if they failed to blackball MedCath.[20]

There is a need to analyze barriers of innovations and how to improve health-care delivery to the community. It is ultimately a country's political system, culture, infrastructure, size, resources, incentive to health-care providers, alignment, and leadership that would decide the type of health-care delivery system to be adopted that is best suited for its citizens. Comparing different systems can reveal hidden obstacles. Developing cross-border collaborations can bring unexpected insights.

COLLABORATIVE APPROACH

An example of East–West collaboration is the setting up of a health-care facility in the Cayman Islands by Narayana Health (NH), based in Bangalore, India, and Ascension, the largest nonprofit and Catholic health-care system in the United States. Both companies have compatible values. NH is committed to care for people regardless of their ability to pay. Ascension is dedicated to furthering its mission of serving community with special attention to those who are poor and vulnerable. The Grand Cayman facility opened its doors in March 2014 with a state-of-the-art, tertiary care hospital. It is a center of excellence in cardiac surgery, cardiology, orthopedics, pulmonary, pediatric, endocrinology, neurology, oncology, and other cutting-edge tertiary care disciplines. Over the next decade, the hospital will expand to a 2000-bed facility, and expects to be a JCI (Joint Commission International)–accredited facility providing care in major specialties. The complex is also planned to have a medical university and an assisted-care living community.

The relationship between Ascension and NH began through TriMedx, a health-care equipment services company that is a subsidiary of Ascension Holdings. TriMedx provides biomedical engineering services to NH in Bangalore, India, through its subsidiary TriMedx International. Ascension is dedicated to the transformation of health care through innovation and excellent clinical care. Ascension Health operates in more than 500 locations in 20 states and the District of Columbia. In fiscal year 2011, Ascension Health managed a total of 16,515 available beds, 70 general acute care hospitals, 2 long-term acute care hospitals, 3 rehabilitation hospitals, and 4 psychiatric hospitals.

In fiscal year 2013, Ascension provided US$1.5 billion in care for persons living in poverty and other community benefit programs while earning US$400 million in income from operations on total operating revenue of US$17 billion.[21]

The Health City Cayman Islands initiative gives the partners the opportunity to positively impact the care being provided in the Caribbean region. Ascension will provide facilities planning, supply chain management, and biomedical engineering services to the project, whereas NH will provide technical input and direction to the Cayman team.

In this project every stakeholder benefits. Patients from the United States get quality treatment at much reduced cost without any waiting near to their country. Ascension wants to learn how to provide quality treatment at much reduced cost back home in the United States. NH would earn revenue. The Indian staff has been given a substantial pay hike compared to Indian levels. The Cayman Islands would get extra employment for locals, a state-of-the-art treatment facility, and revenue by taxes levied.

SUMMARY

Innovations, like good leadership, have been known since ancient times. Until recently, they have been viewed as mysteries, sudden insights by extraordinary people, lucky coincidences, and charisma. The human mind has unraveled many mysteries of nature and created technologies to harness them for the benefit of mankind. In a similar vein, the mysteries of innovation and leadership have been examined to discover patterns and regularities that might enable more and better with less cost. Although it is advisable to humbly admit that there are things that cannot be known, there is still the possibility of advancing the area of things that can be known and successfully managed by determined effort. These are "boxes" of systematic thought that have the potential to advance the innovation process. Occasionally somebody has to think outside of them.

Innovations have a fuzzy front-end that refuses to be captured in systematics. The long and troublesome path to a beneficial application is increasingly manageable by applying what has been learned and summarized into models and thinking tools. In the global world, the area of learning, the number of case reports, and experiences of success and failure in different ecosystems have expanded enormously. In health care both advanced and developed countries face big problems. The case for mutual learning, technology circulation, and cross-border collaboration is stronger than ever.

REFERENCES

1. Daji, B. 1865. Brief Notes on the Age and Authenticity of the Works of Aryabhata, Varahamihira, Brahmagupta, Bhattotpala, and Bhaskaracharya. *Journal of the Royal Asiatic Society of Great Britain and Ireland* 1, 392–418.
2. 5 Things Managers should know about the Big Data Economy. Retrieved from http://www.innovationexcellence.com/blog/2014/05/18/5-things-managers-should-know-about-the-big-data-economy/. Accessed on May 18, 2014.
3. Goldratt, E.M. 2004. *The Goal: A Process of Ongoing Improvement*. The North River Press, Great Barrington, MA.
4. Sergio, R. What is the theory of constraints, and how does it compare to lean thinking? Lean Enterprise Institute, Cambridge, MA.
5. Kubena, M., Okes-Voysey, M., and Vizjak, A. 2012. *Innovation Excellence in Central & Eastern Europe*, Wiley, Weinheim, Germany.
6. Dahlgaard-Park, S.M. and Dahlgaard, J.J. 2002. A Strategy for Building Sustainable Innovation Excellence A Danish Study. *Contributions to Management Science* 2008, 77–94.
7. Retrieved from http://mobilepaper.timesofindia.com/mobile.aspx?article=yes&pageid=6&sectid=edid=&edlabel=ETM&mydateHid=08-04-2014&pubname=Economic+Times+Mumbai&edname= &articleid=Ar00600&publabel=ET. Accessed on May 18, 2014.
8. Four Indians win awards at Harvard competition for startups. Retrieved from http://timesofindia.indiatimes.com/business/india-business/Four-Indians-win-awards-at-Harvard-competition-for-startups/articleshow/34528226.cms http://saathipads.com/. Accessed on May 18, 2014.
9. Gohain, M.P. IIT-Delhi shows cheap can be wonderful. Retrieved from http://timesofindia.indiatimes.com/home/education/news/IIT-Delhi-shows-cheap-can-be-wonderful/articleshow/33624265.cms. Accessed on May 18, 2014.
10. Centre for Health Market Innovation. Solar Ear. Retrieved from http://healthmarketinnovations.org/program/solar-ear. Accessed on May 18, 2014.
11. eRanger Ambulance. Retrieved from http://www.eranger.com/The-eRanger-Bikes/Ambulance.aspx;http://borgenproject.org/motorcycle-ambulance-saves-lives-effective-patient-transport/. Accessed on May 18, 2014.
12. Health min plans to give 50 essential medicines free. Retrieved from http://www.hindustantimes.com/india-news/50-essential-meds-to-be-given-free/article1-1231375.aspx. Accessed on May 18, 2014.
13. US Worst in Developed World in Healthcare. *The Times of India*, June 30, 2014.
14. Bird, J. Wireless, handheld lab analyzes blood in minutes. Retrieved from http://www.fiercemobilehealthcare.com/story/wireless-handheld-lab-analyzes-blood-minutes/2012-09-07. Accessed on May 18, 2014.
15. Design for Learning and Empowerment. IMMUNE–Cell phone based information management system. Retrieved from http://www.id4learning.com/vaccination.html. Accessed on May 18, 2014.
16. World Health Organization. Global Health Observatory (GHO). Retrieved from http://www.who.int/gho/hiv/en. Accessed on May 18, 2014.
17. Continuum Advanced Systems. Retrieved from http://continuuminnovation.com/cas_work/hivaids-point-of-care-diagnostics-system/httpworlddesignimpact.org/projects/project2013/15. Accessed on May 18, 2014.

18. Evaluation of the Information and Communications Technology for Maternal Newborn and Child Health Project. Retrieved from http://villagereach.org/vrsite /wp-content/uploads/2009/08/VR-Exec-Summary-of-CCPF-Eval_Feb-21_FINAL. pdf. Accessed on May 18, 2014.
19. Khosla, V. 2012. Retrieved from http://techcrunch.com/2012/01/10/doctors-or -algorithms/. Accessed on May 18, 2014.
20. Herzlinger, R.E. 2006. Why Innovation In Health Care Is So Hard. Harvard Business School Publishing Corporation.
21. Ascension. Retrieved from www.ascension.org.

17

Innovative Approaches of Affordable Health Care in Emerging Economies

Venkataramanaiah Saddikuti, Mohan Gopalakrishnan, and Saji Gopinath

CONTENTS

INTRODUCTION

Demand for affordable care is forcing health-care providers to improve their operational efficiency, cost control, and quality of care. Government agencies are responding by taking necessary measures to curb the cost of pharmaceuticals and medical devices such as the Medical Devices Regulations Act (MDRA) of 2006, the Drugs and Cosmetics (Amendment) Bill 2013, and the formation of the Central Drugs Authority (CDA). Recent revisions to drug price control are helping patients by improving affordability but adding to the cost pressures on pharmaceutical companies.[1] For example, the price of Omez (for 15 tablets) has been reduced to INR 48 (US$0.80) from INR 75 (US$1.2). As a result, the profit margins of wholesalers have been reduced to 7.25% from 10%, whereas retailers' margins reduced to 13.75% from 20%.[1] These steps show progress toward affordable care.

The Indian health-care industry is adopting information and communication technologies (ICT). ICT-assisted care is estimated to grow at a cumulative annual growth rate (CAGR) of around 22.7% during the period 2013–2015.[2]

The growing middle class predominantly drives Indian health care. This is shown with the following:

> Millions of middle-class families every day came face to face with a harsh Indian reality: the lack of a safety net for health. Few Indians have health insurance and the better private healthcare comes at a premium. These circumstances have given birth to new business models in healthcare financing. Indians can now buy a stent directly from a company in installments or take a loan to finance obesity surgery or cycles of infertility treatment through equated monthly installments (EMI) mode that the middle-class is familiar with. Certain chains of dental clinics, cosmetic clinics, and eye hospitals had begun offering easy monthly installments for not-so-expensive procedures. Multinational medical devices company Medtronic allows patients to pay as little as INR 600 (around US$10) per month and for up to seven years to purchase their cardiac devices. Mya Health Credit in tie-up with Tata Capital offers medical loans of more than INR 70,000 (US$1130) and up to INR 500,000 (US$8000) for procedures ranging from dental implant to bariatric surgery to hair transplant.[3]

Because of pressure from health-care payers, seekers, and regulators, providers are adopting proven productivity improvement practices such as continuous improvement, Lean, Six Sigma, and supply chain management. Both public and private players have shifted their focus toward a more holistic view. In this chapter we highlight the challenges and opportunities, and discuss lessons learned from innovative models for health-care delivery in India.[4] We propose a decision framework considering demand and supply drivers along with issues related to health-care seekers, payers, providers, and regulators. It builds on four As: awareness, accessibility, affordability, and adoptability. We show the framework with a case study pertaining to a fast-growing medical device manufacturing company from India.[5]

CHALLENGES AND OPPORTUNITIES IN HEALTH-CARE DELIVERY IN INDIAN CONTEXT

Many services are based on customer wants, preferences, and trade-offs, whereas health care is a fundamental need. As a result of advances in technology, mass production, and delivery systems, the costs of many products and services are falling. In spite of various revisions of policy and regulations, developments in surgical procedures, and the use of ICT, the cost of health care is increasing. It is becoming less affordable for many and for the poor in particular. In India, the cost of both inpatient and outpatient care has doubled in the last decade.[6] Some reasons are shortage of skilled manpower, lack of indigenous manufacturing, and high dependence on imports.[2,6]

According to a recent study[6] by the Federation of Indian Chambers of Commerce and Industry (FICCI), Indian health care needs to improve in six major areas. These are infrastructure, private investment, quality accreditation, medical education, health insurance, and medical technologies. In this chapter, our focus is on the role of medical technologies in the delivery of affordable health care in the Indian context.

MEDICAL TECHNOLOGIES

As a result of economic growth and improved access, India has attracted many global players. Medical devices imports increased by 1300% between 1998 and 2008 constituting INR 51 billion. A sharp increase in export of medical devices is also observed.[7] In response to growing demand, the government has reduced the import tariff on medical devices from more than 50% in the 1980s, to around 25% during the 1990s, and further to 12.5% during 2003 and 2004. The current tariff rate is around 5% and 4% for cardiovascular devices (CVDs).[7]

In the recent past, the government has negotiated and achieved price reductions. For example, one of the pacemaker manufacturers has reduced its price to INR 30,000 (around US$500) from INR 60,000 (around US$1000) for government hospitals and public schemes, and to INR 45,000 (around US$750) if procured by patients in private hospitals.[8] Although the medical device suppliers have had to reduce their prices, they also suffer long delays in payment, particularly by government hospitals. One of the pacemaker suppliers had INR 10 million (US$0.17 million) and a multinational company INR 30 million (US$0.5 million) accounts receivables from a single government hospital.[9]

The major challenges faced by the device suppliers are the following:[5]

- Low rate of adoption of medical devices
- Lack of indigenous manufacturing and R&D
- Long delays in accounts receivables from hospitals and institutional buyers
- Inadequately skilled workforce at different levels of the value chain
- Complexities in device selection and preference for overseas brands
- Competition from global players
- Limited export opportunities for Indian medical device manufacturers

However, the medical device manufacturers can benefit by focusing on the following opportunities:

- Innovations in product design and development through appropriate R&D and collaboration with technology companies and universities
- Use of ICT in improving payment processes, transparency, and supply chain management
- Training and development for skilled workforce in product design, manufacturing, distribution, sales, and services
- Partnership among stakeholders
- Use of management science approaches

The government is using schemes such as developing the infrastructure for medical device parks that facilitate an ecosystem to promote indigenous product development and manufacturing. It can also support large-scale adoption of devices by special status and tax exemptions.

DECISION FRAMEWORK FOR HEALTH-CARE DELIVERY

In this section, we briefly present the 4As (awareness, accessibility, afford-ability, and adoptability) decision framework for health-care delivery. This is an extension of the 3As (awareness, access, and affordability) framework suggested by Sinha and Kohnke for the global context.[10] In the Indian con-text, the low adoption rate of medical devices means that suppliers are not able to sustain the costs. For this, we suggest a fourth A (adoptability). A brief note about each of the terms is given below and the framework is shown in Figure 17.1.

Awareness[10] primarily focuses on improving the health literacy of the users:

- Know your condition and when you need help
- Know how to prevent illness
- Know what services are available and where
- Know how to express your needs

On the producer side awareness includes innovations in knowledge-pull approaches whereby physicians and allied health professionals can reach out to seek relevant knowledge.

Access[10] to health care refers to provisioning of easy and timely care in urban as well as in remote villages with logistical difficulties. Access includes the following:

- Improvement in physical infrastructure
- Availability of goods and services that enable diagnosis and treatment
- Logistical infrastructure related to travel, transportation, and accom-modation of patients

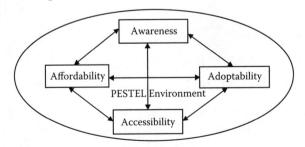

FIGURE 17.1
The 4A decision framework for health-care delivery in emerging economies.

Affordability[10] refers to the cost of health care. Affordability implies that a patient is able to incur, manage, support, or sustain the expense associated with diagnosis and treatment. In the absence of a substantial health insurance, affordability implies cost-effectiveness. The typical enablers are financial services such as health insurance, loans, payment plans, and health savings accounts that enhance the purchasing capability of the patients.

Adoptability[A] refers to the health-care ecosystem that facilitates the delivery of affordable health care in large scale to all segments of society. For example, a patient from a rural area may be aware of treatment but not in a position to take it due to non-cost–related issues or lack of postcare facilities. It is difficult to offer services at affordable prices if volumes are low. This is clear from the Aravind Eye Hospital case.[11] It had to reach out actively to patients to create sufficient demand, so that production efficiency could be achieved. Hence, both service providers and patients need to adopt within the health ecosystem.

Health-care delivery in emerging economies is affected by macro factors such as political, economic, social, technological, environmental, and legal issues (PESTEL). There are many recent examples including election manifestos of political parties assuring quality health care at affordable prices for its citizens. Service providers are also facing numerous problems due to poor legal framework and poor quality of services. Hence, health-care organizations need to consider the macro factors while designing and delivering health care on a sustainable basis.

In the following sections we elaborate on the device-assisted health care and the 4A framework with an example of a medical device manufacturing company.

EVOLUTION OF DEVICE-ASSISTED HEALTH-CARE DELIVERY

Technological developments in devices and advances in surgical procedures help to improve health care across the globe. According to the Food and Drug Administration (FDA) in the United States, a medical device is defined as "any instrument, apparatus or other related article that was intended for use in the diagnosis of disease or other conditions, or in the cure, mitigation, treatment, or prevention of disease."[12] The global market for medical devices is estimated to be between US\$180 and US\$250 billion.[13] The Indian market is growing at a rate of 15%–20% and is expected to continue for the next 5–10 years.[13]

Companies are competing through product and process innovations along with innovations in their business models. For example, Medtronic has introduced equated monthly installments (EMI) options for buying medical devices.[3] GE is developing and offering super value products for emerging economies costing 25% to 40% less than their lowest priced global products. The devices were engineered to focus on core functionalities, leaving superficial and expensive features out. Many organizations are developing skills through partnerships and collaborations. For example, one of the eye care hospitals in Chennai (Tamil Nadu, India) has a collaborative research center with Indian Institute of Technology Madras (IITM).

Product innovation introduces new goods and services for external markets generating sustainable revenues. Process innovation enhances internal production processes and improves quality.[12] Successful organizations innovate continuously around product, process, and service delivery. Consequently, they have to adopt their business models to reach their markets. The medical device industry has introduced many innovative products such as pacemakers, ortho implants, stents, and heart pumps.[14] World-class companies compete by offering both conventional (high volume, low margin) and high tech (high value) products to appropriate segments of the market.

The implantable pacemaker was developed in the 1950s. A pacemaker is a small device, which is placed under the skin of a patient's chest or abdomen to help control abnormal heart rhythms. A battery powers the pacemaker. It has leads (wire-like component) that travel through a large vein to the heart, where the wires are anchored. The leads send the electrical impulses to the heart, as shown in Figure 17.2.[13]

The evolution starting from the first external pacemaker is shown in Figure 17.3. The size of the device is shrinking due to changes in pulse generator technology and advances in batteries while functionality is enhanced through the use of embedded systems. The current devices are as small as 1 in. in diameter and weigh as little as 14 g.[5,14] Biventricular pacemakers are useful for some patients with severe ventricular contractile

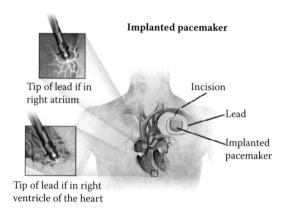

FIGURE 17.2
Pacemaker and components. (From http://www.capanet.org/uploadedFiles/Content/ Resources/Onysko-Richard-revised-powerpoint.pdf, and other sources [www.meditronix .com].)

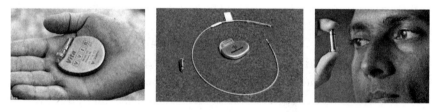

FIGURE 17.3
Evolution of pacemaker. (From http://www.capanet.org/uploadedFiles/Content/ Resources/Onysko-Richard-revised-powerpoint.pdf, and other sources [www.meditronix .com].)

dysfunction. The size of such pacemakers has come down to 24 mm long and 0.75 cm³ volume, enabling their administration without surgery. Advanced pacemakers can be inserted using catheters, reducing cost as well as time for treatment and recovery.[14]

The cost of pacemaker implants in selected countries is shown in Figure 17.4.[15] The average cost in low-cost countries (LCC) is less than 20% of the average in developed countries. Similar trends can be observed in the cost of double chamber pacemakers across seven countries as in Figure 17.5.[15] Frequent introduction of new devices lead to complexity in manufacturing and distribution. Successful organizations are focusing on cost control through management science approaches across the value chain.

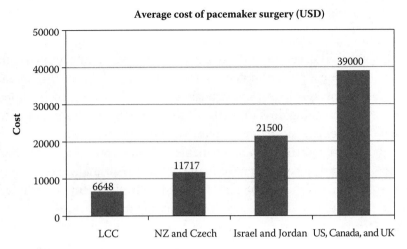

FIGURE 17.4

Average cost of pacemaker implant across selected countries. (From http://www .allmedicaltourism.com/usa/heart-surgery/pacemaker-surgery.)

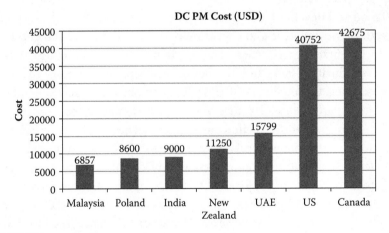

FIGURE 17.5

Cost of double chamber pacemaker implant across selected countries. (From http://www .allmedicaltourism.com/usa/heart-surgery/pacemaker-surgery.)

ROLE OF MEDICAL DEVICES IN AFFORDABLE HEALTH CARE: A CASE STUDY[5]

In this section, we illustrate the 4A decision framework for delivering health care in the Indian context with an example of a pacemaker manufacturing company, Shree Pacetronix Ltd (SPL), located in central India.

Organization and Financial Performance

This case study is based on a medical device manufacturing company, SPL, established in central India in the year 1998 as a private limited company. It became a public limited company in 1993. The company manufactures pacemakers in technical collaboration with a company in United States. The managing director (MD) of the company is the son of a U.S.-based cardiologist. The primary objective of the company was to produce affordable pacemakers for Indian patients, as import processes led to high costs and long delays. SPL started manufacturing pacemakers by importing around 90% of the components required. SPL offer them to the Indian market at around 60% of the average cost of imports.

The firm manufactures single-chamber, multiprogrammable, dual-chamber, and rate-responsive pacemakers. The first pacemaker was single chamber and was introduced in 1993. The company developed a multiprogrammable pacemaker in 1994, a dual-chamber one in 1996, and a rate-response pacemaker in 1998. Except for the first pacemaker all others were designed and developed in-house. The company has achieved substantial growth in the domestic and export markets. It sold around 100 pacemakers in the first year (1993) and more than 4000 units during 2011–12. However, during 2008–2009 the net profit decreased by more than 38% and went negative during 2010–2011. The company incurred losses due to capacity expansion and decrease in sales both domestic and export.

The company adopted innovative approaches such as continuous improvement in manufacturing, partnerships in R&D for high value product design and development, sales and distribution to reduce costs and improve financial performance. The company obtained quality certification from the European Quality Association and an ISO 9001 certificate. Consequently sales improved by around 30% and the losses were covered. Manufacturing capacity has been doubled to meet increasing demand. The company also improved its operational efficiencies across the entire value chain.

Based on its past experience, the company focused on the following for its sustainable growth:

- Product differentiation based on customer needs (basic and high value products in large scale) at competitive prices
- Indigenization in product design and manufacturing, contract manufacturing

- Developing channel partners for efficient distribution and after-sales service
- Partnerships with government organizations and universities for R&D
- Developing affordable information and communication technologies (ICT)
- Developing human capital through suitable training and incentives

Product Design and Development Process

Over the years, the company has developed in-house capability for design and development of advanced products. The company also won a number of national and international awards for its innovative products and services.

In 2010, the company developed a microchip that has been incorporated in their products. With intense efforts, the company successfully developed the screw-in lead and also completely indigenized the rate-responsive pacemakers. The lead is a component in the pacemaker that helps in transmitting the electrical pulses to the heart as required. SPL developed new advanced products such as a dual-chamber rate-responsive (DCRR) pacemaker, a biventricular pacemaker and its leads, implantable neuro stimulators, continuous positive air pressure (CPAP) machines, and deep brain stimulation generators. The company has been working with National Science and Technology Labs (NSTL), Government of India in developing cochlear implants and deep brain stimulation pacemakers and leads. The company is the fourth company in the world to manufacture cochlear implants, which will bring increased revenue and recognition worldwide. Some of the products developed and manufactured by the company are shown in Figure 17.6.

FIGURE 17.6
Selected products manufactured by the company. (From http://www.pacetronix.com/)

The latest pacemaker designed and manufactured by the company weighs 19 g with an estimated life around 12 years. The sales volume in 2009 was 2000 pacemakers out of which 90% were multiprogrammable and the rest dual-chamber and rate-response pacemakers. The company also manufactures pacing system analyzers, pacemaker leads, dental implants and, until recently, mobile x-ray units. The company was the first in Asia to manufacture spine stimulators in 2006. It is an ISO 9001 as well as CE certified company, and has won awards for excellence in manufacturing and services. It supplies pacemakers to government hospitals, private hospitals in India, and exports to European countries and others except the United States because of FDA regulations. It has the capacity to manufacture 4000 pacemaker units annually with a staff of around 60 and a sales turnover of INR 67.6 million (US$1.2m) in 2011–2012. The company is targeting to increase the sales turnover by 50% and exports by a similar 50% growth.

The company has worked closely with government agencies, health-care providers, and other stakeholders through various programs for improving public *awareness* about CVDs and the possibilities of device-assisted health care.

Manufacturing and Distribution

At the time of the study, the manufacturing of a pacemaker was taking about 45 days and consists of various processes depicted in Figure 17.7. Each pacemaker undergoes about 40–45 quality checks. The most time consuming is burn-in, which (bottleneck) takes around 10 days and is done at 90°C. It is critical for the estimated life span of a pacemaker. The final testing will be done at 37°C reflecting the normal body temperature. The company follows world-class manufacturing practices such as quality

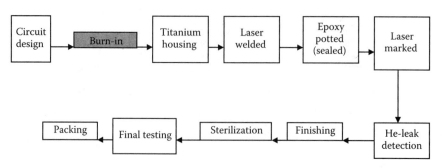

FIGURE 17.7
Pacemaker manufacturing process.

management, continuing education of employees, and collaboration with various stakeholders. The company was able to reduce the overall manufacturing time from more than 60 days (2 years ago) to around 45 days. The company adopted proven approaches such as reducing the manufacturing lead time by addressing bottlenecks in the process through process redesign or capacity expansion, use of visual management control tools, employee education, small group activities, and so on.

Another major cost factor in health-care delivery is sales and distribution cost. The company has direct distribution to hospitals in India and uses distributors for exports, thereby they were able to reduce costs due to middlemen. The company extends the support required in the after-sales period and for service through their own personnel.

SPL restructured its manufacturing and sales and distribution process by adopting proven methods such as world-class manufacturing, and supply chain integration through IT, which facilitated better visibility of inventory across the value chain. The company is adopting various approaches based on the 4A framework suggested in the "Decision framework for health-care delivery" section of this chapter. Supply chain decisions at different levels (strategic, tactical, and operational) on the demand and supply side are given in Table 17.1.

TABLE 17.1

Supply Chain Issues at Different Levels

Decision Level	Supply Side	Demand Side
Strategic	New products by global players, PPP, health-care infrastructure such as medical device parks, reverse innovation by MNCs, and so on.	Aging population, middle income group and its growth, awareness, government support, changing life style, food habits, use of alcohol, increasing medical institutes
Tactical	Number of players in medical devices manufacturing, availability of skilled manpower, reduced import tariffs, collaboration with medical professionals, forecast/ estimation of requirements	Change in rural and urban medical requirements, enabling technologies such as ICT, quality of life, changes in surgical procedures, insurance and paying capacity
Operational	Limited capacity of device suppliers, competition and cost of devices, government regulations and interventions	Number of new players on surgical side, changes in surgical procedures, reduced length of stay

TABLE 17.2

4As of Health-Care Delivery and Their Alignment

Health Care Dimension	Steps/Methods Followed for Alignment
Awareness	Collaboration with health-care organizations in spreading awareness on preventive care on CVDs and device-assisted health care, increase in demand for pacemakers and allied products
Accessibility	Develop high-value products for care delivery and treatment, high-volume manufacturing, customized distribution, and after-sales service through dedicated technical workforce
Affordability	Collaboration in R&D, local talent development, indigenization of product design and manufacturing, contract manufacturing, high-value product development and manufacturing, new product offerings, exports to overseas markets, quality certification, and cost optimization across value chain
Adoptability	Develop world-class products at competitive prices, collaboration with R&D organizations, developing advanced products using microprocessors, dropping complex medical equipment such as x-ray machines and focusing on advanced pacemakers, use of ICT for process improvement at various levels, supply chain integration, partnership/collaboration with stakeholders for delivering care on large scale

The company has taken various steps to align its activities to improve overall performance, which are mapped to the proposed 4A framework. A brief on these is shown in Table 17.2.

███████████

SUMMARY

In this chapter, we described challenges and opportunities for delivery of affordable health care in India. The 4A decision framework has been illustrated with the help of a medical device manufacturing company. *Awareness* of CVDs and preventive care were developed through several steps that improved collaboration and partnerships with different stakeholders. *Access* has been improved by directly supplying devices to hospitals, and support services through dedicated and skilled staff. *Affordability* has been improved through cost optimization, high volume, and product diversification across the value chain. *Adoptability* has been demonstrated through close work with governmental as well as private organizations for improving sales on a large scale through partnerships and collaboration and focusing on high-value products. Patient-focused and technology-enabled health care can benefit all stakeholders.

ACKNOWLEDGMENT

Our thanks are due to Mr. Atul Kumar Sethi, MD, Shree Pacetronix Ltd, for sharing his experience and supplying helpful information.

REFERENCES

1. Kurmanath, K V and Nagasridhar, G (2013). Drug price order-Gain for patients, pain for retailers, Business Line, September 3, 2013. Retrieved from http://www.the hindubusinessline.com/industry-and-economy/drug-price-order-gain-for-patients -pain-for retailers/article5086371.ece. Accessed on September 15, 2013.
2. Healthcare Industry in India (2013). Retrieved from http://www.ibef.org/industry /healthcare-india.aspx. Accessed on September 20, 2013.
3. Iyer, M (2012). Now, loans and EMIs help pay for stents, surgeries. Retrieved from http://articlestimesofindia.indiatimes.com/2012-12-09/india-business/35705325_1 _Instalments-cardiac-devices-patients. Accessed on September 20, 2013.
4. Venkataramanaiah, S, Gopinath, S, and Gopalakrishnan, M (2012). Delivery of affordable healthcare in emerging economies: Challenges and opportunities, a theme based invited session, Decision Sciences Institute (DSI) Annual Conference, San Francisco, CA, November 17–20, 2012.
5. Sethi, A K (2012). Shree Pacetronix Ltd Indore, Madhya Pradesh, India, Information collected through field visits, teleconference and email communications. Retrieved from http://www.pacetronix.com. Accessed on September 2012 and February 2014.
6. FICCI Heal 2008: Fostering Quality Healthcare for All, FICCI, New Delhi. Retrieved from http://www.ficci.com/Sedocument/20107/Recommendations-HEAL-2008.pdf. Accessed on September 15, 2013.
7. Mahal, A and Karan, A K (2009). Diffusion of medical technology: Medical devices in India, *Expert Review of Medical Devices*, 6(2): 197–205.
8. Chakraborty, A (2004). Rs 30,000: That's all for a pacemaker, *Times of India*, March 2004. Retrieved from www.timesofindia.indiatimes.com. Accessed on October 5, 2013.
9. Chakraborty, S (2013). Pacemaker payment delay puts hearts at risk - Foreign gadget supplier stops delivery, indigenous firm threatens to follow suit, *The Telegraph*, August 1, 2013, Retrieved from http://www.telegraphindia.com/1130801/jsp/bihar /story_17178959.jsp#.UrQ0JdIW0sA. Accessed on October 5, 2013.

10. Sinha, K and Kohnke, E J (2009). Healthcare supply chain design: Towards linking the development and delivery of care globally. *Decision Sciences*, 40(2): 197–212.

11. Brilliant, L and Brilliant, G (2007). Aravind: Partner and social science innovator, innovations. Retrieved from http://www.seva.ca/docs/mit_innovations_-_aravind.pdf. Accessed on November 1, 2013.

12. Denend, L and Zenios, S (2006). Drug eluting stents: A paradigm shift in the medical device industry, Stanford Graduate School of Business, Case OIT-50.

13. Martin, M (2012). Cardiac Pacemakers Market: Global industry size, share, trends, analysis and forecasts 2012–2018. Retrieved from http://www.allvoices.com/contributed-news/12404227-cardiac-pacemakers-market-global-industry-size-share-trends-analysis-and-forecasts-2012-2018. Accessed on September 25, 2013.

14. Young, S (2013). World's smallest pacemaker can be implanted without surgery. Retrieved from http://www.technologyreview.com/news/522306/worlds-smallest-pacemaker-can-be-implanted-without-surgery/. Accessed on December 20, 2013.

15. Cost of pacemaker surgery. Retrieved from http://www.allmedicaltourism.com/usa/Heart-Surgery-And-Cardiology/pacemaker-surgery/. Accessed on December 20, 2013.

18

Supply Chain Innovations in Health Care

Atanu Chaudhuri

CONTENTS

INTRODUCTION

Supply chain management encompasses the planning and management of all activities involved in sourcing, procurement, conversion, and logistics. Importantly, it also includes coordination and collaboration with channel partners, which can be suppliers, intermediaries, third-party service providers, and customers. In essence, supply chain management integrates supply and demand management within and across companies.

Three major groups of organizations that comprise the health-care supply chain are shown in Figure 18.1.

1. Manufacturers that produce pharmaceuticals, medical devices, and health-care supplies
2. Intermediaries like wholesale distributors, which help bring health-care products to the marketplace
3. Health-care providers such as hospitals and individual medical practitioners

FIGURE 18.1
Schematic diagram of flow of goods in health-care supply chain.

Pharmaceutical companies and medical device manufacturers are facing increasing competition and dealing with challenges from rising costs and pressure from governments and regulatory agencies. Most pharmaceutical supply chains were originally set up to produce items in high volume, in factories not noted for agility. Consequently, supply chains were structured to avoid stock outs and to meet regulatory requirements. This was achieved by maintaining high inventory levels and carrying costs. Such an expensive and inflexible supply chain further adds to the challenges of pharmaceutical companies. There is a need to redesign the existing supply chain to improve both cost efficiency and responsiveness.

Proliferation of counterfeit products in the entire health-care supply chain is another matter of concern. Supply chain security breaches are threatening patient safety. Such breaches are increasing more than 33% every year, mostly in China, India, and Brazil.[1] Hence, distributors are facing demands from both the manufacturers and the health-care service providers to continuously reduce costs while maintaining high standards of safety.

The medical device industry is also experiencing unprecedented challenges. A typical device company carries a large number of products in its portfolio and has to cater to the needs of health-care service providers on a daily basis. It needs to manage its inventory while meeting the clinical needs of its patients at the lowest possible cost.

Health-care service providers at the receiving end of the value chain need to provide affordable health care for the masses while facing increasing levels of regulatory oversight and patient scrutiny. Patients expect more choice, and demand evidence that treatments really work and lower prices.[2] This is particularly true for countries in India where health insurance penetration is low and large sections of the population pay out-of-pocket for health-care expenses.

In a survey of U.S. health-care professionals, Group Purchasing Organizations (GPO), and distributors respondents indicated that the lack of data standardization and having no visibility into the end-to-end performance of their business processes were their major challenges.[3]

Organizations across the health-care value chain need to improve cost efficiency while being responsive to customer needs. Supply chain innovation is one key enabler to achieve such objectives. The challenges may appear to be disparate and affect only the individual players in the health-care supply chain. It is true that pharmaceutical companies, medical device manufacturers, distributors, and health-care service providers may have to take certain actions to address some of the above challenges. But many of the above challenges impact the entire health-care value chain and will require collaborations for innovation across the chain. In this chapter, we specifically look at supply chain innovations by the individual players in the health-care value chain as well as collaborative innovations amongst multiple players, and provide a road ahead for supply chain innovations in the sector.

IMPERATIVE FOR INNOVATION IN HEALTH-CARE SUPPLY CHAINS

Innovation is an imperative for organizations to gain competitive advantage and improve organizational performance. The challenges across the health-care value chain are creating multiple trade-offs for the firms. Pharmaceutical firms face trade-offs between cost efficiency and growth. Health-care service providers face trade-offs between cost efficiency and providing access to health care as well as between flow efficiency and resource efficiency. Innovation is the means by which the firms can break the trade-offs and position themselves on a different performance frontier. Using cost and responsiveness as two performance measures, Figure 18.2 shows how organizations need to position themselves in different performance frontiers. When they are behind a performance frontier, they face trade-offs: if they strive to cut costs, responsiveness suffers; if they go for responsiveness, their cost position suffers. Breaking a performance frontier is possible only if the organization is able to innovate and engage in series of innovation cycles.

Although some of these innovations can be driven internally by the firms themselves, innovation will require collaboration between players across the chain. Such innovations have to encompass complex sets of processes, and deal with uncertainty in the environment.[4]

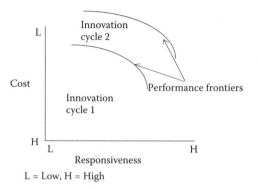

FIGURE 18.2
Need of innovation cycles to break trade-offs.

SUPPLY CHAIN INNOVATIONS BY PLAYERS IN HEALTH-CARE VALUE CHAIN

The pressing challenges in the supply chain have made it imperative for pharmaceutical companies, medical device manufacturers, distributors, and health-care service providers to explore opportunities for innovative solutions. Such innovations typically require design of appropriate processes supported by people and/or technology and can potentially involve collaboration with supply chain partners.

Pharmaceutical Supply Chain Innovation

The pharmaceutical supply chain currently suffers from long manufacturing lead times, high levels of inventory, and long delivery lead times thus making it both unresponsive and cost inefficient.

We look at how a pharmaceutical company leveraged technology to connect people and improve the supply chain. Ratiopharm, Canada, which was acquired by rival Teva Pharmaceutical Industries in 2010, had been finding it increasingly difficult to react to changes in demand for its generic drugs. At times, the company's supply chain unit could be unaware for up to 4 months that manufacturing bottlenecks or quality control issues were causing slowdowns. Information Technology (IT) officials at Ratiopharm determined that better internal communication could alleviate some of the problems. The company decided to use Web 2.0 and social collaboration tools to help employees share information more efficiently. It initially used Microsoft's SharePoint, and later turned to collaboration tools from Strategy-Nets and then software from enterprise social networking firm Moxie Software. The strategy worked and it helped not only in fixing the supply chain problems but also in improving service levels and in saving jobs during the recession.[5] The innovative approach taken by Ratiopharm was to use technology to connect people and improve supply chain visibility, as it realized collaboration between people holds the key to supply chain decision making.

Mr. Tony Martins, Vice President-Supply Chain, Teva Pharmaceuticals, noted that a dynamic business environment requires a supply chain with rapid response. He believes that speed of the supply chain depends to a large extent on people talking to people.[6] The supply chain team is now using social tools. The expertise it has acquired over the past several years has been put to improve processes at Teva Canada. Prior to the Ratiopharm acquisition, Teva Canada was struggling through industry upheaval caused by the recession. Its service level—the percentage of orders filled on time—was below 90%, and its manufacturing cycle was around 80 days. After Teva Canada started using Ratiopharm's tools earlier in 2011, its service level rose to over 95% and its manufacturing cycle time—the period from order to sale—improved from 35 to 40 days.[7]

Medical Device Supply Chain Innovation

The large number of products and customer locations coupled with demand uncertainty and strict regulations make the medical device supply chain extremely complex. Companies face trade-offs between cost efficiency and customer responsiveness under such conditions. Higher responsiveness may result in increased inventory or higher logistics costs while attempts to reduce costs may result in poor responsiveness.

Medtronic is a medical device company that has managed a complex supply chain and improved both cost efficiency and responsiveness. Medtronic's Cardiovascular business unit provides more than 100 different product groups and 12,000 stocking units worldwide.

The diversity of the product portfolio, the uncertainty, and the different delivery methods combined with 4000 hospital locations in the world make Medtronic Cardiovascular's supply chain very complex and dynamic. Achieving a careful balance between optimizing asset management and meeting clinical needs is a challenge for Medtronic. It addresses it by a combined sales and operations planning (S&OP) process and a pull-to-demand-replenishment process that help in sensing short-term changes as well as in preparing for mid- to long-term demand shifts. Medtronic can respond to market signals by aligning its inventory, internal and external manufacturing capacities, and materials to meet the demand at the time it is forecasted. In addition, S&OP includes an iterative risk assessment process that helps senior management to make trade-off decisions between service and cost, wherever required, given the sensitivity around the likely success of forecasting future demand.[8] Medtronic's supply chain demonstrates the power of well-oiled processes in helping decision making by the leadership team. Here, the innovation lies in designing the appropriate order-to-delivery process coupled with the risk assessment exercise that facilitates decision making in the face of uncertainty.

Pharmaceutical Distribution Supply Chain Innovation

Ensuring access to medicines in Africa is a serious challenge for pharmaceutical companies and the various nonprofit organizations involved with the task. To ensure that the medicines reach the appropriate places in the right condition without increasing costs, innovative distribution of medicines has been attempted. In some countries such as Benin in West Africa, health supply chains are leveraging on Coca Cola distribution to improve supply chains for health commodities. Unlike medical and pharmaceutical supplies, Coca Cola is available in every village and at the right condition for the consumers. Coca Cola's expertise has been solicited in the creation of a public–private partnership to expand access to health-care products. The partnership is called Cola Life and its mission is to use the Coca Cola distribution channels to move "social products." An "AirPod" container was created to fit between the bottles in a standard crate of Coca Cola. AirPod container can then be filled with products such as oral rehydration salts, vitamin A, or water purification tablets. As a result of the AirPod, local NGOs or social product manufacturers can "piggy-back" on the strong Coca Cola distribution channels and can have SMS tracking of their products in remote areas. The above approach has been found successful during the pilot in West Africa. It has the potential to be replicated in the hinterlands of countries such as China and India where fast moving consumer goods (FMCG) companies have achieved reasonable success in creating a distribution network.[9] The above example highlights the use of a nontraditional mode and leveraging best practices from a different industry in pharmaceutical distribution.

Health-Care Service Provider Supply Chain Innovation

Health-care providers face a difficult dilemma as they always need to ensure that a patient's life is in no way endangered while driving supply chain efficiencies. Usually health-care providers end up carrying more inventory of medicines and other essential items than needed to cover up for emergencies.

In Mackay Memorial Hospital, Taiwan, the original supply chain comprised two order cycles. Internal health-care units placed orders with the central depot on Monday, Wednesday, and Friday and received the order via an internal delivery system on Wednesday, Friday, and Monday if the item was not out of stock. The ordering logic was a reorder point concept, that is, whenever inventory reduced to the reordering point, the material controller would order a fixed quantity from the central depot via a computerized ordering system. The second order cycle was a computerized ordering system using a similar reordering point concept for monthly orders from suppliers. The problem with this system was that the fixed quantity order often could not meet the real needs, and it would necessitate changes in orders or cause items to run out of stock, which would trigger the emergency ordering procedure. To avoid these problems, a higher stock level was set by the health-care units and logistics department, which was not the ideal solution as it led to higher inventory carrying costs.

Applying the pull-based supply chain design principle to reduce inventory level was finally chosen as the goal of logistics innovation at Mackay Memorial Hospital. The project team decided to choose 70 health-care units in the main Taipei campus for the logistics innovation pilot project. The project team selected 23 high-valued items for pull-based supply chain testing. These items were bulky and supplied by three reliable and reputable suppliers. The final design was a weekly ordering system where all health-care units' orders based on actual planned consumptions are consolidated on Friday and transmitted to suppliers via a computer system. Suppliers delivered products to the central depot on Thursday creating a buffer for the Friday requirements to avoid a potential shortage. In the last stage of the project, all supply chain partners were trained to learn how to work with the new process and computer system. The operational rules and procedures were revised and set during the training period to ensure their correctness in helping supply chain partners to do the correct things. The tacit knowledge of the supply chain partners was also captured and converted to explicit knowledge. The inventory balance was reduced significantly after the introduction of the pull-based supply chain design to the supply chains for the 23 medical supply items.[10] Mackay Memorial Hospital helped break the myth that the pull-based ordering system can work only in manufacturing industries and are unsuitable for industries such as health care. The improvement exercise at Mackay Memorial Hospital demonstrated the need of a systematic approach and the power of a successful pilot to create credibility within the organization.

A rare success story in public health supply chains in India is demonstrated by Tamil Nadu Medical Services Corporation (TNMSC). When TNMSC was set up, drug procurement in the state was scattered, with each public hospital sourcing drugs on its own with no standard procedures. TNMSC, which relied heavily on IT systems and processes to streamline drug procurement, helped in dramatically bringing down drug prices. For instance, the price of 10 strips of antibiotic ciprofloxacin tablets during 1992 to 1994 (before TNMSC) was INR 525. That fell to INR 88 during 2002 to 2003. Similarly, the cost of 100 Norfloxacin tablets fell from INR 290 to INR 51.30 during the same period.

The key to TNMSC's success is its tendering process and a passbook system for distributing drugs. It floats tenders at the beginning of every year to identify suppliers for about 250 drugs, which are the most used and usually cover the treatment spectrum. The purchases follow a two-tier tendering process where first technical bids are evaluated and then price bids decide the supplier. TNMSC follows a stringent testing process—it has about 11 laboratories empanelled with it. These labs test the first batches of every drug supplied and subsequently also random samples picked from TNMSC's 25 warehouses spread across the state. Earlier, drugs used to be supplied in bulk. The corporation put an end to it and insisted on blister packaging and special labeling for it in English and Tamil, which made it difficult to divert them.[11] Thus, TNMSC's innovative approach not only brought down costs but also ensured that the medicines are not tampered with and diverted. TNMSC demonstrates how design of appropriate processes enabled by IT and stringent quality controls can simultaneously improve availability of medicines while bringing down costs.

COLLABORATIVE SUPPLY CHAIN INNOVATION
BETWEEN PARTNERS IN HEALTH CARE

There is a need to innovate across the health-care supply chain with partners sharing objectives and efforts. By its nature, supply chain innovations can rarely be accomplished by a single organization and in most cases require cooperation from the supply chain partners. Health-care supply chain professionals are increasingly accepting the fact that they all share the same supply chain with its own challenges and opportunities and such realization is preparing grounds for future collaborations across the supply chain.[12] Having said that, we must also admit that many collaborative innovations in supply chain demand that the internal improvements are in place before attempting to collaborate with external partners. If an organization finds it difficult to have cross-functional synchronization within its own organization, collaborating with supply chain partners will be far more difficult. The true benefits of supply chain innovations will be accrued if the partners work together to create value for the entire supply chain instead of focusing on individual benefits.

The IT-enabled service delivery innovation demonstrated by K Hospital Group in Taiwan demonstrates the power of collaboration. The K hospital Group identified the target customers as patients who had suffered stroke within the previous year. Services were designed to provide continuous care, 24 hours a day, 7 days a week. The services included monitoring physiological signals, follow-up diagnosis, home visits, home delivery of medicine, applying for social benefits/emergency transfers, and health-care consultation. The K Hospital group deemed community care centers responsible for service operation. Upon discharge from a hospital, patients can use the home health-care system to monitor physiological signals and transfer this data via the Internet to the health-care center for analysis. When patients were discharged from a hospital, K Hospital combined the delivery of services from health-care professionals, hospitals, basic health-care facilities (clinics), social care assistants, and transportation companies. To support these new services, K Hospital established an IT-based health-care service network, which was used to develop services to provide seamless care. The hospital partnered with information system development companies and service providers to form an R&D alliance for code-signing delivery mechanisms and workflows that support these services.[13] For home health-care system, the innovation lies in bringing together all the service providers required for providing care and the development of the IT network that enabled the delivery of service.

SUMMARY

Continuous supply chain innovation can be made possible with supplier cooperation, which in turn can improve organizational performance.[14] To achieve supply chain innovation, organization leaders must nurture an excellent work environment, which includes providing the right resources to support efficient operational processes for high quality of care.[15,16]

The starting point of any initiative to innovate will be identifying the current pain areas, acknowledging that problems exist, and that they can be addressed. This will require that each organization maps its existing processes, collects data, and develops common metrics to understand the areas of improvement. Benchmarking with best-in-class companies across industries can help identify and quantify areas for improvement. Pharmaceutical companies and medical device manufacturers should also map the volume and variety of the products and their existing order to a delivery process. This can be followed by an exercise in understanding the causes of existing inefficiencies, which should lead to a identifying where internal improvements are required and where collaboration with supply chain partners will be essential. Internal improvements, for example, manufacturing lead time reduction for pharmaceutical companies or standardizing the procurement process of a health-care service provider will also require formation of cross-functional teams, top management support, and demonstration of benefits using a pilot project. Collaborative efforts will require identifying a set of products/services for pilot purposes, selection of partners with appropriate capabilities, and willingness to collaborate and set up of agreements for the collaboration that is, sharing of potential benefits.

The complexity associated with clinical care coupled with a large number of products and services across the health-care supply chain make it vulnerable to trade-offs between cost inefficiencies and responsiveness. Organizations across the health-care supply chain must keep a close eye on the organizational and supply chain metrics and make efforts to redesign processes as required while involving people within and across their organizations along with appropriate use of technology. Innovative practices that emerge out of such efforts can help the organizations to break the trade-offs and provide quality care at the right time at an affordable cost. Many of these efforts will be transformational in nature and will require senior leadership commitment and direction.

REFERENCES

1. Thomas S., Erik, S., and Ketan, S. (2013). Strengthening Health Care's Supply Chain: A Five-step Plan. Available at http://www.mckinsey.com/insights/health_systemsandservice/strengthening_health_cares_supply_chain_a_five_step_plan. Accessed October 24, 2013.

2. Merrill, M. (2011). Healthcare Supply Chain Costs: A Tough Pill to Follow. Available at http://www.inboundlogistics.com/cms/article/healthcare-supply-chain-costs-a-tough-pill-to-swallow/. Accessed October 24, 2013.

3. Heather, H. and Edward, A. P. (2009). The State of Healthcare Logistics: Cost and Quality Improvement Opportunities within the Healthcare Supply Chain. Center for Innovation in Healthcare Logistics, University of Arkansas, July 2009.

4. Lee, S. M., Lee, D., and Schniederjans, M. J. (2011). Supply chain innovation and organizational performance in the healthcare industry. *International Journal of Operations & Production Management,* 31(11):1193–1214.

5. Sharon, G. (2011). Social Tools Help Drug Maker Fix Supply Chain. Available at http://www.computerworld.com/article/2550049/internet/drug-maker-fixes-supply-chain-with-social-tools.html. Accessed October 18, 2013.

6. Adrian, G. (2011). Social Media: A Waste of Time or Catalyst for Supply Chain Innovation. Available at http://www.cssl.ws/files/CSSLProg26SocialMediaWasteofTimeAGonzalez.pdf. Accessed October 15, 2013.

7. Sharon, G. (2011). Social Tools Help Drug Maker Fix Supply Chain. Available at http://www.computerworld.com/s/article/358106/Drug_Maker_Fixes_Supply_Chain_With_Social_Tool. Accessed October 18, 2013.

8. Interview with Shannon Crespin, Vice President of Planning, Medtronic Global Supply Chain. Available at http://www.gscreview.com/Mar11_shannon_crespin.php. Accessed October 18, 2013.

9. Mawanda, R. M. (2011). Innovations in pharmaceutical supply chains in sub-Saharan Africa. *Pharmalink,* 11(1): 7–9.

10. Su, S. I. I., Gammelgaard, B., and Yang, S. L. (2011). Logistics innovation process revisited: Insights from a hospital case study. *International Journal of Physical Distribution & Logistics Management,* 41(6): 577–600.

11. Dinesh, N. (2010). Tamil Nadu Medical Services Corporation: A Success Story, Forbes India. Available at http://forbesindia.com/article/on-assignment/tamil-nadu-medical-services-corporation-a-success-story/15562/1#ixzz2dBbroEd8. Accessed October 21, 2013.

12. Heather, N. and Pohl, E. A. (2009). The State of Healthcare Logistics: Cost and Quality Improvement Opportunities within the Healthcare Supply Chain. Center for Innovation in Healthcare Logistics, University of Arkansas, July 2009.

13. Yang, H. L. and Hsiao, S. L. (2009). Mechanisms of developing innovative IT-enabled services: A case study of Taiwanese healthcare service. *Technovation*, 29(5): 327–337.
14. Lee, S. M., Lee, D., and Schniederjans, M. J. (2011). Supply chain innovation and organizational performance in the healthcare industry. *International Journal of Operations & Production Management*, 31(11): 1193–1214.
15. Byrnes, J. L. S. (2004). Fixing The Healthcare Supply Chain. Harvard Business School: Working Knowledge. Available at http://hbswk.hbs.edu/archive/4036.html. Accessed October 21, 2013.
16. Schneller, E. and Smeltzer, L. (2006). *Strategic Management of the Health Care Supply Chain*, Jossey-Bass, San Francisco, CA.

19

Three-Dimensional Health Care: "The Need of the Hour"

Satish Kr. Gupta

CONTENTS

INTRODUCTION

Being poor in a poor country and poor in a rich country are different experiences. A poor person in a poor country often toils from morning to night on unfertile fields or in low-productivity workshops receiving an income that barely keeps malnutrition away. A poor person in a rich country typically is unemployed, idle, and obese.

In a similar vein, being sick in a poor country and sick in a rich country are different things. The sick in a poor country lack essential services and die from diseases to which cures exist. The sick in a rich country would have died, if not for the advances in medicine, antibiotics, and emergency care. Now he survives, but with a chronic condition, that requires continuous monitoring and frequent therapies. Indeed, in rich countries about three-quarters of medical expenditure goes to treating chronic conditions, many of which are lifestyle related. With the beginning of the twenty-first century, the global burden of disease has shifted from communicable to noncommunicable diseases (NCD).[1]

Modern medical science has made tremendous advances in the ability to diagnose and cure. Western medicine emerged out of emergency care and military hospitals. The modus operandi of reactive medicine is, something has gone wrong, now let us make it right again with best available technologies, therapies, and cures. This applies to trauma victims, sudden heart attacks, strokes, curious cancers, and mysterious infections. However, NCD requires low-tech, high-touch medium skills and moderate facilities, and, importantly, that the patient deploys his or her own resources and takes proactive measures. With the growth of NCD, a misalignment between needs and resources has emerged.

Poor countries need to adopt different strategies than the rich. Not everybody needs, nor can afford the care of an expensively trained specialist in narrow fields of medicine. Moreover, to prevent the burden of disease from growing, there is a need to focus on the management of health, rather than the cure of illnesses. In this context, need has arisen for a new comprehensive model of health care that can address the root cause of disease and all the dimensions of a suffering human being, and thereby provide complete and lasting recovery from an illness, physical or mental, leading to a healthy and happy life.

BIOPSYCHOSOCIAL MODEL

There is a growing body of evidence that psychosocial factors play a role in NCD. Type-*A* behavior, anxiety, anger, depression, hostility, social isolation, and acute and chronic life stresses[2-10] can contribute significantly by encouraging unhealthy behaviors such as smoking, atherogenic diet consisting of fast and junk food,[11] sedentary habits (lack of physical exercise),[12] and failure to follow one's biological clock in going to bed early in the night and getting up early in the morning. Besides activating the sympatho-adrenomedullary system, these psychosocial factors can also activate endothelial dysfunction[13] and platelet aggregation, and can become a major impediment in modification of the acquired aberrant lifestyle. Still psychosocial factors continue to be overlooked by clinicians and are frequently underemphasized in modern medical education in India and all over the world. Modern medicine has failed to move beyond the *biomedical model* due to many reasons, such as already overloaded curriculum, inadequate economic incentives, and lack of exposure to the evidence base supporting the role of psychosocial factors in pathogenesis of NCDs.

With the explosion of noncommunicable- and lifestyle-related diseases, Western medicine has turned to the behavioral sciences for help. A lifestyle change, such as smoking cessation, low-fat high-fiber vegetarian diet, daily moderate aerobic exercise, weight reduction, and so on, cannot be administered like a shot of antibiotics or a cardiac bypass. Essentially the patient cures himself/herself, with some aid and support from the caregiver. Such behavioral interventions have been much studied. However, the success rates are nowhere near those of reactive medicine.

Behavioral interventions require a theory, or at least a model of behavior. Western behavioral medicine builds on standard western psychology. It started about a century ago with the behaviorist school, based on Pavlov's famous experiments with salivating dogs. At its extreme, behaviorism reduced human beings to stimulus-response automata. The Freudian school of dynamic psychology looked at the human psyche as a steam engine, where sublime desires create pressure that finds various ways to escape. The current mainstream is focused on cognitive processes drawing on advances in brain research. The eastern tradition has a different conception of what a human being is.

The *biopsychosocial model* and its clinical applications were described by Engel (1977).[14,15] It has become the foundation of primary care. The psychological and social aspects of illness are emphasized in addition to the biomedical disorder. It may be relevant to understanding a variety of clinical outcomes across disorders among primary care patients.

Still, with all the modern gadgetry, knowledge, and technical know-how, why we are not able to provide a cure when dealing with lifestyle disorders such as heart disease, diabetes, hypertension, obesity, gastroesophageal reflux disease, migraine, depression, insomnia, and cancer? Relief yes, albeit temporary and symptomatic.

Can doctors and modern medicine be blamed? I do not think so. They are a hardworking, meticulous set of people who sacrifice a lot to give the best they can. Yet, tools are incomplete. We spend years in medical school learning about the body. Very little time is devoted to the mind and its workings. There is a deficit in our education system. A *human being* is not just a *human body*. The word *human* is derived from *humus*, that is soil, and that is what the body turns into when the *being* (the soul) has gone.

We call it death. So how can we possibly provide a cure or lasting relief to a person when we go on treating his body but not him or her?

Recently, a few well-conducted studies have shown that NCD can be better managed by adopting healthy lifestyle and proper stress management through meditation. Two such studies are briefly mentioned below.

The INTERHEART Study (2004),[16] which included 30,000 men and women in 52 countries over all continents, has shown that modification of risk factors such as reducing mental stress and adopting a healthy lifestyle could prevent at least 90% of all heart disease. Adopting a healthy lifestyle prevents or reverses not just heart disease, but also many other NCDs as well.

Ornish et al.[17] and Jacobs et al.[18] have shown in their studies that comprehensive lifestyle change and intensive meditation training may change gene expression in only a few months by increasing telomerase activity thereby prolonging healthy life. Genes associated with coronary artery disease (CAD), cancer, obesity, and so on were downregulated or *turned off*, whereas protective genes were upregulated or *turned on.*

On the basis of the consistent and observable importance of religion and spirituality to health, Onarecker and Sterling[19] proposed that the biopsychosocial model be revised to include spirituality. The Association of American Medical College (AAMC), the World Health Organization (WHO), and the Joint Commission on Accreditation of Healthcare Organizations (JCAHO) now include spirituality in medical practice and education. This model is consistent with holism, a view that deals with health problems in their physical, psychological, social, cultural, and existential dimensions. Spiritual symptoms may act synergistically with other symptom dimensions in affecting health. Such synergistic effects, however, have not been widely studied. Yet, there still remain many challenges to incorporate spirituality into medicine, such as the lack of a common language for spirituality, as well as concerns regarding boundaries, ethics, and cultural and religious differences.

A disturbed state of mind affects the body. Diseases of the body disturb the being, which in turn disturbs the *mind*, and entity of *soul*, which again adversely affects the body. It is imperative that soul, mind, and body, all three, are addressed whenever a treatment is required or offered for an ailment. The next logical step for medical science is to address all the three aspects of a human being as a *three-dimensional* (3D) *healthcare model.*

Three-Dimensional Health-Care Model

The 3D health-care model has evolved from the author's 33 years of clinical experience and 28 years of spiritual experience with Brahmakumaris Rajyoga Meditation (BKRM). This included extensive literature reviews and intense research into the psychophysiology, psychoneuroendocrinology, and etiopathogenesis of various diseases. This model has been evaluated in more than 5000 angiographically documented heart patients, from India and abroad. They were also suffering from other lifestyle-related illnesses, for example, hypertension, obesity, diabetes, bronchial asthma, chronic obstructive pulmonary disease (COPD), cancer, generalized osteoporosis, autoimmune diseases, and mental health disorders. The present form of the 3D health-care model represents a synthesis of psychological, physiological, endocrinological, clinical, and spiritual experiments with thousands of patients over 16 years.[20,21]

The 3D health-care model has the following principles to be sustained as far as possible in daily living:[20]

- *Self-responsibility through self-empowerment*: The word *healthy* is derived from two words: *heal + thy*, that is, to heal yourself. To heal oneself, one needs to be empowered by appropriate information about the mind–body connection, psychological and conventional risk factors, stress management, diet, exercise, sleep, substance abuse, and usual medical care.
- *Self-awareness:* The Hindi word for healthy is *swasth*, which consists of *swa-*, meaning *inner self*, and *-asth*, meaning *conscious*. The word healthy could also mean *inner self-conscious*. Outer self-consciousness of the mortal body, or ever-changing material things, leads to instability and insecurity, which in turn leads to anger, anxiety, depression, type-A behavior, isolation, and chronic life stresses. Conversely, inner self-consciousness of enduring and immortal spirit leads to stability and security, which in turn leads to peace, love, and happiness. A healthy lifestyle is an *inner self-conscious lifestyle*.
- *Multidimensionality:* The current medical approach addresses only one dimension, the physical body. A new model of health, *3D health care* (soul–mind–body medicine) is called for. As per this new model, health is a dynamic process of harmony in flow of spiritual energy:
  - Knowledge: of truth, purity, peace, love, happiness, and bliss
  - Power: of discrimination, to judge, to withdraw, to pack up, to tolerate, to face, to accommodate, and to cooperate

- Mental energy: positive thoughts, emotions, attitudes, and memories (TEAM)
- Physical energy: healthy diet, exercise, sleep, and medication
- *Biological clock and circadian rhythm:* When activities are in rhythm with one's biological clock, energy expense and stress are reduced, beneficial for the health of the mind, intellect, and body.

MEANING OF SOUL

A very seriously ill patient is brought to the emergency department of a well-equipped hospital. The doctor on duty tries his best to revive the patient, but without success. The patient dies. The doctor tells the relatives he is very sorry and asks them to take away the body. About half an hour back a patient was brought to the hospital, now a body is going out. What has happened when a patient has become a body?

Now assume that, with the consent of relatives, from this body you remove heart, liver, or kidney and transplant them in a histocompatible human being requiring this organ. The organ that did no longer function in the dead body now starts functioning again.

The life force or our true inner self has been termed soul in the Indian literature. The soul uses eyes to see, mouth to speak, ears to hear, heart to pump oxygenated blood to organs, and lungs to oxygenate the blood. In the Indian tradition, soul is a conscient point of spiritual energy. It is located in the center of the forehead between the two eyebrows. Anatomically, soul is supposed to be located at the base of the hypothalamus near the pituitary stalk.

The very word *human being* illuminates the existence of soul. The word *human* derives from humus, soil; the word *being* means life force or soul.

Each *I* is a soul. The soul has no sex, nationality, or race; it is ageless, immortal, and indestructible. We are all visitors to this earth; we are all actors in this world drama. In this way we will see not only our true value, but the true value of others and the true value of this world around us.

In soul-consciousness, the soul is in its rightful place as the ruler of the body, sitting on its throne between the eyebrows. Soul-consciousness also refers to being aware of one's own original state. In body-consciousness, the soul sees a problem as a huge mountain, but in soul-consciousness, the soul sees the same problem as a tiny mound. The problem is the same, but the new perspective has reduced the worry and fear to nothing.

Soul is the master of the physical body in the same way a driver is the master of a car. When soul is inside the body on its seat, all the organ systems are alive and working. When soul leaves the body, all the organs are still there but cannot function.

Subtle Faculties of the Soul

Soul has three subtle faculties to control and rule over the physical body: mind, intellect, and personality traits.

Mind is the thinking power and mental energy of the soul, negative or positive. Mind has four aspects: thoughts, emotions, attitudes, and memories (TEAM).

Soul nourishes each cell of the physical body with its seven spiritual energies: knowledge of the inner self, purity, peace, love, happiness, bliss, and powers through the mind's TEAM. Positive TEAM facilitates the flow of these seven energies to the body cells. Negative TEAM blocks them thereby leading to disease.

The mental energy makes the aura (subtle body) of a person. Soul radiates its spiritual energy to all the brain centers, for example, hypothalamus (thinking center), limbic system (center of emotions and attitudes), frontal cortex (memory center), respiratory center, speech center, visual center, and so on in maximum concentration as these centers are located near the soul. Many scientists the world over are now of the opinion that mind is not only located in the brain but that each cell of the body has mind. That means the mind or mental energy has the same shape as the physical body. It is a well-known fact that each cell of the body has electrical energy that can be measured by various scientific equipment, such as how the electrical energy of brain cells is measured by electroencephalography (EEG), while such energy is measured in the heart by electrocardiography (ECG), and in the muscles by electromyography (EMG).

Aura can be photographed by Kirlian photography and it has been found to be useful in diagnosis of disease in a particular part of body and organ system before it gets clinically manifested in the form of signs and symptoms.

The target organ in a physical body is determined by the interplay of genetic background and environmental factors. Bad actions consume, and good actions increase the spiritual energy. Bad action performed through a particular organ system leads to decrease in nourishing spiritual energy to that particular organ system, which in turn leads to development of disease over a period.

If a person thinks positively most of the time, the aura around him is made up of silvery white light. Such a person is liked by all and radiates all the seven innate qualities around him. Others can feel the soothing effect of these qualities. Positive TEAM opens the flow of spiritual energy and protects cells of the target organ in the physical body from microbes, oxidants, and toxins; it also attracts healing protein molecules, antioxidants, and boosts up the immune system thereby leading to rapid recovery from disease and health-consciousness.

The mind–body connection is very strong. TEAM are electrochemical events occurring in the hypothalamus of the brain. Now, with the help of positron emission tomography (PET), scanning physiological changes occurring in the brain with change in thoughts, emotions, and so on can be seen on the computer screen. After a lot of research in thought chemistry, it has been proved that mental energy gets converted into matter called neuropeptides in the hypothalamus. These neuropeptides have been chemically isolated and identified. They go to each cell of the body through the bloodstream. Each of the 70–80 trillion cells of the body has receptors for them. These neuropeptides act as biochemical messengers. The brain talks to each cell of various organ systems through neuropeptides and cells also talk to each other. In this way, the mind is intimately connected with each cell of the physical body.

Whatever type of TEAM we have in the mind (subtle body), the physical body (cells) cannot escape from its effects, good or bad. If we have a negative thought or emotion, negative neuropeptides are formed in the hypothalamus and they go to each cell of the body, especially the target organ. It leads to release of various stress hormones, for example, epinephrine, norepinephrine, and cortisol, and sympathetic dominance that leads to burning of energy, accumulation of catabolic products, toxins, and oxidants inside the cells (especially the target organ) leading to disease.

On the other hand, if we have a positive thought or emotion, there is a release of endorphins (morphine-like substances released by various cells of the body), encephalin, melatonin, and so on, and parasympathetic dominance that leads to pooling of energy; removal of catabolic products and toxins; and production of antioxidants leading to feelings of well-being, health, and happiness. Negative mental patterns (TEAM) lead to disease and positive patterns lead to health.

Intellect is judging and decision-making power. It is influenced by our old personality traits, resolves, and habits. Intellect can be corrupt when it takes negative decisions, which have a discharging effect on the soul battery. Intellect is correct when it takes positive decisions.

By practicing BKRM, the intellect slowly becomes correct and we start taking positive decisions only and these positive decisions have a charging effect on the soul battery. When the positive decisions are taken again and again these become our new positive personality traits, resolves, and habits.

Personality traits are memories formed by repeated thoughts, speech, and actions. A person starts getting identified by his personality traits and habits; for example, if a person gets angry again and again he is called an angry person, if someone smokes repeatedly, he is called smoker, and if he takes alcohol frequently, he is called an alcoholic. Similarly, if a person always speaks and behaves sweetly, she is called a gentle and sweet person,if he gives money to charity repeatedly, he is called a charitable person.

The supreme soul or God is the ultimate source of all the seven spiritual energies, the powerhouse for all the souls in the universe. We, the souls, consider the supreme soul as our father or mother and our relationship with other people is that of brothers and sisters.

Rajyoga Meditation

Meditation is a method, known in all major religious traditions, of communicating with and attuning oneself to God. All healing and moral guidance ultimately comes from God.

BKRM mediation is an elaborated method that strives to the highest state of consciousness in which the mind is fully relaxed even when the physical body is engaged in daily work. It is the practice of soul-consciousness.

When I try to practice meditation in outer self-consciousness (body, role, material) thoughts of my physical body, relatives, friends, profession, patients, bank account, house, and so on crisscross my consciousness. Instead of achieving peace and happiness, I develop headache and restlessness. Why I am not getting the connection? This *why* leads to disease. The outer self-consciousness leads to negativities such as ego-attachment, greed, anger, lust, jealousy, and laziness. These negative forces are like darkness in the relative lack of spiritual energy. Light has a source, but darkness does not. In the same way, the negative forces do not stem from the real nature of the inner self, but are simply symptoms of relative lack of spiritual energy. As spiritual energy declines outer self-consciousness comes in and negative TEAM appears.

When I practice meditation in soul-consciousness (I am a soul residing within the physical body), I get connected with the supreme soul, the father of all the souls, the ultimate source of spiritual energy, the ocean of all the innate qualities. The full flow of spiritual energy in the form of all the seven innate qualities starts leading to health-consciousness and a feeling of well-being.

BKRM is the science and art of harmonizing spiritual, mental, and physical energy through connection with the ultimate source of spiritual energy (supreme soul) for enjoying ever-healthy, ever-wealthy, and ever-happy life.

A person practicing BKRM takes vegetarian food, regular morning and evening walks, and performs his/her work in home or office in the soul-conscious stage. This is termed a healthy lifestyle.

BKRM can be practiced by any person of any age, cast, religion, and country with eyes open while performing day-to-day work. A person can be trained in BKRM by undergoing a condensed 3-day course.

There are several observed benefits of BKRM. Our face starts radiating all the innate qualities of soul, for example, peace, love, and happiness. We start generating peaceful alpha, theta, and delta brain rhythms, which can be recorded by EEG. There will be better control of hypertension and diabetes. Insulin sensitivity is improved irrespective of diabetic status.[21] There is significant decrease in stress hormone levels in the blood. There is regular and balanced release of happy hormones such as endorphins, melatonin, and dehydroepiandrosterone (DHEA), which give us feelings of well-being, happiness, and pooling of energy. Regular practice leads to parasympathetic dominance that leads to decrease in heart rate, decrease in blood pressure, and opening of blood vessels, increase in skin resistance (GSR), and increase in heart rate variability. Overall, there will be better psychological status: a type-*A* person becomes type *B*, with significant decrease in anxiety, anger, and depression score.[20] We start following healthy lifestyle changes with better compliance.

RESEARCH ON THE THREE-DIMENSIONAL HEALTH-CARE MODEL

To evaluate the efficacy of the friendly 3D health-care model for healthy mind, heart, and body, two multidisciplinary, prospective, randomized, and controlled studies, the Mount Abu Open Heart Trial[20] and Abu Healthy Heart Trial, in 518 CAD patients were undertaken in 1995. The subjects were angiographically documented CAD patients who were also suffering from various other lifestyle-related disorders. Psychologists, physiologists, endocrinologists, cardiologists, clinicians, dieticians, fitness experts, and spiritualists worked hand in hand for more than 16 years. We, at J. Watumull Global Hospital and Research Centre, affiliated with the Brahma Kumaris World Spiritual University, located at Mount Abu, Rajasthan, collaborated with the Defence Institute of Physiology and Allied Sciences, New Delhi. This project was sponsored by Ministry of Health and Family Welfare, government of India, New Delhi and Defence Research and Development Organisation, New Delhi.

The 3D health-care model was put to test with very positive, encouraging, and remarkable results, which have baffled health experts and patients alike. Thousands of heart patients could open their blocked arteries without any percutaneous transluminal coronary angioplasty (PTCA) or coronary artery bypass grafting (CABG). The pumping power of the heart, which was thought to be irreversibly damaged after a heart attack, improved significantly. All this was documented by repeat 2D color Doppler echocardiography and repeat angiography. The results of univariate analysis in these patients indicate that the angiographic changes were attributable to the decrease in weight, triglycerides and management of diet, exercise schedule, and psychosocial stressors through BKRM. The multivariate analysis showed that the independent predictors of CAD regression were not change in weight and lipid parameters as such, but the management of psychosocial stressors through BKRM. The BKRM also motivated CAD patients to adhere more to a healthy diet, exercise, treatment schedules, and smoking cessation.[13]

There were multiple other benefits in terms of improved diabetic control with less medication, better control of blood pressure, and relief from bronchial asthma, migraine, arthritis, depression, insomnia, anxiety, and many other conditions. A total of 93% of CAD patients could open their blocks in the interventional group as compared to only 13.5% in the control group. There was a total positive gain in overall well-being experienced by patients. During the study, the largest data set of its kind was collected on various parameters of the human body (psychological, hormonal, glycemic control, serum lipid profile, 2D ECHO [color Doppler] repeat coronary angiography, and so on.)

Results from the study suggest that CAD patients can be motivated to adopt the 3D health-care model for a fairly long period of 8 years of follow-up, while performing their routine activities outside the hospital.

This program was found to be user-friendly, safe, flexible, and compatible with other treatments in the setting of advanced CAD, with a high degree of compliance. The primary end point of this study was change in percent diameter stenosis. In patients with the most adherence, the average percent diameter stenosis decreased by 18.23 absolute percentage points (29.03% relative improvement), and in patients with medium adherence, it decreased by 11.85 absolute percentage points (19.10% relative improvement), but it progressed in patients with least adherence. Cardiac events were also markedly decreased in patients with the most adherence compared to patients with least adherence. However, more than 50% adherence to the prescribed 3D health-care model is essential to achieve significant regression in percent diameter stenosis and in the number of cardiac events.

The 3D health-care model could modify psychosocial factors by significantly reducing anxiety, depression, anger, and type-A behavior, and improve lifestyles and overall sense of well-being. The modification of psychosocial factors was reflected in better adherence to healthy lifestyle behavior like cessation of smoking, adherence to prescribed diet, and exercise schedules. On physiological analysis of these CAD patients through EEG, it was observed that patients who were found to have dominance of beta rhythm (13–40 Hz) on day 1 changed to dominance of alpha/theta rhythm (4–10 Hz—peaceful and loveful rhythm) on day 7 of the 3D health-care program. It has been observed that brain rhythm corresponds to number of thoughts in a minute. Normally, a person, on average, has 35,000 thoughts per day; it can be reduced to 10,000 thoughts per day within 7 days of practice of Rajyoga Meditation.

Favorable highly significant changes were observed in New York Heart Association (NYHA) function class, angina severity and frequency, drug score, and exercise tolerance by day 7, which were further favorably modified at different stages of follow-up. The long-term reduction in NYHA functional class and nitrate requirements and increased exercise tolerance is on par with what is achieved following coronary angioplasty or bypass surgery.

The improvement in various metabolic parameters in these patients may be due to the low-cholesterol, high-fiber vegetarian diet; physical exercise or BKRM independently, or the synergistic effect of all three. An improvement in the various metabolic parameters after the program are consistent with results found by other investigators who observed that a diet rich in fruits, vegetables,[22] and fiber can reduce the risk factors for CAD due to the presence of a variety of phytonutrients.[11,23] The beneficial effects of exercise on coronary heart disease may be mediated through its effect on the cardiovascular system, on the musculoskeletal system, and by modifying the various cardiovascular risk factors.[12,24] Exercise can also increase vasodilator prostaglandin and decrease levels of plasma rennin activity and blood viscosity.

The cardioprotective effects of BKRM may be mediated through an interaction between the autonomic nervous system and the endocrine system.[25,26] In fact, in these CAD patients the administration of the 3D health-care model also enhanced the alpha activity of EEG and caused a shift of autonomic balance toward relative parasympathetic predominance besides causing a marked reduction in secretion of stress hormones such as epinephrine, norepinephrine, and cortisol.[21,27] Rajyoga is also a training in awareness, which produces definite changes in perception, attention, and cognition. During BKRM, the practitioner remains awake and vigilant but the body enters a state of deep muscle relaxation. It also helps in building strong willpower for compliance to the 3D health-care model as it teaches a holistic lifestyle modification, the benefits of which the participants begin to experience within 7 days of the intervention. Because BKRM also enhances inner strength to lead a stress-free and healthy life it might have caused marked reduction in psychological stressors and favorably modified unhealthy behavioral patterns that in turn may be responsible for regression in coronary atherosclerosis and reduction in coronary events.

The Mount Abu Open Heart Trial[2] was published in September 2011 in the *Indian Heart Journal*. Over the last few years, this study has become the most read and cited article by researchers and the medical fraternity as was informed to us by Biomedlib.com (hit count 23,550,427). The *Mount Abu Open Heart Trial* stands as number one among the top 20 research articles in this category.

From the study we learned that when a human being loses soul-consciousness and is trapped in material consciousness, his mind gets effected by life's situations—favorable or adverse. Eventually, inner peace and happiness are lost. This affects everything; food habits, daily routines, exercise, and social and familial harmony all get changed for the worse and eventually the person is affected by multitude of psychosomatic illnesses. The disease manifests in the psyche (mind) and takes hold of the soma (body).

The disease that has taken hold of the body in turn affects the mind and the soul. A person is caught in a vicious circle of stress, irritation, anger, worry, sadness, and fear, from which it is impossible to escape. It affects not only the individual but also the family and society, not to mention the loss of efficiency at work that translates into significant economic loss to the nation.

In this research, we found that when a human being is given the support of spirituality, he is able to turn from *material consciousness* to *soul consciousness*. He is able to gain back a control over his life, and tackle all that life throws at him without losing peace. He is empowered and in turn empowers those around him by being an example.

SUMMARY

The 3D health-care model is a user-friendly way to address all three aspects of a human being, spiritual, mental, and physical, thereby providing complete health of mind and body. More than 16 years of experiments with thousands of patients suffering from various mental and physical disorders have shown that it is compatible with modern health care and able to provide relief and comfort to patients suffering from any disease of the mind and physical body, especially all the NCDs.

Note: More details on 3D health-care model will appear in the author's forthcoming book.

REFERENCES

1. Global burden of disease study 2010. *Lancet* 2012; 380 (9859).
2. Manchanda SC, Narang R, Reddy KS et al. Retardation of coronary atherosclerosis with yoga lifestyle intervention. *J Assoc Physicians* 2000; 48: 687–694.
3. Rozanski A, Blumenthal JA, Kapan J. Impact of psychological factors in the pathogenesis of cardiovascular disease and implications for therapy. *Circulation* 1999; 99: 2192–2217.
4. Ford DE, Mead LA. Depression as risk factors for coronary artery disease in men: The precursors study. *Arch Intern Med* 2000; 62: 463–471.
5. Kubzansky LD, Kawachi I, Spiro A III et al. Is worrying bad for your heart? A prospective study of worry and coronary heart disease in the Normative Aging Study. *Circulation* 1997; 95: 818–824.
6. Kawachi I, Kubzansky LD, Spiro et al. Prospective study of a self report type A scale and risk of coronary heart disease: Test of MMPI-1 type A scale. *Circulation* 1998; 98: 405–412.
7. Kawachi I, Sparrow D, Spiro AI et al. A prospective study of anger and coronary heart disease: The Normative Aging Study. *Circulation* 1995; 84: 2090–2095.
8. Rozanski A, Blumenthal JA, Davidson KW et al. The epidemiology, pathophysiology, and management of psychosocial risk factors in cardiac practice: The emerging field of behavioral cardiology. *J Am Coll Cardiol*. 2005; 45: 637–51.

9. Chandola T, Britton A, Brunner E, Hemingway H et al. Work stress and coronary heart disease: What are the mechanisms? *Eur Heart J* 2008; 29: 640–648.

10. Hassan M, Li H, Li Q et al. Association of β1-Adrenergic receptor genetic polymorphism with mental stress induced myocardial ischemia in patients with coronary artery disease. *Arch Intern Med* 2008; 168: 763–770.

11. Spieker LE, Hurlimann D, Ruschitzka F et al. Mental stress induces prolonged endothelial dysfunction via endothelin-receptors. *Circulation* 2002; 105: 2817.

12. Lichtenstein AH, Appel LJ, Brands M et al. Diet and lifestyle recommendations revision 2006. A scientific statement from American Heart Association Nutrition Committee. *Circulation* 2006; 114: 82–96.

13. Powers SK, Lenon SL, Quindry J, Meat JL. Exercise and cardioprotection. *Curr Opin Cardiol* 2002; 17: 495–502.

14. Engel GL. The need for a new medical model: A challenge for bio-medicine. *Science* 1977; 196(4286): 129–136.

15. Engel GL. Clinical applications of the biopsychosocial model. *Am J Psychiatry* 1980; 137(5): 535–544.

16. Yusuf S, Hawken S, Ounpuu S et al. Effect of potentially modifiable risk factors associated with myocardial infarction in 52 countries (the INTERHEART study): Case control study. *Lancet* 2004; 364: 953–962.

17. Ornish et al. Increased telomerase activity and comprehensive lifestyle changes. *Lancet Oncol* 2008; 9: 1048–1057.

18. Jacobs TL, Epel ES, Lin J et al. Intensive meditation training, immune cell telomerase activity, and psychological mediators. *Psychoneuroendocrinology* 2011; 36(5): 664–681.

19. Onarecker CD, Sterling BC. Addressing your patients' spiritual needs. *Fam Pract Manag* 1995; May: 44–49

20. Gupta SK, Sawhney RC, Rai L et al. Regression of coronary atherosclerosis through healthy and happy lifestyle in coronary artery disease patients: Mount Abu Open Heart Trial. *Indian Heart J.* 2011; 63: 461–469.

21. Shakun S, Sawhney RC, Gupta SK. Impact of Vegetarian Diet, Aerobic Exercise and BKRM on Hyperinsulemia, Dyslipidaemia and Hyperglycemia in Coronary Artery Disease. PhD Thesis, ACBR Delhi University, New Delhi, India, 2005.

22. Ness AR, Powles JK. Fruit and vegetables, and cardiovascular disease: A review. *Int. J Epidemol* 1997; 26: 1.

23. Howard BV, Kritchvesky D. Phytochemicals and cardiovascular disease. *Circulation* 1997; 95: 2591–2593.

24. Powers SK, Lenon SL, Quindry J, Meat JL. Exercise and cardioprotection. *Curr Opin Cardiol* 2002; 17: 495–502.

25. Cunningham C, Brown S, Kaski J. Effects of transcendental meditation on symptoms and electrocardiographic changes in patients with cardiac syndrome X. *AM J Cardiol* 2000; 85: 653–655.

26. Canter PH. The therapeutic effects of meditation. *BMJ* 2003; 326: 1049–1050.

27. Davidson RJ. Spirituality and meditation: Science and practice. *Ann Fam Med* 2008; 6: 388–389.

20

Innovative Initiatives in Health Care by Indian Government

Vishwas Mehta

CONTENTS

INTRODUCTION

Providing good health care to citizens of a country is an inevitable part of government business, along with external security and internal safety. It is essential for every government to take care of epidemics

289

and provide relief in disasters. In India, the government provides basic infrastructure like hospitals, equipment, and human resources to ensure that there are sufficient resources established equitably to cater to all sections of the society. The private sector would largely be confined to catering to the part of population that can afford to pay for their services.

In India, health is a state subject. Every state government has taken steps to establish hospital facilities in rural areas to take care of the most marginal sections of society.

As illustrated in Figure 20.1, there is a well-established practice of having:

- Health subcenters to look after populations of 5000 people
- Primary health-care centers (PHCs) to look after 25,000–50,000 people

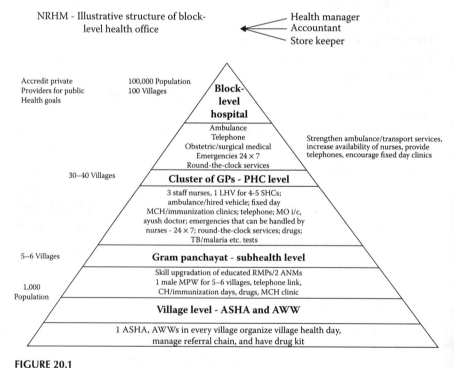

FIGURE 20.1
Indian public health care structure. (From Amarjeet, S., *Crafting a Credible Public System for Health and Nutrition for All: Emerging Issues and Policy Paradigms*, 2009.)

- Community health centers (CHCs) to look after 50,000–100,000 people
- Subdivisional hospitals/district hospitals to take care of 100,000 and above

Currently, in India, the government operates 12,760 hospitals, 4,833 CHCs, 24,049 PHCs, and 148,366 subcenters. This tier structure is supposed to take care of the basic health needs of people and it is expected to work as referral centers. These hospitals have been established by government funding to ensure affordable health care to cover the entire segment of population in the country. However, access varies from state to state depending on locations and infrastructure.[1]

Over the years, several initiatives have been tried in government to achieve the basic objective of providing affordable health care to people. Government, by and large, fails to publicize such initiatives. Therefore, innovations in sustainable health-care management rarely get replicated in other states, even when it is technically and economically possible. India is a vast country with cultural, religious, and geographic diversities, which present huge challenges to policy makers and those engaged in implementing them. Population wise, Uttar Pradesh has 3% of world's population, which is bigger than the fifth most populous country, Brazil. Maharashtra is bigger than Japan and Bihar bigger than Mexico. What works in one state may not work in another state.

This chapter deals with initiatives taken by government with particular focus on Universal Health Coverage, health insurance, health-care delivery systems, human resource management, knowledge networking, a case study of the Rajasthan state government for drug procurement, and the public–private partnership (PPP) model of Kerala.

UNIVERSAL HEALTH COVERAGE

Universal Health Coverage provides a framework for making accessible, affordable, and appropriate health care available to all citizens of a country. It seeks to provide financial protection to people by reducing out-of-pocket health expenditure. To that effect, public financing of health needs to be increased, and better results for the money spent must be achieved. People should have the means to pay for essential services through insurance schemes or other financial arrangements, services should be available and staffed with personnel possessing appropriate skills, and essential drugs should be available at affordable cost.[2]

The High Level Expert Group (HLEG) constituted by the Planning Commission in 2011 has made several recommendations to implement Universal Health Coverage to India. The vision is to cover every citizen under a National Health Package (NHP) for essential primary, secondary, and tertiary health-care services by the year 2020. The NHP would be funded by the government but people can choose between public and private services.[3] Governments can basically take four different approaches to health finance. First, they can choose to do nothing. If so, patients pay the price asked by service providers out of their pockets, or use whatever private insurance is available. This, obviously, results in deprivation of essential services to the poor, and a concentration of resources to serve those with the means. Therefore, out-of-pocket health finance exists only in developing countries, and in rich countries in certain segments considered nonessential, such as cosmetic surgery.

Second, governments can collect funds through taxes and distribute them to service providers in exchange for them providing services to citizens. People pay nothing at the point of service. This is the Beveridge model used in the United Kingdom. Although the tax-based model has intuitive appeal, it removes market competition and leads to producer-centricity, cost inflation, misaligned incentives, poor resource utilization, and long waiting times. Therefore, many governments have realized that even under universal coverage, the money should follow the patient to ensure free choice and competition.

Third, governments can take the role of a general insurer, collecting insurance fees from the public through statutory contributions and providing coverage to everybody. Such national health insurance models are used in Canada and Taiwan.

Fourth, governments can support and regulate the health insurance industry. Insurance companies can be private and compete with each other, but the rules of coverage and premiums are strictly regulated. All citizens must be covered on similar terms regardless of preexisting conditions. For those without means the government pays the premiums. Those willing to pay more for extra coverage are free to do so.

In practice, most countries exhibit mixed models combining elements of all or some approaches. In the United States, all four models are used, depending on state and population segments.

HEALTH INSURANCE

In India, the Ministry of Labour and Employment has launched a health insurance scheme for below poverty line (BPL) families called Rashtriya Swasthya Bima Yojana (RSBY). The beneficiary is any BPL family, whose information is included in the district BPL list prepared by the state government. The eligible family needs to come to the enrollment station, and the identity of the household head needs to be confirmed by the authorized official. RSBY provides cover for hospitalization expenses up to INR30,000 (US$500) for a family of five on a floater basis. Transportation charges are also covered up to a maximum of INR1000 (US$17) with INR100 (US$1.7) per visit. The premium for RSBY differs by districts. The state governments select insurance companies through an open tendering process and the technically qualified lowest bid is selected. The central government pays 75% of the total premium (90% in the case of Jammu and Kashmir and northeast states), whereas state governments pay the remaining premium. Beneficiaries need to pay only INR30 (US$0.5) per family at the time of enrollment.

Most common diseases are listed and made into a package with fixed rates. There is no age limit for getting enrolled. The scheme benefit is available to inpatient treatment only except for a few prenotified day care cases.

The RSBY launched in Kerala was further expanded by the government of Kerala to provide comprehensive health insurance to cover a larger segment of people. Originally, RSBY was only covering 1.17 million BPL (absolute poor) families in the state. The government of Kerala decided to add another 1 million BPL families to extend the benefit of health insurance to cover the most vulnerable segments of societies. Under RSBY, 75% of the premium is paid by the central government and 25% by the state government, while for the additional population covered under the Comprehensive Health Insurance Scheme (CHIS), the state pays 100% of the premium. The competitive premium per family quoted by United India Insurance was INR506 (US$8.4), inclusive of service tax and a smart card used for cashless payments. The scheme launched in 2008 has today enrolled 2.96 million families of which 0.25 million availed medical facilities worth INR800 (US$13.3) million in private and government hospitals as of September 30, 2013.

A unique aspect of the system was that patients were given the freedom to choose a hospital, which created healthy competition between public and private providers. With increased demand, hospitals started to use cashless payment through smart cards to ensure hassle-free treatment to patients and easy processing of claims to the insurance company. The smart card carries the photograph of the head of the family and his/her name in English and the local language. The embedded smart chip within it carries a group photo of all members in the family up to five, and ten impressions of the left and right thumbs of all the members.

After 1 year of implementation, the revenue earned by the 140 empanelled government hospitals was more than that of the 165 empanelled private hospitals. In 2010, INR180 million (US$3 million) was collected by public health institutions through insurance companies and utilized it for improving hospital facilities and service quality, as well as incentivizing staff.

RSBY is in the fifth year of implementation in Kerala. The scheme has rendered free and cashless treatment to more than 2 million people.

UNION GOVERNMENT INITIATIVES IN HEALTH-SERVICE DELIVERY

National Rural Health Mission

India's performance after independence in reducing infant mortality and maternal mortality was a major cause of concern for policy makers. Maternal deaths in India constituted more than 20% of global maternal deaths and neonatal mortality constituted more than 31% of global neonatal deaths. The government of India took serious note of the gravity of the situation, when commitments were made for achieving millennium development goals (MDGs), resulting in the launch of the National Rural Health Mission (NRHM) in April 2005. It was also launched to take care of the rural population that is 70% of the people but was served by 30% of health resources, whereas the 30% of urbanites were looked after by 70% of health resources.

NRHM was the first systematic attempt to bring about major changes with effective decentralization, better financing of public health infrastructure, and human resource development. Villages, blocks, and districts emerged as major units for health action convergence, because it was realized that a top-down approach can be used to control diseases, but it can never guarantee good health. It was also realized that sanitation, clean water, hygiene, nutrition, public health education, gender, and social equality were directly relevant to the quest for better health and well-being of people in both rural and urban areas.

Various health programs were integrated and decentralized. As illustrated in Figure 20.2, the strategy was to increase communities' resources at all levels, improve management and capacity building, introduce flexible financing, and monitor progress against the standards of human resource management.

During the last 8 years, substantial health improvements were made through NRHM[4] as depicted in Figure 20.3. The figure has been constructed from the data of World Health Organization 2010—Trends in Maternal Mortality 1990–2008[4] and Registrar General of India—Sample Registration System (SRS 2001, 2006, and 2012).[5] The projections for 2015 and the graph have been created by the NRHM Division of Ministry of Health and Family Welfare, government of India.

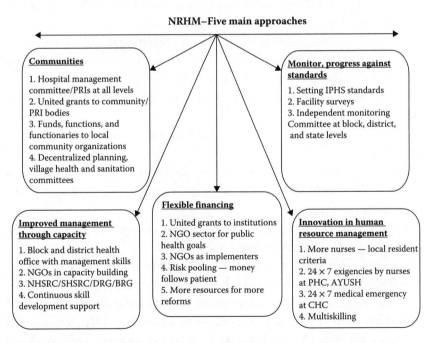

FIGURE 20.2

Main approaches of the National Rural Health Mission. (From Amarjeet, S., *Crafting a Credible Public System for Health & Nutrition for All: Emerging Issues and Policy Paradigms*, 2009.)

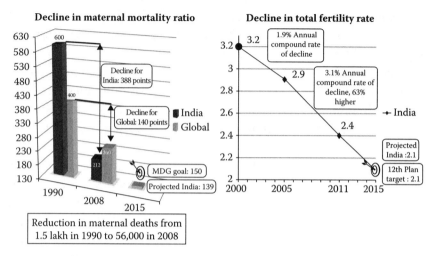

FIGURE 20.3
Improvements in maternal mortality and fertility rates.

- The infant mortality rate (IMR) standing at 58 in 2005 came down to 44 by 2011. However, it still remained well above the target of 30 set for 2012.
- The most remarkable achievement was bringing down the mortality rate of children below 5 years of age from 115 in 1999 to 55. This is still slightly below the global rate of 57.
- The maternal mortality rate (MMR) of 254 in 2005 came down to 212 in 2008.
- The total fertility rate (TFR) of 2.9 in 2005 was reduced to 2.4 in 2009.
- Institutional deliveries that were only 47% in 2007–2008 increased to 73% in 2012 having a direct impact in reducing IMR and MMR in the country.[6]
- Mortality due to malaria and kala-azar dropped to 71% and 84%, respectively, during the last 6 years.
- Leprosy prevalence fell from 1.8 to less than 1 per 10,000.
- Tuberculosis (TB) prevalence and mortality were reduced by 50%.
- The most remarkable achievement was the total eradication of the polio virus from India. According to a survey in 1978, it paralyzed an estimated 150,000 children aged 0–5 years every year. With the launch of the Pulse Polio Campaign along with routine immunization, more than 5 million children were covered all over the country.

The number of polio cases was brought down to 42 by 2010, and no wild polio cases have been reported in India since January 2011.

In the 3 years to 2011–2012, resources and their utilization made a phenomenal jump. Through NRHM 148,000 health workers were added. Outpatient department (OPD) visits increased to 790 from 540 million and inpatient department (IPD) admissions to 40 from 20 million.

With the intervention of NRHM, more than INR1 trillion (US$16 billion) has been spent so far to strengthen the primary health-care system in the country. In the current financial year, central government has kept a provision of INR210 billion (US$3.4 billion) under the National Health Mission (NHM). Despite this, public spending on the health sector is only 1.35% of gross domestic product (GDP), which needs to be increased further.

National Urban Health Mission

The world over, people migrate to towns and cities in search of better opportunities to improve their lives. In India, only 17.3% of the population lived in urban areas in 1951. By 2011, the percentage was 31.2 (377 million people). It is projected that by 2026, 535 million people comprising 38.2% of India's population will live in urban areas. Consequently, the population of urban poor has increased from 326 million in 2001 to 970 million in 2011, with a three-fold increase of population in urban slums. Statistics have shown that IMR and under-five mortality, nutritional standards, and immunization in poor urban areas are even worse than those in rural areas.

The central government has, therefore, decided to have an overarching NHM with two submissions. The National Urban Health Mission (NUHM) was launched to cater to the needs of the urban poor. During the years 2012–2017, it is to cover seven metros and 772 cities with a population of more than 50,000. Its focus is on the most vulnerable populations in slum areas.

It proposes to achieve its objectives by developing an appropriate public health delivery system by

- Creating new infrastructure where none exist
- Strengthening the extant primary public health systems like Urban Family Welfare Centres and maternity homes

- Entering into partnerships with the private sector
- Improving access and building community capacity through provision of community-level institutions like Mahila Arogya Samiti (MAS) and link workers (ASHA), and building capacity of key stakeholders.

In general, the NUHM would adopt a universal health-care approach for the entire urban population, albeit with an emphasis on the poor and vulnerable.

The services provided by urban PHCs will include OPD consultations, basic lab diagnosis and drug/contraceptive dispensing, and delivery of reproductive and child health services. Because the non-communicable diseases (NCDs) constitute a major proportion of the burden of disease in urban areas, the primary health-care system being envisaged under NUHM will screen, diagnose, and refer such cases to the secondary and tertiary level through a referral system. The framework for implementation of NUHM approved by the cabinet on May 1, 2013 provides for both the capital as well as recurring costs of urban PHCs.

Because strengthening of the primary-level institutions and outreach services will bring in a major increase in referrals, the referral hospitals need substantial upgrades. Hence, NUHM will also support creation of 30- to 50-bed urban CHCs for providing inpatient care in cities having population above 0.5 million and 75- to 100-bed urban health centers in the metros. The urban CHCs will act as first referral points for different types of health-care services such as maternal health, child health, diabetes, general surgery, orthopedic and dental surgeries, and mental health. New urban CHCs will be established on the basis of actual need. The total financial requirement for the NUHM submission is about INR225 billion (US$3.7 billion) during the 12th Five-Year Plan of which states will share INR55 billion (US$1 billion). Many states and municipal corporations have proposed for upgrading of the existing maternity homes or referral facilities to CHC level, which implies positioning specialist doctors such as gynecologists, ophthalmologists, and dermatologists in these facilities. In many large cities like Kolkata, Chennai, and Ahmadabad, the existing referral hospitals including maternity homes are not optimally utilized due to want of the required specialist doctors and other support staff. Therefore, the development of human resources is a key concern as in Figure 20.4.

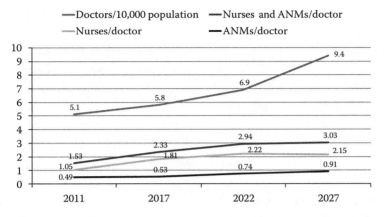

FIGURE 20.4

Projected human resource availability. (From Planning Commission of India, *High Level Expert Group Report & Universal Health Coverage*, 2011.)

ALLIED HEALTH PROFESSIONAL AND SKILL DEVELOPMENT: KEY THRUST FOR HUMAN RESOURCE DEVELOPMENT IN HEALTH

India is one of the youngest countries in terms of population with more than 570 million people below 25 years of age. This huge demographic dividend can be an asset if this young population is educated, skilled, and healthy. It is a liability if they remain illiterate, unskilled, and sick.

Like most postcolonial societies, India had also grown on a rejection of all traditional systems without an adequate expansion of modern systems of care. *The Politics of Health in India* by Roger Jeffery describes how inequalities and hierarchies created civil lines in districts and towns representing islands of cleanliness, hygiene, and sanitation, whereas the sea of squalor, filth, and dirt became part of the lives of the rest. The expansion of modern medicine with trained MBBS doctors at all levels of the health system could never keep pace with the needs of people in a country of 1.2 billion people living in over a million hamlets, villages, towns, and cities.

There is a huge category of allied health workers, loosely called paramedics, who are getting diplomas, degrees, and certificates from all sorts of mostly private institutions. In the absence of a regulating body there is no uniform curriculum, standardization of courses, or accreditation processes. Courses can have varied curriculums offered from 6 months to

3 years. The standards and skill sets are too varied to be easily grouped. No proper data are available.

The Ministry of Health and Family Welfare asked the Public Health Foundation of India (PHFI) in October 2010 to assess the allied health education methods of teaching and training, and suggest strategies to standardize and regulate them.

PHFI carried out a survey of 156 institutions to estimate the needs and gaps. Field visits were organized involving more than 300 experts nation-wide. The recommendations were presented to the ministry in December 2012.[7]

A total of 26 types of allied health professionals were identified. More than 130 courses are offered all over India while maximum demand exists only for about 10 courses like medical laboratory technology, radiography, and optometry. It was assessed that the allied health workforce available in the country is 6.2 million, but the country needs 6.4 million more.

To create human resources in the allied health field, the ministry decided to set up the National Institute of Allied Health Sciences (NIAHS) with eight regional institutes (RIAHS) in various parts of the country. The budget outlay was INR11.5 billion (US$1.9 billion). Once operationalized, this will create training facilities for 10,000 allied health professionals in 33 disciplines.

Simultaneously, steps were taken to establish a National Board for Allied Health Sciences (NBAHS) to develop uniform standards for curriculum, infrastructure, and accreditation of various disciplines. Six states that have set up Para Medical Councils were contacted. Professional associations like Confederation of Indian Industry (CII), Christian Association of India, Federation of Indian Chambers of Commerce and Industry (FICCI), and Skill Councils were invited to share experiences to develop national level quality standards on par with global norms. Efforts have been made through PHFI to also collaborate with premier institutions in the United Kingdom, the United States, Canada, and Sweden to review opportunities to link it with various disease control programs. It was also decided to engage with existing councils like Medical Council of India (MCI), Dental Council of India (DCI), Indian Nursing Council (INC), and other certifying bodies like National Board of Examination (NBE), to estimate their abilities in teaching, training, and skill upgrades to assess gaps in capacities for allied health science.

Currently more than 80 such courses are offered across the country. They are broadly divided into four categories: (1) rehabilitative and therapeutic services; (2) diagnostic and technological services; (3) curative clinical services; and (4) nondirect, ancillary, and community services. The list is by no means conclusive and many more disciplines would be added in due course.

NBAHS should initially be a facilitating body rather than a typical regulator like MCI, DCI, or INC. The existing regulatory councils were all created more than 50 years ago and have evolved hundreds of regulations that are not in tune with reforms needed in modern times. Due care has to be taken to ensure that any apex body created for allied health sciences does not fall into the same rut.

Whatever be the aspirations of middle-class Indians, everyone is not going to become a doctor, engineer, or software expert. There is a huge amount of human resources waiting to be trained in skills for gainful employment within and outside the country. There is no dearth of potential, but what we need is a vision to create opportunities in a systematic manner. Quality comes through standardization that needs to be facilitated rather than regulated.

REFORMS IN MEDICAL EDUCATION

Medical education in India is one of the most sought after and respected vocations. Admission to a medical college is one of the most competitive examinations in India, wherein more than 650,000 students compete for about 50,000 seats. The 5.5 years of medical education are tough and require high levels of intelligence and perseverance, beside hard work and extra-ordinary efforts. Despite having 387 medical colleges, more than anywhere in the world, we produce only about 51,000 medical graduates per year[8] as in Figure 20.5, which is based on data available with the Medical Education Division, Ministry of Health and Family Welfare, India.

The most meritorious students seek admissions in about 181 government medical colleges primarily due to the highly subsidized cost of education. The second category goes into 206 private medical colleges where higher fees, but not so much merit is the main criteria for admissions. The recent mushrooming of private medical colleges has been a major cause of concern, because very often quality of medical education is compromised to meet commercial goals.

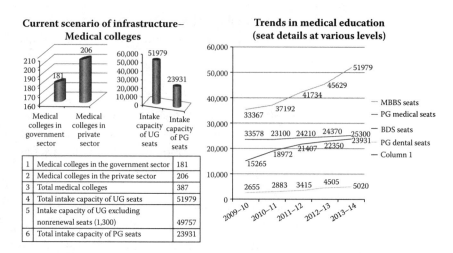

FIGURE 20.5
Current scenario of infrastructure and trends in medical education.

As per the Indian medical register maintained by MCI, there are 867,196 doctors as of January 31, 2013. Hardly 700,000 doctors are available in the country, which gives a doctor–population ratio of 1:1739. As per WHO standards, the ratio should be 1:1000. That would require 1.2 million doctors in India. The current deficit is close to 500,000 doctors. It has taken 65 years to establish 387 medical colleges. Between 2009 and 2014, 97 new colleges were established. Assuming that 20 medical colleges are added every year, it will take 20 years to double the number of medical colleges in India. However, the doctor–population ratio will continue to be adverse because, as per projections, the population of India will reach 1.5 billion people by 2035, and it will be the most populous country in the world, overtaking China.

A total of 64% of the medical colleges are concentrated in the southern and western parts of India. Interestingly, health parameters of these states are far better than in the north and northeast of India.

The principal regulator in India MCI has been responsible for ensuring good standards of medical education in the country. Strict adherence to minimum requirements on infrastructure, faculty, and patients in teaching hospitals makes it is an uphill task to establish medical colleges in India.

The average number of students graduating per medical college per year is 131, which is not very high compared to Europe and the Americas. Many countries have adopted a policy of producing large numbers of graduates without bothering about quality. Large numbers of Indian students, who cannot afford to pay higher admission fees at home, are attracted to these medical colleges in foreign countries to fulfill their aspirations to become a doctor.

Because the quality of medical education varies from institution to institution and from country to country, MCI made a decision in 2002 on a qualifying *screening test* before an Indian graduate can practice in India as a doctor. The current figures show only 20% passing these tests, which is a cause of concern. There is lot of pressure exerted by students, their parents, and even foreign institutions to mutually recognize their medical degrees, but MCI has not relented so far.

The government of India has supported MCI primarily because all countries insist on licentiate exams before medical graduates are allowed to practice. The only exception from the screening test has been made for Indian students graduating from five English-speaking countries: the United Kingdom, the United States, Canada, Australia, and New Zealand.

In India, medical education is a remnant of the hospital- and urban-centric. The textbook education is well supplemented by clinical studies during internship. However, modern technology such as virtual class rooms, telemedicine, simulation models, and computer software are hardly used. Though clinical studies cannot be substituted by technology, such tools can certainly be used to supplement the learning experience.

Quality of medical education and the strict standards insisted by MCI have ensure good quality of doctors in India. They do extremely well in foreign countries where resources and technological advancements are available to them. Indian doctors settled abroad have carved out a niche for themselves all over the world, though at a substantial cost to our national resources and needs.

A medical graduate in India is not exposed to the public health needs of the country, and is hardly exposed to the prevention and cure of common ailments confronting people in rural areas. Naturally, his eyes are set on getting admission to postgraduate (PG) seats, so that he can become a specialist. The 3-year PG course is highly competitive and rigorous but pushes him further away from public health. Once a specialist, he is not fit to work in a PHC, where a generalist is required. Thus, India is producing doctors for hospitals in towns and cities to cater to the urban elite. It is ironic that doctors are not available to work for the 70% of population living in villages.

Various incentives and allowances to encourage fresh graduates to work in rural areas have not been successful so far. Finally, the government of India prompted MCI to come out with *"compulsory rural posting"* of 1 year in PHC as a minimum eligibility condition before admission to a PG course. This was resisted by the Indian Medical Association, a registered body of doctors and medical students, as no one apparently wants to work in villages even for 1 year. However, some young medical graduates have suggested that within the 3-year PG course, 1 year should be compulsory service at a PHC. The critics cannot deny that it is in the national interest to ask graduates to contribute 1 year of their life for public causes before they look for better pastures. Government should also ensure that migration of doctors abroad is restricted to avoid a national waste of precious resources.

Several issues have to be resolved before implementing this decision. There are only 25,000 PHCs for 50,000 graduates and these are not uniformly distributed all over the country. There are several states and union territories like Nagaland, Mizoram, Andaman and Nicobar Island, Daman and Diu, and Dadra Nagar Haveli, which do not have medical colleges but hundreds of PHCs. On the other hand, Delhi has 8 PHCs and 950 doctors to be attached, which brings 118 doctors to be attached to 1 PHC. A small place like Puducherry has 24 PHCs for 1050 doctors, giving an average of 44 doctors to be attached per PHC. Once this is made mandatory, government has to ensure smooth implementation to achieve basic objectives of making doctors available in all PHCs. Medical education needs to be oriented toward public health to ensure that primary health care becomes a priority of the health system in India.

Need for Reforms

MCI has to understand the need for reforms in medical education in conformity with the requirements of modern times. Some of the old regulations, particularly for land, infrastructure, faculty, and OPD and IPD numbers, need to be changed.

Previously, a minimum 25 acres of land was required to establish a medical college. This necessitated finding a huge chunk of land away from towns. State governments or private entrepreneurs would invest large amounts to build teaching buildings, labs, residential facilities, and hospitals. However, MCI never realized that the insisted OPD, IPD, and faculty ratios were impossible to achieve in rural settings. Obviously, this left no choice but to manipulate these to secure permissions. During MCI inspections, truckloads of villagers were ferried to medical college hospitals to be shown as patients, faculty were imported and equipment hired, just to fulfill the MCI requirements. None of these existed on a normal day or during surprise inspections, because newly established medical college hospitals were not viable or sustainable.

Hospitals in medical colleges take years to become functional with sufficient volume of patients, even if such hospitals can provide treatment at affordable costs. Why cannot we attach teaching blocks to government hospitals, which could be on separate pieces of land? Why not allow district hospitals/subdivisional hospitals to be upgraded to mini-medical colleges, when we know very well that there is no dearth of clinical material available in these hospitals. There are currently 422 out of 644 districts (65%) that do not have a single medical college in the district.

Why insist on a one-to-one student–teacher ratio, when we know that we will never be able to provide such large numbers of faculty? Why do we require 40 teaching faculty to start a medical college of 50 seats? Have these medical colleges been created for students or for faculty? Why not encourage senior doctors in public sector to teach? After all, all junior doctors working under them in hospitals are taught by them in hospitals. What about defense services, ESI, railways and public sector undertakings (PSUs), who run and manage huge hospitals all over the country? With some leverage, these fine hospitals providing medical facilities all over the country can be converted into medical institutions of smaller sizes. Drop by drop, these small numbers of doctors created in every nook and corner of the country can provide precious human resources, without sacrificing quality of medical education in the country.

Some of these reforms have begun. The Ministry of Health and Family Welfare (MOHFW) has already suggested to relax infrastructure norms for auditorium, lecture halls, library, residential blocks, and so on besides allowing medical colleges to locate on two separate pieces of land. Some ESI hospitals have been allowed to upgrade into medical colleges. Rationalization of student–teacher ratios in some disciplines resulted in substantial increase of PG seats. Among the districts having no medical colleges, 58 district hospitals/referral hospitals have been selected by the government of India for upgrading them into medical colleges with 100 seats each.

BACHELOR OF SCIENCE (COMMUNITY HEALTH) TO PROVIDE MIDDLE-LEVEL HEALTH-SERVICE PROVIDERS

In 2005, the MOHFW constituted a task force on *Medical Education for the National Rural Health Mission* to examine the possibility of revamping medical education with reference to the requirements of medical professionals under the NRHM. It was also to examine the feasibility of a short-term certificate course in medicine for creating a cadre of health professionals for rendering basic primary health care to underserved rural population.

Community health officers (CHO) deployed to all subcenters will be the first point of contact between health-service providers and patients in rural areas. This cadre of public health providers will be better trained than the ANMs currently managing the subcenters. At the present time, the formal health structure in most of the states does not have any person between the ANM in the subcenter and the MBBS-trained medical officer in the PHC. The CHO will play an essential bridging role. The philosophical underpinning of the model rests on the belief that a sustainable and effective health system has to be located in the community and can be provided only by a middle-level health-service provider. When implemented, this can transform the public health scenario in the country.

The purpose of introducing a 3½-year bachelor of science (community health) (BSc [CH]) course was to enable the state governments to create a cadre of middle-level public health professionals. The students completing the course will be called CHO and be deployed at subcenters to strengthen the public health delivery system at the grassroots level. The curriculum of the course has been designed to impart necessary public health and ambulatory care competencies, give an impetus to public health action in rural areas, and take the core health care closer to people.

The intake of students will be primarily from the nearby district or cluster of districts; they will be trained in the district hospitals, and deployed back to subcenters/rural areas of the same district. These graduates would be an integral part of the three-tier health-care system and function at the first level, that is, the subcenter that is the first point of contact for the poor and vulnerable and is currently manned by an ANM. The second level, that is, PHC/CHC, will comprise MBBS doctors and the third that of specialists. The strength of a CHO is that he will be available at the subcenter and have a degree of formalized education and training much beyond any currently available one to address maternal health, child health, school health, communicable diseases, and also the growing incidence of NCDs. These graduates would be equipped to lead initiatives in preventive health care. The course is thus a step toward the creation of public health cadres in the states as recommended by expert committees and the Planning Commission.

The curriculum for the course has been prepared by a committee of experts constituted by the MCI, which inter alia lays down the criteria for admission, provision for stipend, and accommodation for students. It has been further fine-tuned and finalized by the NBE, which will accredit the course and also prescribe the minimum standards for its implementation. The course will be implemented only in the states who decide to adopt it.

The existing infrastructure will not be overburdened as the BSc (CH) course will be run in specially developed rural health-care schools (RHSs) by the concerned state governments. Although it is for the state governments to decide where and how many RHSs are required to be established, it is expected that the district hospital would provide the locus for the clinical experience required by the students. It will be supported for creating new infrastructure under NRHM.

Teaching of the BSc (CH) students would occur in settings similar to where they will work. Field work and practical skills training will have a major role. Postings in PHCs and health subcenters are a major part of training and internship. Standardized learning resources will be procured or created; tele-education systems and web-based packages will be utilized. Information and communication technology will also be harnessed extensively.

The course would be taught by a mix of full-time and part-time teaching staff. The part-time teachers could be serving or retired faculty of medical colleges, district training centers nearby nursing schools; medical officers, specialists in the district hospitals, CHCs, PHCs; public health officers of the health department; private practitioners; faculty of the Indian Institute of Public Health (IIPS) and the State Institution of Health and Family Welfare (SIHFW); and retired medical, nursing, or dental teachers.

The proposal envisages that the CHOs will be promoted in the public health stream in the state health department and not in the medical doctor or nursing streams. There is no intention of replacing doctors at rural facilities with CHOs. To avoid any confusion regarding equivalence of any kind between MBBS and BSc (CH), the latter has been completely taken out of the ambit of MCI. The BSc (CH) graduates will neither be allowed to prefix the title of *Dr.* to their names nor would have any privileges of a doctor like the right to do private practice. Moreover, the decision whether to adopt the course and implement it would be taken by the respective state governments and it will not be thrust on the states by the center.

NATIONAL MEDICAL COLLEGE NETWORK ON TELEMEDICINE

National Knowledge Network[9]

A government of India initiative, the national knowledge network (NKN), is a state-of-the-art multigigabit pan-India network for providing a unified high-speed network backbone for all knowledge-related institutions in the country. The purpose of such a knowledge network goes to the very core of the country's quest for building quality institutions with requisite research facilities and creating a pool of highly trained professionals.

Globally, research and development activities and innovations are increasingly multidisciplinary, collaborative, and require substantial computational power. The key to successful research today demands live consultations, data, and resource sharing. Therefore, to optimally utilize the potential of institutions engaged in generation and dissemination of knowledge in various areas, it is important to connect them through a high-speed broadband network.

The network is designed to support overlay networks, dedicated networks, and virtual networks. The entire network will seamlessly integrate with the global scientific community at multiple gigabits per second speed. It is protocol independent and is designed to carry multiprotocol traffic. The design follows all the current standards to permit seamless interoperability among technologies and seamless integration among different original equipment manufacturers (Figure 20.6).

The target users for the NKN are all institutions engaged in the generation and dissemination of knowledge in various areas, such as research laboratories, universities, and other institutions of higher learning, including professional institutions. By the end of 2013, NKN has already connected 831 institutions including 151 medical institutions. It aims to connect over 1500 institutions, organizations, and laboratories under various categories throughout the country.

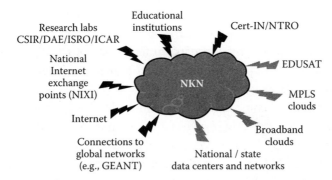

FIGURE 20.6
National knowledge network. (From http://www.knw.in.)

The end-user institutions connecting to the respective points of presence (PoPs) at the core or distribution level will have the option to operate at speeds from 100 Mbps to 1 Gbps per connection. As far as possible, the last mile connection to the respective institute shall be on a protected link.

Various applications envisaged are Countrywide Virtual Classrooms, Collaborative Research, Grid Computing, Virtual Library, Sharing of Computing Resources, Network Technology Test Bed, and e-Governance.

NATIONAL OPTICAL FIBRE NETWORK

At present OFC (optical fiber cable) connectivity is available in all state capitals, districts, HQs, and up to the block level. In October 2011, the government of India approved setting up of the National Optical Fibre Network (NOFN).[10] Funded by the Universal Service Obligation Fund (USOF), it was estimated to cost about INR200 billion (US\$3.5 billion), to provide connectivity to all the 250,000 gram panchayats (GPs) in the country. This would ensure broadband connectivity with adequate bandwidth. This will be done by utilizing existing fibers of PSUs (BSNL, Railtel, and Power Grid) and laying incremental fiber to connect to GPs wherever necessary. The dark fiber network thus created will be lit by appropriate technology thus creating sufficient bandwidth at the GPs. Thus the connectivity gap between GPs and blocks will be filled.

In NOFN, the technology called GPON (Gigabit Passive Optical Network) will be utilized. A passive optical network (PON) is a network architecture that brings fiber cabling and signals to the home using a point-to-multipoint scheme that enables a single optical fiber to serve multiple premises. Encryption maintains data security in this shared environment. The GPON standard differs from other PON standards in that it achieves higher bandwidth and higher efficiency using larger, variable-length packets.

Information and communication technologies (ICT) applications such as e-commerce, e-banking, e-governance, e-education, and telemedicine require high-speed Internet connectivity. NOFN will facilitate this. A World Bank study has estimated that a 10% increase in broadband connectivity leads to 1.38% increase in GDP. Broadband penetration in India at present is less than 2%.

Nondiscriminatory access to the NOFN will be provided to all service providers. These service providers, like telecom service providers (TSPs), ISPs, cable TV operators, and content providers, can launch various services in rural areas.

Bharat Broadband Network Limited (BBNL) is a special purpose vehicle (SPV) set up by the government of India for the establishment, management, and operation of NOFN. BBNL was incorporated as a public sector undertaking (PSU)/company under the Companies Act (1956) in February 2012.

BBNL has embarked on pilot projects in three blocks covering 58 GPs in three different states. These blocks are the Arian Block in the Ajmer district (Rajasthan), Parvada in Visakhapatnam (Andhra Pradesh), and the Panisagar Block in the North Tripura district (Tripura).

The MOHFW has initiated a process to leverage the NKN and NOFN initiatives of government of India, and under the telemedicine umbrella considered establishment of the National Medical College Network (NMCN), National Rural Telemedicine Network (NRTN), and Mobile Health Projects.

All government medical colleges shall be connected in the health education content delivery, skill enhancement, and Healthcare Outreach Services project to be called as NMCN with the services as illustrated in Figure 20.7.

Out of 387 medical colleges, 150 have received NKN connectivity and initially one National-cum-Regional Resource Centre. Five regional resource centers and 35 medical colleges were taken up in Phase-I for the NMCN project.

Besides Health Education Content Delivery, Central Repository of Medical Education Content and Digital Medical Library Network, Technology

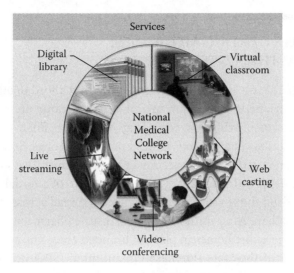

FIGURE 20.7
National Medical College Network. (From http://www.bbnl.nic.in.)

Enabled Skill Transfer and Mentoring, Platform for Interactive Distance Learning in an adaptive environment, tele-consultation, tele Follow-up services, and m-Health shall be initiated under NMCN project.

Virtual classrooms and digital lecture theaters shall be utilized for undergraduate lecture sharing, remote participation in continuing medical education (CME), skill sharing, and open online courses for health professionals.

A Tele-CME Facility shall be located in a hospital near the clinical service areas and meant for continuous professional skills development. A multiconferencing environment—both hardware and web conference with facility for Clinical Case Material Preparation, high-speed Internet access, and end point compatible with video streaming and webcasting—will be available.

Medical colleges shall have access to global knowledge resources through a digital library and every health professional shall have that available for capacity building and skill development. Every medical institution shall have a knowledge park and its web portal would contribute to medical science knowledge hub, nationally and internationally, for becoming a Virtual Health University.

There shall be virtual OPD clinics and virtual IPD rounds in every medical college. The establishment of the project shall help human resources for health development through virtual classrooms, web streaming, video conferencing, and optimal use of other facilities.

LOW-COST GENERIC MEDICINES: THE RAJASTHAN CASE[11]

In Rajasthan, nearly 40% of the population cannot afford to buy drugs. In 2007, the district administration in Chhattisgarh came up with a three-step initiative to provide low-cost drugs to people. First, doctors were asked to prescribe generic drugs instead of patented ones. Second, quality drugs were procured for the government to run cooperative stores. Third, awareness was spread among target groups to avail of affordable drugs.

Low-cost drug shops were set up, which soon spread across 19 other districts of Rajasthan. After initial resistance, private pharmacists too started supplying generic medicines in place of branded ones. The government of Rajasthan asked the State Purchase Organisation (SPO) to procure and distribute initially 45 essential medicines.

Since October 2011, free medicines are being provided to all in government hospitals under Mukhya Mantri Nishulk Dawa Yojana (Chief Ministry Drug Distribution Scheme). Over a period of 3 years, Rajasthan Medical Supplies Corporation has centrally procured 400 essential medicines, 42 surgical items, and 71 drugs prescribed by various national health programs. The procedure was standardized and made transparent.

Increased awareness of the scheme helped increase the number of people visiting government hospitals from 4.4 million to 6.2 million. Today, Rajasthan is appreciated for the supply of generic medicines.

INNOVATIVE SOLUTIONS THROUGH PUBLIC–PRIVATE PARTNERSHIP (PPP) MODEL

PPP has so far not worked very successfully in the health sector. The primary reason is that there are very few win-win situations for both government and private sector. As pointed out earlier, there is a huge gap between demand and supply in health care. Private sector players, from one-doctor clinics to multispecialty hospitals, have commercial aims and objectives. Government on the other hand has to meet the growing need of affordable health care to the most vulnerable sections of society.

One example of successful partnership is found in Kerala in diagnostic services. It has been replicated in other parts of the country as well.

The state of Kerala has made commendable achievements in health standards. The factors contributing to the progress were a wide network of health infrastructure composed of PHCs at the rural level, district hospitals at the secondary level, and general hospitals at the tertiary level. Literate manpower, women's education, general health awareness, and clean health habits are positive influences for health in Kerala.

There are six medical college hospitals, which act as referral and specialty hospitals. The medical colleges are the cornerstone in development of health-care infrastructure in the state by imparting quality medical care to the public and also providing state-of-the-art medical education to the medical students.

In modern medical practice, the magnetic resonance image (MRI) scanner is one of the key diagnostic tools needed to identify a range of medical conditions. It is extensively used by medical specialties, such as radiology, neurology, neurosurgery, orthopedics, and pediatrics. Availability of a MRI scanner is a precondition for obtaining MCI recognition for a radiological diagnosis course in medical colleges. MRI scan was not available at the medical colleges in Kottayam, Alappuzha, and Thrissur; therefore, the courses could not be organized.

Of late, the widely acclaimed Kerala model of health has started showing a number of disturbing trends. Only 30% of the people even from the lower income groups seek medical help from the government hospitals. This is because of the fall in the quality of services at the government hospitals. The requirement for good service with modern equipment and diagnostics has provided the impetus for the growth of private medical care in the state. Features of consumer society are visible in all occupations leading to the commercialization of health care. Health is no more seen as a right but as a commodity to be purchased. The huge remittance of foreign exchange from Gulf countries even to the low- and middle-income households further reinforced this attitude. All these tendencies have led to uncontrolled growth of the private medical care facilities in the state.

This, together with the absence of quality diagnostic facilities at the medical colleges of three districts, has led to the people in the nearby regions to depend on private MRI scan centers. The patients pay exorbitant charges ranging from INR8,000 (US$133) to INR10,000 (US$167). In many cases, patients were unable to avail of this very critical diagnostic tool. This has also led to several unethical practices of the scan centers including providing kickbacks to prescribing doctors.

As discussed earlier, the public RSBY insurance scheme for BPL patients has been rolled out across Kerala. But effective and proper implementation was affected in the three areas because the hospitals had to depend on the private scan centers for MRIs.

The Department of Health and Family Welfare, government of Kerala, considered a new initiative of setting up MRI Scan Centres in the three medical colleges using a PPP model.

HLL Lifecare Limited (HLL) is a government of India enterprise with the motto "Innovating for healthy generations." It is a multifaceted organization with expertise ranging from manufacture of contraceptives, medical devices, and pharmaceutical products to providing procurement services and infrastructure development services in various fields.

Discussions between the government of Kerala and HLL led to a proposal by HLL for providing state-of-the-art MRI scan services at Kottayam, Thrissur, and Alappuzha through its Hindlabs centers. The government of Kerala accepted the proposal and Hindlabs set up MRI Scan Centres with 1.5-T machines at the medical colleges.

The salient features of the proposed outsourcing model were

- HLL will operate the Hindlabs MRI Scan Centre in a partnership model.
- HLL will procure the 1.5-T MRI scanner and associated equipment from its own approved suppliers, and maintain and operate the center with trained manpower.
- The center will be used for teaching purposes of the Radio Diagnosis Department of the respective medical colleges. Cost of consumables used during teaching is to be paid as per predetermined rates.
- The cost of consumables (excluding contrast media), and charges for consumption of utilities for conducting the prescribed tests on the patients will be borne by HLL.
- The charges to patients will be in the range INR3500 (US$58) to INR4000 (US$67) for plain scans.
- The hospital will provide the space on a rent-free basis.
- The hospital will provide the infrastructure required for smooth functioning of the center and the equipment.
- BPL patients will be scanned for free, an amount of 10% of the total patients undertaking scans in the center.
- The agreement will be valid for a minimum period of 15 years.

The first Hindlabs MRI Scan Centre started functioning at Thrissur in August 2009. The second center at Alappuzha was functioning in January 2010, and the third at Kottayam in May 2010. The centers were set up with state-of-the-art equipment from Wipro GE, and the centers were designed to provide a comfortable and modern ambience for patient convenience. A highly trained medical team including radiologists, radiographers, and nurses manned the centers. Through October 2013, Hindlabs have served 54,953 patients.

The following needs of the hospitals were addressed successfully by Hindlabs:

- Affordable and reliable MRI scan services in three government medical colleges
- Impart training to postgraduate students
- Impart training to paramedical and nursing students

The government objective of serving the BPL category patients have been met successfully by the centers by providing RSBY services to 18,686 patients.

Hindlabs operations have a positive impact on the private MRI scan center practices leading to reduced scan charges, quality in reporting, stabilization in pricing, and installation of upgraded equipment. The overall costs of MRI scans have now been reduced for the public thereby reducing the cost of health care as detailed in Table 20.1.

The Hindlabs MRI Scan Centre partnership initiative between the government of Kerala and HLL has helped in reducing the burden on the poor patients of Kerala especially those in the districts of Kottayam, Alappuzha, and Thrissur. This has also upgraded the health-care delivery infrastructure of the medical college hospitals. The benefits are

- Government resources like radiologists and radiographers within the hospital can be used to provide other imaging modalities.
- Better control and implementation of government schemes like RSBY.
- Training to postgraduate and paramedical students of the hospital.
- MRI scan services made available to the public at affordable rates (30%–50% lower than market rates).
- Free service to BPL patients and other certified categories.
- Reduction of the cost of care within the government health-care network.

TABLE 20.1

Before-and-After Comparison of the Hindlab–Government of Kerala Partnership

Before Hindlabs	After Hindlabs
Average private scan rate—INR8000 (US$133) (low Tesla/1.5 T)	Private centers slashed scan rate to INR5000 (US$83) to INR6000 (US$100) at the three districts. Rates for low-Tesla MRI Centers with 02.Y/0.3 T equipment reduced to around INR3000 (US$50) to INR4000 (US$67)
Doctor-centric tariff—scan charges fixed as per needs of the prescribing doctor	Scan charges at stabilized rates
Unethical practice was very high, low quality scans and reporting, performing unnecessary scan procedures	Private centers forced to upgrade quality of reporting services, more ethical practices being adopted
MRI referrals are not justified with clinical symptoms, 60% are normal	More than 94% of the MRI cases at Hindlabs were reported with significant clinical findings
Low-Tesla MRI used widely	Fixed the benchmark as 1.5-T MRI

- Longer opening hours to suit the convenience of the patients and the hospital.
- High uptime commitment of 95% in a year.
- Professional and quality services available 24 × 7.
- Centralized teleradiology hub leading to higher quality reporting.
- Excellent environment for training of medical students and radiology staff on most advanced imaging system.
- Private scan centers are motivated to adopt ethical practices and reduced charges.

The impact of Hindlabs has been recognized by the government of India, a testimony of which is the inclusion of the Hindlabs example as the successful model for PPPs in the Plan Document of the 12th Five-Year Plan.

SUMMARY

Challenges in India are many, but they have to be converted into opportunities. Interventions like NRHM have made a huge difference in changing the health scenario in the countryside. We need to sustain these and continue to target those areas, where impact has not yet been satisfactory. This requires change in strategy and out-of-the-box thinking, particularly for human resources.

Many countries across the globe have looked at the option of deviating from the doctor-centric approach. Midwives in Scandinavian countries and nurse practitioners in the United States have created good impacts in improved health delivery. In India ASHAs, even though less competent, have successfully changed health-service delivery in rural areas. Middle-level health providers can substantially improve the health-care system in India. Creating community health officers can usher in a new era of public health cadres in the country. Doctors will still be required, but let the middle-level health-service providers and allied health professionals take care of basic jobs, and enable the highly educated professionals to concentrate on tasks only they can do.

The last six decades have seen unprecedented reforms in the Indian health sector. We need to keep pushing for reforms, so that in coming decades, we can show to the world that we are capable of delivering good quality health care despite the huge challenges.

DISCLAIMER

The views expressed in this article written for academic purpose are personal and have nothing to do with the official position of the author. Every effort has been made to ensure accuracy of facts and figures, however, mistakes, if any, are purely accidental.

REFERENCES

1. Amarjeet S. (2009). *Crafting a Credible Public System for Health & Nutrition for All: Emerging Issues and Policy Paradigms.*
2. Planning Commission of India. (2011). Why Universal Health Covering for India and How Can It Be Achieved? www.planningcommission.gov.in.
3. Planning Commission of India. (2011). High Level Expert Group Report and Universal Health Coverage for India. www.planningcommission.gov.in.
4. World Health Organisation. (2010). Trends in Maternal Mortality 1990–2008. http://whqlibdoc.who.int/publications/2010/9789241500265_eng.pdf.
5. Registrar General, New Delhi: Sample Registration System, SRS Bulletin Vol.35 (2001) Vol.41 (2006), Vol.47 (2012) and Special Bulletin on Maternal Mortality in India–2011.

6. National Rural Health Mission. (October 5, 2013). Newsletter.

7. Public Health Foundation of India (PHFI) Report, 2012–National Initiatives for Allied Health Sciences.

8. Ministry of Health and Family Welfare Highlights–Five Years (2009–2014) Achievements and New Initiatives.

9. National Knowledge Network. http://www.knw.in.

10. National Optical Fibre Network. http://www.bbnl.nic.in.

11. Centre for Innovation in Public System (CIPS). (2013). One World Foundation India Access of Low Cost Generic Medicines: A Case Study with Details of Rajasthan for Replication. http://www.cips.org.in/database-of-innovative-practices?category=Health&state=Rajasthan&submit=Submit.

21

Indovation: Frugal Innovation in Indian Health Care

Sandeep Bhalla and Nimisha Singh Verma

CONTENTS

INTRODUCTION

Indovation is an abbreviation of Indian innovation. It was conceptualized in 2009 by Navi Radjou, the executive director of the Centre for India & Global Business at the Judge Business School, University of Cambridge. A related term is *jugaad*, a Hindi word meaning creative ideas providing a quick, alternative way of fixing a problem by creating an improvised arrangement or work-around. Like the Japanese words *kaizen* and *muda*, jugaad has entered the Anglo-Saxon business vocabulary. It should be noted that jugaad has two different and to an extent contradictory meanings. A work-around means the root cause of a problem is not solved. Instead, a way to get around it is created, thus complicating the flow of work. On the other hand, jugaad can mean to use what is available to generate a good enough solution, better than the alternative of no solution at all. We prefer the second usage, and think of Indovation as an Indian way of frugal innovations attempting to make best use of available resources.[1] Thus the opposites of Indovation are imported, over-engineered, costly, and economically unsustainable solutions.

As the saying goes, "Necessity is the mother of invention." Pure deprivation, however, is not a sufficient condition. Humanity has suffered for millennia of abject poverty. Only after the Industrial Revolution affluence has slowly trickled down to the masses. Poverty alone is not enough. Technologies and solutions must exist, together with a belief that change is possible and that risky innovations may have a huge payoff. When the escape from poverty and disease is technically possible, it becomes a necessity.[1]

Most of the current burden of disease is curable and preventable. But in many parts of India, even though incomes are rising, resources are not available. That leaves three possible development paths. The first is the traditional capitalist way through free markets, investments, and higher productivity. With higher incomes people start to buy health care, education, sanitation, and security. As demand tends to create supply, providers will come with their offerings. Needs are fulfilled, but first to those with the means and understanding to make use of them.

The second way is to expect someone else to pay and provide the services, be it the government, United Nations, or charitable organizations. Over the past half-century, billions of U.S. dollars have been spent on such efforts with slim results.

The third way is to tinker with possible, available, frugal, and good enough solutions. Using the terminology of Lean production, the core customer value, and the minimum necessary value stream to achieve it, is identified. Then the processes, technologies, and equipment needed for production are reverse engineered and squeezed to the minimum. For example, light is a necessity, if one wants to work or study after dark. Light bulbs produce light, but need the backing of an electric grid and power plants, all which demand huge investments. Cheaper, frugal technologies, however, have been developed, using locally available biowaste, a simple gasification process, standard generators, and a local grid. The solution may not be elegant, but it works better than the alternative of burning oil. Many such social enterprises, companies that combine sound business methods with social objectives, are sprouting all over India.

Health care is rich in evidence-based innovations. Yet, even when such innovations are implemented successfully in one location, they often disseminate slowly—if at all.[2] For many consumer products with easily perceivable value, such as mobile telephony, a new innovation spreads like a wildfire through competitive markets. Although hospitals have long been quick to adopt breakthrough technologies in medical devices, procedures, and treatments, far less attention has focused on innovations in service delivery, distribution, processes, networking, and communications.[3]

NETWORKS, ECOSYSTEMS, AND PARTNERSHIPS

Health care can be depicted as a network, or set of networks connecting various players. The connections are more or less formalized trading relations, such as insurers collecting fees and reimbursing providers for services offered to patients. There are, however, relevant connections that are not formalized as relations. For example, the design, cost, and availability of bike helmets have an impact on how much and what kinds of head injuries appear at emergency departments (EDs). Helmet manufacturers do not trade with EDs, nevertheless they are part of a health ecosystem. Ecosystems in business, as well as in nature, are the breeding grounds of new mutations and combinations.

As illustrated in Figure 21.1, in health care there are three basic types of players: government (central and local), ordinary for-profit businesses, and charities.

Governments have the power to collect taxes and impose enforceable regulations. Governments exercise power, legitimately if they can, using force if they must. Governments can prohibit or promote. Authorities can

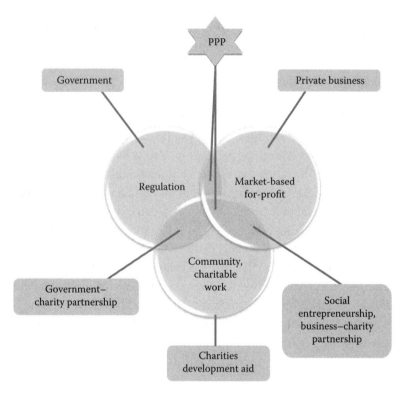

FIGURE 21.1
Public–private partnership model/health-care ecosystem players.

establish and run health service production where markets do not work. Governments, both central and local, however, have as their primary task the execution of power. Therefore, their organizational architecture is laid out with the intention of making power transparent, legitimate, and orderly. Governments need to listen to the people on election days, but in their daily dealings they treat citizens as subjects, not as customers. Therefore public production, be it of food, automobiles, or health services, tend to be overly bureaucratic and unresponsive.

Business corporations enter health care like any other area where profits can be made. Limited liability companies are organized to accumulate investments, acquire technologies, produce, market, and sell for a profit. Where markets are open and competitive, companies depend on their customers for their revenue stream. Therefore, corporate organizational architectures are designed for flexibility and open to innovations.

Charities, such as foundations, NGOs, and religious bodies are organized to fulfill a mission. Typically they have charismatic founders and loyal followers. They receive their initial funding through voluntary donations; sometimes, but not always, donors also cover their operating expenses. Many charities have achieved good results in fulfilling their missions. However, lacking public authority and reluctant to use economic incentives to motivate their staff, they are dependent on voluntary action. Because they typically do not have corporate style management control systems, they tend to be inefficient. Because charities depend for their capital on a donor base that soon will be exhausted, they seldom have the resources, or the capabilities to expand.

Each of these types has its strengths and weaknesses. Therefore, it is natural that various combinations arise, as depicted in the overlapping areas of Figure 21.1.

Government-business combinations are usually called public–private partnership (PPP). Government determines the mission and makes the funds available, but outsources production to private entities. Thus, the inherent constraints of governmental organizational architecture can be avoided and production is run following market principles. In a similar vein, governments can employ the services of charities.

Business-charity combinations are called social enterprises. They are, like charities, founded on a social vision to provide solutions to pressing needs. However, they adapt a business-like organizational architecture, founded on the idea that the realization of value requires that the benefactors and customers, perceive the value of their offerings and are willing to pay. As long as value is delivered, the social enterprise is economically sustainable. When the perceived value no longer exceeds production costs, the enterprise goes out of business. Contrasted to government programs and charities that tend to outlive their usefulness; a social enterprise cannot survive without value.

Imagining health care as an ecosystem and as a set of networks makes it possible to envision a variety of innovative combinations. In the following, we look into some examples from India.

INNOVATION INITIATIVES BY GOVERNMENT

The Indian government is often perceived as bureaucratic and inefficient. However, historically it has played a major and in most cases a singularly positive role. Despite explosive population growth, the average literacy rate in India grew from 18% in 1950 to 65% in 2001 thanks to concerted government efforts; female literacy rose from a mere 8.9% to 53.7% in the same period. Some sectors of the Indian education systems are performing very well. According to the Global Competitiveness Report 2007–2008, the quality of mathematics and science education in India is ranked as 11th best in the world, far ahead of Japan (29th), Germany (36th), the United States (45th), and the United Kingdom (46th).

In the following, some examples of government initiatives toward innovation are described.

National Innovation Foundation

The government of India started the National Innovation Foundation (NIF) in March 2000 by providing a corpus fund of INR200 million (US$3.3 million). NIF is an autᵒonomous body under the Department of Science and Technology. NIF is developing a National Register of Green Grassroots Technological Innovations and Traditional Knowledge. It also seeks to develop a new model of poverty alleviation and employment generation by helping convert grassroots innovations into enterprises.

National Innovation Council

National Innovation Council (NIC) is a think-tank under the chairmanship of Sam Pitroda. NIC discusses, analyses, and helps implement strategies for inclusive innovation in India. NIC has suggested a road map for innovation 2010–2020 as the President of India has declared this as the decade of innovation. NIC brings together various domain experts and stakeholders in council innovation centres (CICs). NIC has sectorial and state-level innovation councils to harness local resources and capabilities.

Innovation Hub

The India Inclusive Innovation Fund has been created with INR5 billion (US$8 million) with the idea of financing for incubating new innovative methods. Health is the number one priority. This will scale to INR50 billion (US$83 million) in the next 2 years.

Health Innovation Council

The Ministry of Health and Family Welfare, government of India has formed a sectorial council called the Health Innovation Council to encourage and facilitate innovations in health care. Federation of Indian Chambers of Commerce and Industry (FICCI) is the industry member of the council, including participants from service providers, medical devices, medical electronics, medical education, clinical research, and pharmaceuticals. The main aim is to improve the existing skill set available and provide recommendations and guidelines.

ROLE OF PUBLIC–PRIVATE PARTNERSHIPS IN DRIVING INNOVATION

The term PPP describes a relationship in which public and private resources are blended to achieve a goal or a set of goals judged to be mutually beneficial both to the private entity and to the public. PPPs are contractual agreements between a public agency and a private sector entity that allow for greater private participation in the delivery of public services. The partners share risk, reward, and responsibility for a shared investment.

In India, the public sector accounts for only around 20% of the total health-care expenditure, representing around 1% of the GDP—among the lowest in the world. India's public health care is underfunded and small in size to meet the current health needs of the country. The contribution of private sector in health-care expenditure in India, around 80%, is one of the highest in the world. Almost 94% of this amount is out-of-pocket expenditure. The private sector contributes 60% of all inpatient care, 78% of outpatient visits, 58% of the hospitals and employs, and 81% of the doctors in India. Therefore, government needs to harness private initiatives for service production, and use private financial instruments, such as insurance, to create and manage demand.[4]

Health issues having wider ramification at the national level, such as food and drugs, family planning, medical education, and vital statistics, come under the central government. Items like public health, hospitals, and sanitation fall under the state governments. Mostly through national health programs the central government pumps in around 15% of the total funds in the health-care sector. The government health projects are implemented through the states, with the Department of Health facilitating access to external aid.

PPP initiatives in India have spanned several areas, such as disease surveillance, purchase and distribution of drugs in bulk, contracting specialists for high-risk pregnancies, national disease control programs, social marketing, management of primary health centers, collocation of private facilities (blood banks, pharmacy), subsidies and duty exemptions, joint ventures, contracting out medical education and training, engaging private sector consultants, pay clinics, discount vouchers, self-regulation, R&D investments, telemedicine, health cooperatives, and accreditation. The idea of PPP as a scalable and long-term solution to Indian health care brings up some key thrust areas where private sector participation will have the maximum impact. Opportunities for private players can be broadly classified along the following key areas:[5]

- Development and strengthening of health-care infrastructure that is evenly distributed geographically and at all levels of care
- Management and operation of health-care facilities for technical efficiency, operational economy, and quality
- Capacity building for formal, informal, and continuing education of professional, para-professional, and ancillary staff engaged in the delivery of health care
- Creation of voluntary as well as mandated third-party financing mechanism
- Establishment of regional and national IT backbones and health data repositories for ready access to clinical information
- Development of a maintenance and supply chain for ready availability of serviceable equipment and appliances, and medical supplies and sundries at the point of care

In the following, we give some examples of models and initiatives, where the principles of indovation have been used. These models are recognized and widely used in India and some of the examples have been accepted by the global community.

Comprehensive Annual and Total Checkup for Health (CATCH) program

CATCH program was initiated by the government of Sikkim. It aims to make Sikkim the healthiest state in India by 2015 by providing comprehensive preventive care. Free annual checkups of all citizens in the state are performed at their door steps. The program was launched in August 2010 and has covered almost 90% of the state's population so far. Camps are organized wherein a team of health-care providers take medical histories, do physical checkups, and screen for major health problems. In case a disease is detected, the patient is sent for free consultation and counseled on how to maintain a healthy lifestyle. A database of the health status of each individual is maintained. A microchip-based smart health card will be provided to all individuals. Also, a file is maintained with the health information of the area like common causes of death and major ailments, which help the community leaders to apply appropriate collective interventions. State referral hospitals, medical college, district hospitals, primary health-care centers (PHCs), and sub-PHCs are working toward this initiative. It has been beneficial especially for the below poverty line (BPL) families and senior citizens who are not able to travel long distances in the hilly terrain. Through October 2013, more than half a million complete checkups have been conducted.[6]

e-Mamta

e-Mamta is a mother and child welfare tracking system to reduce infant and maternal mortality by using mobile technology. It was launched in 2010 in Gujarat by the State Rural Health Mission of the Health and Family Welfare Department.

The program is divided into five phases:

1. Data entry of all the individuals of Gujarat by Accredited Social Health Activist (ASHA) workers.
2. Verification and validation of the data.
3. Registration of pregnant mothers, children in the age group of 0–6, and adolescents.
4. A unique ID is provided to all expecting mothers to ensure complete delivery of antenatal care (ANC), child birth, postnatal care (PNC), immunization, nutrition, and adolescent services.
5. Tracking of services through monthly work plans and follow-up of the left outs.

ASHA workers are health-care professionals who work as a bridge between the expectant mothers and the medical staff to ensure timely prenatal and postnatal care. The state government has provided a computer with Internet connectivity to each PHC and SIM cards to health workers. ASHAs collect and validate health-related data of their areas. The registration and other details are fed into a centralized system, which sends timely updates to all ASHA workers and mothers on their mobile.

The online tracking software has been developed by the National Informatics Centre (NIC) in consultation with the Ministry of Health and State of Gujarat's Family Welfare Division.

Since 2010, the e-Mamta program has reached more than 20,000 villages in 26 districts of Gujarat, covering 1090 primary and 283 community health centers (CHC) in the state.

The National Rural Health Mission (NRHM) is piloting the model in others states such as Himachal Pradesh, Uttarakhand, Jammu & Kashmir, and Jharkhand.[7]

- *Chiranjeevi Yojana* is a PPP health financing scheme implemented by the government of Gujarat in 2005 in five districts. It offers emergency obstetric care and emergency transport services for women in the BPL category and tribes. This is done by covering their out-of-pocket costs incurred on travel to reach the nearest health-care facility and by providing financial support to the accompanying person for loss of wages. The scheme has now been extended to the entire state.

The medical officers and the ASHA of the respective subcenters undertake the responsibility of identifying, motivating the community, and bringing the expecting mother for institutional delivery at the nearest impanelled gynecologists/hospital. For this, ASHAs are paid INR200 (US$3.3) from the ASHA incentive fund. The trust hospital/private local gynecologists sign a memorandum of understanding (MoU) for providing services for normal and complicated deliveries at their health facilities. The obstetricians/gynecologists are paid by the government INR280,000 (US$4647) for 100 deliveries, which includes normal, cesarean section, and complicated deliveries. If the private gynecologist offers the services in the government hospital, then INR86,500 (US$1435) is paid for every 100 deliveries.

The beneficiary is provided INR200 (US$3.3) for transportation and does not have to bear any type of charges related to delivery, medicine, anesthesia, laboratory investigations, or operation. The scheme allows for a 48-hour stay after delivery.

Until March 2012 in 26 districts, around 646 obstetricians/gynecologists were enrolled and total deliveries conducted were 769,418. Out of which 682,976 were normal deliveries, 47,946 cesarean deliveries, and 38,496 complicated deliveries.

This scheme has been awarded the Asia Innovation Award and Prime Minister's Award in 2009.[8]

- *Yeshasvini Cooperative Farmers Health Care Scheme* is a microinsurance program run by a private trust formed by the government of Karnataka since 2003. The trust was set up by regrouping several public and private individuals with the principal secretary of the cooperative department acting as chair of the trust. The program targets poor farmers who are members of the cooperative societies. Yeshasvini is one of the largest self-funded health-care schemes in the country.

Each beneficiary is required to pay a prescribed rate of annual contribution every year of INR210 (US$3.4). Yeshasvini was initially originated in the mind of Dr. Devi Shetty and designed to pay only for surgical procedures. The Yeshasvini plan covers about 823 surgeries at 476 networked private/public hospitals. These hospitals enter into an understanding in accordance with the guidelines and criteria fixed by the trust for providing a cashless facility to the beneficiaries under the scheme at predefined tariffs for each surgery. The surgery package includes the cost of medicine, consumables, operation, and bed charges. These hospitals are teaching/government hospitals that have capacity to address a large population. In addition, out of patient diagnosis is provided free of cost and some diagnostic tests are performed at discount rates. The tariff is 40%–50% off the actual tariff applied by these hospitals. Once a patient requiring surgery gets admitted to a network hospital, a preauthorization is sent for approval. The trust arranges the payment to a network hospital. More than 3 million farmers are contributing and enjoying coverage to date. On the basis of the success of this model, other states such as Andhra Pradesh and Tamil Nadu have launched similar schemes.[9]

- *Voucher scheme for institutional delivery and immunization* to promote institutional delivery and to enhance routine immunization coverage. The state government started a voucher scheme in December 2005 in all 22 districts of Jharkhand. This scheme is implemented by a auxiliary nurse midwife (ANM), Anganwadi worker (AWW), and Sahiyya, the village-level link health worker. Vouchers are issued to BPL pregnant women at the time of registration of pregnancy. The AWW and Sahiyya are responsible for the registration of pregnant women in the community. At the time of registration, INR100 (US$1.6) is given to the pregnant woman as an incentive. A hundred tablets of iron and folic acid (IFA) and two doses of tetanus toxoid (TT) are provided to the registered pregnant woman at the subcenter. At around 8 weeks before the expected date of delivery, another voucher of INR700 (US$11.6) is issued to the woman, which entitles her to have delivery at any government hospital or network private health facility and in case of cesarean section INR1500 (US$24.9) is issued. After the delivery, the woman is encouraged to visit the health facility or Anganwadi center for the immunization of the newborn. After complete immunization schedule of 1 year the woman is rewarded with a cash incentive of INR300(US$5). The AWW/Sahiyya and ANM are issued two vouchers each for INR100 (US$1.6) on completion of immunization of the newborn.[10]

- The *NICE foundation* operates in Andhra Pradesh and Rajasthan providing proper health care to mothers, children, and infants. The organization serves around 453 tribal villages in Andhra Pradesh. The foundation runs two programs in Andhra Pradesh—the Schoolchild Healthcare Plan and the Tribal Reproductive Child Health.

The Schoolchild Healthcare Plan ensures complete health care at no cost for poor children who attend government schools. The PPP with the Andhra Pradesh government allows it to cover common ailments to cardiac surgery for US$4 per child per year. The foundation holds comprehensive health camps, school-based patient clinics, and dedicated inpatient specialty hospital. This plan operates in Hyderabad in Andhra Pradesh and three districts of Rajasthan covering approximately 200,000 children.

The Tribal Reproductive Child Health program provides quality maternal, neonatal, and child health services to the tribal population at no cost. The foundation works on a three-tier level. Health awareness sessions on preventive aspects are conducted on a regular basis at the village level. At the mandal (county) level, basic equipment and ambulance service are provided and at the specialty hospital level all specialized care is given.[11]

- *GVK Emergency Management and Research Institute (EMRI).* In April 2005, GVK EMRI, a nonprofit organization, was established with an aim of providing comprehensive emergency response services such as medical, police, and fire in many states in India like Andhra Pradesh, Gujarat, Uttarakhand, Rajasthan, and so on. EMRI is a PPP model between GVK and state governments. There are over 6668 ambulances including 770 drop back ambulances and geographic information system (GIS)-based software and back-end support from the call center, which helps to provide emergency care and management. EMRI also conducts research related to emergencies and offers various emergency management training programs. About 54,000 calls are received a day. In Andhra Pradesh, 600,000 lives have been saved through telemedicine and reaching an accident spot within 15 minutes of a call. Various awards such as the NASSCOM Social Innovation Honours 2012 award, an Innovation for India award in 2012, Global CSR Excellence and Leadership award, and so on have been awarded to EMRI.[12]

- *Lifeline Express* is the world's first hospital on rails funded by the Impact foundation, corporations such as Mahindra, and other charitable organizations in collaboration with Indian Railways and Ministry of Health and Family Welfare. It started in 1991 and its mission is to eradicate avoidable blindness, deafness, and physical handicaps. The express halts for 3 weeks across rural India during which major surgeries have been performed to restore movement, hearing, sight, and correction of clefts with the help of over 80,000 surgeons and 100,000 volunteers. Over 600,000 disabled poor in rural India have been benefited till December 2010. The train has air-conditioned coaches, operation theaters, wards, a sterilizing room, power generators, pantry, accommodation for staff, and storage for medical equipment and supplies. There is a main operation theater (OT) with three operating tables and one stand-alone secondary OT with two operating tables. The theaters are equipped with a circuit camera that is used in providing training to local doctors by showcasing live surgical procedures. A six-bed recovery room is situated next to the main theater. The second theater is powered by a diesel generator and can be detached to form a stand-alone operation theater, which can be used during disaster management. The villages and nongovernment organizations offer assistance to the train by providing food, laundry services, and crowd control management.[13]
- *Akha Boat Clinic.* The innovative health initiative of the Centre for North East Studies and Policy Research (C-NES) is aimed at providing health care to the population of nearly 2500 islands of river Brahmaputra. In May 2005, the mobile boat clinic (Akha Boat) was launched with support from the Dibrugarh district health administration, C-NES, and other organizations. The boat clinic has provision for providing routine primary health-care services, as well as emergency services especially for women and children. In 2006, UNICEF partnered with C-NES by providing startup support (such as consumables and fuel for running the boat) during the floods. In 2008,

C-NES signed a MoU with the government of India under the NRHM program to provide health-care services to the riverine islands in five districts of the state. By 2010, the initiative was scaled up to 13 districts through 15 boats. In 2004, Akha received World Bank's India Development Market Place Award for innovation in transforming the lives of rural communities and INR900,000 (US$18,000) of startup capital. This health intervention has expanded to an additional 12 districts, reaching 218,000 beneficiaries in 2010–2011.[14]

- *LifeSpring Hospital* is a 20- to 25-bed private hospital with an objective of delivering world-class maternity care at remarkably low cost around Hyderabad. LifeSpring has delivered more than 22,000 babies across the 12 hospitals in Hyderabad. LifeSpring is a 50-50 joint venture owned by HLL Lifecare (a government of India enterprise) and Acumen Fund (a U.S.-based social venture capital fund). It offers normal deliveries at INR5,000 (US$83) and a cesarean delivery costs INR12,000 (US$200) in the general ward, which is about one-fifth of the price at any private hospitals. The delivery package includes hospital stay, medicines, doctors' charges, and any government-supplied free vaccination. The doctors perform four times as many operations a month as their counterparts. Around 100–120 deliveries per month are performed as compared with 30–40 in similar-sized private hospitals.

The hospital is highly standardized, process driven, and follows international quality standards. It focuses on service specialization, high asset utilization and para-skilling by using its midwives to provide maternity care that helps the doctor to manage more patients and focus more on the cases requiring doctor's attention. The hospital also maintains low operating cost and has cut down cost by providing basic services and equipment, outsourcing a few of the services, and referring complicated cases to other hospitals, hence providing no frills to the patients. It has implemented a tiered pricing system where those with the ability to pay subsidize care for the poor. The chain's first hospital broke even after 18 months of operations. The hospital plans to expand to 200 hospitals by 2015 so as to provide low-cost maternal care to those where almost 60% of births are still unattended by a health worker. The hospital has been honored with World and Business Development Awards, Frost & Sullivan award, and ET Now *leap of faith award*.[15]

- *Karnataka Internet-Assisted Diagnosis of Retinopathy of Prematurity (KIDROP)* by Narayana Nethralaya in 2008. Retinopathy of prematurity (ROP) is a condition of nondevelopment of blood vessels within the retina. This PPP project between Narayana Nethralaya and the government of Karnataka applied teleophthalmology techniques to diagnose ROP in young children.

By 2009, the project had screened over 6500 babies and offered free consultation and treatment who those who could not afford the treatment. The mobile vehicle with high-end portable digital imaging camera travels on fixed days to screen the babies. Trained technicians perform screening by capturing the retinal images and storing them in the server. The doctor accesses the images using his PC, smart phone, or tablet and also gives live diagnosis of infants screened in the rural areas. Recently, *Decision Support* on the mobile platform has been added. For instance, standard images when used along with some image enhancement tools have helped the clinician in routine work and research possibilities.[16]

- *Vaatsalya Hospitals*, founded in 2004, became the largest private hospital network serving tier-II and tier-III cities in India. It provides low-cost primary and secondary health care to 400,000 patients across two states, Karnataka and Andhra Pradesh, through 17 hospitals. The hospital prices are 15%–20% of the average urban hospital. Vaatsalya's core specialities are gynecology, pediatrics, general surgery, and general medicine so as to address 70% of the local population. Vaatsalya raised US$16 million in venture capital and private equity from Aavishkaar India, the Oasis Fund, the Aquarius India Fund, and the Seed Fund. Capital expenditure was minimized by leasing the facilities and procuring basic equipment such as x-ray, ultrasound, and ventilator, centrally and in bulk, which resulted in cost savings of more than 20%. No-frills services such as cafeteria, air-conditioning, simple furniture, and interiors were incorporated. The diagnostic center is on a revenue-sharing basis with local partners who make the capital investment to set up the center on hospital premises. Most of the staff is locally hired. To attract and retain the consultants, a revenue-sharing model is used by the management. To reach to the lowest strata of population, Vaatsalya decided to partner with government and accepted state and central insurance programs. The hospital has a capacity utilization of 80% and earned revenues of INR25 million (US$0.4 million). On average, the hospital earned 15%–18% in operating profits. The hospital has been the recipient of the Sankalp Award 2009 for health-care inclusion,

Frost and Sullivan Award for health-care excellence in 2010, Winner of the BiD challenge India 2007, and Lemelson Recognition and Mentoring Program (LRAMP) award 2008 in the enterprise category.[17]

- *Health Management and Research Institute (HMRI)* is a nonprofit organization based in Hyderabad, supported by the Piramal Foundation and government. It leverages information and communication technologies as well as public–private partnerships to provide low-cost quality care to maximum number of people. The program has three components: health information helpline, mobile health services, and telemedicine. The health information helpline 104 advice is an initiative wherein anyone can seek medical information, advice, counseling, directory information, or lodge a service complaint against any public health facility. The qualified and trained doctors and paramedics provide services to 28 million callers. The technical support is provided by Tech Mahindra company. Since its inception, there has been increase in the number of calls from 200 per day to an average of 50,000 per day. The received calls are tracked and analyzed to identify the disease pattern that is helpful for the government.

HMRI deploys 104 mobile health units (MHUs), that is, vans equipped with technology, medical devices, medicines, and health workers, to rural poor once a month. Primary focus is on chronic diseases, maternal and child health, and minor ailments. The MHUs provide screening, patient education, medication, monitoring, and follow-up. Telemedicine services are also used by HMRI to reach the unserved population.[18]

- *Low-cost diabetes screening system and test strips.* India is home to 65 million diabetics and by 2030 it is expected to cross the 100 million mark as reported by the International Diabetes Federation (IDF). Union health minister launched the indigenously developed diabetes screening system and test strips in January 2014. The product is developed by Birla Institute of Technology (BIT), Hyderabad and Indian Institute of Technology (IIT), Mumbai with funding from the Indian Council of Medical Research. It will be manufactured by Bio Sense Technologies and available in the open market in the next 6 months. The glucometers will cost between INR500 (US$8.3) and INR1000 (US$16.6) as against the price of INR1000–INR2500 (US$16.6–US$42) for the imported instrument. Each glucostrip will be at a price below INR5 (US$0.08), which is 20% less than the available strips in market. This new technology will make screening for blood sugar affordable and help in early detection. Approximately 29,000 glucometers, 58 million glucostrips, and 67 million lancets were supplied while screening population in 11 states under the national program on prevention and control of cancer, diabetes, CVDs, and stroke. The imported testing strips used while mass screening makes it expensive and difficult to use.[19]

- *GE Healthcare India.* GE healthymagination is a US$6 billion strategy to provide better health for more people at lower cost through powerful technology, innovation, and people talent. As part of its healthymagination initiative, GE Healthcare India came up with cheap, portable, and easy to use electrocardiogram (ECG) machine, MAC 400 and MAC I ECG. They make early detection of cardiac diseases very easy at the bedside of the patient. It is particularly suited for rural India where health care is delivered through primary health clinics or individual physician clinics. The MAC 400 is priced at one-third that of imported ECG machines. A variant, the MAC I ECG, where *I* stands for India, was introduced at half the price of MAC 400. Product development was done locally and commercially available chips were used instead of customized processors. The battery was redesigned to withstand local conditions. General Electric (GE) also focuses on process innovation. To penetrate rural India, it tied up with State Bank of India to provide interest free-loans for rural doctors to purchase ECG machines. The cost of an ECG scan has dropped to US$1 per patient.

Lullaby Baby Warmer is an Indian innovation for newborns. It costs 70% less compared to a similar imported product making it affordable for more clinics. The device is a bed with an overhead heater, showering the newborn with delicate warmth while the baby is bathed after birth and checked for its first vital statistics. Another innovation worth mentioning is the pocket-sized ultrasound V-scan, which is battery driven and extremely easy to operate.

GE Healthcare is the first company in the industry to successfully create and replicate PPP models. GE Healthcare signed a MoU with government to ensure that medical colleges in Indian states such as Gujarat, West Bengal, and Maharashtra have advanced diagnostic facilities such as computer tomography (CT), magnetic resonance image (MRI), ultrasound, and x-ray within their premises.

To date, GE Healthcare has brought out 11 "Designed in India, for India" solutions. GE Healthcare is in the process of developing many more such solutions locally, studying the local conditions and requirements to bridge the health-care gaps.[20]

- *Life line drug stores* (LLDS) were conceived by SMS Hospital, Jaipur, Rajasthan, in 1996. The store provides quality drugs and surgical items at the lowest possible rate leaving a profit for the private contractor to run the pharmacy store. The Rajasthan government's Medicare Relief Society (RMRS) is the controlling authority, which does the bulk purchasing of drugs. A list of essential drugs was created by a technical committee of RMRS. Through an open tender process, RMRS selects the suppliers and the contractors of the drug stores. The bidders have to fulfill certain eligibility criteria to apply. The selected contractor operates the store 24 × 7 with a fixed salary and 1% commission on sales. This PPP contract is valid for 2 years. The hospital provides the medicine and surgical item stock to the store, and the contractor sells it to the patient at the rate fixed by the committee. The contractor has no power to purchase or sell medicines on its own. LLDS provides medicines cheaply—often 30% lower than in the market. The medical superintendent of the hospital is in charge of monitoring the store and its functioning. The success of this initiative encouraged the government of Rajasthan to start such stores within the premises of district hospitals, CHC, and even at PHC.[21]
- *Jaipur foot.* In 1968, Ram Chander Sharma, a craftsman, under the guidance of Dr. P. K. Sethi conceived the original Jaipur foot. By using rubber, wood, and tyre cord, he designed and manufactured a prosthetic foot for under US$45. Other prosthetics were priced up to US$12,000, completely unobtainable for the majority of Indian population. Over the years, the Jaipur foot has been improved. Now it is made up of polyurethane that has better movement capability and enables squatting, sitting cross-legged, and walking on uneven terrain. It is water resistant, has a life-like foot feel, and is easy and quick to fit. The Bhagwan Mahavir Viklang Sahyata Samiti (BMVSS) fits the Jaipur foot for free. Donations and the government of India supports it with financial aid. About 60,000 individuals each year receive a free Jaipur foot. There are mobile clinics in 26 countries around the world. To date, BMVSS has rehabilitated more than 1.3 million patients. BMVSS has agreements with various

universities such as Stanford University, Massachusetts Institute of Technology (MIT), Indian Space Research Organisation, and Indian Institute of Technology (IIT) for research and development. In 2009, BMVSS and Stanford University codeveloped the low cost, US$20, Jaipur knee made of oil-filled nylon, which is easy and quick to fit.[22]

- *Swasthya Slate* was launched by Public Health Foundation of India (PHFI) and the government of India. Swasthya Slate is an affordable diagnostic kit, which has bridged the gap between doctors and patients. The kit includes an Android tablet, interface unit, and a peripherals bag containing all the diagnostic equipment and disposables like ECG electrodes. The Bluetooth interface unit is attached to the diagnostic devices, which are used to take the patients vitals. The tablet has a free app called Swasthya Slate that allows health-care workers to take demographics and a brief history of the patient that is stored in the internal memory of the tablet. The kit is GPS enabled and can take pictures, which helps in recording patient coordinates. Once the interface unit is connected to the software, it allows the tablet to monitor, store, and display the diagnostic information. The following tests can be conducted: blood pressure, blood sugar, blood hemoglobin, heart rate, water quality (total suspended particles in water), ECG, body temperature, urine protein, and urine sugar. The results are available within minutes and uploaded to a central server via Internet. In case of no Internet connectivity, the patient database is stored within the tablet's internal memory. The result can be sent as mail or SMS to the doctor and the patient. The software is available in several languages, which enables the use of the kit in rural areas. The software also has features like a decision support system capable of suggesting recommendations for treatment of the patient. The kit is easy to use and health-care workers like ASHAs and ANMs are trained and empowered to use the kit. It allows them to provide recommendations and guide the physicians through phone/videoconferencing. This will help to monitor health of the population at large and also refer high risk cases to the doctor. Swasthya Slate currently costs around INR30,000 (US$498) and is expected to cost around INR15,000 (US$250) after it enters mass production. Swasthya Slate has been introduced in nine states of India. Outside India, the device has been used in the United States, Europe, Nigeria, and Canada. The overall cost comes to around INR78 (US$1.3) for the primary group of tests out of which INR50 (US$0.83) is the cost of materials used, such as sampling strips and disposable needles. The remaining amount of INR28 (US$0.46) goes to the health-care worker administering the tests, giving them a monetary incentive as well.[23]

- *Operation ASHA* is a registered nonprofit organization that works closely with the government of India and other funding agencies to eliminate TB. It operates in over 3000 villages and slums in 8 Indian states and in 2 provinces in Cambodia. TB treatment centers are set up in the community. Local health workers are trained to identify new patients, ensure adherence to the drug schedule, and carry out educational awareness camps. In collaboration with Microsoft Research, a biometric system was launched called e-compliance. Whenever the patient is administered the drug, the fingerprint is scanned and the visit is recorded. The visit logs are available to monitor medication delivery. Any missed dose triggers an SMS to the health-care worker, who in turn ensures timely administration of medication by following up with the patient within 48 hours. OpASHA is expanding to over 225 centers around the world. To date, 4,931 patients have been enrolled, 105,557 supervised doses have been logged, and 89% of patients have successfully completed their prescribed treatment matching World Health Organization (WHO) standards. The cost of treating a patient for the entire therapy is US$80. An estimated US$115 of donated tuberculosis medicines, hospital care, and diagnostic services from the government is received. OpASHA spends the majority of the remaining US$80 on salaries and program expenses for the providers and community partners. A grant for providing TB treatment and other TB services is received after 2 years of opening the center, which fully covers the operating costs. Various awards such as the Innovation and Entrepreneurship Award 2013 and Wall Street Journal Technology Innovation Award 2012 have been received.[24]
- *The wooden incubator* was developed by Dr. Sathya Jeganathan, a pediatrician at Chengalpattu government medical college, a rural hospital in southern India. At the hospital, infant mortality rate was high. On average, 39 out of every 1000 infants died at birth. Dr. Jeganathan reviewed that the incubators available in market were expensive and difficult to maintain. So, she designed her own incubator that was inexpensive and easy to use. The incubator was designed from a wooden table made of locally harvested wood, and standard 100 W bulbs to maintain the infant's temperature. The incubator costs around US$100 and has cut down the infant mortality nearly by

half at the medical college. Dr. Sathya and the Lemelson Foundation are working together to further develop the product design.[25]

- *JANMA Clean Birth Kit.* In India alone, 78,000 women and nearly 1 million babies die each year from pregnancy and childbirth complications. According to WHO, approximately 60 million women in developing countries give birth each year with the help of an untrained attendant or with no help at all. The unhygienic environment during birth leads to the risk of contracting an infection, which is a leading cause of nearly one in five maternal deaths. To achieve Millennium Development Goal to reduce maternal and infant mortality rate, institutional deliveries are encouraged. However, many institutes lack infrastructure and trained professional. Ayzh, a for-profit social venture, which provides health and livelihood solutions to impoverished women worldwide, launched the JANMA clean birth kit to provide a safe, clean, and hygienic delivery experience at home or at institution. JANMA is a birth kit that provides clean and sterile instruments recommended by WHO for use during childbirth at a cost of US$2. The kit provides the *Six Cleans*: clean hands, clean perineum, clean delivery surface, clean cord cutting and tying instrument, and clean wraps for mother and baby. JANMA is sourced and assembled by Indian rural women in a biodegradable jute bag. Ayzh sells the kit to for-profit organizations such as network of local pharmacies, clinics, and hospitals, and to nonprofit organizations. More than 20,000 units have been sold throughout India and Africa. Ayzh is also committed to education, training, and evaluation programs in collaboration with the Harvard School of Public Health, measuring the effect clean birth kits have on clean birth practices. Various recognitions, such as Ashoka Changemakers 2010, Clinton Global Initiative 2010, Echoing Green 2012, and World Healthcare Congress Award 2011, have been awarded.[26]
- *Provision of essential maternal and child health services in tribal areas.* ARTH (Action Research and Training for Health), an NGO, started a reproductive and child health (RCH) clinic in 1997 in Rajasthan. The program has now expanded to cover a total of 50,000 population covering 45 villages. The program is funded by the Sir Ratan Tata Trust and MacArthur Foundation. ARTH recognized the need for affordable health care for women in small towns and rural areas. Five nurse-midwives manage two health centers and provide 24-hour delivery and obstetric first aid services. Each health center has a health worker cum driver with motorbike to assist the midwife and

help in commuting for home visits and for referrals at night. Clinical and counseling training is imparted to the midwives, so that they can interact with the community. Drugs and consumables are supplied at the health center and a doctor visits nurse-midwife clinics one to two times every week. Subsidies are provided to poor women and children who need referral to a district hospital and arrangement is made by the midwives. Community volunteers are also encouraged in helping the nurse-midwife. There was an increase in institutional delivery from 12% to 38%, nurse–midwife conducted delivery increased from 1.6% to 20.7%, stillbirth rate of 28.9 and neonatal mortality rate (NNMR) of 37 per 1000 live births respectively from 1995 to 2005.[27]

- *VisionSpring*, formerly Scojo Foundation, is a social enterprise founded by Jordan Kassalow and Scott Berrie in 2001. VisionSpring in India was launched in 2005 to provide affordable eyeglasses to every individual. According to a study, 703 million could have their vision restored with a pair of glasses.

VisionSpring trains local people and employs them as vision entrepreneurs. They perform eye screening and distribution of affordable reading glasses to the population. VisionSpring employs a hub and spoke approach where the optic shop functions as hub and vision entrepreneurs act like spokes. VisionSpring's optical shops have an optometrist who conducts eye exams and each optical shop has a team of vision entrepreneurs associated with it. Vision entrepreneurs travel to educate the community about eye care and bring awareness about free vision screening at the VisionSpring optic shop by providing marketing material. The vision entrepreneurs set up the screening room on the day of a vision camp. As a lot of illiterate people come for the screening, the tumbling E-diagram chart is used, which enables individuals to simply point in the direction that the *E* is facing. After the screening is done, a prescription for reading glasses or a referral for an advanced eye screening and treatment are provided. Around 1200 vision entrepreneurs distribute more than 100,000 pairs of glasses in 13 countries.[28]

- *Smiles-on-Wheels Program* is a national mobile hospital run by a not-for-profit organization, the Smile Foundation. It caters to underprivileged children and women in remote rural areas and urban slums. The program has 19 operational projects in 265 remote villages and urban slums across India, benefiting 231,000 lives directly in a year. Five vans visit two to three villages to deliver health care at a nominal cost to the community. The vans are staffed by specialized medical personnel and equipped with an x-ray machine, ECG machine, basic pathological services, antenatal and postnatal services, and an outpatient department for common ailments. The staff performs routine medical examinations, distributes condoms and oral contraceptive pills, and transports severe cases to superspecialist clinics. The team also carries out awareness programs on health and hygiene and preventive health care.[29]

- *Neighborhood network in palliative care (NNPC)* is a community-led initiative aiming to provide home-based palliative care to all those in need in Kerala. Local community volunteers from local and national government, schools, universities, religious groups, and nongovernmental organizations are trained to identify problems of the chronically ill and dying patients and to intervene effectively with support from a network of trained professionals. NNPC aims at empowering locals by involving them in designing, delivering, and evaluating services. The initiative has attained coverage of over 60% in many areas and provides care to approximately 2500 patients per week.[30]

- e-*Choupal health* is a program designed to address issues related to lack of access to quality health information and products. It is supported by ITC Limited and the USAID funded market-based partnerships for health (MBPH). Its objective is to create awareness regarding family planning, child health, nutrition, and hygiene. Also, it facilitates in providing health products to improve health outcomes. In 2000, e-Choupal was initially introduced for farmers to access markets directly for marketing their production. Later, it extended to providing basic health-care services.

In 2005, e-Choupal health built rural information centers. The center situated at the choupal (a common meeting place of people in a village) level is managed by a village health champion (VHC). The VHC is the first point of contact and its role is to disseminate health awareness and information through choupal portal and radio. The VHC also helps in selling health-care products. Each center serves five villages, which is connected to a single district hub called the Choupal Saagar (rural mall), which is equipped with a clinic, pharmacy, and an automated laboratory. The hub clinic has a telemedicine facility for teleconsultation with specialists and trains locals for providing preventive health care and conducting awareness programs. The health products are stored at the hub clinic and distributed to the VHCs for selling it to the community. The health products such as condoms, oral contraceptive pills, sanitary napkins, nutritional supplements, and reading glasses are supplied by health partners such as Ranbaxy, JK Ansell, Royal Hygiene, Vision Spring, and Wyeth/Pfizer. All the partners pay a fee to ITC for utilizing their network.[31]

- *World Health Partners* (WHP), a nonprofit organization that uses social franchising to link and train existing village-level providers through business relationships and technology to provide quality health care to rural communities. The organization has launched pilot program in three districts of Uttar Pradesh. It works by bringing together formally and informally qualified private providers. Each village has a local informal qualified provider called as Sky Care providers. The main responsibility of the Sky Care provider is to refer patients to the Sky Health Centre. The rural providers consult and refer the patients to the urban providers. The rural providers also provide family planning service to the population. The Sky Health Centres are the most important component of the referral chain. The major responsibility includes facilitation of teleconsultation of the patient. Sky Health centres are linked to nearby urban qualified providers at WHP-owned or approved franchised clinics, which are existing clinics in close vicinity of Sky Health Centre. Each Sky Health Centre also has a Sky Med Centre, which has generic drugs and family planning products stored. Intrauterine device (IUD) insertion and lab collection is also available in Sky Health Centre. WHP has tied up with laboratories that can provide diagnostic services for Sky Health patients. Services are subsidized by WHP, which is supported by donors or from government pro-poor programs. At 60% less cost, IUD coverage has increased by 11 times and sterilization by 5 times in these areas. There is also an increase in the number of consultation with the rural providers.[32]
- *Frugal Digital's Clock Sense* is a cheap screening device that measures the amount of oxygenated hemoglobin in the blood. Designed in Copenhagen, Denmark, after research in India, it uses components that are easily available, such as an analog alarm clock, two LEDs, and a simple light sensor from a TV remote. The clock meter has a USB port, which is a connector plugged into a family of sensors that can measure temperature, blood pressure, pulse, respiration rate, oxygen saturation, and so on. The clock dial has three readings: (1) green means you are healthy, (2) amber means you need a checkup, and (3) red means you need to visit the doctor/hospital. This device

is easy to use for the frontline workers. The designing team does not want to manufacture this product, but plans to share the knowledge and tie up with manufacturers and developers so that it can reach 250,000 health workers in India.[33]

- *Low-cost standard therapeutics (LOCOST)*, founded in 1983, is a public nonprofit charitable trust registered in Gujarat. It makes essential medicines at affordable price especially for poor and people in remote areas. LOCOST manufactures over 60 essential medicines in 80 formulations (liquid, capsule, and tablet). The medicines are bought in powder form in bulk from the bulk drug manufacturers. Tablets, capsules, and syrups are then formulated in its own small-scale factories. The medicines are not made from the first stage of chemical formulation. It conforms to the strict quality standards prescribed by the WHO and has an in-house quality control laboratory. The organization is able to sell the drugs at one-fourth or one-tenth of the market price and still make 10% profit. For example, Atenolol 50 mg, a drug used to treat high blood pressure, is available for INR20–INR25 (US$0.33–US$0.41) as a strip in market, LOCOST sells the same strip for INR3 (US$0.05). LOCOST supplies drugs to over 100 civil society organizations (CSOs) and charitable organizations for the past 23 years, which provide drugs to the poor without thinking of profits, unlike the retailers. The organization also brings awareness among the people about profits made by branded drugs prescribed by doctors. The doctors and patients are encouraged to buy LOCOST drugs that are cheaper and of good quality. LOCOST has a presence in three other states of India.[34]

- *ToucHb* is a portable needle-free anemia screening tool that requires no expensive equipment and little training to use. It was conceived by Mr. Myshkin Ingawale and developed by Biosense Technologies. Anemia is one of the leading causes of death in developing countries especially in women and children during childbirth. Anemia can be treated if a simple test and treatment is taken on time. The ToucHb allows local health workers to test patients and immediately read results so that treatment can be started. Biosense plans to sell devices to every clinic in India and eradicate deaths due to anemia by 2020. The design is simple, easy to use, and dust-proof to last in rural areas. The device is equipped with a rechargeable battery and a hand crank mechanism for operation in areas with infrequent electric supply. There are no recurrent costs, such as needles, lancets, microcuvettes, and blotting paper, other than the batteries that can be recharged and are expected to last for more than 100 tests. Biosense aims to sell the machines for between US$200 and US$300 and the cost of an individual test will be INR5 (US$0.08). The readings can be sent to central server using the Android app made by Biosense. The device is undergoing testing in a pilot project with 3000 women in Maharashtra. Biosense has won the Emerging Award for innovative key entrepreneur ideation in health care at Sankalp 2009, India's largest Social Enterprise and Investment Forum.[35]

Apart from indovation examples, few innovations are worth mentioning, which were specifically applied first time in India but the idea was conceptualized abroad.

- *Embrace* is a durable, reusable, safe, and low-cost sleeping bag-like product. It was designed by four graduates, Jane Chen, Linus Liang, Naganand Murty, and Rahul Panicker at Stanford's Institute of Design in 2007. It has a removable heating element and a pouch of phase-change material (PCM), a waxy substance. It requires only 30 minutes of electricity to warm and maintains the desired temperature of 37°C (98.6°F) for up to 6 hours without electricity. Unlike traditional warmers, it also ensures the close contact between mother and child, which is also referred to as kangaroo care. After 4 hours, the PCM pouch could be *recharged* by submerging it in boiling water for a few minutes. The infant warmer costs about US$200 and has helped save more than 22,000 low birth weight and premature infants' lives. It is portable and easy to use; hence it works at all levels of health care, that is, rural as well as urban. Furthermore, it has no moving parts, which minimizes the risk of failure. The entire sleeping bag can be sanitized in boiling water making it reusable. The Embrace organization has also set up educational programs to address the root causes of hypothermia. GE Healthcare has partnered with Embrace for the distribution of this infant warmers.[36]
- *A behaviour changing (ABC) syringe.* Accounting for 83% of all the world's injections, India is the largest consumer of syringes in the world. According to WHO, unsafe needle injections cause an estimated 1.3 million early deaths and an annual burden of US$535 million in direct medical costs each year. It is also estimated that up to 40% of the 40 billion injections administered each year are delivered with syringes reused without sterilization, causing 5% of

all new HIV cases, 32% of all hepatitis B cases, and 40% of hepatitis C cases. Syringes are being reused because of poverty and often by mistake. Dr. David Swann of Huddersfield University, Huddersfield, England, invented the ABC syringe. It is nitrogen-filled package that is colorless and once it is exposed to air (CO_2), it activates an o-crestholphthalein that changes the syringe from colorless to irreversible red within 60 seconds of exposure. The red syringe warns the patient and doctors that the syringe has been used and is not to be reused. The syringe was tested in India with 100% accurate response to the red coloration. The ABC syringe costs only half a cent extra than an ordinary syringe in India. It is estimated that 700,000 unsafe injections can be prevented and save 6.5 million life years and US$130 million in medical costs in India alone.[37]

- *Odon device.* The device was conceived by a car mechanic Jorge Odón from Argentina. The low-cost simplified device helps in assisted vaginal delivery, which protects babies and mothers, when labor is prolonged. It is made of film-like polyethylene material. The device is positioned around the baby's head and the lubricated sleeve is gently inserted around the baby's head. Once a marker on the device indicates that it has been positioned properly, the inner compartment of the sleeve is inflated, providing a strong grip on the baby's head. The inserter is taken away and the sleeve can be pulled with up to 19 kg (42 lb.) of force to pull out the head and allow for delivery of the baby. The device is under clinical trial in health-care facilities of Argentina and rural South Africa. Becton Dickinson has agreed to manufacture and distribute the unit and estimates the cost as US$50 per unit. This device is potentially safer as the risk of infection and injury is less. It is easier to use with minimal training than using forceps and vacuum extractor. It is a safe alternative to few cesarean sections in areas with limited access. So far, the device has been safety tested only on 20 women in Argentina with uncomplicated pregnancies. The WHO is assisting in further testing of the device on more than 250 women in China, India, and South Africa with both normal and complicated pregnancies. It has received research grants from the United States Agency for International Development and Grand Challenges Canada.[38]

- *Certificate course in evidence-based diabetes management (CCEBDM)* has been developed by PHFI in collaboration with Dr. Mohan's Diabetes Education Academy, Chennai, with a grant from MSD Pharmaceuticals in 2010. CCEBDM is a uniquely designed once-a-month training program for primary health-care physicians. The objectives of the course are to develop core skills and competencies in primary care physicians for the practice of evidence-based diabetes management. The course is spread across a year with 12 training modules, held once a month on a Sunday to better suit the schedule of busy physicians. It follows a strong monitoring mechanism by PHFI for overall smooth conduction of course with the help of observers all across the country. More than 5000 doctors have already been trained. Recently, this model has also been adopted by various government agencies. There is a dedicated website for this course at www.ccebdm.org.[39]

This is one of the biggest capacity building initiatives in the field of diabetes management for primary care physicians. Recently, IDF recognized PHFI for excellence in providing diabetes education to health-care professionals with this CCEBDM model. This is the only recognized course by IDF for primary care physicians for building their capacity in diabetes management.

SUMMARY AND ANALYSIS OF INNOVATIVE MODELS

The various innovative models by different organizations are summarized in Tables 21.1 through 21.5.

TABLE 21.1

Government Health-Care Models

Innovation Health-Care Models	Development Area	Implementing Agency	Funding Agency	Program Outreach	Verified Results
CATCH program	Comprehensive preventive care	State government of Sikkim	State government of Sikkim	5,19,968 Checkups conducted (October 2013)	Covered almost 90% of state population
e-Mamta	Mother and child welfare tracking system by using mobile technology	State government of Gujarat	State government of Gujarat	Reached more than 20,000 villages in districts of Gujarat (since 2010)	NRHM is piloting the model in several other states

TABLE 21.2

PPP Health-Care Models

Innovation Health-Care Models	Development Area	Implementing Agency	Funding Agency	Program Outreach	Verified Results
Chiranjeevi Yojana	Health insurance	State government of Gujarat	State government of Gujarat, private hospitals	646 obstetricians enrolled and total deliveries conducted is 769,148 (March 2012)	Asia Innovation Award and Prime Minister Award, 2009
Yeshasvini Cooperative Farmers Health-Care Scheme	Microinsurance program	State government of Karnataka	State government of Karnataka, private trust, farmers cooperatives, private providers	823 surgeries at 476 network hospitals. More than 3 million farmers benefited	Other states like Andhra Pradesh and Tamil Nadu implemented the model
Voucher scheme for institutional delivery and immunization	Institutional delivery and routine immunization	State government of Jharkhand	State government of Jharkhand Public and private hospitals	22 Districts of Jharkhand	—
NICE foundation	Schoolchild Healthcare Plan, Tribal Reproductive Child Health	State government of Andhra Pradesh and Rajasthan	State government, NICE foundation	Covering around 200,000 children	Serves around 453 tribal villages in Andhra Pradesh

(Continued)

TABLE 21.2 *(Continued)*

PPP Health-Care Models

Innovation Health-Care Models	Development Area	Implementing Agency	Funding Agency	Program Outreach	Verified Results
Emergency Management and Research Institute (EMRI)	Comprehensive emergency response	GVK	State government and GVK	Saved 600,000 lives in Andhra Pradesh state, reaching an accident spot within 15 minutes of a call	Awards—NASSCOM Social Innovation Honours 2012, Innovation for India awards 2012, Global CSR Excellence and Leadership
Lifeline Express	World's first hospital on rails	Indian Railways & Ministry of Health and Family Welfare	Indian railways, NGOs, and villages	Over 600,000 disabled poor in rural India benefted (December 2010)	—
Akha Boat Clinic	Mobile boat clinic	Center for North East Studies and Policy Research	C-NES, UNICEF, government of India, NRHM	Providing health care to the population of nearly 2500 islands of river Brahmaputra	World Bank's India Development Market Place Award for innovation 2004
LifeSpring hospital	World-class maternity care at remarkably low cost	HLL Lifecare (government of India enterprise)	HLL Lifecare and Acumen Fund (U.S.-based social venture fund)	More than 22,000 babies delivered across 12 hospitals in Hyderabad	World and Business Development Awards, Frost & Sullivan award
Karnataka Internet-assisted diagnosis of retinopathy of prematurity	Internet-assisted diagnosis of retinopathy of prematurity	Narayan Nethralaya and state government of Karnataka	Narayan Nethralaya and state government of Karnataka	By 2009 screened over 6,500 babies and offered free consultation and treatment	—

Innovation Health-Care Models	Development Area	Implementing Agency	Funding Agency	Program Outreach	Verified Results
Vaatsalya Hospitals	Health-care services	Vaatsalya	Vaatsalya partner with government and various private companies	Provides low-cost primary and secondary health care to 400,000 patients across two states through 17 hospitals	Recipient of BiD challenge India 2007 and LRAMP Award 2008, Sankalp Award 2009, Frost and Sullivan Healthcare Excellence Award 2010
Health Management and Research Institute (HMRI)	Health information helpline, mobile health services and tele-medicine	Piramal Foundation and Indian government. Technical support by Tech Mahindra	Piramal Foundation and Indian government	Increase in the number of calls from 200 per day to an average of 50,000 per day	—
Low-cost diabetes screening system and test strips	Indigenously developed diabetes screening system and test strips	Birla Institute of Technology (BIT), Hyderabad and Indian Institute of Technology (IIT), Mumbai. Manufactured by Biosense Technologies	Indian Council of Medical Research	Expected usage: ~29,000 glucometers, 58 million glucostrips, and 67 million lancets supplied while screening of population in 11 states conducted	—

(Continued)

TABLE 21.2 (Continued)

PPP Health-Care Models

Innovation Health-Care Models	Development Area	Implementing Agency	Funding Agency	Program Outreach	Verified Results
GE Healthcare India	Affordable equipments	GE Healthcare	GE Healthcare and state governments	—	Low-cost ECG, baby warmer, and pocket-sized ultrasound scanner
Life line drug stores (LLDS)	Store provides quality drugs and surgical items	SMS Hospital, Jaipur, Rajasthan	RMRS suppliers and distributors	Provides medicines 30% lower than the market price	Implemented in other CHCs and PHCs of Rajasthan
Jaipur foot	Prosthetic foot	Bhagwan Mahavir Viklang Sahyata Samiti (BMVSS)	Government of India and donation	About 60,000 individuals each year receive a free Jaipur foot and there are mobile clinics in 26 countries	Benefited over 1.3 million people with physical disabilities
Swasthya Slate	Diagnostic kit	PHFI and government of India	PHFI and government of India	Implemented in states of India and various countries	—
Operation ASHA	Ensuring administration of TB dose to patients	Operation ASHA	Government of India and other funding agencies	It operates in over 3,000 villages and slums in 8 Indian states and 2 provinces in Cambodia	Recipient of Innovation and Entrepreneurship Award 2013, Wall Street Journal Technology Innovation award 2012

TABLE 21.3

Private and Charitable Health-Care Models

Innovation Health-Care Models	Development Area	Implementing Agency	Funding Agency	Program Outreach	Verified Results
Wooden incubators	Affordable equipments	Innovation at a government medical college by Dr. Sathya Jeganathan	Dr. Sathya Jeganathan and Lemelson Foundation	Tested at Chengalpattu government medical college	The incubator costs around US$100 and has cut down the infant mortality nearly by half
JANMA Clean Birth Kit	Affordable equipments	Social enterprise	Ayzh, for-profit social venture	More than 20,000 units sold throughout India and Africa	Recognition such as Ashoka changemakers 2010, Clinton global initiative 2010, Echoing green 2012, and World healthcare congress award 2011
Essential maternal and child health services in tribal areas	Reproductive and child health (RCH) clinic	ARTH (Action research and training for health)	Sir Ratan Tata Trust and MacArthur Foundation	Expanded to cover total of 50,000 population covering 45 villages	Increase in Institutional delivery from 12% to 38%, nurse–midwife conducted delivery increased from 1.6% to 20.7%, reducing Stillbirth rate and NNMR
VisionSpring	Affordable eyeglasses	Scojo Foundation	Social enterprise	1,200 Vision entrepreneurs distribute more than 100,000 pairs of glasses in 13 countries	—

(Continued)

TABLE 21.3 *(Continued)*

Private and Charitable Health-Care Models

Innovation Health-Care Models	Development Area	Implementing Agency	Funding Agency	Program Outreach	Verified Results
Smiles-on-Wheels Program	National mobile hospital	Smile foundation	Community-led initiative charity	19 Projects in 265 remote villages and urban slums in India, benefiting 231,000 lives in a year	—
Neighborhood network in palliative care (NNPC)	Home-based palliative care	Community-led initiative	Charity, volunteers	Coverage of over 60% in different areas and provide care to 2,500 patients per week	—
E-Choupal health	IT services	ITC	ITC and USAID funded market-based partnerships for health (MBPH)	—	—
World Health Partners (WHP)	Social franchising via Sky Health Centres	Services are subsidized by WHP	Supported by donors or from government pro-poor programs	At 60% less of the cost, IUD coverage has increased by 11 times and sterilization by 5 times	—

Innovation Health-Care Models	Development Area	Implementing Agency	Funding Agency	Program Outreach	Verified Results
Frugal digital's Clock Sense	Affordable equipment (hemoglobin screening)	Designed by frugal digital. Plans to tie up with manufacturer	—	—	—
Low-cost standard therapeutics (LOCOST)	Low-cost quality drugs to the poor	LOCOST manufactures the drugs. For distribution through various charitable and civil society organization	LOCOST	Presence in Indian states—Gujarat, Madhya Pradesh, Maharashtra, and Karnataka	—
ToucHb	Affordable equipment (hemoglobin screening)	Biosense Technologies	Biosense Technologies	Undergoing testing in a pilot project with 3,000 women in Maharashtra	Won the Emerging Award for innovative key entrepreneur ideation in health care at Sankalp 2009

TABLE 21.4

Innovation Conceptualized Abroad and Applied in India

Innovation Health-Care Models	Development Area	Implementing Agency	Funding Agency	Program Outreach	Verified Results
Embrace	Affordable equipment (infant warmer)	GE Healthcare	GE Healthcare with Embrace	Costs about US$200 and has helped save more than 22,000 low birth weight and premature infants lives	—
A Behaviour Changing Syringe (ABC)	Affordable equipment	Invented by Dr. David Swann of Huddersfield University	PPP	—	—
Odon Device	Affordable equipment	Becton Dickinson and WHO	WHO, USAID, and Grand Challenges Canada	Under clinical trial. 20 women in Argentina tested in first phase testing	—

TABLE 21.5

Innovative Capacity Building Health-Care Model

Innovation Health-Care Models	Development Area	Implementing Agency	Funding Agency	Program Outreach	Verified Results
Certificate course in evidence-based diabetes management (CCEBDM)	Education and training of physicians in evidence-based diabetes management	PHFI in collaboration with Dr. Mohan's Diabetes Education Academy	MSD Pharma	5082 PCPs enrolled under the program. Model adopted by various state health departments	IDF recognizes PHFI for excellence in providing diabetes education to health-care professionals

LESSONS LEARNED AND CHALLENGES

The concepts of health ecosystems and PPP help governments become more inventive by envisioning and creating a space outside the government structure that allows innovation to flourish. It helps to inject a broader set of skills and talents, as well as a more diligent and responsive work culture into the government machinery. Private capital investment and market-based revenue streams help generate more resources beyond those available through government. PPPs help private companies bring together new financial resources and business skills to help open the door for the creation of new industry clusters. PPPs allow private companies to engage in large-scale projects that go far beyond their traditional capacities and reduce the risks associated with investing in new technologies. Within an ecosystem, various players can simultaneously drive the development of new services, applications, and solutions that do not yet exist. PPPs often deliver services and solutions more cost effectively than traditional government approaches, and provide objectives and coordination better than purely market-driven initiatives.

Indovation requires synergistic use of cumulative efforts of industry, government, educational system, R&D environment, and customers. The Indian innovation system has adopted selected features of other countries to improve the effectiveness of its national innovation system. The government has been increasing the science and technology outlay every year and allocating higher funds for cutting-edge technological development. Suitable policies are being formulated as needed by the government to suit innovation. For unleashing the huge innovation potential, India needs to develop a strategy that focuses on increasing competition as a part of improving investment climate, supported by stronger skills, better information infrastructure, and more finance from public and private sectors. It also needs to strengthen its efforts to create and commercialize knowledge, as well as better diffuse existing global and local knowledge, and increase the capacity of smaller enterprises to absorb it.

RECOMMENDATIONS

Probable recommendations to overcome the challenges faced and strengthen the Indian innovation system are as follows.

Creation of Expert Panels and a Database on Innovations

Constitution of subject-wise expert panels in technical institutions around the country can facilitate screening and evaluation of ideas. Evaluation reports from these panels in a standard format could then be processed further for support. Creation of a database on innovations, which is made accessible to the prospective innovators as well as the expert panels, would not only avoid processing of new applications on ideas already considered in the past, but would also lead to cross-fertilization of ideas. Such a database would also serve as a tool to the expert panel in proper screening and evaluation of ideas.

Innovation Awareness Campaign

To make people aware about various funding mechanisms, awareness campaigns could be launched by holding seminars/exhibitions of successful innovators and screening of videos/CDs/documentary films on innovative projects at technical institutes/colleges/schools and industrial clusters in different parts of the country. Also, sensitization camps for innovation awareness, targeted at executives and professionals could be organized. A standard innovation awareness creation module could be evolved at the central level, which could be utilized by institutions and NGOs in the country.

One of the innovative examples is Healthcare Technology Innovation Centre (HTIC) of IIT Madras, which is an R&D center established through a joint initiative of IIT Madras and Department of Biotechnology (DBT), government of India. Since its inception in 2011, HTIC has evolved into a unique and leading med-tech innovation ecosystem in the country bringing together more than 20 medical institutions, industry, and government agencies collaborating with HTIC in developing affordable health-care technologies for unmet clinical needs. HTIC's technologies are reaching the field, touching lives, enabling business, and benefiting society.

HTIC runs an annual innovation fellowship program aimed at creating innovators and innovations in health-care technology to address the growing health care needs of India. The 18-month fellowship program is designed for interested candidates from diverse backgrounds, such as engineering, medicine, business administration, public health, and social sciences, both fresh graduates and ones with work experience.

User-Friendly Funding Mechanisms

The assessment and processing time of proposals in any funding mechanism could be made optimum by evolving well-defined parameters in consultation with experts as well as user groups. Terms and conditions of funding could be such that support is liberal and on easy terms, when the risk involved is high, that is, during the birth and survival phase of innovation, and support is partial with appropriate sharing by innovator when risk is relatively less, that is, during the growth phase of innovation. Also, terms and conditions could be flexible for projects in high priority areas. Further, the adopted mechanisms should conform to internationally accepted benchmarks and best practices, for example, the innovation evaluation process (IEP) model followed by the National Science Foundation, the United States.

One of the examples is the GE Healthcare and HTIC multidisciplinary R&D center at IIT Madras, which have come together to develop a range of affordable health-care solutions.

This 3-year collaborative research and development initiative will address the needs in the areas of mother and child health, cardiology, and cancer. GE will provide a grant of INR7,500,000 (US$12,400) to HTIC toward research and development of these solutions for emerging markets.

Intellectual Property Rights Infrastructure and Training

To make the filing of patents simple and easier, efforts should be made for setting up more extension centers of patent offices around the country, for example, in industry associations, and providing linkages among them. More and more intellectual property rights (IPR) awareness-cum-training programs should be organized to mitigate the myths about patents, designs, trademarks, and copyrights in the minds of people and also train them in drafting patent claims, filing patent applications, and so on. Training is also essential in drafting MoUs/agreements to avoid IPR-related disputes at a later stage.

Marketing Support System

Providing a platform to the innovators in national and international exhibitions to exhibit their developments would help in attracting investors for commercialization of innovative products/processes. Internet portals of government departments and industry associations can also play a useful role in providing publicity to the innovative products/processes.

Coordination through National Innovation Foundation

The NIF should play a national role as a coordinating body between various departments/agencies operating innovation support mechanisms. NIF should maintain a record of all completed projects, whether they result in prototypes, pilot plants, or commercial products and then forward them to other relevant agencies for taking them further in the innovation chain. NIF should also maintain a panel of technical experts and testing laboratories at approved rates, whose facilities could be utilized by innovators/organizations.

SUMMARY

Indovation can be viewed as an ecosystem that is exhibiting rapid evolution. It is continuously adapting itself to the newer ways of sustainable development. It is keen to adopt select features of innovation systems in other countries to improve its effectiveness, and eager to participate in a global innovation system, wherein an idea is generated in one part of the world, a prototype is developed in another, and it is commercialized in yet another part of the world for global consumption. There is an increased thrust on public–private partnership models to nurture and support the entire innovation chain in the country.

REFERENCES

1. Anderson, N., C. De Dreu, and B.A. Nijstad. 2004. The routinization of innovation research: A constructively critical view of the state-of-the-science. *Journal of Organizational Behavior*, 25: 147–173.
2. Berwick, D.M. 2003. Disseminating innovations in health care, *Journal of the American Medical Association*, 289: 1969–1975.
3. Gupta, A., 2008. Prescription for Change. *Wall Street Journal*, 20: R6.
4. Aggarwal, M. and B. Ladda. 2010. PPP in Education: Workshop on PPP in Urban and Social Sectors. CRISIL Risk and Infrastructure Solutions Limited, 21 May. CRISIL Infrastructure advisory. Available at http://www.crisil.com/pdf/infra-advisory/6-ppps-ineducation.pdf.
5. Akkawi, A. 2010. INSEAD—PPPs as Policy Instruments. November 29. Ernst & Young. Available at http://campuses.insead.edu/abu_dhabi/events/PPPPresentation 29.11.10.pdf.
6. CATCH program. Available at http://sikkimhealth.gov.in/CATCHH.docx; http://www.sikkim.gov.in /Government%20Missions/CATCH.aspx.

7. E-Mamta. Available at http://informatics.nic.in/news/newsdetail/newsID/276.
8. Chiranjeevi Yojana. Available at http://www.gujhealth.gov.in/chirnajivi-yojana.htm.
9. Yeshasvini Cooperative Farmers Healthcare Scheme. Available at http://www.yeshasvini.kar.nic.in /about.htm.
10. Voucher scheme for institutional delivery and immunisation. Available at http://hsprodindia.nic.in /listdetails.asp?roid=122.
11. NICE foundation. Available at http://healthmarketinnovations.org/program/nice-foundation; www.nicefoundation.in.
12. Emergency Management and Research Institute (EMRI). Available at www.emri.in.
13. Lifeline Express. Available at www.impactindia.org/lifeline-express.php.
14. Akha Boat Clinic. Available at www.unicef.org/india/10._Akha_Boat_Initiative_in_Assam.pdf.
15. LifeSpring hospital. Available at http://www.lifespring.in/about-us.html; http://forbesindia.com/article/breakpoint/lifesspring-hospitals-saves-mothers-and-newborns-using-a-low-cost-model/33492/1; http://healthmarketinnovations.org/program/lifespring-hospitals-private-limited-lhpl.
16. Karnataka Internet Assisted Diagnosis of Retinopathy of Prematurity (KIDROP) by Narayana Nethralaya. Available at www.narayananethralaya.org/com_eye_care_rop_pro.html; http://www.kidrop.org/pdf/jibr.pdf.
17. Vaatsalya Hospitals. Available at healthmarketinnovations.org program vaatsalya-hospitals; www.vaatsalya.com.
18. Health Management and Research Institute (HMRI). Available at www. hmri.in; http://healthmarketinnovations.org/program/health-management-and-research-institute-hmri.
19. Low cost diabetes screening system and test strips. Available at http://www.thehindu.com/sci-tech/health/medicine-and-research/pursefriendly-diabetic-testing-kits-launched/article 5575433.ece.
20. GE Healthcare India. Available at http://www.healthymagination.com/.
21. Life line drug stores. Available at www.hsprodindia.nic.in/retopt2.asp?SD=21&SI=7&ROT=1; www.hsprodindia.nic.in/files/PROD135/LLDS_SIHFW%20Excerpts.doc.
22. Jaipur foot. Available at www.jaipurfoot.org.
23. Swasthya Slate. Available at www.swasthyaslate.org.
24. Operation ASHA. Available at http://www.opasha.org/ http://healthmarketinnovations.org/program /operation-asha.
25. Wooden incubators developed by Dr Sathya Jeganathan. Available at http://articles.economictimes.indiatimes.com./2012-07-28/news/32906719_1_indian-innovations-frugality-incubator; http://www.allameri canspeakers.com/speakers/Sathya-Jeganathan/387775.
26. JANMA Clean Birth Kit. Available at http://www.ayzh.com/sites.path.org/mchn/files/2013/06/Path_1-pager_-JANMA.pdf.
27. Provision of Essential Maternal and Child Health Services in Tribal Areas, Rajasthan. Available at http://cbhi-hsprod.nic.in/listdetails.asp?roid=106; http://nipccd.nic.in/mch/fr/pi/pi1.pdf.
28. Vision Spring. Available at visionspring.org/en.wikipedia.org/wiki/VisionSpring.
29. Smiles-on-Wheels Program. Available at smilefoundationindia.org/smile_on_wheels.htm.
30. Neighbourhood Network in Palliative Care (NNPC). Available at http://india.ashoka.org/fellow/suresh-kumar.

31. E-Choupal Health. Available at mbph.in/e-choupal-health.html;healthmarketinnova tions .org /program/e-choupal-health.
32. World Health Partners (WHP). Available at worldhealthpartners.org/healthmarket innovations.org /program/world-health-partners-whp.
33. Frugal Digital Clock Sense. Available at http://www.wired.co.uk/magazine/archive/ 2013/05/ features/frugal-innovation; Frugaldigital.org.
34. Low Cost Standard Therapeutics (LOCOST). Available at http://www.locostindia. com/ http://healthmarketinnovations.org/program/low-cost-standard-therapeutics-locost http://infochangeindia.org/public-health/stories-of-change/locost-affordable-drugs-for-everyone.html.
35. ToucHb. Available at http://healthmarketinnovations.org/program/touchhb, http:// www.biosense.in /touchb.html, http://www.bbc.com/news/technology-17199877.
36. Embrace. Available at http://www.embraceinnovations.com/products/the-problem/; http://embrace global.org/main/product?section=howitworks.
37. A Behaviour Changing Syringe. Available at http://nominateforindexaward. dk/Presentation/read /id=MTg0Nw==; http://worlddesignimpact.org/projects/ project2013/2/.
38. Odon Device. Available at http://en.wikipedia.org/wiki/Od%C3%B3n_Device#cite_note-NYT2013-1; http://www.odondevice.org/index.php.
39. CCEBDM. Available at http://www.ccebdm.org or http://www.idf.org/public-health-foundation-india-phfi.

22

Emerging Health-Care Innovations

Preethi Pradhan and Keerti Pradhan

CONTENTS

INTRODUCTION

Innovation is implementing an idea for creating an impact.[1] This could result in disruption of the status quo. In this chapter, we will take a sweeping view of 10 innovations as depicted in Figure 22.1 that have the potential to change the future of health-care delivery. The ones that have made it to this list are those where explorations are underway but the full value is not yet realized. Neither are the entire spectrum of their applications and possible side effects fully known. Although several of these can be seen as technological innovations, their usage requires changes in the health-care delivery process both from the provider perspective as well as the patient experience. Some of these innovations have already rewritten the business model of how health care is provided.

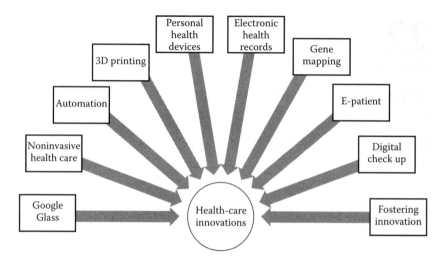

FIGURE 22.1
Ten emerging health-care innovations.

The 10 innovations described in this chapter can be divided into four categories. First, there are technologies, such as Google Glass and three-dimensional (3D) printing. They were developed for consumer or industrial use, but are finding useful applications in health care. Second, there are technologies that are specifically developed to solve known problems within health care such as health records, noninvasive health care, and ways to foster innovation itself. Third, there are innovations whose primary function is to empower patients by providing them with more and better information about their health and assist in finding appropriate help such as personal health devices and assistive robotics. Fourth, advances in financing may assist in converting ideas to fruition faster.

The innovations are listed in the order of the buzz it has managed to create in the current era of technological breakthroughs.

GOOGLE GLASS

Google Glass is being explored by the medical fraternity to determine its health-care applications. In a recently published article[2] by Muensterer et al. surgeons made the observation, after using Google Glass continuously for 4 weeks, that it allowed hands-free photo and video documentation, and provided the ability to make hands-free telephone calls.

It is also expected to play a role in medicolegal cases to provide evidence as it can record surgery very well. During emergencies, the front line health staff can stream data for the specialist in the hospital to receive advice on what care to be provided to the patient on site or during transport.[3] The ability to pull up radiographic images without leaving the surgery site was perceived as an important advancement for surgeons.

Another surgeon who evaluated this product[4] noted it will be useful in the operating room as an adjunct device in delivering necessary information, but opined that it has miles to go as a product. Drawbacks encountered with the current equipment were low battery endurance, data-protection issues, poor overall audio quality, as well as long transmission latency combined with interruptions and cutoffs during Internet videoconferencing. Also the images could be seen better in low ambient lighting whereas during surgery it is not possible to switch off lights. For maintaining an absolutely sterile environment it was felt that a hands-free Google Glass that relies only on voice commands would be better than the current version which requires swiping for commands. The other concern is that currently Google Glass works on wireless Internet connectivity[5] and does not provide point-to-point transmission between an in-house computer and the device. This raises concerns of patient data security.

Philips Healthcare[6] is viewing Google Glass as hardware to which they are providing software solutions termed "glassware" so that it will be easier for the medical fraternity to make the most of this device. In collaboration with Accenture Technology Labs and tested with doctors, Philips Healthcare has proactively reviewed how Google Glass could aid doctors. Their initial feedback was that it has the potential to give a live view of critical patient monitoring data such as pulse rate, temperature, respiration rate, and blood pressure. Philips is contemplating Glass integration to allow surgeons to access a presurgery safety checklist; give doctors the ability to view the patient in the recovery room after surgery; conduct live, first-person point-of-view videoconferences with other surgeons or medical personnel; and record surgeries from a first-person point of view for training purposes.

A Boston hospital is the first to use Google Glass technology to treat patients despite privacy concerns. At Beth Israel Deaconess Medical Center eyewear is being worn by medics to look up patients' records and check things online. Google Glass has been described as the "holy grail" of hospital technology. In January, it helped to save a patient's life who needed drugs to stop bleeding. The hospital has not yet outlined how it will seek the permission of patients to be filmed by the device's built-in camera.

Even in a developing country like India, it has been used for the first time in a privately run hospital in Mumbai for open heart surgery in June 2014. These glasses are still not locally available. The private hospital besides using it during cardiac surgeries is seeking to develop telemedicine applications for Google Glass which will be Android-based.

In short, this device is going to spin off a lot of innovations that are going to have a high potential in health care. It will be interesting to see how the balance will tilt between its potential easy access to all health-care stakeholders barring the cost factor versus the privacy and ethical dilemmas it poses and how they are resolved in the days to come.

NONINVASIVE HEALTH CARE

There are several inventions that enable a shift toward noninvasive health care.[7] Injections are expected to give way to pills. Monitoring blood parameters without drawing blood is also possible with the user wearing a device on the arm like a wristband. This has huge implications especially for those who are required to frequently test their blood and would otherwise be subjected to numerous puncture on their arms.

Another innovation expected to have significant contribution in detection as well as providing treatment is nanorobotics: "nanobots" and nanomedibots[8] as they are referred to for their particular usage in health care. They have the potential to give early warning of organ failure, take biometric measurements, detect areas of arterial weakness, and deliver medicines to the exact area in the body. MRI machines are projected to position them in the right places within the body to mark the size of tumors as well as provide treatment for cancer or break down kidney stones. As this innovation evolves, it is expected that nanomedibots will have capacity to replicate as well as self-destruct inside the body once their mission is accomplished. Although it holds potential, there are concerns due to their microscopic size whether they will trigger some other problems that are not yet foreseen. Apprehensions are also there regarding wrong usage if they get into the wrong hands.

Implantable, multiprogrammable brain stimulators that save the patient from surgical operations are already on the market for epilepsy and other debilitating neurological disorders. Similar applications have also been identified in cardiology for the identification and prediction of life-threatening episodes.

The other area where noninvasive care is expanding is with virtual endoscopy.[9] Being a noninvasive procedure, it is carried out without resulting in complications. It also costs less than the conventional endoscopy as it does not require any additional infrastructure or resources.

AUTOMATION IN HEALTH CARE

Automation of health care is becoming intrinsic in a variety of ways. Deploying robotics is one key method by which it is being done. They are expected to check the patient vitals and notify the appropriate source in case of variations. This is yet another example of an innovation that addresses staffing shortages in health care. Robotics has already gained deep inroads in health care to perform tasks in a sterilized, infection-free environment thereby totally eliminating the usage of human hands. The examples of these include packing of drugs, preparation of medicine dispensers, transporting medicines to the bedside,[7] providing treatment, and administering medicine to ease pain. Robotic surgery is also being experimented with.

Humans make amazing health-care professionals but machines can make the reach far and wide with high quality and precision. From using drones to delivering medicines in remote African villages to telemedicine, the increasing innovation happening in the field of nonhuman care interventions is something to watch out for.

Assistive robotics has gained increasing attention in the last decade.[10] Although initially conceived for human motion augmentation purposes, wearable powered robots have been gradually proposed as a technological aid for motion rehabilitation and assistance, and functional substitution in patients suffering from motor disorders. Live Braille,[11] a wearable glove developed by a student of Chitkara University, is another example which is expected to ease the challenge of mobility not just for blind patients but also for the increasing number of low-vision persons.

3D PRINTING

3D printing, also known as additive manufacturing,[12] is a recent technological innovation that is making huge inroads in health care. It is used to make customized objects with no additional tooling or material waste.[13] Dentistry and orthopedics have seen a great uptake of this. Printed implants have a more precise and personalized fit. Printed models of a patient's bone structure allow a surgical team to practice the process before actual intervention. Patient education is also expected to be better with the use of such prototypes.

A further area of specific development is that of bioprinting.[14] Bioprinted tissue is expected to become commercially available for both drug development and therapeutic purposes. Through this method, prosthetics are created that resemble the body part that is replaced or supported. New drugs can be tested using printed tissues, and customized drugs can be printed. A replica of a patient's living tissue can be printed out as a strip, which can then serve as a test site for administering a variety of medications to find the most efficacious one. 3D printing is also being investigated as a potential source to repair or replace defective organs, such as kidneys, heart, or skin. This may also alleviate the shortage of organ transplants, where finding a tissue match and avoiding rejections are key concerns. These will become nonissues if organs could be printed and grown using cells from the patient's own body.

A future has already been envisaged when a vaccine could be delivered to a pharmacy via e-mail, then printed and administered. Maintaining the cold chain would then be a thing of the past, thus bringing down costs radically.

PERSONAL HEALTH DEVICES

Smart watches and fitness trackers are for more than just telling time. Heartbeat, cholesterol, or blood pressure can be monitored through gadgets one wears.[15] From headsets that measure brainwaves to clothes that incorporate sensing devices, personal health monitoring is the wave of the future. Technological advances and the emergence of novel adapted technologies such as wearable technologies with considerable reduction in size, cost, and energy consumption are becoming an accessible solution to provide assistive services to humans. There are several remote monitoring systems that are based on wearable technology as well as ambient sensors and gesture-based technology.

Physicians will now be able to know how much a patient jogged or how much sugar was eaten. Examples of these include Fitbit and Android Wear. Life Vest[16] by ZOLL Medical recently was the recipient of a Wearable Championship for health-care technology. Life Vest responds to some of the estimated 920,000 people in United States who are expected to suffer a heart attack.

Phones in the pocket are no longer just devices for calls and messaging. Qualcomm, Nvidia, Google, and Apple are now able to track a person's health movement and activities from one's pocket. The next-gen chips such as the Apple M7 chip[17] are expected to be more powerful to handle all this data that will highlight the currently unknown facets of a person's daily life. Patients can input their health and biometric data from consumer monitoring devices that measure basic parameters such as blood sugar, weight, and hypertension (to name a few) into smartphones or PCs, which then safely integrates into the electronic health record (EHR, PHR, EMR) facilitating instant communication and feedback from the health-care providers. Caregivers can enlist the help of digital pill boxes[18] to monitor whether medication has been taken.

This in turn will help the health-care professionals to better understand what people actually engage in as part of their routine. The long-term stability and biocompatibility of these wearable and implantable monitoring devices are not yet fully researched.

There are plenty of mobile phone health-care outreach innovations as well. Mediphone[19] provides immediate care for nonacute and minor ailments with appropriate advice over the phone. Airtel has formed a strategic alliance with Healthfore (a division of Religare Technologies) to provide Mediphone services in India.

mDiabetes, Arogya World's diabetes prevention SMS program,[20] is a diabetes prevention mobile health (mHealth) initiative being implemented in association with Nokia. It reaches one million consumers in rural and urban India educating them about diabetes and its prevention through SMS, twice a week in 12 languages. Nokia Life Healthcare Service's Nokia Life Tools enables users to access health information related to maternal and child health, health and fitness, and general health using their mobile phones.

ELECTRONIC HEALTH RECORDS

Innovations in record keeping range from advancements in mobile electronic medical records (EMRs), use of open-source medical records, and EHRs for every individual. EMRs have been around for a long time and they have grappled to find a good fit within the health-care system as well as acceptance by the health-care professionals. Now with the popularity of mobile devices, EMRs are more friendly and usable compared to the experiences of yesteryear. They have also contributed to making health care increasingly paperless.

An example of open-source medical records innovation is OpenNotes[21] wherein patients have easy access to their own records that previously the physician had control over; they were not shared with the actual patient. This allows patients to better understand what the treatment plan is, helps in better educating the patients, and moderates their expectation as well as increases patient compliance.

Individual EHR is the concept of a passport merging with the individual's family tree applied to health care. Similar to a passport that provides each individual their identification data, this will provide an individual their health-care identity. Not only will the individual be able to maintain their own health record but by applying the family tree concept, it can be linked to other family members' health passports. This will particularly be of great benefit in the case of genetic disorders. It is also expected to have great predictive ability. This health-care passport becomes portable across geographical zones and across health-care facilities.

GENE MAPPING

Gene mapping[22] will be integrated into EHR seamlessly. It is not just a person's gene but also the family genetic history and even perhaps the potential for a population's genetic history that could be linked. For example, if a person has a genetic mutation that makes a person 15 times more likely to develop Alzheimer's disease, the information could be found far ahead and passed on to the family. Risk markers can then be identified at the individual level as well as the family level.

E-PATIENT

The e-patient movement[23] is trying to get the patient back into the center of health-care delivery. The patient is no more viewed as a mere entity who is worried, desperate, and in a bad shape, where he or she cannot think and must be told what to do. Today, the medical fraternity recognizes that the patient needs to be considered as an active partner in the healing process and the maintenance of health. International hospital accreditation processes such as Joint Commission International (JCI) insist on patient empowerment as a key activity. The e-patient movement offers the voice of the patient to be heard center stage in all forums where traditionally the patient was not a part. This includes conferences, doctors, meetings, continuing education programs, internal meetings of the hospitals, and the boards of health-care organizations. This perspective allows for several new insights which in turn unleashes potential innovative ideas. The patient is very much part of the innovation development process providing feedback until an innovation meets the required criteria.

DIGITAL CHECKUP

Very soon the diagnostic lab might be on a chip.[24] DxBox is a lab-on-a-card[25] approach currently being developed by a consortium. It is a single instrument that is capable of running both immunoassay and nucleic acid-based assay tests. It has several advantages over existing technology such as minimal sample volume requirements (one to two drops of blood), automation of whole blood processing, and immunoassay and molecular testing with a single instrument. The other advancements are diagnostic solutions that minimize the size and bulk of required instrumentation.

Direct analysis of patient breath is also being explored, which would be a major breakthrough in the early diagnosis of respiratory diseases. Portability of diagnostics also increases dramatically when assays can be performed without an instrument. Furthermore, simplification of an assay to the point where no equipment is required removes the need for maintenance and essentially ensures that the readout is visual based, which currently requires the least amount of training to use and interpret. One of the most innovative "point of care" (POC) platforms that is emerging is paper-based diagnostics. Paper-based platforms eliminate the need for bulky plastic disposables, dramatically reducing the size and weight as well as the cost of a novel POC test.

Seventh Sense Biosystems, an early-stage company based in Cambridge, Massachusetts, is also working with the concept of POC diagnostics that do not require an instrument. The company is at an early stage of developing diagnostics that can be worn directly on the skin ("on-skin") or temporarily imprinted into the skin ("in-skin"). Seventh Sense's "in-skin" diagnostics are compatible with a qualitative yes-no, or threshold response, whereas the "on-skin" diagnostics are expected to be fully quantitative. The most significant potential of both types of diagnostics, once developed, is that users will be able to self-monitor various conditions outside of the traditional health-care system. Although early in development, this concept has the ability to be applied in multiple indications with no need for lab infrastructure or lab personnel, thus it is relevant in both developing and developed worlds. The "on-skin" diagnostic patch is adhesively applied to the skin, and the patch functions by drawing a small amount of interstitial fluid or blood from the patient for analysis. The "in-skin" diagnostic is enabled by a biocompatible assay reagent that can be temporarily imprinted into the skin and then sloughed off over several weeks. The discovery of relevant biomarkers for diseases of the developing world has been difficult. The basic science that leads to biomarker discovery often falls under the purview of academia because the extended timeline, high investment, and lack of financial return do not provide sufficient inducement to the industry.

INNOVATIVE FINANCING MODELS FOSTERING HEALTH-CARE INNOVATIONS

A very big challenge in fostering innovations relates to organizing the finances required to pursue the complete link from translation of innovative ideas into a demonstrable concept. This is now being addressed by those pursuing health-care innovations quickly raising the finances through a model called crowdfunding or raising money from the masses.[26] Indiegogo, Rockethub, and Kickstarter are striking examples of these models. These reduce the paperwork for innovators and help them to quickly put together the resources and get the innovation up and going in the shortest possible time.

The other innovation in this model is the concept of "living labs"[27] to foster research and innovation with active participation of the end users in cocreating the product.

Way Forward

To meet the demands of the market, thrive, and be sustainable, each new technology application[28] must answer the following questions:

- At what price will it be available in the market?
- Is it a niche product or for everyone's usage?
- Would there be any side effects in the long run?
- Does it impinge health-care ethics in any manner?
- Does it further patient empowerment and patient comfort in the health-care delivery process?

Most countries have strict regulatory regimes for new pharmaceuticals and devices. Many of these new innovations blur the line between consumer electronics and medical devices. In some cases, markets can be expected to work properly, in others regulatory supervision is necessary. India, like several of the developing nations, does not have a Health Technology Assessment Council that on one hand may accelerate the adaptation of innovations, and on the other, could lead to risks associated with unproven technologies.[29]

SUMMARY

Health care is a field with immense pressing needs awaiting breakthrough solutions to address ever-increasing health-care burdens for the communities and the health-care providers. For health service producers, these existing and emerging technologies provide a window of opportunities for innovative applications for bettering care delivery, outcomes, and patient experience.

The tide needs to turn from a trickle of health-care innovations to a deluge of innovations. This can happen only when variety of stakeholders are involved. Interdisciplinary work will quicken the pace of innovations and, therefore, bring about the much needed change in health care. Yet, one needs to bear in mind that innovation alone is not the panacea for all the problems that plague health care. However, it does offer a bright ray of hope for the quickness and speed with which it can make change happen.

REFERENCES

1. Dabholkar, V and Krishnan, R. *8 Steps to Innovation*, Collins Business. HarperCollins Publishers, India, 2013.
2. Oliver, JM, Lacher, M, Zoeller, C, Bronstein, M, and Kubler, J. Google Glass in pediatric surgery: An exploratory study. *International Journal of Surgery* 2014; 12(4): 281–289.
3. Glauser, W. Doctors among early adopters of Google Glass. *Canadian Medical Association Journal* 2013; 185: 1385.
4. Fast Company. A Surgeon's Review of Google Glass in the Operating Room. Retrieved from http://www.fastcompany.com/3022534/internet-of-things/a-surgeons-review-of-google-glass-in-the-operating-room, accessed January 21, 2014.
5. Google: GLASS FAQ. Retrieved from https://sites.google.com/site/glasscomms/faqs, accessed January 21, 2014.
6. Fast Company. How Philip's Digital Accelerator is Hacking Google Glass for Surgeons. Retrieved from http://www.fastcompany.com/3024202/how-philips-digital-accelerator-lab-is-hacking-google-glass-for-surgeons, accessed January 21, 2014.
7. Schwartz, A. Health Care of the Future: Non-Invasive Blood Tests, Brain-ConnectedAvatars, Digital Pill Boxes. Retrieved from http://www.fastcompany.com/1763785/health-care-future-non-invasive-blood-tests-brain-connected-avatars-digital-pillboxes, accessed April 13, 2014.
8. Strickland, J. HowStuffWorks.com. How Nanorobots Will Work. Retrieved from http://electronics.howstuffworks.com/nanorobot.htm, accessed April 29, 2014.
9. Dunkin, BJ. Flexible endoscopy simulators. *Seminars in Laparascopic Surgery* 2003; 10(1): 29–35.
10. Johnson, DO, Cuijpers, RH, Juola, JF, Torta, E, Simonov, M, Frisiello, A, Bazzani M, et al. Socially assistive robots: A comprehensive approach to extending independent living. International Journal of Social Robotics 2014; 6(2): 195–211.
11. LIVE BRAILLE "Light for the Blind": Abhinav S Verma at TEDxYouth@ ChitkaraSchool. Retrieved from http://tedxtalks.ted.com/video/LIVE-BRAILLE-Light-for-the-Blin;search%3Atag%3A%22tedxyouth-chitkaraschool%22, accessed April 25, 2014.
12. Schubert, C, van Langeveld, MC, and Donoso, LA. Innovations in 3D printing: A 3D overview from optics to organs. *The British Journal of Ophthalmology* 2014; 98: 159–161.
13. Wohlers Associates. What is 3D printing? Wohler's Report 2013. Retrieved from http://www.wohlers associaes.com/3D-printing.html, accessed April 29, 2014.
14. Mukherjee, S. The Five Most Promising uses of 3D Printing in Medicine. Retrieved from http://www.thinkprogress.org, 2013.16.
15. Patel, S, Park, H, Bonato, P, Chan, L, and Rodgers, M. A review of wearable sensors and systems with application in rehabilitation. *Journal of Neuroengineering and Rehabilitation* 2012; 9: 21.
16. Baum, S. And the Wearables Championship for healthcare technology goes to: ZOLL Medical. Retrieved from http://medcitynews.com/2014/04/and-the-wearables-championship-for-healthcare-technology-goes-to-zoll-medical/, accessed April 13, 2014.
17. Talbot, D. What Apple's M7 Motion-Sensing Chip Could Do. Retrieved from http://www.technologyreview.com/news/519531/what-apples-m7-motion-sensing-chip-could-do/, accessed April 12, 2014.

18. Tate, R. Apple's Upcoming Health App is the Start of Something Huge. Retrieved from http://www.wired.com/2014/03/apple-healthbook-is-just-the-beginning/, accessed April 13, 2014.

19. Dass, R. Replicating a simple model of providing basic healthcare access. Retrieved from http://www.ipihd.org/mediphone/, accessed April 25, 2014.

20. Saligram, N. Diabetes: How cellphones help tackle India's ticking time bomb. Retrieved from http://edition.cnn.com/2012/10/11/health/nalini-saligram-diabetes-mobile, accessed April 13, 2014.

21. Oster, NV, Jackson, S, Dhanireddy, S, Mejilla, R, Ralston, J, Leveille, S, Delbanco, T, Walker, J, Bell, S, Elmore, J. Patient access to online visit notes perceptions of doctors and patients at an urban HIV/AIDS clinic. *Journal of the International Association of Providers of AIDS Care (JIAPAC)* 2014.

22. Hart, S and Muenke, M. Genetics and genomic medicine around the world. *Molecular Genetics & Genomic Medicine* 2014; 2(1) 1–2.

23. Bhargava, R and Johnmar, F. *ePatient 2015: 15 Surprising Trends Changing Healthcare.* IdeaPress Publishing, 2014.

24. Riva, G. Application of Virtual Environments in Medicine. Retrieved from http://w.cybertherapy.info/MIM_0161_Riva.pdf, accessed April 13, 2014.

25. Mehta, P and Cook, D. The Diagnostics Innovation Map: Medical Diagnostics for the Unmet Needs of the Developing World. Retrieved from http://www.bvgh.org/LinkClick.aspx?fileticket=-a1C6u2LE4w%3D&tabid=91, accessed April 13, 2014.

26. The Basics of Crowdfunding (2013). Retrieved from http://www.entrepreneur.com/article/228125, accessed April 25, 2014.

27. Bergvall-Kåreborn, B, Holst, M, and Ståhlbröst, A. Concept design with a living lab approach. *Proceedings of the 42nd Hawaii International Conference on System Sciences:* 2009.

28. Khangura, S, Polisena, J, Clifford, TJ, Farrah, K, and Kamel C. Rapid review: An emerging approach to evidence synthesis in health technology assessment. *International Journal of Technology Assessment in Health Care* 2014; 30: 20–27.

29. Fleuren, M, Wiefferink, K, and Paulussen, T. Examining the evidence: A series presenting findings from a systematic search of the literature on a specific topic and offering quantitative or qualitative analysis of these findings: Determinants of innovation within health care organizations: Literature review and Delphi study. *International Journal for Quality in Health Care* 2004; 16(2):107–123.

Afterword

V. K. Singh and Paul Lillrank

The history of innovations shows that certain ingredients are necessary, but recipes are hard to replicate. India has the ingredients: the needs, the rising purchasing power, space to grow, and hungry entrepreneurs connected to the world. So far, there is no spectacular recipe comparable to Japanese Lean management. But there are themes that resound in the chapters of this book.

A lot can be done with little.

In India, there are millions of people with poor or no health service at all. In the past, these people succumbed to their fate or started insurgencies. Now mass media and the ubiquitous mobile phone convey the message of alternative solutions. Entrepreneurs and NGOs ask what can be done with what is available. Even the union government has realized that the traditional path through full-blown medical schools and highly educated doctors at super-specialty hospitals will not solve India's health problems anytime soon.

A country with moderate means can mass the resources needed to take care of acute needs and provide decent public health. Indeed, the progress of public health measured as life expectancy starts to flatten out when the per capita health expenditure reaches US$1000. At the current US$61, India still has a long way to go. On the progress toward the US$1000 mark, India needs to innovate, import, copy, edit, and paste. But it makes sense to start looking further.

The deepening health crisis in rich countries does not invite followers. Who wants rampant health cost inflation together with worsening public health? Trying to do more with more ends up accomplishing less with more.

In rich countries, if you get hit by a truck or get struck with an aggressive form of cancer, you can, by and large, count on being well taken care of. But if you have several interconnected ailments or develop a chronic condition, be prepared to encounter hassles.

The health crisis in advanced countries is not in the super-specialties categories. It is driven by the high volume and long duration of diseases, which require low tech, high touch, and easy access. A system still entertaining the world view of emergency medicine cannot cope. Primary care is the problem.

Regardless of the level of regulation, physicians and capital drift toward the specialized highs, leaving the primary care doctors behind in both compensation and status. It is not a conspiracy of greed but a natural reaction to the fact that the primary care sector is too heavy and expensive in relation to demand and outcomes. The Indian insight is that there can never be enough highly specialized and handsomely paid doctors to deliver super-specialized affordable care to the masses. Therefore, health care needs a management revolution akin to the revolution in retailing in the 1990s driven by Walmart and other innovators of logistics, purchasing, and supply chain management. Health service distribution is the key.

Adopting Lean and improving production efficiency is the most obvious "what to do differently next Monday" advice to service providers. However, the literature of Lean is dominated by descriptions of battles against entrenched legacy cultures. Obviously, only the successful cases ever get into print. Going from obese to Lean is difficult. Therefore, the take-home message for India is: how about not acquiring that bulk at all? Apply preventive management and frugal design, be Lean from the start. Frugal design is like proactive prevention, whereas Lean is like reactive treating of diseases. Although existing providers can learn a thing or two from India, the main message is to entrepreneurs searching for new ideas.

Index